Wedged between the Battles of the Somme and Passchendaele, the Battle of Arras has often been termed 'The Forgotten Battle' with little in the way of supporting literature. *A Taste of Success* is aimed at filling that void – giving the reader an insight into a battle that clearly showed the development of the British and Commonwealth Armies over the early years of the First World War, and how far they still had to go to achieve victory. Why Arras became a focal point and the political background is covered in depth – being controversial and giving the reader an insight into the divide between the military and their political chiefs. *A Taste of Success* shows us how infantry tactics had improved and how the use of artillery had become a fine art in supporting the men as they attacked; how a preliminary artillery bombardment left the German defenders shattered, but also created the conditions that would hinder any kind of rapid movement once the first lines were broken. The key role of the Royal Flying Corps, how tanks were used and the vital role of support units such as the Royal Engineers are all examined in detail. As the story unfolds, it becomes clear that the initial success – based upon excellent planning and training – was followed by a chaotic confusion of command and control. It soon becomes evident that the development of the British Army in April 1917 had reached a point where in the Battle of Arras, they could stage a successful assault – applying perfect planning, but lacking the forethought to plan and carry out the follow-up phases. Controversially, although the performance of the soldiers carrying the fight is never questioned, that of many of their commanders is – it being clear that they were not yet ready to win the war. A great deal of the work is based upon primary material, with both British and German sources being used to deepen the analysis of events and also to challenge myths and previous descriptions of the battle. *A Taste of Success* presents a fresh and important reassessment of this important, yet generally ignored, battle as we approach its centenary. This book contains 16 pages of colour images and maps – in addition to many illustrations, maps and diagrams throughout the text.

Born and raised in Sheffield, Jim Smithson always had a love of the countryside. He initially pursued outdoor instruction as a career prospect, but was soon persuaded that his interpersonal skills and personality were best suited to teaching. Graduating in 1980 from Durham University, he entered the teaching profession and, following a few years teaching in West Yorkshire, relocated to Germany to teach in the British forces schools. After over 32 years' teaching he achieved the post of deputy head teacher at a secondary school. Jim has had a keen interest in military history since his days as a teenage wargamer. Thus began his interest in the World Wars which led to visits to related battlefields at every available opportunity. This enduring passion led to the purchase of a house near Arras in 2007. Thus situated, the opportunity to explore the former battlegrounds of the Western Front on a daily basis presented itself. With the 2014 closure of the military school system in Germany, Jim retired to his Artois home. Since then he has been employed as a battlefield guide. Sharing his enthusiasm with others whilst developing an appetite for primary research, the result has been the acquisition of a deep knowledge and understanding of the First World War from both sides of the wire. It should come as no surprise then that his first book has as its subject, the very battlefield on which he now resides. Combining original research with daily walks around Arras and vicinity has provided Jim with a unique insight into the spring 1917 campaign.

A TASTE OF SUCCESS

The First Battle of the Scarpe 9-14 April 1917 The Opening Phase of the Battle of Arras, 9-14 April 1917

Jim Smithson

Helion & Company

Helion & Company Limited
26 Willow Road
Solihull
West Midlands
B91 1UE
England
Tel. 0121 705 3393
Fax 0121 711 4075
Email: info@helion.co.uk
Website: www.helion.co.uk
Twitter: @helionbooks
Visit our blog at http://blog.helion.co.uk/

Published by Helion & Company 2017
Designed and typeset by Mach 3 Solutions Ltd (www.mach3solutions.co.uk)
Cover designed by Paul Hewitt, Battlefield Design (www.battlefield-design.co.uk)
Printed by Short Run Press, Exeter, Devon

Cover: MKII tank C47 (*Lusitania*) passing through the environs of Arras on 9 April 1917.
(IWM Q3184)

ISBN 978-1-911096-40-5

British Library Cataloguing-in-Publication Data.
A catalogue record for this book is available from the British Library.

For details of other military history titles published by Helion & Company
Limited, contact the above address, or visit our website: http://www.helion.co.uk

We always welcome receiving book proposals from prospective authors.

To Frances and Philippa.
Who could wish for more amazing children.

Contents

List of Illustrations

List of Maps in Text

Colour Maps and Images

Acknowledgements

Although in the modern era a great deal of information can be acquired from the Internet there remains much to be accessed in more traditional depositories. The staff of both the National Archives, Kew and Imperial War Museum, London were always most helpful especially as much of my work required a constant stream of different pieces of archive material. My thanks go to those staff and the trustees of both organisations for giving permission for the reproduction of images and the quoting of texts from material therein.

Similarly, I would like to thank staff at the *Deutsche Nationalbibliothek* in Leipzig for their cooperation in obtaining texts for me and supplying copies of documents I required.

Working in France has always been inspirational in the writing process. Being able to walk the battlefields of Arras at will brings much of the material to life, especially when visiting the resting place of so many of those who lost their lives in the area. My thanks must go to those who during this process kept me on the straight and narrow, putting up with my constant obsession with the Arras battles. Tim and Gill for their precious friendship and hospitality on many occasions and especially Tim for getting me on two wheels around the battlefields. He also kindly allowed me to photograph two sets of his medal collection for use in the colour pages. Thanks to Ken and Karen for making me feel so welcome as a newbie in the ex-pat community (and the cake, mustn't forget the cake) and of course all others in that very particular group of people for their friendship. Thanks also to Andy Pay who provided a lot of material on his beloved 14th (Light) Division in the early days of my research and Peter Doyle for his kind permission to reproduce a photograph of a document he took at the National Archives in my colour section.

A very special thank you to George Anderson for his conversion of my amateur maps into quality renderings for inclusion. Any errors therein are mine and mine alone. Also a big thank you to my good friend Jon Nicholls for agreeing to write the foreword.

My heartfelt gratitude to Duncan Rogers and Dr Michael LoCicero at Helion Books knows no bounds. I thought I was tilting at windmills to approach them at the Great War Forum conference some time ago now with my pitch for a book but they have been a constant source of encouragement and support in taking a fledgling author through the minefield of publishing a piece of work. I only hope I have not let them down.

I have endeavoured to source all the material I have used and please accept my sincere apologies if I have failed to acknowledge anyone in the footnotes.

Finally, a word for Jenny who came into my life as this work was requiring that final push to completion and has been a constant source of love and support during that process.

Jim Smithson
Boiry-Becquerelle
November 2016

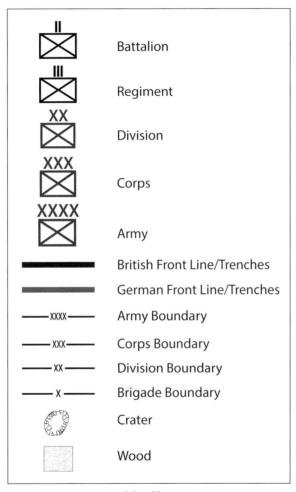

Battalion

Regiment

Division

Corps

Army

British Front Line/Trenches

German Front Line/Trenches

Army Boundary

Corps Boundary

Division Boundary

Brigade Boundary

Crater

Wood

Map Key.

Preface

GOOD-MORNING; good-morning!' the General said
when we met him last week on our way to the line.
Now the soldiers he smiled at are most of 'em dead,
and we're cursing his staff for incompetent swine.
'He's a cheery old card,' grunted Harry to Jack
as they slogged up to Arras with rifle and pack.
…
But he did for them both by his plan of attack.

The General[1]

Captain Siegfried Sassoon had personal experience of a battle that, if the general public are questioned today, remains in the shadow of those of greater fame or maybe notoriety, which descriptor depending upon the attitude of the responder. Placed in the first half of 1917 it has been, in the past, condemned to those shadows by the far more widely known battles of the Somme and Third Ypres, the latter more commonly known as Passchendaele. Even that most esteemed military historian, David Chandler, in his guide to the battlefields of Europe,[2] relegated Arras to a description of the minor conflict between the small British contingent and Rommel's *7th Panzer Division* in May 1940, although Flanders, the Somme, Mons and Cambrai are included. As this volume is written, nations are commemorating the centenary of what was initially called the Great War until a further global conflict rendered it merely the First World War. The British Government decided that Arras should play no official part in those commemorations and therefore a veil has remained held over the battle. Yet the Battle of Arras in April and May 1917 was a pivotal moment in the development of the British and Commonwealth Army in its quest to play its part in winning this most devastating and desperate war. One which had advanced into the kind of conflict nobody, even the most imaginative, had foreseen. Lessons had been learned during the Somme battles and these were being tried out for the first time in a major set piece offensive and on the first day they worked! The dichotomy of that initial success and subsequent deterioration into the same kind of slogging match of the previous year was one that at the time deserved attention if the learning was to continue. That, in spite of new tactics and increased artillery capability, the battle should have a daily casualty rate greater than that of any other British battle in the war,[3] should surely have merited closer inspection. Unfortunately, it was not to receive the attention it should have and that was the initial step in casting the battle into the shadows. Simple excuses were found for the failure to turn a break-in into a breakthrough and attention moved to Flanders. This volume is an attempt to investigate those first days where success quickly became failure and as to what lessons were perhaps missed which could have proved valuable later in the year. There is, lamentably, very little previous literature on the Battle of Arras, a reflection of its Cinderella like position in the historiography of the First World War. As well as the British Official History volume dealing with the first

---

1   Sassoon, Siegfried, *Counter attack and Other Poems*, (New York: E.P. Dutton, 1918). p. 26.
2   Chandler, David, *A Guide to the Battlefields of Europe*, (Ware: Wordsworth, 1998).
3   A daily rate of just over 4,000 casualties, against around 3,600 for the final offensive in 1918, around 2,900 for the Somme and around 2,300 for Third Ypres if each campaign is taken as a whole.

half of 1917 and the German equivalent for the April offensive, only Edward Spears' *Prelude to Victory* dealt with the period until the 1990s. An excellent anecdotal volume, *Cheerful Sacrifice*, was added to the literature by Jon Nicholls in 1990, which remains one of only two easily accessible accounts of the Battle of Arras. Peter Barton and Jeremy Banning added a beautiful addition to those wishing to see more with their Arras volume in the series of Great War panorama photographic books in 2010 but with coverage of the whole of the battle and concentration on photographic interpretation of the battlefield, there remained a place for a more detailed investigation. Some more detail can be found amongst Pen & Sword's 'Battlefield Europe' series with Monchy-le-Preux, Oppy and Gavrelle taken in isolation as elements of the larger battle, in addition of course the ability to wander the battlefield with Paul Reid's *Walking Arras*. There are a small number of French volumes, some translated into English, for example *Somewhere on the Western Front* by Girardet, Jacques and Letho Duclos. Other available secondary literature was found within the annals of unit histories, at both regimental and divisional level. When considering the background to the battle the breath of secondary literature increases as the political domain is investigated. The relationship between the military chiefs and their political masters has been the focus of many texts over the years and it was not difficult to find a plethora of opinion on how and why this influenced events.

Primary source material was, of course, in plentiful supply and having assimilated all the published material it was to this I turned. War diaries of the units involved are all readily available at the National Archives under WO95 and at the Canadian Archives, the latter fortunately online and accessible. Although variable in quality these do allow one to triangulate events and make some sense out of a battle; that most bewildering and incompressible activities humankind can be involved in. Poring through masses of this material, I gained an increasingly deep impression that there were many aspects of the battle that had not been fully explored and needed to be aired. Questions were forming in my mind that I wanted to shape at least some answers to and this book is a result of that quest. In many respects I wanted to bring the battle into its rightful place as one of the three major attritional battles of 1916 and 1917 and remove its rather orphan like position in the development of the British and Commonwealth forces. I also found that primary and secondary literature were in conflict on occasions and that a number of myths had grown around the battle that the public may wish to question.

A decision at an early stage was that the book would concentrate on the First Battle of the Scarpe, thus limiting the scope of the work but allowing more detail and analysis than might be allowed in a volume covering all three battles. In no way should that be read as a qualitative appraisal of the overall 1917 campaign around Arras. The Second and Third Battles of the Scarpe are equally worthy of study but their conduct and failings are not dissimilar to many other battles on the Western Front, both before and after spring 1917. What was much more fascinating being those first five or six days of the opening battle. Why success and failure were such bed partners and what went wrong, if indeed anything did. In order again to limit the book in its scope I have not included the battle at Bullecourt on 11 April. The battle did not have any effect on the main offensive mainly due to the total failure to make any real inroads into the formidable Hindenburg Line defences around the village. The battle is well-documented in the book *The Blood Tub*[4] by Jonathan Walker should you wish to learn of that day and subsequent attacks on the village which lie outside the dates of this volume.

There were many lessons to be learned from those first days but it remains a moot point as to how many of them were assimilated by the higher echelons of the command structure of the British Army. Many were, however, recognised by lower rank commanders and although it did take time, these considerations percolated upwards to move the British and Commonwealth forces towards

---

4   Walker, Jonathan, *The Blood Tub* (Staplehurst: Spellmount Ltd, 1998).

the more efficient and decisive force it became in the autumn of 1918. As one example; artillery was used with sufficient weight and careful forethought and planning, both enabling the majority of attacks on the 9 April to be successful and rendering the opposing artillery near to useless. Where it was not used effectively failure ensued. Attacks on subsequent days to the 9th, hastily prepared and with poor artillery support, invariably suffered substantial casualties for little or no gain. Small wonder that the attrition rate climbed so horrendously. Unfortunately, poor weather conditions and the subsequent state of the ground made a ready excuse for the poor showing of the artillery in the period immediately following the first day, perhaps masking other failures that were not attended to for another year or more. There was no substantial review of the battle, certainly not one that looked carefully at leadership at divisional and higher level along with the work of the staff officers which fell far short of a reasonable level of competence between 10 and 14 April. I hope that in the work I show that there were considerable failings at these levels without the necessary remedial work during the months afterwards that might have been possible with more detailed analysis.

I have included far fewer contemporary anecdotal personal accounts than is common in recent literature, primarily to allow space for analysis without making the work too long. I hope those long gone soldiers forgive me that decision. I spend a great deal of time paying my respects amongst those who were left behind in the area, having given their all, so I feel pretty sure that I will be forgiven. I have them in my heart even if not taking centre stage in my work.

Modern visitors to the Arras battlefields will meet a mixture of industry but also tranquil and reflective areas. Some of the front line area which bore witness to the events of April 1917 has been disturbed by the onset of modern trade and transport systems. Motorways and new fast rail lines can play havoc to intrepid visitors following the path of this or that unit; obstructing sight lines that would have been clear in those turbulent times. Factories unfortunately sit on parts of both British and German front lines of 9 April 1917. Nowhere down the front line of that momentous day, however, is the story impossible to follow. In fact, in many locations, the whole narrative of battalions surging forward or meeting their fate on the wire can be followed on the ground almost yard by yard. Visitors are not as common as on the Somme or Ypres battlefields and therefore one can experience glorious tranquillity when either walking the less built up areas or visiting the many CWGC cemeteries dotted around the whole countryside. Some of the latter are as poignant and beautiful as any on the more famous fields of battle. Whilst this is not a battlefield guide I hope that by infusing the odd comment about the ground as it is seen today, plus as much map and diagrammatical content as possible, the reader can begin to recognise the area, if and when he or she is able to visit. Such a visit I would heartily recommend.

All the chapter introductions are extracts from poems by Edward Thomas (1878-1917). Thomas cannot be regarded as a 'War Poet' as much of his poetry was written whilst in the United Kingdom before going to France and rarely hints at the war. He was killed on the morning of 9 April as the offensive was getting underway; many modern poets lamenting his early death as his work was showing immense promise. His remains were interred at Agny Cemetery, not too far from where he died.[5]

Accommodation can be readily found in Arras itself which, poised in the centre of the whole campaign, is ideal as a place from which to explore. Being on an offshoot of the TGV link from Lille to Paris and also just off the A1 and A26 motorways allows for easy access from the United Kingdom. It is, besides, a lovely city and summer evenings on *Place des Héros* are an absolute pleasure following a hard day touring the fields.

---

5   There was a myth about his being killed by a shell without leaving a mark but a letter from his commanding officer later said he was shot and killed instantly. As the latter is common to spare relatives the real horror of many deaths, it may never be known exactly how Thomas died.

Foreword

On this 2016 remembrance weekend, I watched England play South Africa a thrilling game of Rugby Football at Twickenham. England's sturdy foot soldiers made several elementary mistakes in the opening stages of the intense forward battle but nevertheless, fought through and won a stunning victory of 37 points to 21. They achieved what they had set out to do and although they let South Africa back into the game via counter attacks, it was for England – who had not beaten the Springboks since 2008 – a taste of success.

A comparison can so be drawn between that elusive Rugby victory and the dramatic events of 9 April 1917, the first day of the Battle of Arras, described by Captain Cyril Falls as 'One of the great days of the war.' It was indeed, in spite of some basic errors, the most successful stroke yet delivered by the British Army in that most awful war. Allenby, the manager and commander of the 3rd Army, was shortly after to leave France to gather greater renown by his triumphs in the Holy Land. The German retreat to the Hindenburg Line and America's declaration of war had keyed up the players to a high level of expectation. Indeed, the French Minister of War, Monsieur Painlevé, had visited our front just before and had commented on the vivid impression he had received of an assured confidence in victory. Allenby had an immediate tactical objective, the capture of Vimy Ridge. As a strategic objective he needed to rupture the enemy switch line by which the Hindenburg Line linked itself with the old defensive system north of Lens. To reach this, an advance *deeper* than had yet been attained would be necessary. The initial point of attack and the force employed were larger than those of 1 July on the Somme, almost 16 divisions against 14, but the casualties were 32,000 against 70,000 suffered on the Somme. Arras was a relatively short battle which would have been broken off sooner but for the misfortunes of the French which led to the 'most savage infantry battle of the war' – the most lethal offensive battle, based on a daily casualty rate – where worn out, British divisions were re-sent into the fray. However, 9 April did finally bring that much longed for taste of success. It caused Ludendorff to wryly remark "The consequences of a breakthrough of 12 to 15 kilometres wide and 6 or more kilometres deep are not easy to meet … a day like 9 April threw all calculations to the wind." Any subsequent failure at Arras lay not in the first day of battle but in the next, which was a real *day of delay*. Nevertheless in the short duration of the battle leading up to 3 May, 32 of the best German divisions had been engaged, or double the number engaged on the Somme for the same period.

The main cause of the victory of 9 April was the immense improvement in the tactical handling of British troops. Training facilities and coaching methods had improved. The town of Arras had been made avast underground repository for reserves. Medieval caverns had been expanded, cellars interconnected and lit by electricity. Almost 25,000 troops emerged from them into the communication trenches. The approaches had been largely freed from congestion by the laying down of a large number of converging plank roads. Thus fresh divisions were readily available to pass through the original attacking troops and to continue the advance without interruption, a manoeuvre known as 'leap-frogging.' On Easter Monday the infantry progress fulfilled all reasonable expectation. Though held up in places by strongpoints and resolute riflemen, they overran a large number of enemy batteries, taking 200 guns and 13,000 prisoners on the first day. In spite of dreadful weather conditions, the creeping barrage and aircraft liaison worked admirably. The Canadians took the Vimy Ridge in a magnificent feat of arms and due east of Arras the 4th Division gained a footing in the enemy's last line at Fampoux. The opposition had taken a battering and the way to the Hindenburg switch line was now open, albeit on a narrow front.

The problem of a continued success was accurately expressed by a soldier of the time, Lieutenant-Colonel Charles Jerram (Royal Marine Light Infantry) who stated that some recent writers:

> Ignore or simply notice the *only* thing that matters and without which you cannot begin to criticise, i.e., the fact that it was the only war ever fought without voice control; which came back in Second World War with walkie-Talkie and without which the modern soldier is as completely lost as we were. Nobody recognises that once troops were committed to the attack, *all* control was over. Why didn't our Generals go up and take charge, see for themselves and give the necessary orders? What the hell use would they have been? The ONLY place where it was possible to know what was going on was at the end of a wire, with its antennae to Brigades and Artillery.

When I wrote *Cheerful Sacrifice: The Battle of Arras 1917* in the 1980s I did not have the advantages of the modern day writer, when all the relevant information could be obtained sitting in front of a computer screen. I spent several weeks encamped at the National Archives (Kew) at considerable cost (the relevant war diaries cost 25p per page!). However, I did have one distinct advantage. Many of the men who had fought in that battle were still around, both British and German. I sought them out and spent many hours 'on the streets' interviewing them and taking some back to their old action spots, on the Arras battlefields – a treasured memory.

Jim Smithson will show in this new book, the progress of a set-piece battle in precise terms. It is to the advantage of the modern historian, armchair or professional, to understand the problems of a great attack like 9 April 1917 and it is all here. The determination and sheer grit shown by the soldiers can be associated with the tenacity of the England players yesterday. It was a real 'taste of success.' It's a pity our soldiers did not possess the fabulous wireless communication system available to Eddie Jones and his staff.

Jonathan Nicholls
Remembrance Sunday
13 November 2016

1

The Race to Arras

Roads go on
while we forget, and are
forgotten like a star
that shoots and is gone.
Roads

The Great War came in earnest[1] to the villages east of Arras on 1 October 1914 when elements of *Infanterie-Division 8* of Crown Prince Rupprecht of *Bavaria's 6th Army*, moving west towards Arras met French troops racing to cover their left flank. This was a small element of that leapfrogging activity often referred to as 'the race to the sea'; the name, commonly used to describe the period, being a misnomer as the intention was never to get to the sea but to outflank the opponent. Both sides simply ran out of land as they reached the Channel. To the modern reader, with an image of trenches and mud engrained within the historical montage of the First World War, the image of mobile units fighting an encounter battle is unfamiliar. This was, though, still October 1914 with both sides eager to gain an advantage on the field and as yet ignorant as to where this would lead.

The heady days of August and September had cost France dear in both men and French soil. The French and to a much smaller extent British, on the Marne, had dislocated the German attempts at a knockout blow to match that of 1870, but had not defeated them. Both sides imagined outflanking the other, the Germans hoping to drive to the west, reinvigorating their attempts at a knockout blow; the French with similar dreams but eastwards to Berlin. Taking part in these manoeuvres was a newly constituted French Army, the 10th. It had, as its commander, General Count de Maud'huy. The war began with de Maud'huy commanding a brigade but, following the disasters of the early weeks, his courage and 'incomparable magnetism'[2] soon found him commanding XVIII Corps on the Marne. Spears speaks of him, after his taking over of 10th Army:

> I remember a very uncomfortable afternoon spent with him at Arras. The Germans were shelling hard. Whenever a shell fell de Maud'huy walked to the spot and began a conversation with whoever he could lay his hands on. Example he called it, no doubt excellent, but this sort of thing cost the French dear.[3]

de Maud'huy's army had been formed to attack in a south easterly direction against the German right flank but before it had even concentrated around Arras it became clear that the Germans

---

1   The Germans had briefly entered Arras during autumn 1914, but subsequently withdrew after several days.
2   Spears, Edward, *Liaison 1914* (London: Cassell, 1930), p. 458.
3   Spears, *Liaison 1914*, p. 455.

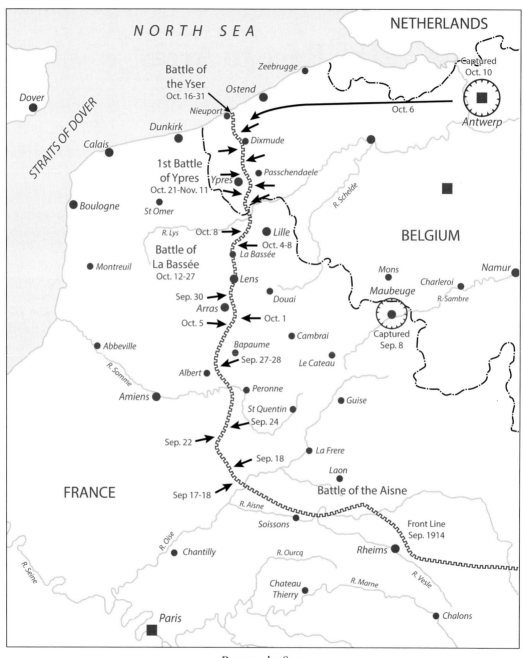

Race to the Sea.

were already in front and that a desperate blocking action was required if 10th Army was not itself to be enveloped.[4]

The division to which the defence of Arras was to fall was named at first after its leader Général Ernest Barbot.[5] The *Division Barbot*, eventually to become the *77ᵉ Division Alpine*, was made up of the *159ᵉ and 97ᵉ Régimentd Infantrie Alpins* and four battalions of *Chasseurs à Pied*. The fighting that occurred between these units and those of the Prussian *8th Infanterie-Division* at first centred on trying to take or hold Monchy-Le-Preux.

Général Barbot's imposing statue in Souchez. (Author)

Général Ernest Barbot in 1915. (Author)

---

4   Edmonds, Brig.-Gen. Sir James E., *Military Operations, France and Belgium 1914* (London: Macmillan and Co., 1922), p. 459.

5   Barbot was killed fighting near Souchez on 10 May 1915; he is buried in the cemetery at Notre Dame de Lorette and is also commemorated with a statue in Souchez.

This village, perched on the one significant hill of the area, would eventually pay for its prominent position in being totally destroyed by the end of the war. At this juncture, however, it was whole and still populated, leading to an incident which, at the time, seemed to confirm to the French the nature of their opponents. The French were about to counter attack Monchy when:

> Officers and company runners used their field glasses and pointed out to him [the Colonel] the edge of the village. Men, women and children were kneeling or standing along practically the whole length. Behind them, Germans in their field-grey uniforms were gesticulating.[6]

The counter attack could not take place and of course the Germans were accused of using civilians as a human shield. In actual fact after the war it became clear that as the Germans drove the French out of the village, the civilians wanted to escape and their obvious direction towards safety was west, which brought them directly out facing their own troops about to counter attack. The image of the reprehensible Bosch seemed, however, at the time, to be confirmed.

The German forces were convinced that they only faced cavalry or weak territorial units and pressed on to take Arras. Local resistance was fierce and the advance could only proceed slowly. Barbot's division was, however, eventually pushed back into the suburbs of Arras after Neuville Vitasse, Tilloy-les-Mofflaines and then Feuchy to the north fell to the Germans.

The 5th of October saw two changes. For the French, General Foch arrived to coordinate the operations of all the French forces in the area. He demanded a much more offensive approach from his troops leading to counter attacks which, if not stopping the Germans, certainly gave them something to think about.

The strenuous efforts of Barbot's men on the Arras – Cambrai road had left them in a precarious position. To their right Beaurains had fallen, units of General Rogerie's *20ᵉ Division d'Infanterie* falling back into the Saint Sauveur area of Arras, less than a mile from the railway station. Meanwhile further north, *70ᵉ Division d'Infanterie* under Général Fayolle was also fast losing ground; villages east of Vimy Ridge all falling to the advancing Germans with the ridge itself lost on 5 October. Along with German advances south of Arras, the French positions were fast becoming a salient and in danger of being enveloped. This led to thoughts of withdrawal behind Arras, thus abandoning the city. A combination of pressure on de Maud'huy from Foch and the determination of Barbot not to abandon Arras, led to the determined fight to give no ground; this resistance leading, as a consequence, to the Germans pausing to await heavy artillery.

To the north, the *I. KöniglichBayerisches Reserve-Korps*, made up of *1. & 5.Bayerische Reserve-Divisionen* continued to push hard on the heels of the Fayolle's men, taking Souchez, Neuville-St.-Vaast and Thélus, and then moving up onto the Lorette Spur. It was the determined efforts of the men of *70ᵉ Division d'Infanterie* which saved Arras, fighting over every village east of Vimy Ridge and then, in spite of losing those heights, not folding under pressure and thus allowing the Bavarians their head. Had the Bavarians been able to push them to one side, advance along the Lorette Spur and beyond, any troops in Arras would have had no option than to fall back and leave the city open.

This was not to be, however, and that was the second change on 5 October. The Germans now recognised that this was not a hole into which they could rush their army. Arguments between *Generaloberst* Falkenhayn, Chief of the Imperial German General Staff and *Generalmajor* Konrad Krafft von Dellmensingen, Chief of Staff *6. Armee*, arose out of a perceived lack of aggression on

---

6   General Mordacq quoted in Girardet, Jacques and Duclos, *Somewhere on the Western Front* (Arras: Degeorge, 2007). p. 10.

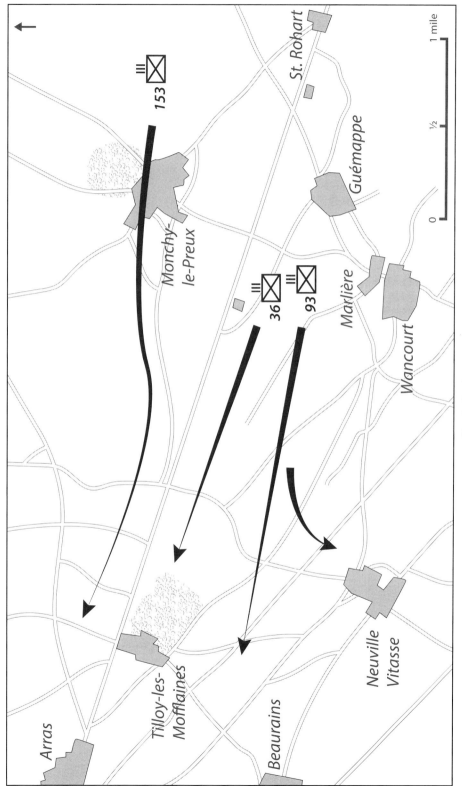

Battle for Arras.

behalf of the Bavarians but the truth was that forces were now beginning to be matched and no German reserves were on hand.

Certainly on 6 October the French in the Ronville and Saint Sauveur suburbs of Arras were still expecting a stiff fight:

> The southern and south-eastern edges of the suburbs were organised for defence, as were the railway tracks and the station. Construction of barricades on the two bridges either side of the station was begun, as well as in the streets of Arras which would be stubbornly defended, if it came to it.[7]

Indeed, for 6 October, orders were to push on Arras from all directions, including the north. Here, *5. Bayerische Reserve-Divisionen* was to provide flank cover whilst all other units were to attack Arras. This meant the Lorette Spur had to be held against increasing French attempts to dislodge the Germans who had entrenched there. Although some progress was made out of Neuville-St.-Vaast and towards Ecurie and Roclincourt, by the 7th this limited advance was brought to a standstill.

On the River Scarpe, Athies was taken but elements of *Kgl. Bayerisches Reserve-Infanterie-Regiment Nr. 1 & Nr. 2* could not take St. Laurent. Orders continued to arrive over the next few days from *I Bavarian Corps* such as:

> Roclincourt is to be captured tonight by 1st [Bavarian] Reserve Division (7 Oct.).
> On 20 October, 1st [Bavarian] Reserve Division is to capture Roclincourt, the high ground around Maison Blanche and St. Laurent East.' (19 Oct.).[8]

Such offensive actions, however, came to naught and over the next weeks into November the lines became more or less static. That is not to say that all offensive action ceased as the OHL[9] wanted French forces pinned whilst further north the battles around Ypres raged on.

The final positions achieved by the Germans by the end of 1914 were over many sections of the front ideal for defence, lying as they did on the high ground. Thus any movement by Entente forces was constantly under observation. This was especially true on the front north of Arras where, although tenuous, the German positions on the heights of Notre Dame de Lorette were very commanding of the countryside around. Alongside positions on Vimy Ridge the Germans must have felt very much in control of the area. It was thus natural that in planning offensives for 1915, the French Commander-in-Chief General Joseph Joffre, would target these heights as essential objectives if the required breakthrough was to be successful. If Vimy Ridge was to fall, however, it was essential that the Germans be first ejected from the heights to the west. Although many sections of the front around Arras had settled to their respective positions, this was not to be the case on the Lorette Spur. The first months of 1915 followed closely the pattern of the previous ones. Lines south of the Scarpe were relatively quiet, but north of the river the precarious position of the Germans led to continuous aggressive trench warfare.

---

7   Lieutenant August Villeman quoted in Girardet et al., *Somewhere on the Western Front*, p. 12.
8   Sheldon, Jack, *The German Army on Vimy Ridge 1914–1917* (Barnsley: Pen & Sword, 2008), p. 28.
9   *Oberste Heeresleitung*: General Staff of the German Army.

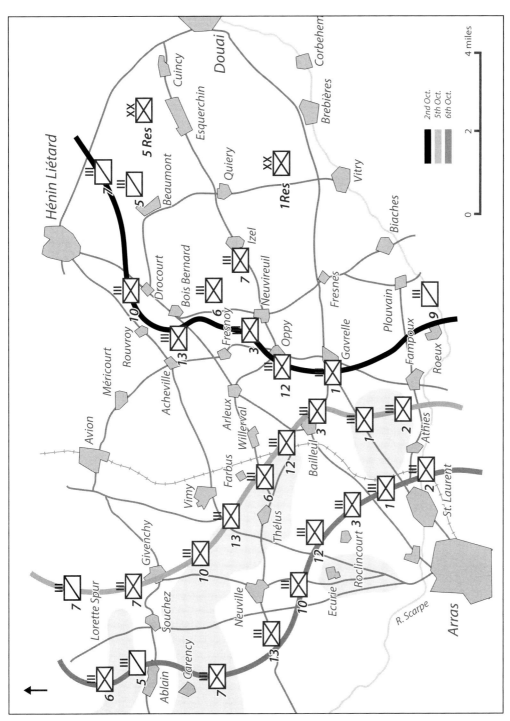

The German advance north of Arras over Vimy Ridge.

Particular dates, such as 16 and 17 January and 3 to 5 March 1915 stood out as occasions when the fight for the Lorette Spur was particularly intense, but it is impossible to look back at the period and to isolate genuinely quiet periods.[10]

1915 was the year, as far as General Joffre was concerned, during which the Germans would be pushed off his native soil and defeated. Sir John French (commanding British forces in France) concurred as made clear in his memo to the government of January 1915: "the utmost importance that we should take the offensive and strike at the earliest possible moment *with all our available strength*" [emphasised in original].[11]

General Joffre's plan was to attack on three fronts, one of which concerns us in our particular area:

> An advance from the Artois plateau eastwards, driving the Germans from its western border, north and South of Arras, and thence across the plains of Douai, would reach the centres of the communications of the German forces in the Noyon salient between Rheims and Arras.[12]

At first there were difficulties putting sufficient forces in place for these offensives. General Joffre wanted the British not only to take part in the offensives but to take over more of the line (that around Ypres). Without these extra forces, the French general argued, the northern offensive could not take place. Sir John French could not meet all these demands, not having the men necessary for both. Thus the combined effort was delayed although the British did 'go it alone' in March by attacking Neuve Chapelle. This limited offensive, although not gaining any strategic objectives, did increase the French's opinion as to the British Army. No longer did their commanders see them as only good for holding parts of the line to release French reserves for the offensive, or for minor diversionary attacks, but as effective partners in planned general offensives.

On 24 March General Joffre again contacted Sir John over a combined offensive; however, he also stated that this would need time if it was to be prepared with any hope of success. Thus it was to be the end of April, at the earliest, before the major effort could be made. The earlier demand that a part of the French line be taken over was also repeated and this time Sir John was able to comply. Ironically it was this move that put British troops into Ypres just at the point in time that the Germans began their offensive there. The ferocious fighting around Ypres did not deter General Joffre from his plans; on the contrary, he felt that the best way of deflecting the enemy from their actions in the north was to carry out the already carefully prepared offensives. Detailed planning continued and although the British and French attacks were not originally planned for the same day the usual delays meant that the date of 9 May was set for both. The British attack is the one usually termed the Battle of Aubers Ridge and was not successful at all; in fact, it was nothing short of a disaster. A lesson learned at Neuve Chapelle was that as long as there was "thorough previous registration of the enemy's trenches by our artillery, it appears that a sector of the enemy's front line defence can be captured with comparatively little loss."[13] This of course relied on sufficient artillery and sufficient ammunition. Neither was present at Aubers Ridge and therefore the capturing of very limited amounts of the front line trenches, subsequently all given up, was with considerable and not, as foreseen, little loss. The lack of ammunition was to have

10   Sheldon, *The German Army on Vimy Ridge*, p. 45.
11   TNA: Cab 42/1: Memo from Sir John French, 3 January 1915.
12   Edmonds, Brig.-Gen. Sir James E. and Wynne, Capt. G.C., *Military Operations, France and Belgium 1915 Vol. 1* (London: Macmillan and Co., 1927), p. 68.
13   Edmonds, Brig.-Gen. Sir James E., *Military Operations, France and Belgium 1915 Vol. 2* (London: Macmillan and Co., 1928), p. 18.

consequences in two ways. On the one hand it triggered a crisis in the UK Government when the whole artillery shell situation became a public scandal. On the other hand, it delayed any continuation of the offensive by the British 1st Army on 10 May and for some days afterwards; leaving the Germans only one area that it needed to send reserves to, the one attacked by the French.

To their south the French *10th Army* was tasked with not only removing the Germans from Vimy Ridge but then in subsequent operations to advance onto the plain with the objective line Cambrai – Douai. This was to be led by no less than five corps, 21st, 33rd, 20th, 17th and 10th on a front of 19km. The basic objective was to push the Germans off all the high ground of the Lorette and Vimy Ridges and onto the Douai Plain beyond. A glance at the map will show that there was considerable ground to be taken, including the fortified villages of Ablain-St.-Nazaire, Souchez, Carency, Neuville-St.-Vaast and Thélus even before the heights of Vimy could be attempted.

After a number of days of bombardment and a two-day delay in the attack due to bad weather, the time for the attack was to be 10.00am on 9 May.

The 33rd Corps had the major role of taking Souchez and Vimy Ridge.[14] The attack of the Moroccans was very successful, storming all the initial German trenches and reaching Hill 140[15] by around 11.00am; an advance of nearly four kilometres, with elements of *1ᵉ régimentétranger* (Foreign Legion)[16] and *7ᵉ tirailleurs* even having troops reach Givenchy and Petit Vimy.[17] However, the two battalions that should have been lending immediate support were eight kilometres back in Mont-Saint-Eloi and Acq. In spite of being asked for at 10.45am only one was released at 11.30am, too late and too far in the rear to prevent the Moroccans being pushed back off the hill by German counter attacks. Both flanks were also insecure due to the whole of Neuville-St.-Vaast not being taken on the right and a similar situation on the left in Souchez. The *77ᵉ Division d'Infanterie*, on the left, had been as successful as the Moroccans at first, some elements reaching Givenchy but again, too stretched and without immediate reserves they were eventually pushed back. In the south, *20ᵉ Corps d'Armée* attacked with *11ᵉ Division d'Infanterie* but after German counter attacks by the *Bayerisches Reserve-Infantry-Regiment Nr. 10* could only hold onto part of Neuville-St.-Vaast. Next to the French *20th Corps, 17th Corps* and also *10th Corps* made absolutely no progress towards Thelus or Bailleul. This remained the situation for some days, in spite of repeated attacks by the French, until both Neuville-St.-Vaast and Souchez were reduced to rubble, amongst which men fought desperately, often hand to hand. A similar area of desperate fighting was in a complex net of trenches known as the Labyrinth. This lies just south of Neuville-St.-Vaast and in the area of the fields behind the present day German Cemetery. This disputed area of trenches would take the French days to master with reports from *53ᵉ Division d'Infanterie* that they had used over 20,000 bombs[18] over a three-day period.[19] Attacks all along this front continued for some weeks until, on 8

---

14   The corps consisted of, from the left, *70ᵉ D.I., 77ᵉ D.I.* and *Division Marocaine.*

15   Care has to be taken with comparing French accounts with later British and Canadians ones, as what for the latter was Hill 145 (i.e. where the Canadian Memorial is situated) was for the French, Hill 140 as this was the height shown on contemporary French maps.

16   Interestingly this regiment also included a company of Czech and Slovak volunteers and another of Polish. The Nazdar Company, fighting in the hope of a defeat of the Austro-Hungarian Empire and thus the creation of a nation state for themselves. A memorial and cemetery for the Czechs has been created on the land they attacked over not far from Neuville-St.-Vaast on the road to Souchez. On the other side of the road is a monument to Polish troops who fought in the war.

17   Le ministère de la Défense, Memoire des Homes, 26 N 463/11, *Division Marocaine* War Diary.

18   The standard name for what is today named as a grenade was, in the First World War, a bomb. All future references to bombs or bombing are to be understood as using grenades in modern parlance.

19   Le ministère de la Défense, Memoire des Homes, 26 N 366/2, *War Diary of 53ᵉ Division d'Infanterie.*

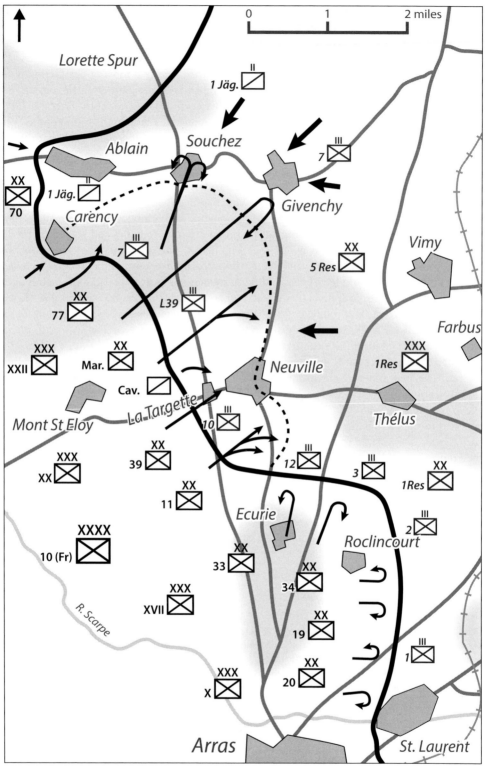

The French offensive towards Vimy Ridge in May 1915.

The village of Carency after the French recapture. (*The War Illustrated*, June 1915)

June the *5ᵉ Division d'Infanterie*[20] was brought into the line opposite Neuville-St.-Vaast. Over this and the next day the *39ᵉ Regiment d'Infanterie* finally, house by house (or what remained of them), took the whole of the village.[21] By 25 June although progress had been made in the taking of the plain in front of Vimy Ridge and clearing the Germans off the Lorette Ridge, it was clear that an exhausted army could do no more and the offensive was brought to a halt.

Small scale fighting continued throughout the summer but in September the French decided to make a further assault on the ridge. Although still planned as a major attack, again to include British support, in essence this was a subsidiary attack to a major battle to be fought further south in the Champagne region. The *10ᵉ Army* was basically told to complete the task given to them in the spring. Resources in terms of men were similar to those in May; however, due to the attack further south, significantly there was less heavy artillery than was available for the earlier assault.

Intensive bombardment began on 19 September but poor weather delayed the attack until it was finally fixed for 25 September, the same day as the beginning of the Champagne assault and the British attacking in concert a few miles north at Loos. Curiously the attack went in during the afternoon of the 25th at 12.25pm, the wet weather making conditions awful underfoot. The

---

20 Commanded by Général Charles Mangin, relatively unknown at this point but to acquire notoriety in future years for his aggressive nature, earning him the nickname; 'The Butcher' or sometimes 'The Black Crusher' due to his advocating the use of colonial troops as first line assault units. For all this he did become an army commander by the end of the war.

21 Le ministère de la Défense, Memoire des Homes 26 N 366/2, War Diary of *39ᵉ Regiment d'Infanterie*. Also for a German view of the ferocity of the fighting I would highly recommend Sheldon, *The German Army on Vimy Ridge*, pp. 55-84.

Germans, mainly Silesians in the southern sector, were manning the same trench lines as in the spring due to the lack of any French progress there. Again in fighting around Roclincourt and Ecurie the French failed to break into the German lines. Further north the fighting was more desperate for the Germans as they were now manning lines that were further back than those earlier in the year. This led to three major disadvantages for the Saxons of *123. Infanterie-Division* that had taken over the line. First of all, there were no completely formed trenches with adequate dugouts, secondly there was now very little scope for defence in depth as they were now near to the foot of Vimy Ridge and finally, having lost the Lorette heights they were badly overlooked.[22] In spite of heavy losses the French managed to slowly push the German defenders back and at times seemed to threaten to take the whole of the ridge. The wooded area between Souchez and Givenchy, known to the Germans as *Gießlerhöhe* was an area of intense fighting but was held by the Germans in no small part to the fact that reserves were on hand. A significant factor in the eventual defence of the heights was the arrival from the Eastern Front of the Guards Corps who, although depleted, were thrown immediately upon arrival into the fighting. Over the next few days and weeks it was this body of men which thwarted all attempts by the French to take the whole of the ridge, although they did succeed in taking Hill 119 which will be met later as the Pimple. Worsening conditions and lack of progress, in spite of heavy losses, began to drain the impetus of the French and there were clear indications to the Germans of low morale.[23] Eventually on 14 October Joffre called off any further offensive action both in the Artois and in the Champagne.

An important result of the French autumn offensive around Vimy was that the German defences now occupied an even narrower strip of the ridge than before. Their defences had been pushed back to within a mere few hundred yards of the rear of the ridge where it fell far more precipitously than on the western side. The consequences of this will be discussed in more detail when the German defences before the April 1917 assault are discussed.

What followed in the months afterwards was a combination of limited attacks by the Germans attempting to improve their narrow positions and a variety of operations carried out underground. The weather had turned foul and keeping trenches in any kind of suitable condition was an almost full time occupation. Notwithstanding these conditions the German forces did carry out a number of attacks in January of the New Year under the overall operational name of 'Rupprecht'. Although there was a need to try and create more defensive room on the ridge there had also been an order from Army High Command to carry out diversionary attacks in the area to distract attention away from the building of forces in front of Verdun.[24] These attacks demonstrated to the Germans that morale in the French Army was at an even lower point than in October, a combination of the failed offensives of 1915 and poor conditions.[25] One further operation in February, coinciding with the opening of the assault at Verdun on 21 February was significant for our purposes as it resulted in the retaking of Point 119 by *Infanterie-Regiment Nr. 163*.

Early in the war it had been realised that as the front stagnated into virtually a siege type of trench warfare, one method of attack was by tunnelling; simple reference to medieval techniques sufficed for intelligence here. The need to dig underground was also recognised for protective purposes. Tunnelling underneath opposing trenches in order to blow mines was by 1915 commonplace on almost two thirds of the front. Indeed, the blowing of mines in front of Carency in May

---

22   Sheldon, *The German Army on Vimy Ridge*, pp. 109-110.
23   Sheldon, *The German Army on Vimy Ridge*, p. 130.
24   Rupprecht, *Kronprinz von Bayern, In Treue Fest. Mein Kreigstagebuch, Erster band*, (Berlin: Mittler & Sons, 1929), p. 422. Rupprecht complains about later orders to do the same in February. I have failed to find this first order (he does not reference it in the work) and it seems strange as the first date set for Operation Gerichte, the attack at Verdun was 8 February.
25   Sheldon, *The German Army on Vimy Ridge*, p. 141.

French who remain in the soil below Vimy Ridge. (Author)

of that year had been part of the French attack on the village. It did not take long for both French and German tunnelling companies to get to work attempting to gain dominance over the battle-field between Vimy Ridge and the Scarpe Valley by using such a method of warfare. For protection both sides also looked to the fact that much of the area was already blessed with a large number of underground quarries or *Carrières*. Since medieval times locals had used underground quarrying techniques to provide building material for their houses and almost every village in the area had such an underground facility. Today's visitors to Arras can visit exactly such a place when going down into *Les Boves* from their entrance in the Tourist Information section of the Town Hall. All through 1915 offensive and defensive mining continued unabated. The former being charged with undermining the opposition lines and setting explosive charges, the latter being the act of defending against exactly such acts by the opposition.[26] The 'Rupprecht' series of attacks by the Germans previously mentioned used the detonation of mines to aid the assaulting troops. At the same time digging went on to create underground systems for headquarters and other important facilities, safe from artillery. Fighting also took place during this period actually within some of the quarries or *souterraines* as they were called by the French as described by one of their officers:

> The passages in which we were advancing were eighteen feet deep, and often twenty-four feet or more … One burrow, 120 feet long, took us thirteen days of ceaseless fighting to conquer entirely … And all this went on in complete darkness. We had to use pocket lamps and advance with the utmost caution.[27]

---

26 An excellent description of the experience of the men underground at this time can be found in Sheldon, *The German Army on Vimy Ridge*, pp. 189-193.

27 Cave, Nigel and Robinson, Philip, *The Underground War: Vimy Ridge to Arras*, (Barnsley: Pen & Sword, 2014), p. 25.

Evidence of such fighting can still be seen in Aux Rietz cave at the La Targette crossroads.[28]

Into this arena of close proximity of trenches, heights dominated by the Germans coupled with constant mining operations going on north of the Scarpe, came the British in March 1916. The pressure of Verdun meant that within days of the German attack, General Joffre was asking the British to relieve two corps of his 10th Army. General Haig now commanding British forces, immediately agreed to this and acting on advice from Maj.-Gen G.M.W. Macdonogh, Director of Military Intelligence at the War Office, decided he could take over the whole of 10th Army's front. Thus when Joffre, realising that Verdun was indeed the major German offensive, asked for this to happen, plans were already in place.[29] The British 14th and 5th Divisions of 3rd Army extended their front northwards, to be met by 23rd, 46th and 51st (Highland) Divisions of 1st Army extending their line down from the north. The area south of the Scarpe had seen very little activity over the previous year therefore British units taking over were able to settle in with little disturbance. This was not, however, the case in the Vimy sector. Here the recent aggressive activities of the Germans and the general condition of the line made taking it over a difficult undertaking. The comments from British troops taking over the line were not complimentary; "merely shell holes joined up; hastily organised positions in mine craters; straight trenches without traverses. The whole ground is a quagmire, practically impossible for attack at present."[30]

Alarmingly, it was also quickly discovered that the Germans had by far the upper hand underground with workings much further advanced than those taken over from the French, including being under the British front line. Haig had given Allenby instructions to only hold the old front line with outposts and create a better line[31] and it would have been sensible to draw some way back. This was politically not possible though, given the effort and blood shed by the French taking the ground now held. April and much of May, therefore, was a frenzy of activity on the British side as endeavours were made to wrest the initiative underground away from the Germans. Large numbers of tunnelling companies were drafted in to create both defensive traverses[32] to protect the line and also tunnels towards the German lines from which mines were exploded and subsequent craters, or at least the near lip of them, taken by infantry.[33]

> An enormous effort had been put in by the British tunnelling companies to 'win' the mining war on the Ridge in 1916 and generally speaking they had reached an acceptable degree of success by the early summer.[34]

A German response came near the end of May. Although the Germans had succeeded in matching the efforts of the British underground they were always at a disadvantage as the latter began digging at a lower level and therefore getting deeper was easier. If an attack could take the trenches from which tunnels were being dug, then the problem would be alleviated. In addition, the German *6th Army* was under pressure from High Command to do something active to relieve pressure at Verdun. Operation Schleswig Holstein was devised to do both of these. Initially delayed by

---

28   Cave, Nigel and Robinson, Philip, *The Underground War: Vimy Ridge to Arras*, pp. 26-27.

29   Edmonds, Brig. Gen. Sir James E., *Military Operations, France and Belgium 1916, Vol. 1* (London: Macmillan and Co., 1931) pp. 36-37.

30   Edmonds, Brig. Gen. Sir James E., *Military Operations, France and Belgium 1916, Vol. 1*, pp. 211-212.

31   Edmonds, Brig. Gen. Sir James E., *Military Operations, France and Belgium 1916, Vol. 1*, p. 212.

32   This was an underground tunnel, parallel to and in front of your own front line, designed to detect tunnelling activity by the enemy.

33   For a vivid description of this period from a German perspective see Sheldon, *The German Army on Vimy Ridge* pp. 205-206 and 210-211.

34   Cave, Nigel; Robinson, Philip, *The Underground War: Vimy Ridge to Arras*, p. 19.

poor weather, on the evening of 21 May, elements of *18. Reserve-Division*, supported by *5. Garde-Regiment zu Fuß*,[35] attacked and overwhelmed the British front line positions, which, it must be remembered were only held by isolated outposts.[36] Although initially the German troops advanced as far as Zouave Valley, this area could not be permanently held and eventually the front line was advanced by around 500 yards on a 1,500-yard frontage. The effect was to increase the distance from the newly established British front line to Hill 145 from around 500 yards to nearer to 1,000 yards.

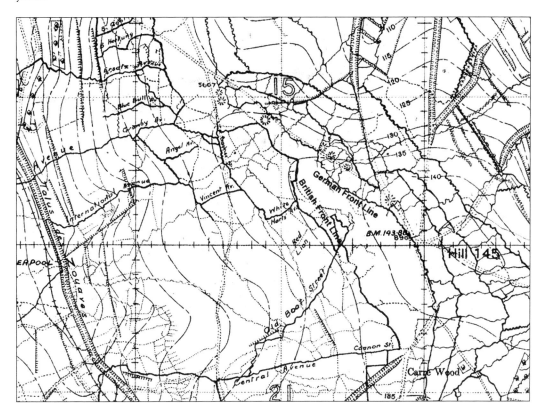

Trench Map early 1916, before the German attack. (Author)

The tunnelling war, although never totally quiet, settled down at this point and allowed the British to concentrate their efforts more on creating underground subways and accommodation for their men. This included on Vimy Ridge the creation of a series of subways leading from Zouave Valley to the front lines, thus creating a safe passage for troops moving under the gaze of the Germans on the high ground. By 9 April the four Canadian divisions between them could use a total of 13 major subways varying from the shortest, Gobron, at 870 feet to the longest, the Goodman/Pylones system, at 5,649 feet.[37] South of Vimy Ridge smaller subways were used by

---

35   Foot Guards.
36   British troops here were 140th Brigade of 47th Division.
37   Cave, Nigel; Robinson, Philip, *The Underground War: Vimy Ridge to Arras*, p. 38. A visit down part of one of these systems, the Grange Subway, can be arranged today through the Canadian Visitors Centre in the Memorial Park on Vimy and comes highly recommended.

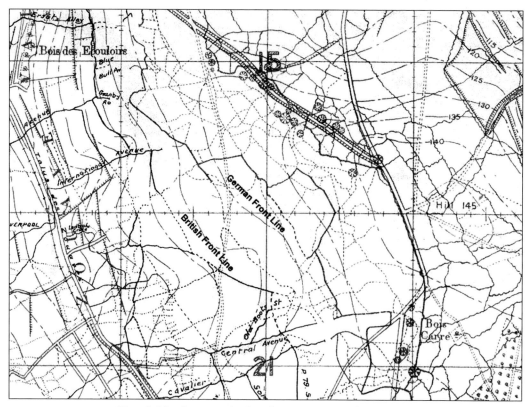

Trench Map June 1916, after the German attack. (Author)

a number of divisions but it was in Arras that another major work was completed. Historically Arras had used the stone beneath the city in the same way as many villages as quarry material for building. A village may have a small *souterraine* beneath its buildings but Arras and its suburbs had created enormous caverns in the process of building during the previous centuries. During the latter part of 1916 it became clear that if these underground quarries could all be connected to the *Boves* beneath the city then a combination of large scale protected accommodation and movement to the front could be created. A number of tunnelling companies were eventually involved in the creation of this system but the prime movers (literally, when the amount of chalk removed is considered) were the New Zealand Tunnelling Company. A glance at the map of the completed system gives some indication of the extent of this work which, could house some 20,000 troops as well as providing covered movement for many more.

> Well before Zero Day (finally fixed for 9 April 1917), all the arrangements were completed. The caves had all been levelled and made safe, the lighting completed, bunks, cook houses, washing places and latrines installed, gas-tight doors fitted to all entrances and routes, galleries and exits signposted.[38]

---

38   Cave, Nigel; Robinson, Philip, *The Underground War: Vimy Ridge to Arras*, p. 180. When touring the area, a visit to the *Carrière* Wellington where one of these underground caverns can be inspected is not to be missed. You can find the Wellington cave on the map in the Ronville system.

The Subway & Cave System in Arras. (Falls, Captain Cyril, *Military Operations, France and Belgium 1917 Vol. 1*)

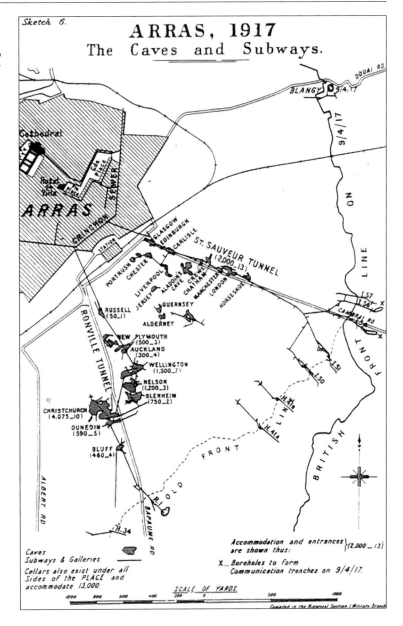

With the eyes of the Germans on Verdun and then increasingly on the Somme and those of the British turning, almost exclusively, to the latter, it was to be the beginning of a relatively quiet period on the Arras front. The lines were now in the positions that are going to be found when the background to and preparations for the coming offensive in spring 1917 are described. The Germans had, however, one last trick up their sleeves.

The failure of the Verdun campaign to provide the kind of results promised by General Falkenhayn as Chief of the General Staff, compounded by the allied attacks astride the Somme led to the General's demise and as August came to a close he was replaced by the architect of success in the east, Paul von Hindenburg. Hindenburg was accompanied by his Chief of Staff Erich Ludendorff who took the title of *Ersten Generalquartiermeister* (First General Quartermaster) and

Hindenburg (left) and
Ludendorff. (Author)

Kronprinz Rupprecht
von Bayern. (Author)

in essence became the leader of the German Army with Hindenburg as his front man. Meeting all the leading generals of the Western Front in Cambrai on 7 September it became clear to Ludendorff that the battles of the year so far had cost the German Army a great deal. However, arrangements for reliefs of fighting units and the creation of a new system of reserves discussed at Cambrai came to nothing as the Somme offensive went on into October.[39] As autumn turned to winter, the entry of Rumania into the war and Russian offensives in the east added to the German High Command's concerns. It became clear that the army was close to breaking point, "We were completely exhausted on the Western Front."[40] Although by the end of the year there had been success in defeating the Rumanians and bringing all other fronts to a standstill the situation was identified as critical. In this atmosphere it was clear that where some kind of realignment of the front could be achieved and thereby release men and resources, then it should be considered. This had already been in the minds of the two leaders and as such they had already marked out and made a start on defensive positions to do just that. Work began on a defensive line from Arras in the north, running between Bapaume and Cambrai down to St Quentin and beyond in the autumn of 1916 and this made the decision to retire in the new year that much easier. The prime mover behind the decision was the commander of the Army Group responsible for the whole of the area under consideration, Crown Prince Rupprecht. As British pressure on the Ancre increased, this led the Prince to demand on 28 January that a retirement to the Hindenburg Line should take place. The planning had already been set in motion; all that was required was the permission to move. After some prevarication OHL gave in and the order was signed by the *Kaiser* on 4 February. The plan was given the name "Alberich"[41] and was timed over 35 days. The first day planned was 9 February and a number of marching days designated. At first what was supposed to happen was that material and stores were removed before troops. However, pressure from the British, especially the attack at Miraumont and others astride the Ancre put such a strain on the Germans in the area that they could wait no longer. The first real signs of the withdrawal came on 24 February when 55th Brigade of 18th Division pushed into Petit Miraumont.[42] A message was sent to II Corps pointing out the surprising turn of events. Similarly, on V Corps front at Serre, of infamous reputation from the previous year's fighting on and after 1 July, the village was entered to the Army Commander, much to General Gough's disbelief at first. This was not, however, a retreat without planning and organisation. Rear-guards and a number of resistance lines had been set up in advance and as British and Australian units of 5th Army attempted to harry the enemy they were at times dealt a bloody nose.

There is a general impression given by many authors of a withdrawal of the Germans, the creating of a devastated area by their troops and subsequently a British follow up. That gives a completely wrong impression of some of the fierce fighting that had to be undertaken by 5th Army in their advance towards Bapaume. There was a series of three lines of resistance, R1 to R3, all of which were designed to be held at some strength. They mostly consisted of lines that already existed as support lines should there be a breakthrough and were therefore wired and fairly strong. Even some of the villages on the way and existing trench systems such as Irles and Grévillers Trench required attacking with substantial artillery support. The result, on 10 March being that the German defenders were overwhelmed and the objectives taken. This methodical advance was necessary; however, it did slow the whole process and thus when the bombardment of the R1 line

---

39   Ludendorff, General Erich, *Meine Kriegserinnerungen*, (Berlin: Mittler & Sons, 1919) p. 217.
40   Ludendorff, *Meine Kriegserinnerungen*, p. 230.
41   Given that the Hindenburg Line was to the Germans the *Siegfried-Stellung* it was only natural to choose another name out of the *Niebelung Saga*; Alberich being the malicious dwarf in the traditional tale.
42   Two days before, men of the 7th Royal West Kents had found no Germans on the crest south of Petit Miraumont, but this was not recognised as a general withdrawal.

Stizze 15. „Alberich-Bewegung" zwischen Arras und Soissons März 1917.

Operation Alberich, the German withdrawal; Ludendorff, General E. (1919).
(*Meine Kriegserinnerungen.* Berlin: Mittler & Sons)

had been completed it was found that the Germans had already moved back to the R2 line. That corners could not be cut was made clear when a hurried attack on a strongly defended Bucquoy by 91st Brigade of 7th Division and 137th Brigade of 46th Division failed with heavy casualties. Both divisional commanders had complained that the attack should be delayed but to no avail.

Meanwhile further south on 4th Army front and then in the French area it was soon evident that a withdrawal was taking place. At an Army conference on 17 March, Field Marshal Haig did not make many remarks regarding the process of following up the withdrawal. He did though approve Rawlinson's plan of using advanced guards covered by cavalry, establishing a line on the Somme south of Péronne and remaining there until his communications had caught up. It seems he was fully aware of the danger of rushing into German rear-guard actions with an army very unused to working in an open field of conflict. The French, in the form of the *G.A.N.*[43] on 4th Army's right, were under orders to be able to pass to the offensive at 10 days' notice. Commanding, General Franchet d'Espèrey, had therefore made comprehensive preparations for an offensive. Therefore, as news arrived at d'Espèrey Headquarters of German withdrawals, he was eager to launch an attack as soon as possible to disrupt the German retreat. General Nivelle, unfortunately, would not recognise that the retreat was a major one, nor how far it would go. He refused to give the necessary permission, not wishing his overall plan to be modified. This was unfortunate in the extreme and was a clear demonstration that Nivelle was following that very worst of leadership directions, that is where a commander is blind to changing circumstances and has not the courage to abandon cherished plans.

In the area of most concern to this work, that of 3rd Army, it was not until 17 March that some signs appeared that seemed to show that the withdrawal was not confined to the armies in the south. There was no R3 line north of Achiet-le-Grand and therefore as 5th Army made progress through the R2 line further south the German salient north of Bucquoy was no longer tenable and therefore the withdrawal was very rapid. Over the next three days, villages such as Boisleux au Mont, Boyelles and Boiry Becquerelle were occupied. Soon afterwards the divisions of 3rd Army were up to the Hindenburg Line northwards to Hénin-sur-Cojeul and Neuville Vitasse which were both held in strength and lay in front of the German main defences. Shortly north of here the Hindenburg Line ended as it reached the fortified area on Telegraph Hill called The Harp. The Germans had given up their positions close to Arras in Beaurains and retreated to this stronghold which was then connected to the village of Tilloy-les-Mofflaines. It was at this point that the old line remained in place, no withdrawal occurring from that village northwards.

The German withdrawal was accompanied by a scorched earth policy laid down by the German High Command. The whole area retreated over was to be left as a desert, with all the infrastructure normally to be found in a developed country to be destroyed. This meant that all structures were destroyed, trees cut down, roads made impassable and even wells to be filled in or polluted but not poisoned.[44] What was to be even more of a problem for advancing troops, however, was the laying of booby traps in abandoned trenches and dugouts. The soldier's partiality to souvenirs was to cost some lives before orders came out warning of the dangers of a casually left helmet or other valuable items. Even wooden steps and boards were booby-trapped and it became a full-time job for engineers to inspect and clear dugouts before they could be used. The most catastrophic example of such a booby trap was the result of one laid in the Town Hall at Bapaume. Here a large device

---

43   *Groupe des Armées du Nord.*
44   There are no confirmed cases of poisoning; however, well corruption with animal carcasses or excreta was common which is very close to the same idea.

on a long term delaying fuse,[45] exploded on 25 March killing a number of Australian soldiers and two French deputies. Rupprecht did not approve of the scorched earth policy, the order originating from higher levels of command. Nor did some local German commanders approve of the setting of such devices, as in some areas of the front none were found.

The Germans had thus, for the overall strategic plan of the Allies for 1917, thrown an enormous spanner in the works. Although time was short, the plans for the British contribution to the year's major offensive were not unduly disrupted. The disappearance of German troops in front of the French *G.A.N.* and British 5th Army, however, was another matter and this has to be borne in mind in the next chapter where the development of the operational plans are described.

---

45   Using acid corrosion to avoid the obvious ticking of a clock, a similar device in Behagnies did not detonate until the following July.

2

Background

That I was happy oft and oft before,
awhile forgetting how I am fast pent,
how dreary-swift, with naught to travel to,
is Time? I cannot bite the day to the core.
The Glory

The walls of the Chateaux at Chantilly, if such were possible, would have been experiencing a decidedly acute sense of déjà vu in November 1916. Was this not the same scene as that being played out 12 months previous? The actors seemed the same. There was that imposing figure of General Joffre, but was he wearing a different mask to that of last year? Certainly his grand schemes for 1916 had floundered before they could even begin; drowned in the torrent that fell upon his armies at Verdun. Was he looking older than the one year that had passed? Alongside him, upright figure as ever, General Haig. New boy at such a meeting last year but now seasoned campaigner having carried out as much of last year's plans as had remained, north of the River Somme. The torrid year that was 1916 had seen success. Verdun had been saved and the British (and the French who could be spared) had bled the Germans badly over the course of July to November. The cost in human lives and suffering had, however, been great. Could the Entente consider another year with such a butcher's bill? This was, however, to be the general thrust of the conference. A concentrated effort on all fronts would finally put the beast to the sword. If all members of the Entente could synchronise their offensives, then the subsequent results would lead to victory. Discussion worked around the timings of such offensives and here there was some discord as Joffre, anxious that the Germans may renew their efforts at Verdun, wished for an early start date; Haig being more supportive of May 1917. The final main proposals, taken to the Paris meeting of heads of government could be summed up as follows:

1. Offensive operations to be continued throughout the winter, dependent upon climactic conditions.
2. The Coalition to be ready to undertake joint offensives from the first fortnight of February 1917.
3. If possible, offensives should be synchronised (no more than three weeks apart).
4. Bulgaria should be put out of action, with The Allied Army of the East (in Salonika) raised to 23 divisions.

What should be noted is that the military chiefs had been asked to postpone their meeting by a week in order that the political conference should have been completed and the political will of the Entente would therefore have been central to the military discussions. This was refused and thus when the army chiefs reported to Paris it was in essence a fait accompli.

That this was a war, not of cut and thrust and grand movements of armies, but of attrition was becoming a common theme on the side of the Entente. The first intimations of this becoming an essential element of grand strategy came as early as 1915 when the first note made by Hankey, at

Field Marshal Haig. (Author)   General Joffre. (Author)

the time secretary to Asquith's War Committee, after an Anglo/French Conference in Calais was, "1. The general policy of a war of attrition is to be continued."[1]

In his appraisal of the situation on the Western Front of January 1916 the Chief of the Imperial General Staff, William 'Wully' Robertson painted a positive picture of the Entente's position for the year. Admitting that 1915 had not seen the breakthrough required for victory, he puts forward the argument that lessons had been learned and that now, with better and more guns and ammunition, the Allies were ready to act in a decisive manner. The ominous statement within his report, however, is:

> At the same time I wish it to be clearly understood that it is highly improbable that the enemy will be completely defeated as the result of a single great effort. On the contrary, we must expect prolonged fighting, a great expenditure of ammunition and heavy losses, even when his defence lines have been penetrated.[2]

In the same paper Robertson makes a claim to be often repeated in the coming year, that the Germans "are approaching the limit of their resources, both as regards men and materials."[3]

---

1   TNA: Cab 28/9 Lt Col. Hankey's draft of the conclusions of the Anglo-French conference held at Calais Tuesday 6 July 1915.
2   TNA: Cab 24/2 G-47 'The Question of Offensive Operations on the Western Front' Note by the Chief of the Imperial General Staff, W.R. Robertson, 1 January 1916, p. 4.
3   TNA: Cab 24/2 G-47 'The Question of Offensive Operations on the Western Front', p. 4.

General Sir William 'Wully'
Robertson. (Author)

Thus 1916 was set up to be the continuation of an offensive policy towards an enemy that would shortly be on its knees. When the Germans pre-empted all such plans by launching their Verdun offensive, strategy took on more of a reactive nature. Joffre put enormous pressure on Haig to adhere as much as possible to the plans for an offensive. It would have been very difficult for him to use changed circumstances as an excuse for altering his own strategy. Thus the die was cast for five months of offensive action where small, almost insignificant at times, gains in territory were exchanged for huge casualty lists on all sides. That the respective Commander in Chiefs could sit around a table and consider more of the same can be viewed in different ways from the perspective enjoyed today. It could also be perceived in different ways by contemporaries of the Generals and it is this that needs to be considered if proceedings in the first three months of 1917 are to be fully understood.

One view, popular for a significant period of the 20th century was that of callous generals, carelessly throwing away the flower of their respective countries' men in a slogging match; such as one might see between two heavyweight boxers who have no idea how to defeat their opponent other than to keep punching, whatever the cost to themselves. Sat in comfortable châteaux, ignorant of the suffering caused by their lack of imagination and skill to carry out the war effectively; these were Alan Clark's incompetent donkeys leading the lions in the trenches.[4] If this view is taken then it could be considered that a continuation of such a policy stands on very shifty moral sand and that its perpetrators should have been removed and more suitable candidates found. From a more modern perspective this view suffers from the knowledge that the approach taken did indeed play a significant part in the collapse of the German nation and that there was little or no alternative.

---

4   Clarke, Alan, *The Donkeys*, (London: Hutchinson, 1961).

There certainly was no viable alternative to the British C-in-C at the time. The Western Front was where victory was eventually won and the tough path that the armies of the Entente had to follow, to learn how the war could be won, paid off in the successes of the 100 days at the end of the war.

What about the perspective of a political leader in December 1916? It is an almost impossible task for a modern reader to place themselves in the mind-set of the leaders of the day, both political and military; hindsight being a barrier difficult to surmount. The arguments over how the war was to continue to be fought had raged at the highest political level from the day it was declared. A continuing fight was between those who felt the war had to be won on the Western Front, any other action being a waste of resources and those who sought other means of attacking the enemy; the so called 'westerners' against the 'easterners'. Other fronts had been opened (and in one case subsequently closed) but the lack of any clear successes had led to a growing distaste, especially amongst military quarters, for such endeavours. Some sympathy can be had for those who had favoured other avenues of attack when Cabinet papers are examined for the period 1915 through to 1917. Early in 1915, the then Secretary of State for War, Field Marshal Kitchener was perfectly happy to accept the need to look at distant shores, suggesting the Dardanelles was "worth trying"[5] At the same meeting Sir John French C-in-C of the British Expeditionary Force (BEF), attending in order to discuss the present situation, entered the debate:

> Complete success against the Germans in the western theatre of war, though possible, was not probable. If we found it impossible to break through, he agreed that it would be desirable to seek new spheres of activity – in Austria for example.[6]

It is therefore not surprising then that political leaders, hearing such advice from their military advisors at the highest level, should support endeavours away from the Western Front. It is a matter of idle and not particularly useful speculation as to whether the course of events in 1915 and 1916 would have run differently in France had there been no diversion of effort. On the other hand, the failure on all such fronts, including France and in spite of advice given, could have done little to promote a high level of confidence in their military leaders by any of those Cabinet members who sat in meetings throughout those months. To be faced with decisions by their respective army commanders which were paramount to 'more of the same' must have seemed less than satisfactory. The general feeling of politicians at the mid-November Paris Conference of political leaders in 1916 can only be described as gloomy. The notes of their meeting are enveloped in an air of despondency and lack of direction. Quite simply, they could not conceive of a method of winning the war. Thus when the military leaders joined them, the plan coming out of Chantilly was accepted almost without question.

There is one other result of the Entente discussions that must be borne in mind when the events of spring 1917 are studied. It is clearly evident from Haig's diaries that Joffre was offering him the offensive he held dearest to his heart; that of clearing the channel ports with an attack in Flanders.[7] Haig was always adamant that an offensive in the north was imperative for both the security of the English Channel and his own forces in Belgium and France. There are very clear and valid grounds for this strategy and the eventual outcome of events in the autumn of 1917 east of Ypres,[8] when this approach was carried out, must not be allowed to colour an analysis of the options available.

---

5   TNA: Cab 42/1/16 Notes of a Meeting of a War Council, 13 January 1915.
6   TNA: Cab 42/1/16 Notes of a Meeting of a War Council, 13 January 1915.
7   TNA: WO 256/14 Diaries of Field Marshal Sir Douglas Haig, entry for 10 December 1916.
8   The Third Battle of Ypres which, although a continuation of the reduction of the German Army's strength was, for reasons outside the scope of this book, a drain on the British in many ways. In popular parlance it is generally known as "Passchendaele".

What it meant for this particular period of time was that there were two specific strategic areas on Haig's mind throughout these months. The one dictated to him by the decisions of the Entente with subsequent coalition plans and the other, to him more important, possibility of success in the north. Another point made in that day's diary entry of interest, again when later events are studied, is that he was glad that Joffre had come around to the idea of Haig (or someone else British if necessary) leading the whole force, including a French contingent. December though was to see major political shifts that would to some extent nullify the Chantilly meeting, or at the very least, cause a re-evaluation of intent.

The political temperature in Britain had risen somewhat over previous months. The shell scandal of 1915 had already been a major contributor to the fall of the original Liberal government under Herbert Asquith; leading to the formation of a coalition government under the same Prime Minister. This was then put under intense pressure during December 1915 by the conscription debate; one which split the Liberals and only large scale compromises on both sides allowed Asquith to keep hold of the reins. As 1916 progressed the Prime Minister's position became more and more difficult and he was reporting to a friend his own deteriorating state of mind; the death of his son exacerbating the process.[9]

By the autumn of 1916 the whole governmental process of decision making had become engulfed in continual crisis management. The internal power struggle was reaching almost epic proportions, a very sad state of affairs at any time, but when the country is at war, potentially catastrophic. There was the Chancellor of the Exchequer, Reginald McKenna on one side of the spectrum and the Secretary of State for War, David Lloyd George on the other; Asquith standing as a lonely figure trying to hold these two very disparate ends together. Adding to this was the growing influence of the press. "It marked an evolution in distrust: even more than the war, newspapers were the continuation of politics by other means."[10]

The Unionists or Conservative press was of the more popular type with large circulation whilst that of the Liberals was not. Thus, the message was clear when pressure for change came, that it was for a leadership which would bring victory in the war, not one that seemed to be prognosticating over policy and averse to consent to the total commitment of the whole nation, willing or not. Liberal ideals were to have no further place in the running of this war.

Everything came to a head when Lloyd George promoted the idea of a War Cabinet,[11] comprising of very few members, to drive the war forward and end the prevarications he felt endemic to the War Committee in its present form. An interesting manoeuvre, typical of the ambitious Lloyd George, was that the Prime Minister should not be in the chair but that it should be the Secretary of State for War, namely himself, holding this position. Clearly a rebuke and a reflection upon Asquith's handling of the war so far, this was of course unacceptable to the Prime Minister. The usual threats of resignation, so common over the last months, with an extremely fragile coalition, led unerringly and rapidly to a change of leadership.[12] At first the premiership was offered to Bonar Law[13] but he had no heart for such a poisoned chalice. It was then offered and accepted by Lloyd

9   Asquith to Pamela McKenna, 20 September, 24 October 1916, quoted in Farr M., Winter and Discontent: The December Crises of the Asquith Coalition, 1915-1916 *in Britain and the World* (Edinburgh: University Press, 2011), p. 130.

10   Farr, Winter and Discontent, p. 132.

11   Farr, Winter and Discontent, p. 134.

12   Farr, Winter and Discontent, pp. 135-137; a fascinating insight into the political world of the day and essential reading if a fuller understanding is required of this change of leadership.

13   Andrew Bonar Law was leader of the Conservative Party at the time and a mutual trust between him and Lloyd George would prove invaluable to the prosecution of the war. His two eldest sons were killed in action during 1917.

Herbert Asquith. (Author)   David Lloyd George. (Author)

George and thus the scene was set for the last years of the war. The position of Prime Minister in what was still a fragile coalition government did not come without cost in terms of agreements and compromise. One important condition from the perspective of this study was that set by the Conservatives who insisted that there be no change in the military leadership of British forces in France.

What was the situation as inherited by Lloyd George? Too often a campaign is studied without the reader being fully aware of the political and strategic situation away from the centre of action. In the case of 1917 it is folly to analyse the offensives of April without an understanding of the origins of the plans and under what constraints and theoretical strategic goals they lay. The British Government were almost immediately faced with two developments which had to be dealt with urgently. One, the threat of Greece openly siding with the Germans and thereby threatening the security of Entente forces in Salonika; the second being peace overtures presented by the Germans to the American Government. The former was dealt with quickly and efficiently, in spite of the French being in somewhat of a panic with one significant result being a fairly strained relationship between Paris and London. The second was more serious than many modern commentators perceive as the relationship at this moment in time with the United States was a fragile one. This becomes evident when what was a clear attempt by the Germans to present a totally unacceptable proposal became known to the Entente nations. All the nations were one in condemning the proposal but making it clear that an outright refusal to consider it would be playing into the German's hands. War Cabinet records present a high level of concern that, to be deemed to be dismissing the proposals out of hand would lead to the United States taking some kind of punitive action against Britain. The Cabinet were well aware that the financial situation was, at present, extremely worrying and that any action by the USA would be of a financial nature and could lead to collapse.

On the prosecution of the war Lloyd George was faced by a military establishment that was clear about their strategy for the New Year. As already mentioned, he had faced this at the Paris Conference before he held the reins and now he hoped to use his more powerful position to change the minds of those in charge. He knew the impossibility of that task with his own General Staff and therefore he looked to his political allies to try and put plans on a different course. The French came over to London in December, primarily to persuade the British to support them with increased numbers in Salonika, but, at the same time, being wary of General Sarrail's (the French C-in-C of forces in the region) motives for the increased level of troops. The British prevaricated, naming transport issues as a barrier to lending greater aid and this allowed Lloyd George to successfully suggest a meeting to re-evaluate the policy for the coming year in Rome to allow Sarrail to attend. His objective was to use this meeting to again try and deflect the military from a continuation of their attritional policy on the Western Front. Thus he entered into 1917 still hopeful of being able to influence the course of events at a strategic level.

Not only in Britain had progress, or perceived lack of any in the war led to political upheaval. In France, Briand's government was put under extreme pressure following what was seen as a disastrous 1916. He had been forced by the Chamber of Deputies, earlier in the year, to form secret committees to take more control of the military. A vote on 7 December by one such committee, reviewing the actions of Joffre, forced Briand to move the General from his post to that of little more than a ceremonial one, that of technical advisor to the government. Briand then went on to form the 6th of his governments with changes reflecting those having just occurred in Britain, that is to say a small war cabinet. His plan failed, however, as this small group was not awarded the executive power of its counterpart in London and in addition Joffre resigned with "a marshal's baton to sweeten his retirement"[14] once it became clear to him that his new position lacked any power. Briand thought he had the ideal replacement for his fallen Marshal of France; namely the younger and recently successful General Nivelle. Being championed by Briand, however, was not a strong hand to have been dealt; Briand's leadership being constantly under question and his position of power in the land not at all secure. Added to this was his appointment of the fiery General Lyautey as Minister of War. For the first time in the war, power of decision was with the minister, not with the C-in-C of all French forces. In fact, Nivelle was not given the same position as Joffre at all, being limited to being commander of the armies of the north and north east of France. Both Lyautey and Nivelle found themselves in posts that were way above their experience level. This was all going to have significant repercussions as the first months of 1917 passed by.

The scenery in France had therefore, in the last days of 1916, been subtly but appreciably transformed. On the one hand a leader who wanted (and needed, politically) to see results in 1917 emerge very differently from those of the previous year and on the other a military leader who promised just that. General Nivelle had been successful in a number of relatively small scale offensives on the Verdun front over the few months prior to his appointment and this had bolstered his already immoderate sense that he had the answer to the stagnation of trench warfare. The more obvious contenders for replacing Joffre: Foch, Petain or Castelnau had, for one reason or another, been disregarded. Foch had played a political game during 1916 which eventually cost him all forms of command, albeit temporally;[15] Petain was seen as too defensively minded and Castelnau as being too close to Joffre, having been his Chief of Staff. Haig in his diaries saw the reasons otherwise, showing just a little contempt for the French:

---

14   Bernard, Philippe, *The Decline of the Third Republic 1914-1938* (Cambridge: University Press, 1985), p. 37.
15   See Greenhalgh, Elizabeth, *Foch in Command: The Forging of a First World War General* (Cambridge: University Press, 2011), pp. 192-207.

Prime Minister Briand. (Author)   General Nivelle. (Author)

> Foch was objected to as the successor to Joffre because he has a Jesuit brother and is a church
> goer. Also his handling of the French in the Somme battles was much criticized [sic]. Petain
> because he was brought up by Dominicans and is also a church goer. Castelnau is still more
> objected to because he goes to Mass and is very Catholic.[16]

This left the dynamic and confident Nivelle a clear field to persuade all before him that his
methods, practised at Verdun, would have similar effects on a wider scale, bringing the Entente
the breakthrough and victory they desired.

The new central dramatis personae had now become Generals Nivelle and Haig along with
Lloyd George. The new Prime Minister is included as a leading component at this point as he was
to have a significant impact upon the relationship between the two military men over the coming
months. The initial meetings between these players were positive to say the least. Nivelle's mother
was English and thus he spoke the language perfectly; allowing him to use his full persuasive
powers, especially upon Lloyd George, over his plans for the forthcoming year. Haig's first diary
comment on the French commander reads: "I was quite favourably impressed with Nivelle."[17]

Much has been made in some quarters of Haig disagreeing with the plans[18] and the ideas that
Nivelle presented, but this is not borne out by contemporary evidence, either from Haig's own
diary or from the correspondence between the two generals. After reading Nivelle's plans, Haig's
diary, recording his meeting with the general regarding them, details: "That I was in agreement

---

16   TNA: WO 256/14, Haig diaries, entry for 13 December 1916.
17   TNA: WO 256/14, Haig diaries, entry for 31 December 1916.
18   Cassar, George H., *Lloyd George at War, 1916–18* (London: Anthem Press, 2009), pp. 89–90.

with his principles of action." Also, "That I believed he would be successful, but it is possible he might not get as far as he hoped"[19]

It is also notable in this day's entries that Haig was quite happy with taking over a length of line from the French to aid the operation with a proviso that the full extent of the request could only be carried out when Haig was sure of receiving extra divisions from England. Not the words of someone altogether unhappy with the plans. The two generals had already in December begun to discuss and come to certain agreements over plans for 1917. These discussions, mostly by mail, it has to be noted, were not shared with London although it is clear that they were shared with the Paris administration. A letter from Nivelle to Haig dated 21 December outlined the General's plans for the forthcoming year in terms of the offensive they had discussed in a meeting the day before.[20] The objective of the letter is to ask the British to take over more line to allow the formation of the necessary forces for an attack. Haig's answer to this, on Christmas Day indeed, was a general agreement with the principles outlined by Nivelle, but with the provisos mentioned above in Haig's diary.[21] Further letters from Nivelle then go into more detail regarding his plans but also there is the impression, even at this point, of a little frustration, especially in the letter dated 27 December, that the British general[22] is creating problems that are not insurmountable within present resources.[23] The density of troops holding the front line are compared between the two armies with a claim that the British have a greater number of troops for a given length of line. This argument was going to linger and reaches a governmental level when the two political bodies of the allied nations met at a conference in London over the days immediately following Christmas. The Conference was to primarily look at the Salonika question and the German-American peace notes but the French added the offensive and thereby the extension of the line in France, to the agenda. This surprised the British who only found out about what had been transpiring in France on the eve of the conference. Lloyd George, when the conference considered this item on 27 December, quite correctly holds that he needs to consult with his military commanders before he can commit to what is proposed by a very assertive Ms Ribot, Minister of Finance, standing in for the ill French Premier.[24] Ribot, in a not too veiled criticism on Haig's playing for time, raises the density of troops issue, claiming there are adequate troops already in France. The following interchange is quite remarkable in the way Ribot constantly insists upon an instant reply to the astonishment of the entire British contingent. He even claims the British Government knew of such demands two months previously, a rather preposterous claim, given that the Chantilly Conference had not even taken place at that point. This meeting gives ample evidence that Lloyd George and his ministers were not going to make decisions over their Commander-in-Chief's head. It is also, however, evidence of how much the British Cabinet were sometimes kept in the dark over military discussions at GHQ level. The point is emphasised here to bear in mind when the political manoeuvrings of the next three months are considered.

The chain of events moved into the New Year, with the chief participants all collecting in Rome for the conference of British, French and Italian delegates. This was dominated on two fronts. The first of these was the main reason Lloyd George had manoeuvred the Conference to Rome. He distributed a memorandum (more in the way of a lengthy essay) to Conference members

---

19   TNA: WO 256/14, Haig diaries, entry for 31 December 1916.
20   TNA: WO 158/37, Sir Douglas Haig and General Nivelle: Correspondence, Nivelle to Haig, 21 December 1916.
21   TNA: WO 158/37, Correspondence, Haig to Nivelle, 25 December 1916.
22   Haig is created Field Marshal on 1 January 1917 should the reader be confused by his rank changing as the narrative develops.
23   TNA: WO 158/37, Correspondence, Nivelle to Haig, 27 December 1916, 2 January 1917.
24   TNA: CAB 28/2 IC 13(b) Minutes of the Anglo-French Conference, 26 December (morning) 1916.

during the morning of the first day outlining where he felt the situation lay and some possible ways forward. One of these was to provide extra heavy artillery to offset any possible attack by the Central Powers now that Rumania was out of action or even to mount an attack of their own. Cassar[25] would have us believe that Lloyd George was proposing an Italian/French/British attack but that is not supported by the actual memorandum in which it is clear that extra heavy artillery is all that is being put forward as support to a purely Italian offensive. The beginning of a Lloyd George's policy of letting someone else do the bulk of the fighting is starting to take shape.

The other was a continued effort on behalf of the French by Briand to encourage more participation in Salonika; Lloyd George commenting upon his speech as follows:

> If eloquence would carry two divisions to Salonika M. Briand's speech at the conclusion of the previous evening's Conference would have accomplished the task. Unfortunately, however, ships were needed and these we had not got.[26]

The idea of an Italian offensive backed by extra heavy guns fell on stony ground. The Italian Chief of the General Staff, General Cadorna was clearly not willing to commit himself to action siting the need to return the guns within a time period as being a reason for not attacking.[27] Lloyd George called this bluff by asking what if the guns did not have to be returned but Cadorna was not to be drawn. It was clear that the generals, in their separate meeting, had literally closed ranks. Thus the British Prime Minister's plans for diverting attention from the Western Front were in tatters and he had to turn his thoughts towards how to prosecute the war on his own terms by other means.

Nivelle wanted to arrange a meeting with Lloyd George whilst he was in France but the latter, thinking the discussion was over the extension of the British front line, declined the invitation, not wanting to do so without Haig present and instead invited the general to London.[28]

Lloyd George was very taken by the new French Commander-in-Chief. Finding himself in need of someone who was coming up with plans promising some level of success in the coming year he welcomed Nivelle with open arms, even accepting the idea that the Western Front was the place for a major effort. Nivelle's promise that the action would be brought to a halt should there not be a breakthrough and the fact that French forces would be the main combatants both being characteristics very attractive to the British Prime Minister. Nivelle came to London, as requested, for two War Cabinet meetings on the afternoon of 15 January and morning of the 16th. At these meetings the general plan as discussed by the two military leaders was put in writing and signed by them.[29] It is worth, at this point, quoting in some detail Haig's interpretation of the agreement, as he set it out for conformation to Nivelle in a letter sent to the French General on 6 January:

> In your letter of 2 January you divide the operation into three phases. In the first phase you propose that strong attacks shall be made by our respective armies with the object not only of drawing in and using up the enemy's reserves, but of gaining such tactical successes as will

25   Cassar, *Lloyd George at War,* p. 86.
26   TNA: CAB 28/2 Secretary's Notes of Allied Conferences held at the Consulta, Rome on 5, 6 and 7 January 1917.
27   TNA: CAB 28/2 Secretary's Notes of Allied Conferences held at the Consulta, Rome on 5, 6 and 7 January 1917.
28   Hankey, Lord, *The Supreme Command 1914-1918,* (London: Allan & Unwin, 1961), p. 613.
29   TNA: CAB 23/1, War Cabinets 34 & 35, Jan 15 & Jan 16 1917. The author has only been able to find the French version of the document as signed; the content is very much agreeing to an offensive as agreed by the two commanders and as outlined by Field Marshal Haig in his communication which is quoted in the text.

open the way for decisive action on the fronts of attack, either immediately or – later on – as a result of success obtained by you in the second phase. During this first phase adequate reserves are to be held ready either to exploit success immediately, or to continue to use up the enemy's reserves, according to the development of the situation. I have already agreed to launch such an attack as you describe, but not to an indefinite continuation of the battle to use up the enemy's reserves. Such continuation might result in a prolonged struggle, like that on the SOMME this year and would be contrary to our agreement that we must seek a definite and rapid decision. In the second phase you propose that my offensive shall be continued while you seek a decision on another front. This I have also agreed to on the definite understanding that your decisive attack shall be launched within a short period – about eight to fourteen days – after commencement of the first phase; and, further, that the second phase also will be of very short duration. You will remember that you estimated a period of 24 to 48 hours as sufficient to enable you to decide whether your decisive attack had succeeded or should be abandoned. The third phase, as described in your letter of 2 January, will consist in [sic] the exploitation by the French and British Armies of the successes previously gained. This is, of course, on the assumption that the previous successes have been of such magnitude as will make it reasonably certain that by following them up at once we can gain a complete victory and, at least, force the enemy to abandon the Belgian coast. On that assumption I agree also to the third phase on the general lines described in your letter.[30]

Haig then talks of the importance of clearing the Belgian coast and quite clearly states that should this not arise as a consequence of the French/British offensive, "then I not only cannot continue the battle but I will look to you to fulfil the undertaking you have given me verbally to relieve on the defensive front the troops I require for my northern offensive."[31]

It is very important at this stage in the proceedings to take three points from this agreement:

a)   There is never any change to this fundamental premise upon which Haig agrees to attack in the spring. Even with the change in French circumstances that will arise later.
b)   The emphasis that Haig repeatedly confirms with Nivelle is that there is to be no prolonged battle.
c)   Haig's objective is abundantly clear, to liberate the Belgian coast and if Nivelle's offensive fails to succeed in this task, he wishes the means to do it himself.

The other part of this agreement was that the British Army takes on more of the French front line, down to the line of the Amiens – Roye road. This Field Marshal Haig agreed to, but he did so only after obtaining an undertaking from the War Cabinet that his divisional strength on the Western Front be increased from 58 to 62 divisions. "These must either be sent from England, or I must reduce the strength of my attack."[32] In the present climate it was no surprise that the Field Marshal received his undertaking. It seems at this stage that the British Government were willing to do all in their power to comply in all ways in order that the French offensive should take place.

During January one particular aspect of the preparations for the coming offensive begins to rise to the top of the agenda; Haig's at least. He writes to Nivelle on 24 January outlining his deep concern for the state of transportation in France, especially with regard to the condition of the railways.[33] In the previous year the Battle of the Somme had highlighted the dire straits to which

---

30   TNA: WO 158/37, Sir Douglas Haig and General Nivelle: Correspondence, Haig to Nivelle, 6 Jan 1917.
31   TNA: WO 158/37, Correspondence, Haig to Nivelle, 6 January 1917.
32   TNA: WO 256/15, Haig diaries, entry for 15 January 1917.
33   TNA: WO 158/37, Sir Douglas Haig and General Nivelle: Correspondence, Haig to Nivelle, 24 Jan 1917.

transportation had fallen: "Transportation remained an essentially ad hoc construct based on the old Field Service Regulations Part II (1912), and had ceased to be equal to the task."[34]

Transportation was not the only area experiencing the problems resulting from the expansion of the war effort from those days of the two corps BEF in France to a global world war; with an army increasing from an initial 160,000 troops to an army of over 1.4 million by this point. The creation of the Ministry of Munitions under Lloyd George and the subsequent appointment of Sir Eric Geddes, previously Deputy Manager of the North Easter Railway, was a turning point for the whole machinery of war in Britain. Brought in by Lloyd George whilst the latter was Minister of Munitions, Geddes initially put his expertise to the war effort in the better provision of munitions. As the crisis in the creation of sufficient armaments began to abate there arose the question of actually getting them to the troops. The situation had been worsened in France as the French were now asking the BEF to take responsibility for the transport necessary to maintain their forces, a result of the severe manpower crisis that now prevailed. Thus, when Lloyd George became Secretary of State for War he took Geddes with him and on 24 August 1916 sent the businessman to France to investigate the situation. Although met with hostility by many members of GHQ (he was, it must be remembered, a civilian) a short 2-day examination of the area allowed the team to come to the conclusion that a lack of central control led to inefficiencies on a grand scale. His findings, although sceptically received by many of the military, gained a positive response from the one man that mattered; Haig on this occasion highlighting the ability of the C-in-C to embrace new ideas and innovations. With his backing Geddes and a team were able to carry out a much deeper survey into the problems which were clearly severe, as pointed out by Sir Eric, the newly appointed (1 September 1916) Director of Military Railways, when writing to Lloyd George two weeks into his mission:

> It is beyond argument that there is today no one who controls the continuous transit from this country to the front. There is no one who can tell you throughout where his weak places are, or coordinate the policy and resources, present and future, of the various means of transit. It is not possible for the Commander-in-Chief or Quartermaster-General in France to do it; it is alone a big job for the best man you can find.[35]

Haig was so taken by the man and his findings that he asked that he be immediately made Director-General of Transport in France. In the end Geddes held both appointments and set up a headquarters in France not far from GHQ in Montreuil in what was eventually to be nicknamed "Geddesberg". As the latter appointment was in principle a military one, he was given the honorary rank of Major-General:

> There is a good deal of criticism apparently being made at the appointment of a civilian like Geddes to an important post in the army. These critics seem to fail to realise the size of this Army and the amount of work which the Army required of a civilian nature.[36]

34   Brown, Ian Malcolm, *British Logistics on the Western Front: 1914-1919*, (Westport, Connecticut: Praeger, 1998), p. 140.

35   Quoted in Phillips, Christopher, 'Managing Armageddon: Sir Eric Geddes and the Impact of Transport Management on the Western Front', University of Leeds, unpublished Doctoral Thesis, p. 5.

36   Haig's diary Friday 27 October 1916 from Sheffield, G and Bourne, J., *War Diaries and Letters 1914-1918*, (London: Orion, 2005), p. 248.

The task was an enormous one and by January 1917 it was clear that problems remained. In reply to Haig, Nivelle[37] rather petulantly points out at length that the French had been telling the British that they would have to look to their own means for over a year. Geddes reported to the Cabinet in February[38] in person that the whole situation was on something of a knife edge with the French on the one hand making promises and on the other stating that the British had not fulfilled their part in the decisions made the previous year. Those British undertakings were being implemented, Geddes reported; however, it would all take time. The whole matter was raised again by Robertson at the Cabinet meeting[39] of 13 February with reference to a memorandum drawn up by the Imperial General Staff.[40] The result was a message to the French Government from the Foreign Office stating that, having supported the French against the wishes of the British generals to some extent:

> His Majesty's Government accordingly feel that they have incurred a heavy responsibility, and they cannot but express their disappointment at the present unsatisfactory situation in regard to the railways, which, from a telegram received today from Sir Douglas Haig, has as yet undergone no improvement.[41]

The upshot of all this was the first mention of the possible requirement for a conference where both government representatives and military chiefs should meet in order to discuss the situation. Over a couple of Cabinet meetings on the 20 and 21 February[42] and after correspondence with Paris a meeting was decided upon. Finally, at a fateful meeting on 24 February the following statement was decided upon by Cabinet:

> The War Cabinet discussed the questions to be raised at the forthcoming Anglo-French Conference and the general line which the Prime Minister should adopt in regard to them. It was stated that the questions to be considered were as follows:
> 1. The French Railways.
> 2. The operations on the Western front.
> 3. The scope of the Salonika operations.
>
> Having regard to the great importance of avoiding any misunderstanding with regard to the forthcoming operations in the Western theatre, and of preventing any recrimination after the operations, the War Cabinet authorised the Prime Minister to ask General Nivelle and Field Marshal Sir Douglas Haig to give him a full explanation of their plans for the campaign of 1917; to use his best endeavours to ascertain any points on which there might be a difference of opinion between the two Commanders-in-Chief; in concert with M. Briand to decide any such differences of opinion on their merits; and to aim more especially at the adoption of such measures as might appear best calculated, as the result of the discussion of the Conference, to ensure unity of command both in the preparatory stages of and during the operations.[43]

---

37 TNA: WO 158/37, Sir Douglas Haig and General Nivelle: Correspondence, Nivelle to Haig, 26 Jan 1917.
38 TNA: CAB 23/1, War Cabinet 59, 9 February 1917.
39 TNA: CAB 23/1, War Cabinet 64, 13 February 1917.
40 Interestingly, the figure of 200,000 tons requirement for importing was suddenly raised to 250,000 tons in this document (included in the minutes of the meeting). Geddes' investigation had arrived at the former figure therefore some level of opportunism by Robertson et al can be identified here.
41 TNA: CAB 23/1, War Cabinet 65, Appendix II, 14 February 1917.
42 TNA: CAB 23/1, War Cabinet 75 & 76, 20 & 21 February 1917.
43 TNA: CAB 23/1, War Cabinet 79, 24 February 1917.

Normally the War Cabinet was attended by the three standing members, Lloyd George, Curzon and Bonar Law plus whoever was felt to be concerned with the agenda items. Balfour (apart from secretary Hankey)[44] was the only other person there. Where any discussion regarding military matters was concerned, either Robertson, as Chief of the General Imperial Staff or Major General Maurice as Director of Military Operations, would normally be in attendance. That neither were asked to come is significant in the analysis of what follows. Where this meeting had been discussed in Cabinet previous to this date only the French railway problem had been mooted as the reason for the conference. Now more military matters were to be discussed, without telling the responsible men that this was planned. Clearly surprise was a planned element of the forthcoming conference.

Meanwhile Haig had been called to fend off criticism due to an interview that had taken place with French journalists. The resultant articles caused something of a stir in Britain, leading to questions in the House of Commons. It was made clear that the Field Marshal had been misrepresented, but feedback from Maj. The Hon. Lytton[45] to Haig, having represented him at a Cabinet meeting, also pointed towards the way the Prime Minister had used the incident to undermine the latter; as Haig recalled in his diary; "What concerns me is the desire of certain people, including the PM [Lloyd George] to make capital out of a trivial incident and to misrepresent the actual nature of the so-called interview in order to rouse public opinion against me and then to order my recall."[46] Haig also had meetings with the French Minister of War, General Lyautey where they exchanged mutual dislike of politicians: "He [Lyautey] spoke most frankly and said he felt quite at home with me and my staff, whereas he distrusted 'the politicians' [sic]."[47]

The first indications of the German retreat also came through to Haig on the 25 February and therefore he is travelling to the conference in Calais, set for the 26 February with a feeling of distrust for Lloyd George intensified by the recent incident, reinforced by a leading military man from France and with a disquieting piece of news from the front. Not a frame of mind to readily receive a shock.

The meeting to be held in Calais on the 26th at the Hotel Terminus must be regarded as one of the most controversial and far reaching of the war. Not only did it decide upon procedures for the upcoming offensive but it also fundamentally changed the relationship between the British Prime Minister and his military chiefs. Yet the sources used to describe this meeting are all, in one way or another, apart from the official notes themselves (depending how much you can trust such things), suspect.

The official papers will be taken first to put all other discussion in context.[48] On the first day, 26 February, the meeting began at 3.30pm. Representing the British were Lloyd George, Robertson, Haig and Geddes. For the French Briand, Lyautey, Nivelle, Albert Claveille (Under Secretary of State for Transport), General Ragueneau (in charge of military transport in northern France) with three of the General's staff officers. The initial part of the meeting discussed the railway situation with Geddes laying out the requirements and the French baulking at the numbers. One interesting aspect of this discussion is the claim by the French that the British requirements (in terms of wagons) for the offensive seemed to be far more than the French who had far more troops involved.[49] At this point Lloyd George intervenes as the discussion is clearly going nowhere and

---

44   At the time Lt. Col. Sir M.P.A. Hankey, KCB, Secretary to the War Cabinet.

45   Major the hon. Neville Lytton, a member of Haig's staff.

46   TNA: WO 256/15, Haig diaries, entry for 22 January 1917.

47   TNA: WO 256/15, Haig diaries, entry for 23 January 1917.

48   TNA: CAB 28/2, I.C.-17(a), Notes on an Anglo-French Conference Held at the Hotel Terminus, Calais, on 26 & 27 February.

49   Haig was, in fact, building up stores and material in the Ypres area as well as for the coming offensive therefore there was a little subterfuge here but not on a grand scale.

asks the railway experts to go and debate amongst themselves and find a solution. Briand agrees with him and the meeting adjourned for a short time. The military members of the group reconvened at 5.30pm. beginning with Briand stating that "it was not the business of the two Prime Ministers to make plans. It was their business, however, to know and understand the plans and to assent to them. He proposed, therefore, that the Generals should be asked to state their plans and conclusions."[50]

Nivelle laid out his reasons for moving away from the plans of General Joffre and then the details of his own; not printed in the notes "owing to the extreme importance of secrecy."[51] It is at this point that Lloyd George intervenes with a strange speech about there should not be any misunderstandings, there being a key phrase within it: "He [Lloyd George] asked what preparations General Nivelle would propose for complete success, and whether he desired any alterations in the present arrangements."[52]

He then made a number of comments pushing Nivelle to come out with what he wanted hoping "that he would feel no delicacy or reserve."[53] Briand then joined in making a key comment:

> He [Briand] fully agreed with Mr. Lloyd George in wishing that General Nivelle and Field Marshal Haig should speak their whole minds and state exactly what they considered was required to ensure complete cooperation and the best possible disposition for our forces. If the two Generals are in agreement, the Governments had no more to do than express their agreement.[54]

Nivelle went on to say that he feels the he and the British C-in-C work very well together and could foresee no problems as they were "veritable brothers in arms."[55] He did express a wish, however, for certain rules. Lloyd George pushed Nivelle on giving details of these, but the latter wanted Haig to have the chance to speak first. Haig demurred and so Nivelle continued. In a somewhat confusing and rambling manner, Nivelle stressed how well the two sides had always worked together but then used an example from an earlier discussion to show that at times duality of command can lead to difficulties.[56] Haig's response concurred over the 'most intimate'[57] of relationships and that he could not see how this would not continue. The British C-in-C and Nivelle then disagreed over the example used by the French general allowing Lloyd George to interrupt, saying that as civilians they were not competent to express an opinion (it is not difficult to imagine Haig and Robertson looking at each other and supressing a wry grin at that statement) and that Nivelle should "put down on paper the rules which he considered ought to guide the two generals."[58] Briand had the last word in this meeting with a closing phrase that must have put both Haig and Robertson at some unease, saying that he "had confidence in both the commanders-in-chief, either in one or the other, but that he did not feel confident in a system of duality."[59]

---

50   TNA: CAB 28/2, I.C.-17(a), Notes on an Anglo-French Conference Held at the Hotel Terminus, Calais, on 26 & 27 February, Second Session.

51   TNA: CAB 28/2, I.C.-17(a), Notes on an Anglo-French Conference. Amusing given the often leaky nature of the French Government and High Command as will be seen.

52   TNA: CAB 28/2, I.C.-17(a), Notes on an Anglo-French Conference.

53   TNA: CAB 28/2, I.C.-17(a), Notes on an Anglo-French Conference.

54   TNA: CAB 28/2, I.C.-17(a), Notes on an Anglo-French Conference.

55   TNA: CAB 28/2, I.C.-17(a), Notes on an Anglo-French Conference.

56   The example is not given in the minutes but according to Haig's diary entry for the day it was Nivelle disagreeing with Haig over attacking Vimy Ridge.

57   TNA: CAB 28/2, I.C.-17(a), Notes on an Anglo-French Conference.

58   TNA: CAB 28/2, I.C.-17(a), Notes on an Anglo-French Conference.

59   TNA: CAB 28/2, I.C.-17(a), Notes on an Anglo-French Conference.

The Conference then closed for the day but the action did not. The rest of the evening, not being part of the conference, relies upon those that were there for a description of events. The chain of events is reasonably clear, sources agreeing on the chronology; however other aspects are not. At around 8.00pm Briand, Nivelle and Lyautey came to see Lloyd George and handed him a written proposal for the joint command of the French and British forces. The Prime Minister simply saw it as the French being in overall command and that seemed to fit with his wishes. When Hankey saw it, however, he was shocked as, being a military man, he could see the implications of the proposals; namely the reduction of Haig's level of command to that of no more than an Army commander and certainly no longer a Commander-in-Chief.

The origins of this proposal are confidently stated by many to be the result of collusion between the French Government and Lloyd George to create a unified command and force Haig to either accept the situation or resign. That there was some form of communication over the role of the Conference to create a unified command is clear from the behaviour of the two leaders in the meeting of the 26th and in the minutes of the War Cabinet meeting. The scale of this is, however, thrown into some doubt by a number of factors. All the evidence for it being a conspiracy to remove Haig comes from one major source, a telegram, supposedly sent on 16 February by Commandant Bertier de Sauvigny, Chief of the French Military Mission in London, to both Nivelle and Lyautey. The contents of the telegram are given in full as an appendix in Spears[60] but he does not site a source. Civrieux[61] mentions an earlier telegram (than that of the 19th, see below) but it is not to be found in any of the French archives. According to the version in Spears, quoted in full, it describes a meeting which took place in London. Sauvigny was meeting with Hankey when Lloyd George joined them and made it clear that he intended to place all the forces under Nivelle, giving Haig secret instructions to this effect if required. Neither Hankey nor Lloyd George make any mention of such a meeting. Unfortunately trust in Spears on this point is shaken when the latter part of the same appendix is read in which a further telegram from Sauvigny is reported. It is partially quoted by Spears as follows: "The War Cabinet intends to unmask its batteries against Haig's plans. Proposals will be made by Mr. Balfour for 28 February."[62]

The actual text of this telegram does exist and was supplied to Edmonds for the Official History by the French Historical Services. It was sent as a response to Haig's comments that a meeting of governments was no longer necessary as he had come to an agreement with Nivelle over transport. The equivalent passages read in fact:

> The War Committee has decided to unmask its batteries by bringing about a reunion, in the course of which he will ask you whether the projects of Sir D. Haig have in fact your approval.
> [and]
> These proposals will be made to-morrow, the 20th, by Mr Balfour to the ambassador, unless between now and then I should receive notice of your wishes.[63]

These discrepancies do place the entire episode in waters that are less than clear and the emphasis changes somewhat.[64]

Whatever the origins of this first proposal, when shown to Robertson and Haig, it was clear what their feelings were. They went to see Lloyd George, both angry at the proposal, leading the

---

60   Spears, Brig.-Gen E.L., *Prelude to Victory*, (London: Jonathan Cape, 1939), Appendix IX, p. 546.
61   Civrieux, Commandant de, *L'Offensive de 1917* (Paris et Bruxelles : Van Oest, 1919), p. 40.
62   Spears, *Prelude to Victory*, Appendix IX, p. 546.
63   Falls, *Military Operations, France and Belgium 1917 Vol. 1*, (London: Macmillan, 1940), p. 537.
64   See the Note on Sources for a detailed review of *Prelude to Victory* and how much Spears can be relied upon in his accounts of the dealings between Lloyd George and the military chiefs.

Prime Minister, probably displeased that the plans to create a unified command were going astray, to react badly and Hankey felt that "he more than hinted that Haig would have to resign if he didn't come to heel."[65]

Thus the evening came to an end with a great deal of anger and frustration in the air. Hankey wanted to see both Robertson and Haig afterwards but they wouldn't see him, so he retired to his room and drafted what he thought would be a possible compromise, acceptable to both sides.

Next morning Hankey persuaded Lloyd George that the French proposal was not the way forward and when asked to produce something better handed him his typed up proposal from the night before. This the Prime Minister accepted, called for Robertson who, according to Hankey's diary extract,[66] also accepted it, as did Haig "after palaver".[67] Spears claims[68] that the clause in the proposal, that the British C-in-C could appeal to London, came from the military side but as Haig's diary[69] does not mention it and as it contradicts Hankey's diary entry it is difficult to accept.[70]

It may never be known exactly what exactly happened in Calais, or what level Lloyd George's involvement was, prior to the event. What is clear, however, is that the British Prime Minister did wish to clip the wings of his military arm in some way. In one aspect he succeeded as he obtained some kind of agreement creating a unified command. By working in an underhand manner, what he also succeeded in doing unfortunately was confirming, in both Haig's and Robertson's eyes, the distrust that they had in Lloyd George and politicians in general. Thus the British efforts in the war were still to be controlled by two camps which, whilst remaining generally civil, were not working in harmony.

What followed in the next few weeks can only be described as a West End farce and unbecoming to allies engaged in a deadly conflict. The first sign of trouble was when communication from Nivelle's headquarters arrived on Haig's desk at 6pm on the 28 February. The Field Marshal's diary clearly shows how he felt about it:

> Its language was couched in very <u>commanding</u> [underlined in original] tones. He asked for a copy of my orders to my Armies for the forthcoming offensive, …
>
> … and it also one [sic] which certainly no C-in-C of this great British Army should receive without protest.

He then makes a point that he only comes under Nivelle's orders after the battle commences.[71]

The letter was unfortunate as it was couched in exactly the terms a C-in-C would use when addressing a subordinate. In asking for the orders to Armies it is implying an element of possible criticism and Haig would have it clear in his mind that the Calais agreement unmistakably gave him freedom of choice on how to employ his troops.[72] He immediately forwarded the letter to Robertson along with a covering note and a memorandum to be placed before the War Cabinet. The paper also pointed out the potential dangers now faced by the British, mainly in the north, as a result of the, now confirmed, German retreat towards the Hindenburg Line. Much of what the note said was based upon no real intelligence information and was a very scaremongering

---

65   Hankey, *Supreme Command*, p. 616.
66   Hankey, *Supreme Command*, p. 616.
67   Hankey, *Supreme Command*, p. 616.
68   Spears, *Prelude to Victory*, p. 152.
69   TNA: WO 256/15, Haig diaries, entry for 27 February 1917.
70   The full text of the agreement can be found in Appendix I.
71   TNA: WO 256/15, Haig diaries, entry for 28 February 1917.
72   See clause (4) of the Calais Agreement in Appendix I.

document, designed with one purpose and that was to derail all the plans for the year. The War Cabinet already had in its hands a paper by Robertson from 23 February[73] showing a difference of 940 battalions in favour of the Entente with a new reserve being built by Germany of up to 300 battalions. In it he states that there are no indications of an offensive such as seen the previous year at Verdun. Politicians in the Cabinet would have to weigh up the two documents and judge the effects of the German retreat in a climate of distrust in what their military chiefs were telling them.

Thus he was presenting a double blow, firstly pointing out the unacceptable behaviour of the French and then within a matter of days after the Calais Agreement, invoking Clause iii)[74] by arguing that his left flank was in danger and therefore he had to have control of his reserves without reference to Nivelle. Haig then replied on 4 March to Nivelle without betraying his true feelings, excusing the delay in replying by writing that he was "studying the possibilities arising out of the enemy's withdrawal on my 5th Army front."[75] Given Haig's memorandum to the War Cabinet the letter is on the surface supportive of Nivelle. He wishes to point out that the German retreat removed a whole section of the plan of attack and thus the British 5th Army would not have the role it had previously being given; this then allowing reserves to be moved from this front to reinforce his left flank in the north. Also that the attack at Arras, if carried out in isolation, would have "no more than a local effect"[76] and therefore asking that Nivelle clarify what his intentions are given the new situation. He goes on, however, to deal two body blows to Nivelle when he says further that he cannot now, in the changed circumstances, see Cambrai as a feasible objective for the British and that he does not see preparations being ready for 8 April. He answers the demand for a British mission with a need for further discussion as to its role and that relations with des Vallières[77] at GHQ were such that he could see no reason for "duplication of the existing arrangements".[78] Spears is critical of Haig at this point, claiming that his maintaining a soldierly manner had "blinded him again to General Nivelle's real attitude and blind he remained."[79] This may be true but with this approach Haig was following a path of his own making and with careful deliberation had managed to undermine the whole Calais agreement within a week of its inception. He attached a copy of his memorandum to the British Cabinet to ensure that Nivelle was under no illusion as to the strength of the Field Marshal's intentions.

If Nivelle was not 100 percent sure of what he was hearing from the British, an additional communication from the very man whom Haig regarded as his effective link with the French, des Vallières, arrived dated 5 March; reporting on an interview he had with the British Field Marshal. The report must have confirmed all Nivelle's suspicions that Haig was trying to derail the whole year's plan. The problem was that in many ways Haig was correct. The German retreat was severely disrupting all previous plans and a rethink was clearly necessary. Unfortunately, des Vallières, in his report, concentrated on the movement of troops to the north and what he regarded as a clear reluctance on the side of the British to mount any offensive at all; claiming, rather disingenuously, that even the Arras attack was not going to be carried out à fond (in full).[80] Evidence was now

---

73   TNA: CAB 24/6, GT 49 – Germany's Intentions.
74   Within which the British C-in-C could refuse to conform to French commands should it endanger the safety of his Army. See Appendix I.
75   TNA: WO 158/37, Sir Douglas Haig and General Nivelle: Correspondence, Haig to Nivelle, 4 March 1917.
76   TNA: WO 158/37, Sir Douglas Haig and General Nivelle: Correspondence, Haig to Nivelle, 4 March 1917.
77   General des Vallières, Head of the French Mission at GHQ in Montreuil.
78   TNA: WO 158/37, Correspondence, Haig to Nivelle, 4 March 1917.
79   Spears, *Prelude to Victory*, p. 166.
80   Correspondence of des Vallières to Nivelle, 5 March 1917, translation printed in Spears, *Prelude to Victory* p. 560. Haig never said anything of the attack at Arras not going ahead as planned; this was the French liaison officer allowing his imagination to extrapolate what was really said.

mounting in Nivelle's mind that the British had every intention of going their own way with an attack in Belgium at some stage during the year; worse still, that any Anglo-French attack would be weakened in order to save troops for that operation.

When this was presented to the French Cabinet on 7 March there was deep resentment at what was seen as a total disregard for the agreement formulated in Calais. Prime Minister Briand had, for once, a united Cabinet although General Lyautey did try to calm waters somewhat by suggesting that Nivelle had shown a lacking in tact in how he had handled matters since Calais. Correspondence with London duly followed so that by 8 March the British Cabinet was faced with both sides of the argument between the Commanders-in-Chief. Lloyd George was not blind to Haig's manoeuvrings but the tone of the communication from Paris incensed the rest of the Cabinet so much he had little choice but to act on his Commander-in-Chief's behalf.[81] A further conference was therefore called by the British Government. This was at first rebuffed by the French; nevertheless, Lloyd George insisted and both sides convened in London on 12 March. Briand did not travel to London, sending Ribot, Minister of Finance to lead the delegation. The French Prime Minister was very unsure of his position at home with considerable forces working to remove him, therefore he must have felt that absence from Paris would be dangerous.

The meeting had been brought about by factors on both sides. On the one hand Haig had, it would seem, quite deliberately, made every effort to derail the plans for the year. Initially by placing great emphasis on the rail problem, much of which was true but exacerbated by the increased traffic to 2nd Army in the north (which the French were unaware of) and then by over emphasising the dangers created by the German retreat. On the other hand, Nivelle, by holding to an interpretation of the Calais Agreement far beyond that which was sensible and by poor handling of subsequent communications, handed the baton to Haig, giving him sufficient ammunition to stir the British Cabinet. In addition, his inability to recognise or at least properly acknowledge the possible consequences of the German retreat had put doubt in Lloyd George's mind as to how much he was to be trusted to command. This is evident when the minutes of the London Conference are examined.

The first day of the conference[82] was essentially the politicians meeting at 10 Downing Street and the military at the War Office. Spears describes this initial split as a triumph for Robertson with the politicians adjourning without deciding anything whilst the military went away to sort things out. Unfortunately, whatever Spears' used as a source for this information erred. What actually occurred was that Lloyd George met both generals, initially individually and then together and fed the contents of this meeting back to the Conference when it met in the afternoon. In the meantime, GHQ advocates went to the War Office to discuss strategy. Spears' error can be easily identified when he describes Lyautey's contributions to the military meeting in his usual flamboyant way, when in actual fact the French Minister of War was where he should have been and that was at the meeting of politicians. Lloyd George reported to the meeting that both sides had now agreed on most points with such matters as the British liaison mission and some of the worries that Haig had over, for example, whether Nivelle would come and inspect British troops without permission. Lyautey tried to claim that the agreement now removed the clause allowing Haig to appeal to the British Cabinet (Clause 2(3)), but this impression was quickly dismissed and the clause confirmed by Lloyd George. The tone of the communications sent by Nivelle was raised, Lloyd George replying that they had discussed this and Nivelle had laid the blame on subordinates having written the letters. This face saving device was accepted by all at the meeting although it is not difficult to imagine what the real feelings were. The job was done though in terms of bringing

81   Spears, *Prelude to Victory,* p. 180.
82   TNA: CAB 28/2, I.C.-18 & 18(a), Notes on an Anglo-French Conference Held at 10 Downing Street, London, on 12 & 13 March 1917.

the two generals together and ironing out the differences between them, removing the ability of either to use such differences to derail the planned offensive. When the Conference reconvened the next morning with the military members present, it was merely an exercise in confirming the discussions of the previous day. The French did attempt yet again to remove clause 2(3) but this was rebuffed by Lloyd George. Concerns over whether planning would cease should Haig refer to the Cabinet over anything were also eased by pointing out that during the recent dispute preparations had proceeded without pause and would do so in any similar circumstances in the future. Finally, there was agreement over sending General Wilson to the British Mission at French GHQ; Haig conceding this request of the French on advice from Robertson who felt there were larger battles to win.[83] Thus another document was created which really only clarified aspects of the Calais Agreement with some protective clauses for the British.[84]

The period from mid-February to the end of the London Conference really does look to anyone peering at it from the distance of time as one of wounded pride, pompousness and anything but the behaviour of major players within a world in crisis. Lloyd George had made his bid for a major change in the leadership of the British Army not realising the strength of the Field Marshal's hand, nor his guile in playing it. He had even asked Hankey to prepare an argument for the removal of Haig and who the successor might be. The result of this is an intriguing hand written memo[85] from Hankey to Lloyd George on 8 March. The content of Hankey's memo makes a great deal of sense; criticising aspects of Haig's behaviour but coming to the conclusion that firstly, it would cause the fall of the government should Haig be removed and secondly that there was nobody of quality to replace him. Hankey also makes it clear that he has lost confidence in Nivelle and that Haig is in principle correct in his judgement over the German retreat. In Hankey's own words "the conclusion differs from that which I expected to reach".[86] The most important piece of advice, which it seems, from subsequent events, the Prime Minister took on board, was to now place total confidence in the C-in-C and that "there should be a complete reconciliation".[87] Hankey read the memo to Lloyd George the next day (which is why it cannot be found in a typed form) and it is goes a long way to explaining why the Prime Minister's behaviour over the next few days (and in fact months) is very different to that of a few weeks previous. For Haig's part, he very intelligently used everything in his power to put the proverbial spanner in the works. Why he did so though stands up to the most careful scrutiny as being a concerted effort to protect his army in what he saw as a volatile and changing situation. His attitude towards the Calais Agreement was not beyond criticism and his (and Robertson's) memoranda to the Cabinet must have been difficult for Lloyd George to swallow (Hankey calls his attitude "uncivil and almost insubordinate.")[88] Haig used the "danger on the Channel Coast" card very well, but his diaries do betray a real fear from that quarter, one that cannot be disregarded by those not ever having responsibility for over a million men.[89] Whilst it could be said that Haig's motives were for the most part admirable, he also knew he had strong backing and not only from politicians. He had informed the King privately of his unhappiness at what had transpired in Calais and on 9 March was visited by Col. Wigram, the King's Personal Secretary. Wigram informed Haig of the King's support for him and it is not difficult to imagine a private meeting between King George and Lloyd George where the Prime Minister was informed of His Majesty's displeasure at having found out about proposed

83   TNA: WO 256/15, Haig diaries, Letter from Robertson to Haig 6 March.
84   The contents of this agreement can be seen in Appendix II.
85   TNA: CAB 63/19, Lord Hankey Papers, No. 50.
86   TNA: CAB 63/19, Lord Hankey Papers, No. 50.
87   TNA: CAB 63/19, Lord Hankey Papers, No. 50.
88   TNA: CAB 63/19, Lord Hankey Papers, No. 50.
89   TNA: WO 256/15, Haig diaries, 2 March 1917.

changes to the leadership of his army without his knowledge.[90] Lloyd George was a shrewd enough politician to know when to change tack. Nivelle, on the other hand, does not seem to have had the same level of ability to see when plans need to be reassessed. This was precisely the moment when a much greater commander, or even a reasonably competent one, might have conceded that the overall strategic plan for 1917 had been completely disrupted by the withdrawal of the Germans. Admittedly there was a commitment, especially to the Russians and Italians as part of the overall strategic plan for the year, for offensive action on all fronts. On the other hand, adding to the complicated situation were events in Russia where the Tsar had abdicated on 15 March and as such could the Entente be sure that any kind of offensive action was coming from that direction until the political situation had been resolved. Closely following, five days later, was the resignation of French Prime Minister Briand after his minister of war Lyautey had resigned on the 15th. Lyautey, seemingly frustrated by what he saw as a poor sense of security within the government refused to discuss particular secrets during a closed session of the Chamber of Deputies and this caused an outcry. In losing Briand, the major supporter of Nivelle throughout the difficult process of bringing his plan to fruition was gone, only opponents remained. This was the point at which proceedings could have been brought to a halt and the overall strategy for the year reviewed. A new French Government was formed under Alexandre Ribot, his 4th visit to the Prime Minister's position, an example of how volatile French politics was in the 3rd Republic. He appointed Paul Painlevé as his Minister of War but only after he agreed to work with Nivelle. Painlevé was not a supporter of Nivelle, favouring the less flamboyant approach of General Pétain and also being an avid supporter of General Sarrail, currently commanding the forces in Salonika; "there was even speculation that he might now bring back Sarrail to replace General Nivelle as commander-in-chief on the Western Front."[91] Painlevé met Nivelle on 22 March and put all of his doubts over the coming offensive to the General, concluding that it should be called off. One major doubt, in addition to all those raised by the German withdrawal, was the fact that it was clear that the whole action had been compromised and that the Germans knew exactly where and when it was all going to occur. In February the Germans had carried out a major raid during which bundles of paperwork were retrieved. "Found within the captured material were orders to the French 2nd Infantry Division that clearly indicated a large scale offensive on the Aisne in April."[92]

Painlevé himself, despite not previously in the government knew many details of the offensive and thus he argued, the Germans must also be fully aware. Nivelle was not to be moved and knowing that the Germans would now be reinforcing the front, turned the argument around, according to Spears, by saying; "I do not fear numbers. The greater the numbers the greater the victory."[93] Greenhalgh sites a number of sources[94] that point to Painlevé probably replacing Nivelle soon after taking over, with Petain then taking charge. A meeting was called for 6 April attended by Ribot, Painlevé, (Minister of Armaments), (Minister of Marine), Nivelle and the four Army Group Commanders (d'Espèrey, Micheler, Pétain and Castelnau). Although it seems this meeting did nothing but undermine the whole strategy, resulting in Nivelle offering his resignation, this was declined and nothing was decided. An opportunity for completely reassessing the strategy for the year had been missed; however, given the lateness of the day (the British artillery bombardment was already underway) the momentum for the offensive had taken on a life of its own and would have been very difficult (but not impossible) to stop. Painlevé himself, when reporting back

90   This is speculation as these meetings are never recorded in any form; however, it is hard to imagine the King not mentioning something in his regular meetings with the Prime Minister.
91   Dutton, David, *The Politics of Diplomacy*, (London: Taurus, 1998), p. 122.
92   Ludendorff, *Kriegserinnerungen*, p. 324.
93   Spears, *Prelude to Victory*, p. 338.
94   Greenhalgh, *The French Army and the First World War*, (Cambridge: University Press, 2014), p. 184.

to the French Parliament in secret session on 29 June compared stopping the offensive to halting an express train by standing in front of it.[95] What Painlevé did believe though, after the meeting, is of great interest when later evaluating decisions taken as the offensive was underway. He wrote the day after that,

> it is not a question of pursuing at any cost a battle in which all our resources would be committed; rather the battle would be stopped as soon as it seemed that it would impose excessive losses on our army, likely to weaken it profoundly for insufficient and hazardous results.[96]

It was under this impression that Painlevé allowed the offensive to go ahead. Thus the great machinery of war, already on the move, was allowed to continue following a plan, now not merely doubted by some in the French military, but one cobbled together having reacted to events out of its control and with the full knowledge of the German High Command.

---

95   Greenhalgh, *The French Army and the First World War*, p. 185.
96   Quoted in Greenhalgh, *The French Army and the First World War*, p. 185.

3

Plans Made and Unmade

Now all roads lead to France
and heavy is the tread
of the living; but the dead
returning lightly dance.

Roads

It is now important to examine how the plans that had caused so much consternation at the political level had developed over the months after General Nivelle had taken over command. In essence Nivelle wanted to do much more than was planned by Joffre and others at the Chantilly Conference. He felt that he had the solution to the problem of breaking through the German lines and achieving a conclusive victory in 1917. Basing this on the successes he had achieved at Verdun he saw no problem in enlarging the resources and tactics used there and doing exactly the same across a front measuring hundreds of miles. The perfect vision of historical hindsight questions this belief and condemns it to the scrapheap of military nonsense. However, the morale of many a politician and not a few military men has already been examined and an end to the war was as far removed from the perceptions of leaders as it had ever been. The plan as outlined to Haig can be best seen on a map and compared to that created in the November meetings.

The differences can be seen between centre of thrust and emphasis on exploitation. Whereas Joffre and Haig had envisaged a continuation of the pressure either side of the River Somme with only secondary attacks in the south, Nivelle's was based upon a far bolder conception. The British Armies would attack first in the north, pinching off the salient created by the 1916 attacks on the Somme and then threatening Cambrai, thereby drawing off German reserves from other armies. Around the same time the *G.A.N.*[1] would also attack and then after a period of time of maybe 10 days the main assault would be launched by the *G.A.R.*[2] on the Aisne. These plans were under discussion and the fundamental overall strategy agreed between Field Marshal Haig and General Nivelle when the events already described above dislocated them. Firstly, the timing was put in question by, on the one hand, the railway problem being raised in the first place and on the other the transportation problem itself. Then Lloyd George managed to poison the whole situation with the leadership question and finally the nail in the coffin caused by the German withdrawal. Nivelle's inability to see past his own precious plan led to no major change in his thinking, the southern element of the offensive simply gaining in importance with everything now depending upon the success of the *G.A.R.* The one major result of changes to the plan which altered British planning was the much reduced role now given to 5th Army south of the Arras front. The 4th Army had no role in the original plan, other than taking over more of the line to their right to relieve French forces as agreed by Field Marshal Haig before the withdrawal. The difference now

---

1   *Groupe d'armées du Nord.*
2   *Groupe d'armées du Reserve.*

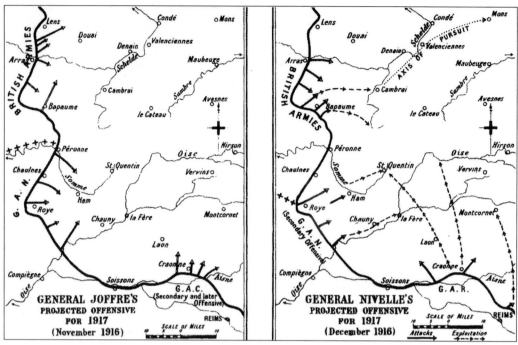

Nivelle's change of plan. (Falls, *Military Operations 1917 Vol. 1*, Sketch 1)

being that instead of extending down to the old front line at Roye it was now to be on the Amiens to St Quentin Road. In the original plan 5th Army was to attack on 3rd Army's southern flank, towards Achiet-le-Grand. All that area was evacuated by the Germans therefore 5th Army was instructed to aggressively follow the German withdrawal to the Hindenburg Line and then to plan an attack on those defences between Quéant and Écoust and to support the offensive of 3rd Army. This led to the dreadfully mismanaged and tragic First Battle of Bullecourt, which due to its failure, had little or no effect on the endeavours in 3rd Army area. Troops that had been released by the straightening of the line allowed Haig to make some changes to his dispositions before the commencement of the offensive. He was able to increase 3rd Army to 18 divisions and also 1st Army to 13 divisions by moving XIII Corps to it from 5th Army. In doing this he was able to think of that corps as a reserve to exploit success in the direction of Douai, cover 3rd Army's northern flank if it advanced on Cambrai or, rather interestingly, reinforce 2nd Army at Ypres. He had not dismissed the dangers he felt still existed on his Belgian flank.

For the offensive 1st Army was providing the Canadian Corps of four divisions, 1st to 4th, with the British 5th Division attached to it as a reserve. The main British effort would be made by 3rd Army under General Edmund Allenby. It is worth taking a moment to look at both the character of this man and also his relationship with Haig. At 6ft. 2in. with a barrel chest and a very quick temper he received the nickname "The Bull". Taking over command of 3rd Army in October 1915 he was therefore in command of the disastrous diversionary attack at Gommecourt on 1 July 1916. At this time one of his staff officers was Archibald Wavell, who would eventually be one of the leading generals of the Second World War and in 1941 published a biography of Allenby. With no diary and few personal papers, bar letters home for this period, from Allenby, Wavell's first-hand experience of the man is invaluable. Allenby, a man known for his violent temper is shown by

Wavell to have a gentler side but this was more towards children and the sick.[3] It seems that at a military level he was quick to criticise and would loudly admonish anything he took a dislike to:

> These unfortunate outbursts, often over some comparatively trivial breach of discipline, did much to destroy the good impression that the sight of the Army commander in the front trenches made, and to confirm the legend that "the Bull" was merely a bad-tempered, obstinate hot-head, a 'thud-and-blunder' general.[4]

Allenby's association with Haig is an important one as the campaign being studied here has to be seen within that context. It was quite simply a cold relationship having its roots in rivalry that stretched back to Staff College many years previous. Neither man being comfortable in conversation led to this never being reconciled. Indeed, the animosity between was obvious in public:

> At the periodical conferences of Army commanders, it was obvious that Allenby's opinion carried little weight, and received scant attention, especially if Gough, commander of the Fifth Army, had a different view. Often Sir Douglas Haig would turn to one of the other Army commanders and ask his opinion on some point while Allenby was still speaking.[5]

The result of this was that Allenby would follow orders but there would be no active discussion between two experienced leaders as to the best way forward should plans go astray or even what the next steps might be should they go well. It was not the best leadership scenario to be in place at the outset of a major offensive.

Both in this chapter and all subsequent ones when the action begins, the narrative is going to move from north to south on the map. This is contrary to military 'doctrine', as laid out in the Official Histories but, because of the nature of the plans and fighting, far more reasonable for the reader to follow. The Official History describes events which did not happen until well after those it subsequently portrays, bringing an element of disorientation for the reader. Thus plans and events will follow the order of Canadian Corps in 1st Army, followed by XVII Corps, VI Corps and finally VII Corps of 3rd Army.

All the plans were devised with particular objectives expressed in lines, each of which

General Edmund Allenby. (Author)

3   Wavell, Archibald, *Allenby: A Study in Greatness: The Biography of Field-Marshal Viscount Allenby of Megiddo and Felixstowe,* (New York: Oxford University Press, 1941), pp. 168-169.
4   Wavell, *Allenby: A Study in Greatness: The Biography of Field-Marshal Viscount Allenby of Megiddo and Felixstowe,* p. 166.
5   Wavell, *Allenby: A Study in Greatness: The Biography of Field-Marshal Viscount Allenby of Megiddo and Felixstowe,* p. 170.

was awarded a colour to distinguish them. These were, in order from the British lines outwards were the Black, Blue, Brown and as a final objective line in some places for the first day, Green. This varied a little on the Canadian front with the order being Black, Red, Blue, and then Brown; with more limited final objectives for the day. The particular shape of the planned offensive led to decisions regarding timings that can cause confusion when you read that units adjacent to each other attacked at very different times. Before going into detail it is perhaps best to see the line as a whole to begin with.

It can be seen that as you move south of the River Scarpe the line begins to turn from an almost north-south axis to one facing north east. The direction of attack for the units from the 14th Division southwards was much more in this direction, not eastwards. If all units had jumped off at the same time, there was a risk of 14th and 56th Divisions attacking across the units of those further north. Thus the decision was taken to make the British front line in the south the Black Line. In other words, they were already on the first objective and therefore would only attack later in the day. The fact that units on the far right of the offensive had even later start times will be discussed when the more detailed planning in that area is reached.

Another complication for British planners was the retreat of the Germans as described earlier. The old lines running from Tilloy-les-Mofflaines through Beaurains and further in this direction had been abandoned. This had left the advancing British the problem of creating jumping off trenches for the offensive under the noses of the Germans. It also meant that southwards from the complex trench system near to Tilloy named The Harp, the Germans were in the newly built *Siegfried Stellung*, or to British planners, the Hindenburg Line. These positions will be discussed in greater depth when the situation is described as seen by the Germans. It cannot be said though that the retreat badly disrupted planning for the offensive. There was sufficient time for all facets of the planning to be completed before the required start date. There is no evidence that haste played any part in possible errors that might be found in the arrangements at all levels, from Corps down to individual units.

The overall plan was that XVII Corps, VI Corps, and VII Corps of 3rd Army would attack astride the river Scarpe with the general direction, as agreed with Nivelle, of Cambrai. This offensive was to be supported by an attack by the Canadian Corps of 1st Army on Vimy Ridge in order to support and protect the left flank of the main effort.

The nature of the front line being attacked and other reasons (which will be discussed later) led to a complicated timing of the assault when compared to other offensives such as the first day on the Somme. All the forces north of the Scarpe had 5.30am as zero hour, as did VI Corps south of the river. To the right of the southernmost division of the latter unit, however, began the complications. These entailed a delay in the start time of varying proportions. It was at Tilloy-les-Mofflaines that the old German front line, as noted earlier in describing the March retreat, diverged from the one about to be attacked. Here 3rd Division had the complex task of dealing with the taking of the area in front of Tilloy, the village itself and a stronghold on Telegraph Hill to the south of it. This redoubt was named the Harp, clearly from its shape resembling the instrument. 3rd Division shared the task of taking the Harp with 14th Division of VII Corps on its right. Looking at the map you can see that a slight change in direction of the new German lines and the tasks to be dealt with before the Harp could be attacked meant that 14th Division had to have a delayed start time. This was understandable if unfortunate, as the element of surprise mentioned earlier would thus be lost. There then began a complicated time lapse as you moved right down the line of VII Corps. Both 14th and 56th Divisions to its right had the later 7.30am start time. 30th Division, attacking with two brigades, had a different start time for each of them. On the left of the division, 21st Brigade had 12.55pm as their jump off time whilst 89th Brigade on the right shared the 4.15pm time with 21st Division on their right.

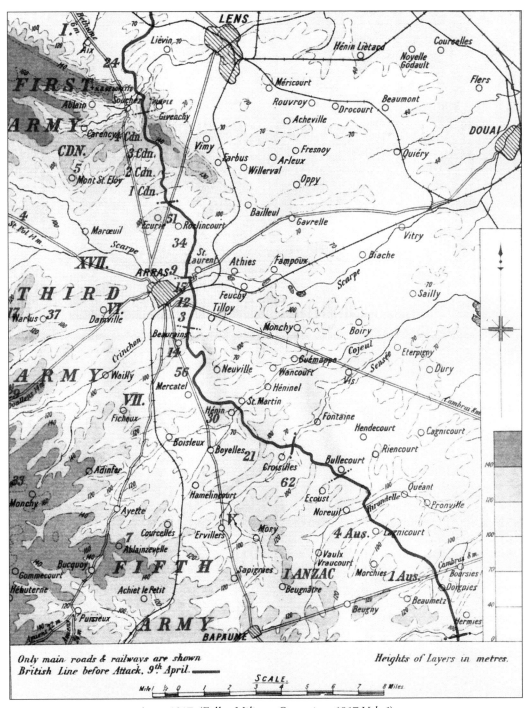

Arras 1917. (Falls, *Military Operations 1917 Vol. 1*)

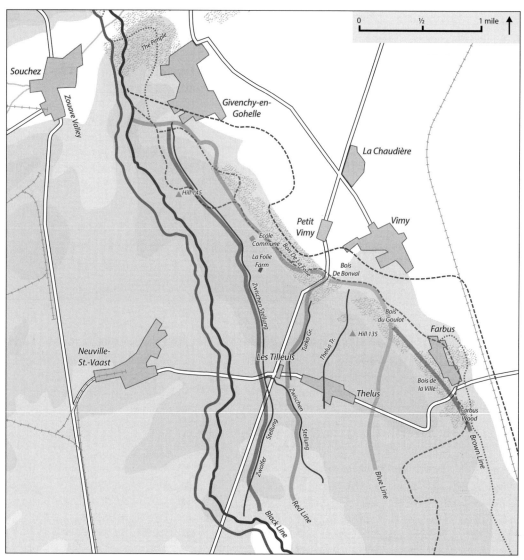

1st Army objective lines.

This arrangement was, to some extent, a compromise solution to a disagreement between Allenby and Lieut.-General Sir T. D'O.Snow, VII Corps commander. Snow had not wished to attack the Hindenburg Line directly on the right, using instead his left two divisions (14th and 56th) to break through at Telegraph Hill and Neuville Vitasse and come behind the Hindenburg Line; meanwhile only making spoiling attacks to the south without confronting the line directly. Allenby disagreed and told Snow he had to attack. In reply Snow asked for the Brown Line to be brought back. To fit in with all the timings for the Brown Line this led to the very late start time on the very right. The very fact that Allenby was insistent on this attack should have led to sufficient resources being given to Snow to attack what was in many ways the strongest German positions on the whole front. This will be seen not to be the case and directly led to the consequences that will be discussed later. Thus, in the planning stage were laid foundations for problems that would eventually lead to an inherent flaw in the attack.

The allocation and command of reserves for the attack was somewhat complicated. When the German withdrawal had released a number of divisions to Haig he rearranged the allocations of many of them, turning XVIII Corps under Lieutenant General Sir Ivor Maxse into a reserve for 3rd Army. At this planning stage this was seen as a breakthrough corps, to be used under its own corps command to follow up successes and had four divisions. The other element of the reserve was the Cavalry Corps with 2nd and 3rd Cavalry Divisions and 17th Division allocated. 4th Cavalry Division had been allocated to 5th Army for use in any potential breakthrough in that area and 1st Cavalry Division kept under direct GHQ control; however, it was kept in 3rd Army area. Although Maxse's Corps was under Allenby's 3rd Army it could not be used without GHQ permission, an unusual situation for an Army commander to be in. It also lost one of its divisions on 6 April, reducing the reserves available to Allenby to four infantry and two cavalry divisions.

What about the opposition? Many of the positions held by the Germans were those taken in October 1914 and held ever since. North of the Scarpe the French had managed, as has been seen, to regain some lost territory but from Roclincourt to the Scarpe the lines were as they had been two and a half years before. Also south of the Scarpe the German front line was as close to Arras as they had come in 1914. Only south of Tilloy-les-Mofflaines, where the German withdrawal had changed everything, had those old trenches been abandoned and that move had been to place troops into bastions such as The Harp and the Hindenburg Line. Time and resources then had been ample for the Germans to turn this part of the front into a highly sophisticated and deep position of strength. Although it must be noted that the Hindenburg Line was not as completely finished as the Germans would have liked. When faced with a similar situation 10 months earlier on the Somme, the British first attacks had foundered. This must be kept in mind when later following the narrative.

It was the German *6th Army* under that occupied the positions to be attacked, within the overall area of *Heeresgruppe des Kronprinzen Rupprecht von Bayern*. Once it was clear that the Arras region was going to be attacked Rupprecht ordered a rearrangement of units within the armies under his control and a reinforcement of the front. The right wing of *1st Army* to the south of Arras was transferred to *6th Army* to ensure that there was uniformity of command in the coming offensive. *23. I.D.*[6] and *24. I.D.* were withdrawn from the positions on both sides of the Scarpe and replaced by *14. Bayerische. I.D.*[7] north of the river and by the four divisions of *IX Reserve-Korps* south of the river as outlined below. Some of these new units had come from comparatively quiet areas and had received some rest but many were still suffering from one or more spells of action on the Somme in the previous year and also found themselves providing labour to rapidly finish the work on the Hindenburg Line. They were far from fresh units coming into the line. The only compensation was that the number of reinforcing units now allowed the divisions to reduce the number of men at the front and introduce more regular rotation of units.

Falkenhausen's army was split into a number of groups according to location. *IV Armee-Korps* made up *Gruppe Loos*, which was situated beyond the geographical scope of this book. Next southwards was *Gruppe Souchez* consisting of *VIII Reserve-Korps* led by *Gen.der.Inf.* Wichura and holding the line from Loos to Givenchy-en-Gohelle. This was made up of *56. I.D.* (*Generalmaj.* von Wichmann), *80.R.D.*[8] (*Generalmaj.* Körner) and in the south *16. Bayerische. I.D.* (*Generalmaj.* Möhl). The left wing of this *Gruppe* would be attacked by the Canadian 4th Division on 9 April. On the main Vimy Ridge from Givenchy-en-Gohelle down to the Scarpe was *Gruppe Vimy*, made up of the *1 Bayerische. Reserve-Korps* under the leadership of *Gen.der.Inf.* Ritter von Fasbender.

---

6   From this point on *I.D.* will be used as the abbreviation for the German *Infantrie-Division*.
7   Abbreviation for *Bayerische Infantrie-Division*.
8   *Reserve-Division*.

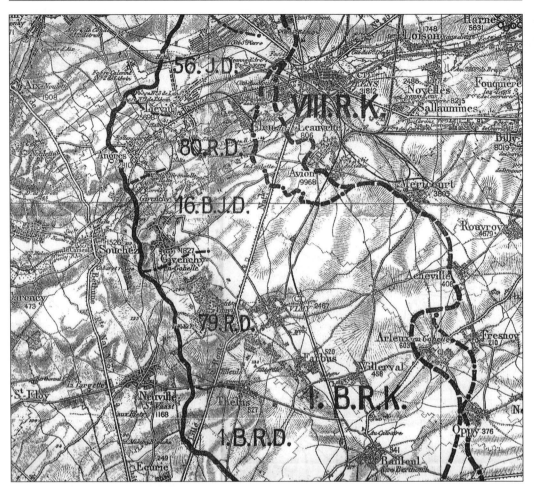

German defenders on Vimy Ridge. Note the Gothic capital I and J are the same which is why the *16. Bayerische I.D.* appears as *B.J.D.* (*Die Osterschlacht bei Arras 1917 I. Teil*)

This northern group consisted of *79. R.D.* (*Gen.der.Inf.* von Bacmeister), then *1 Bayerische R.D.* (*Generalmaj.* Freiherr von Pechmann), and on the banks of the Scarpe, *14 Bayerische. I.D.* (*Generallt.* Ritter von Rauchenberger).

South of the Scarpe was the group that was to face the whole of the attack of the British VI and VII Corps, *Gruppe Arras*, consisting of *IX Reserve-Korps* under the leadership of *Generallt.* Dieffenbach. Adjacent to the Scarpe was *11 I.D.* (*Generallt.* von Schöler), then *17 R.D.* (*Generalmaj.* von Reuter), *18 R.D.* (*Generallt.* von Wundt) and finally down to Croisilles *220 I.D.* (*Generalmaj.* von Bassewitz). In reserve *6th Army* had three divisions, *17 I.D., 18 I.D. and 26 I.D.* with call on two divisions of what had been *1st Army*, namely *1. Garde-Reserve-Division* and *4.Garde-Infanterie-Division*.[9]

Some of these units had moved to this front during early March and as far as Rupprecht was concerned it created a much stronger defensive position than was previously the case. Some of the

9   Behrmann, Franz & Brandt, Archivrat Walther, *Die Osterschlacht bei Arras 1917 I. Teil* (Oldenburg: Stalling, 1929), p. 22.

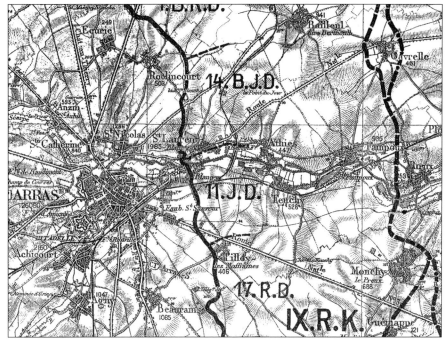

German defenders east of Arras. (*Die Osterschlacht bei Arras 1917 I. Teil*)

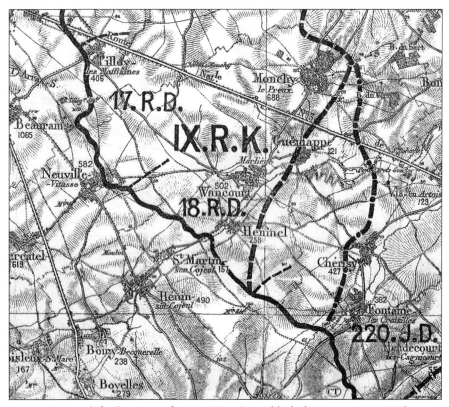

German defenders west of Arras. (*Die Osterschlacht bei Arras 1917 I. Teil*)

units were replacements for those that had spent a reasonably long period of time in the line. It seems that this was not before time as the passive nature of some of the front seems to have led to the deterioration of some of the defences. In the front line near to Tilloy-les-Mofflaines *I.R. 51*[10] was part of the relief of *24. R.D.* by *11. I.D.* during the last days of March. The history of the regiment is far from complementary about what they found:

> The Communication trenches, to be used to reach the front from the valley behind the railway bridge were so blocked with mud that large sections had to be traversed above them. Other connecting and communication trenches were only knee deep, so that movement in them by day was not possible. The fighting trenches were very neglected. Only the front trench was defensible and this only in sections. Between B1 and the company on our right, was a hundred-metre stretch that was unoccupied and filled with barbed wire, making it impassable. On the left were similar 50 and 200 metre impassable lengths of trench.[11]

The liturgy goes on to describe how the wire in front was wide but very damaged and had not been repaired. They only had scant days to do anything about the situation with poor weather and a very active patrolling enemy to deal with.

Problems were not confined to the trenches that had been in place for many years. Even the units moving into the Hindenburg Line found that in their haste these incredibly strong positions were not always ideal. *R.I.R. 84. (18. R.D.)* arrived in the newly constructed trenches in the middle of March and immediately made comment upon them.

> The front trench (fighting trench) was unusually deep, on average 3-4 m. Fire positions and fire steps were almost non-existent.It was also the case that the communication trenches, between the front and second line trenches were unusable. In total contradiction to the extremely deep main trenches these were only knee deep. However good the Siegfried Stellung was the experienced front-line soldiers soon saw all these problems, to which must be added the complete lack of communication trenches leading back from the front lines. How, in daylight fighting, were reserves to be moved forward when they would have to move, clearly observed, over the high ground between Wancourt and Chérisy.[12]

Great Britain was not the only combatant nation to look carefully at its performance on the Somme and learn from it. The Germans too had a hard year of fighting both on the Somme and at Verdun to reflect upon and it led to a change of thinking in how to plan for an enemy offensive. Overall planning for 1917 was seen by Ludendorff almost immediately to be defensive in nature. New ideas for how this was to be done were formulated and supported by Ludendorff. They were circulated in two orders, *Abwehrschlacht* (defensive fighting) and *Ausbildungsforschrift für die Fußtruppen im Krieg*, (training regulations for infantry) which laid out a change in how a line was to be defended. Instead of regular and easily recognizable lines the defence was now to be organised in deep formations with the front line being far less densely held. Instead, counter attack formations were to be formed, the front lines would give way under pressure and then be retaken by these specialist units. This was planned at all levels, all the way up to that of division. Reserve

---

10   *Infanterie-Regiment Nr. 51.*

11   Nollau, Oberstlt. a.D. Herbert, *Geschichte des Königlich Preußischen 4. Niederschlesischen Infantrie-Regiments Nr. 51*, (Berlin: Kolk, 1931), p. 157.

12   Speck, Justiczinspector William, *Das Königlich Preußische Reserve-Infanterie-Regiment 84* (Zeulenroda: Sporn Verlag, 1937), pp. 171-172.

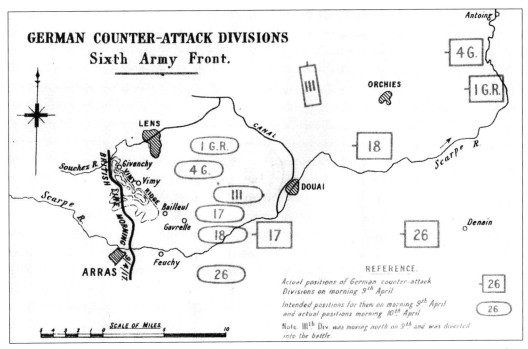

The position of the five reserve divisions on the morning of 9 April shown as rectangles as opposed to where they should have been. (Falls, *Military Operations 1917 Vol. 1*, p. 241)

divisions were to be seen as counter attack divisions, their task being to retake the terrain occupied by offensive enemy troops whilst they were still disorganised from the attack.[13]

Ludendorff himself accepted that in the early months of 1917 this new doctrine had only partially filtered down to units of all levels. A glance at a map of reserve division positions on the eve of the battle makes it abundantly clear that the system was not as yet fully understood or implemented.

The impact of the placement of reserves and the controversy that reigned almost from the first day of the offensive will be examined at the end of the book. For the Vimy Ridge defenders, whether they wished to follow the new 'defence in depth' orders or not, the position they held made it almost impossible. With a second line system sitting at the foot of the ridge, it meant that should there be counter attack troops, as laid down, they would be carrying out that task up the steep slopes of the eastern side. Local commanders saw the immense difficulty of this and therefore were forced to man the trenches actually on the ridge far more densely than they would have liked; in fact, even more densely than they would have done in other circumstances before the new orders. The situation was recognised by the Germans and they had plans for an attack (code-named "Munich") to push the Canadians back. Rupprecht had some doubts about the operation; however, he makes it clear in his diary that he also felt the position of the troops on the ridge to be

---

13 Ludendorff, *Meine Kriegserinnerungen* pp. 306-307.

vulnerable: "Nevertheless, I approved the operation, which aims to strengthen our positions in a *particular vulnerable point* [author's italics]."[14]

The operation was delayed and was overtaken by events when the Canadians attacked first. Another piece of evidence which demonstrates the weakness of the position and not its impregnability, as many have claimed, came in a conference on 18 March. At the meeting, Corps commander Fasbender made the following point; "Geographical Setting of our Position. Unfavourable. Total lack of depth. Initial enemy success [would be] extremely difficult to rectify."[15]

---

14   Rupprecht, *Kronprinz* von Bayern, *Mein Kreigstagebuch, Zweiter Band,* (Berlin: Mittler & Sons, 1929), p. 115.
15   Quoted in Sheldon, *Vimy Ridge*, p. 252.

4

Preparations

When I look back I am like moon, sparrow, and mouse
that witnessed what they could never understand
or alter or prevent in the dark house.
One thing remains the same – this is my right hand
The Long Small Room

It could be said that the offensives in 1917 had been two and a half years in the making. Certainly the experiences of the previous 10 months had been central to the make-up of the army that was about to take to the field. "The five-month Somme battle taught the BEF many lessons and transformed it from a largely inexperienced mass army into a largely experienced one."[1] To understand why things worked and why they did not in the upcoming offensive some background to the level of development within the British Army and its allies has to be considered.

The Men

The resources that Field Marshal Haig put in place for the offensive were considerable. To give some comparison in terms of divisions, on the first day of the Somme in the previous year (Gommecourt diversionary attack exclusive), 12 divisions had attacked on the first day. On the first day of Arras, 14 divisions plus one brigade from two other divisions were to be involved in the attack.

Although a description of a battle in the First World War can be divided neatly in actions by different Corps, that large formation was not a permanent collection of units and could change its composition on a daily basis. Later in the war, only the Canadians and Australians could train and work as a Corps. All other corps were a temporary housing facility for the main fighting high level unit, the division. Orders emanated from Army command, such as 3rd Army and would be directed at the corps within that Army. Corps would then take what would essentially be very strategic and general orders and allocate them, still at a more general level, to the divisions within its command at that moment. Some aspects, such as elements of the artillery and tanks could well remain under the direct command of the corps H.Q., but generally the division was where the more detailed plan for carrying out the general order was formulated. The division was designed to be a fully self-supported organisation with: three infantry brigades (each usually of four battalions), artillery, engineers, signals and a whole plethora of other units necessary for continuing a battle for some time. Although units could be moved from one division to another, essentially it was primarily within the division that some level of training and what is often called 'esprit de corps' could be established. Divisions gained reputations over the course of the war, some deserved, others possibly not. High Command also, on occasions, demonstrated a level of

---

1   Griffith, Paddy, *Battle Tactics of the Western Front, The British Army's Art of Attack 1916-18,* (New Haven & London: Yale University Press, 1994), p. 65.

prejudice for or against certain types of division. Without going into too much detail the British divisions could be broadly separated into three types: Regular, in existence at the beginning of the war; Territorial, part of the Territorial Force, created in 1908 to bring together all the local units of what could be loosely called 'part-time soldiers', mainly designed for home defence; and New Army, those divisions raised as a consequence of the massive recruitment drive, instigated by Field Marshal Kitchener in the early months of the war. Regular units were those in existence at the beginning of the war, with long traditions but no longer, after two and a half years of attrition warfare, containing very many men who were pre-war soldiers. Twelve such divisions were eventually formed after scraping together Regular units from around the world. Regular battalions were also no longer always brigaded together or all together in the same division but remained the core of the British Army. There were eventually 32 Territorial divisions, eight of which were for home defence. All Territorials had the choice not to serve overseas and those that chose not to formed those latter divisions. During 1915, as the first Territorial divisions entered the fray there was an element of prejudice against them from some higher echelons of command.[2] They soon, however, showed themselves as brave and capable as any of the Regular units. Unlike many of its continental neighbours, Britain had never moved to a 'nation state' by conscripting its available men, training them and then releasing them on condition that they would regularly be asked to attend training and would be called upon when required to join the colours. The outbreak of war in 1914, therefore, posed the problem of where the large army, very quickly recognised as a requirement, would come from. Secretary of State for War Lord Kitchener, very well-known throughout the nation for his previous exploits, was recalled shortly before returning to Egypt by Prime Minister Asquith and made Secretary of State for War. Unlike many around him he did not regard the blossoming war as likely to be a short affair and he set about creating a much larger force with which to fight it. Following Asquith's request of parliament to provide half a million more men, Kitchener announced his call for an immediate 100,000 volunteers. This was the beginning of a process that would eventually lead to five new armies being formed, usually designated by the codes K1 to K5 for obvious reasons. By the end of December, the number volunteering had risen to almost 806,000, allowing the formation of K1 to K4. All these were to be organised around the original regimental system, battalions thus formed being termed service battalions. Using the senior line infantry regiment,[3] The Royal Scots, as an example its battalions looked something like this:

A)   Three Regular battalions; 1st, 2nd and 3rd Royal Scots, the last being a training battalion always based in the United Kingdom.
B)   A number of Territorial Force battalions: first line such as 1/4th,1/5th up to 1/10th; second line such as 2/4th, 2/5th up to 2/10th and third line reserve 3/4th to 3/10th.
C)   New Army service battalions; 11th (Service) up to 17th (Service).
D)   A small number of other reserve or pioneer battalions.

The call to arms was deliberately organised in the early part of the war on a localised basis. In addition, battalions could be raised by local individuals or municipalities. One early example of this was the result of a meeting between General Henry Rawlinson, Director of Recruiting at

---

2   Kitchener himself was very opposed to these 'amateur soldiers' and that was the reason for his building completely new armies upon embarking on the recruiting drive and not using the existing structure as a baseline.
3   The Royal Scots were originally designated as 1st Foot and was thus the senior infantry regiment of the army after the Guards.

the time and Major the Hon. Robert White, a veteran of earlier wars. The meeting led to White raising a battalion of men from the financial houses of the City of London which eventually became the 10th (Stockbrokers Battalion) Royal Fusiliers. The same regiment would eventually, in addition, have Sportsman and Public Schools battalions. It was Lord Derby, chairman of the West Lancashire Territorial Association that would have the greatest and lasting impact on this phenomenon though. After lunching with Kitchener, and obtaining permission to form a battalion from business houses in Liverpool, the numbers of volunteers swelled so much that three battalions could be raised, then in October a fourth. These became the 17th to 21st King's Liverpool Regiment; soon the idea of forming local battalions, where the men came from the same area and will often have been friends, spread to Manchester, Birmingham and beyond. The nature of these groups of local men and friends soon led to them being termed 'Pals Battalions'. Referring back to the example above from the Royal Scots, 16th (Service) Battalion (2nd Edinburgh) was created largely out of the staff and supporters of the Heart of Midlothian Football Club at the instigation of Lt-Col. G. McCrae, MP and became known as McCrae's Battalion. In summary, of 557 battalions raised under the New Army umbrella, 215 were locally raised. It was not long before divisions of the New Army found themselves in Gallipoli and on the Western Front with a baptism of fire for some at Loos in September 1915. The 9th (Scottish) Division performed splendidly on the first day of the offensive, but a different fate awaited 21st and 24th Divisions. Thrown into the battle as part of the reserve, scarcely days after having reached France, this was not an auspicious beginning for them, casualties were high and their performance came under, somewhat unfair, criticism. The most famous, in modern culture, event which was to be attached to the units of the New Armies, was to be the Battle of the Somme, or more correctly in mythological terms, the opening day of that battle on 1 July 1916. The horrendous losses of some of the locally raised battalions came to dominate the cultural and historiography of that day and still does to the present day. Summed up in the most poignant of ways by John Harris in his fictional book Covenant with Death; "Two years in the making. Ten minutes in the destroying. That was our history."[4]

Into the British sector of the Battle of Arras came a mixture of all the types of unit described above. From, for example, the Regular 3rd Division, through the Territorial 56th Division and then New Army 9th Division, all were to play their part in the coming days. Barely distinguishable by this point of the war they would all be made up of a combination of hardened veterans who had maybe already experienced Ypres, Loos and some aspect of the long campaign on the Somme, alongside recently arrived conscripts with only training to guide them through the experience. Training was much more advanced within the British and Commonwealth Army by April 1917. Lessons had been learned from the Somme battles and at the lowest level embodied in a new set of instructions for how the basic elements of a battalion should function. A Training Directorate had been set up and Brigadier A. Solly-Flood put in charge. He was one of a number of officers, which included Maj-Gen. Currie O.C. of Canadian 1st Division, that had attended the French 4th Army training school in Chalon, all returning with a new perspective on how units should fight. GHQ had already, as a reaction to the fighting on the Somme, issued a number of pamphlets on a variety of issues. One of the most important in November of 1916 was S.S. 135 *Instructions for the Training of Divisions for Offensive Action*, which laid out in great detail how a division was to prepare for an attack. Solly-Flood built upon these manuals and using his French experience as a base, produced, in February 1917, S.S. 144 *Instructions for the Training of Platoons for Offensive Action*. These two documents began the process of producing a far more coherent template upon which units could train for and then carry out an attack. Much of it was a product of experience, many units already

---

4   John Harris, *Covenant with Death*, (London: Hutchinson, 1961). Harris, a Sheffield man, used conversations with veterans of the Sheffield Pals Battalion as a basis for the experiences of the characters in his book.

carrying out several of the techniques in the latter months of 1916. Several divisional commanders on the Somme had advocated a change in tactics, including Deverell (3rd Division), Stephens (5th Division) and Maxse (18th Division); Stephens going as far as to advocate the kind of platoon structure eventually seen in S.S. 144.[5] There was to be a standardised method for planning an assault, which is clearly reflected in many of the Operation Orders seen in the unit diaries leading up to April 1917. These covered a plethora of areas from timings to attack boundaries, down to dealing with prisoners. A number of key statements from S.S. 135 are worth quoting and bearing in mind when accounts of the attack are read. "No battalion can be expected to carry out more than one heavy attack in a day."[6] Also, "All movement must be over the top of the ground."[7]

Finally, there is a section on exploiting success which, in light of what is to encountered later, requires a full examination here:

1.   Although a commander's first duty on reaching his objective is to make every effort to secure it against recapture by the enemy, this does not imply that he should adopt a purely defensive attitude. On the contrary, he must continue his offensive with any troops available after the needs of consolidation have been provided for.

2.   The enemy is bound to be in confusion immediately after our successful assault; a few men boldly handled will then usually be able to seize, at practically no cost, important tactical points beyond the objective. If immediate advantage of the enemy's state of confusion is not taken, the opportunity will be lost, as he recovers very quickly; tactical points that might have been had for the asking will have to be taken later at considerable expense.[8]

The section goes on to describe how this may be done but the key phrase comes mid-way which is that; "The decision must be left to the man on the spot."[9] That this instruction should have been devolved all the way to battalion commanding officers is interesting when some of the occasions are examined on the 9th where officers complain of not being able to press forward when the opportunity arose.

What S.S. 135 also laid down, which was particularly important, was that the platoon was to be the basic unit of assault. This was a move away from a whole company advancing in waves to some distant objective. Experience from the Somme battles showed that if initial objectives could be taken by the first troops over, further men following behind were far more equipped to then move through and take the next. This idea was extended from platoons advancing through, then to companies and fresh battalions passing through and finally in two places in the overall attacks a whole division passing through another in order to create fresh impetus.

S.S. 144 did something more radical in changing the make-up of the platoon in its new enhanced role as the basic unit. As new weaponry had been introduced over 1915 and 1916 such as better bombs (grenades in modern parlance), rifle grenades and Lewis guns, there had been a tendency to create special sub-units within a battalion or company leaving a platoon as a rifle and bayonet unit and therefore not always capable alone in dealing with a problem. This lack of flexibility was recognised and S.S. 144 was not only concerned with how a platoon is trained but also how it should be organised. Usually a battalion was made up of four companies, each of four platoons,

5   Robbins, Simon, *British Generalship on the Western Front*, (London: Frank Cass, 2005), p. 100.
6   S.S. 135, *Instructions for the Training of Divisions for Offensive Action* (London: H.M.S.O. 1916), p. 14.
7   S.S. 135, p. 27.
8   S.S. 135, pp. 40-41.
9   S.S. 135, p. 41.

each of four sections, a section being around 9 men. The sections were now to all have a specific role within the platoon. S.S. 143 gave as an example an average Platoon of 36 men plus an H.Q.:

> Headquarters – One Officer and four O.R.
> One section bombers – One N.C.O. & eight O.R. (inc. two bayonet men and two throwers)
> One section Lewis gunners – One N.C.O. & eight O.R. (inc. Nos. 1 & 2)
> One section riflemen – One N.C.O. & eight O.R. (picked shots, scouts, picked bayonet fighters)
> One section rifle bombers – One N.C.O. &eight O.R. (inc. four bomb firers)
> All N.C.O. and men should carry a rifle and bayonet bar the Nos. 1 and 2 of a Lewis gun team and the rifle bombers if they were using a cup attachment.[10]

There were a number of very important points made in the manual and must be borne in mind when reading the accounts of the offensive later in this book. First of all, the idea of waves was not dropped, more revolutionary tactics of platoons working in 'clumps' or 'blobs' being felt to be too difficult to train troops for in a short length of time. What was different is how the waves were made up as can be seen on the diagram from the manual. Bombers and Lewis gunners are put on the flank of the attack to facilitate the outflanking of any difficult opposition, such as a machine gun nest, that pinned the riflemen down. What is made very clear in the text, however, is that in the attack from trench to trench; "No further comment is necessary, other than to lay stress on the point that waves must go direct above ground to their objective",[11] thus reinforcing the directive in S.S. 135. When movement had to be carried out some distance from the enemy, and not in direct line of fire, a different system was used, namely the artillery formation. The thought behind this particular formation was that it would minimize casualties from artillery fire, thus the name, but it was also an easier formation to control when moving over some distance. The remainder of the booklet is dedicated to advice on how men could be trained to ensure the best performance in an attack. Technology had increased the complexity of weapon systems available and experience had begun to show their best usage. At the same time new arrivals into a unit were now, in the main, conscripts with, on average, 13 weeks training but it was reported that some arrived with as little as six. It was imperative then that men should be assimilated into a unit as quickly as possible and it was training that allowed that to happen. As often as possible then, units were taken out of the line for exercise in rear areas in preparation for the attack. This usually consisted of daily routines involving musketry, bomb throwing, moving in formation but in many cases also included moving over a taped area made to resemble the exact terrain a unit would be attacking over.

There is great emphasis in some works, especially those emanating from Canada,[12] of Maj-General Currie's influence on the way the Canadians attacked Vimy Ridge. In actual fact the leaders and men of the Canadian divisions followed the doctrines laid out in S.S. 135 and S.S. 143 in the same way as did the remainder of those assaulting on the morning of 9 April.[13] Operation orders –filtering down to company commanders – who would then discuss the attack with their platoon leaders. The platoon leader becoming a pivotal role, not merely as in the past to inspire and lead his

---

10   S.S. 143, *Instructions for the Training of Platoons for Offensive Action* (London: H.M.S.O. 1917), p. 9.
11   S.S. 143, p. 12.
12   P. Berton, *Vimy*, (Toronto: McClelland & Stewart, 1986) is a notorious example of this, full of inaccuracies and laying down the dubious claim that the Canadians invented the whole doctrine, showing the way to the rest of the British Army.
13   See Mark Osborne Humphries, Old Wine in New Bottles: A Comparison of British and Canadian Preparations for the Battle of Arras in Hayes, Geoffrey, et al (eds). *Vimy Ridge: A Canadian Reassessment*, (Ontario: Wilfred Laurier University Press, 2009), for a more detailed analysis of this topic.

20   TRAINING OF PLATOONS FOR OFFENSIVE ACTION.

APPENDIX I.

The Platoon, Taking an Average Strength of 36 and H.Q. 4—
Formation for Trench-to-Trench Attack.

(Showing 2 platoons in 2 waves, with the right the outer flank.)

·100ˣ·

□□□□♠□□□□♙ ○○○○♙○○○○ *1st Line*

15ˣ
to
25ˣ

♙   *1st WAVE*
⊠

♦♦♦♦♙♦♦♦♦ ▨▨ ▨▨♙▨ ▨□▨ *2nd Line*

10ˣ
to
15ˣ

▲▲▲▲▲▲▲▲ ⊠ ▲▲▲▲ ▲▲▲ *3rd Line (Moppers up for the Objective
allotted to the 2nd Wave)*

50ˣ
to
100ˣ

♙
⊠

□□□□♠□□□□ ○○○○♠○○○○ *4th Line*

15ˣ
to
25ˣ

3   *2nd WAVE*

♦♦♦♦♙♦♦♦♦ ♙□▨□□♙▨□▨ *5th Line*

Key :—

♙ Platoon Commander.   □ Rifleman.   ♦ Rifle Bomber.
♙ Platoon Sergeant.   ▨ Lewis Gunner.   ▲ Mopper Up.
⊠ Section Commander.   ○ Bomber.   ⊞ Platoon H.Q.

NOTES.

Two platoons are depicted, showing the different positions of leaders in first and second waves.

The platoon is the unit in the assault, moves in one wave of two lines, and has one definite objective.

Every man is a rifleman and a bomber, and in the assault, with the exception of the No. 1 and No. 2 of the Lewis gun, fixes his bayonet. Men in rifle sections must be trained either to the Lewis gun or rifle bomb.

Bombing and Lewis gun sections are on the outer flank of platoons.

Platoon in trench to trench attack. (Page from *Training of Platoons for Offensive Action*, War Office 1917)

men forward, but also with a sound understanding of the objectives ahead of him. Also under his command the means to change tack and bring different arms to bear should difficulties be faced during the attack. In this way the men were well prepared for the task that lay ahead of them, or at least the initial phase of the attack.

In the northern element of the attack 1st Army was responsible for the taking of Vimy Ridge as far down as the vicinity of the village of Thelus. For this task, General Sir Henry Horne in command of 1st Army, allocated his Canadian Corps, now comprising of all four Canadian

Platoon in artillery formation. Page from *Training of Platoons for Offensive Action*, War Office 1917)

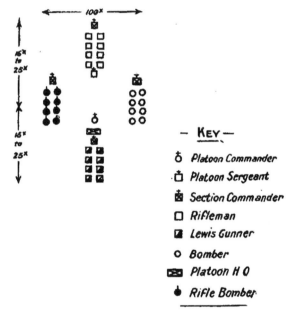

TRAINING OF PLATOONS FOR OFFENSIVE ACTION. 21

In assembly, the distance between lines and waves may conveniently be reduced to lessen the danger of rear waves being caught in enemy barrage, the distance being increased when the advance takes place.

"Moppers up" follow the second line of a wave and precede the unit for which they are to mop up. If the numbers are large, they must be found from a different company or battalion. Small numbers are preferably found from the unit for which they are to mop up. They must carry a distinctive badge and have their own commander.

G.S.
O.B. No. 1919/T

APPENDIX II.

The Platoon in Artillery Formation with the Right the Outer Flank.

— KEY —

♂ *Platoon Commander*

⚲ *Platoon Sergeant*

🛡 *Section Commander*

□ *Rifleman*

▨ *Lewis Gunner*

○ *Bomber*

⬚ *Platoon H Q*

♦ *Rifle Bomber*

NOTES.

Sections move in fours, file, or single file, according to the ground and other factors of the case.

Platoon H.Q. moves with that column best suited for purposes of command.

divisions with the temporary addition of the British 5th Division to provide an additional brigade for the attack and to act as a reserve. For additional operations just to the north of the ridge the right of I Corps would be involved with the remaining part of 1st Army holding the line and joining in some form of artillery demonstration during the lead up period to the offensive.

The Canadians, comprising the bulk of this northern force, had gone through, at times, a difficult growth as a fighting body of men. Although the corps had been officially formed in September 1915, up to this point they had never fought as a complete corps, all divisions together, but had been partnered with British units. A complex history of political machinations and difficulties over commanding officers at all levels had finally been ironed out by this stage and Lt-Gen Hon. Sir

Support troops moving up in artillery formation. (IWM 5115)

Julian Byng as corps commander had begun to create a very effective force. A cavalryman at the beginning of the war Byng led IX Corps in their successful withdrawal from Gallipoli, returning to the Western Front to briefly command XVII Corps in 1916 before in May of that year taking over the Canadian Corps. By the spring of 1917 motivation in the corps was at a high level with the prospect of attacking as a combined force. Byng had been careful to ensure that proficient staff officers such as Alan Brooke, John Dill and Edmund Ironside[14] joined the corps, sometimes to offset political appointments from Canada. For example, Major Brooke as Staff Officer Royal Artillery was the prime planner of the artillery for the corps as in his words the Commander Corps Royal Artillery "… was full of bravery and instilled the finest of fighting spirit in the whole of the artillery under his command but as regards the tactical handling of artillery he knew practically nothing."[15]

The formations comprising 3rd Army were a good representation of the mix within the British Army by this point in the war. Along the line could be found original Regular army units, units of the Territorial Force and New Army formations. Also to be found were units from all corners of England, a proportionally large number of Scottish and a smattering from Ireland and Wales. To be added to that amalgam was a brigade of South Africans. Many of the units had fought on the

---

14   All of whom were to eventually rise to the rank of Field Marshal and become Chief of the General Staff.

15   Liddell Hart Centre for Military Archives, Papers of Field Marshal Viscount Alanbrooke, 5/2/13, *Notes on My Life*, p. 59, quoted in Fraser, David, *Alanbrooke*, (London: HarperCollins, 1982), p. 123. The CCRA was Brigadier W.E.B. Morrison who had been appointed by controversial Canadian Prime Minister Hughes. For a more detailed analysis of the leadership problems for the Canadian Corps caused by their politicians see Paul Dickson, The End of the Beginning: The Canadian Corps in 1917 in Hayes, *et al* (eds), *Vimy Ridge, A Canadian Reassessment*.

Somme and so the alterations in tactics described above had already, to some extent, been practised in the field. With many of the units having some period of rest over the winter months and with additional extra training, morale was seen to be high indeed. Losses experienced in that last campaign had been made good to a large extent and it could be generally said that divisions were in a good condition for the offensive.

Artillery

By the early spring of 1917 the severe problems faced by the British and Commonwealth Army in fighting what had become an artillery war, had to a large extent being overcome. The shell shortages of 1915, the lack of enough heavy artillery in 1916 and the poor quality of shell were now not the concerns they once were. In his initial planning for the offensive Allenby wanted to be fairly radical. The artillery plans he and his GOCRA[16] Maj-Gen. A.E.A. Holland forwarded to GHQ on 7 February 1917 was based around a 48-hour intense bombardment. Haig was unhappy with this suggestion, replying on 12 February citing the wear and tear on the guns, the fatigue of the men and the doubt that it would sufficiently cut the wire or severely affect the morale of the defenders. Allenby continued to defend his decision and answer Haig's concerns. Lending support to the C. in C.'s apprehensions however was the artillery advisor at GHQ, Maj-Gen J.F.N. Birch. To Haig's argument he added the inexperience of much of the artillery and perhaps most importantly additional factors about the wire; that observation of wire cutting would prove difficult and that the field artillery had no instantaneous fuse. This latter point requires some explanation as it will prove to be a deciding factor and influence a great deal of what happens when the offensive begins. All the way through the war so far fought, whenever the attacking troops came up against uncut wire almost invariably the attack failed, often resulting in a high number of casualties. The initial tool to cut wire was the shrapnel shell. These are shells filled with almost 400 small lead balls designed to be propelled upon detonation whilst in the air onto troops below. Designed essentially as an anti-personal shell it was thought for a long period in the war that it was also the most effective method of wire-cutting. Within a short span of ranges this could be true; however, if the range was too short, below 1,000 yards, or beyond 2,500 yards, the effect was diminished and it was thought brought to almost nil at 3,000 yards. It also required skilled gunners and most importantly, observation so that fuses could be timed to ensure shells were exploding correctly for maximum effect. An alternative shell was high explosive. Used increasingly as the war developed into one akin to siege tactics and destructive on trench systems, it was not an effective wire cutter. The fuse used would mean detonation after a short delay and buried in the ground, tending to throw the wire in the air not destroying it, leaving behind an equally tangled mess. What was required was an instantaneous fuse, exploding in the wire and thus destroying it. Such a fuse, No. 106, was developed during 1916 but was only available in any substantial numbers in early 1917 and then only for 6", 8" and 9.2" howitzers. It was also not available in sufficient numbers to satisfy demand.

The initial reply by the 3rd Army commander was to argue the reasons for his case but to no avail. To ease the situation Holland was promoted to command I Corps and his place was taken by Maj-Gen. R St. C. Lecky, an advocate of a longer barrage. This disagreement out of the way, planning could go ahead. No equivalent argument took place in 1st Army, in fact the bombardment was planned to be even longer in this sector. The first phase of the bombardment in the 1st Army area began on 20 March with half the available pieces at that point firing. Therefore, the German defenders on Vimy Ridge were already undergoing a quite severe bombardment well before their

---

16   GOCRA: General Officer Commanding Royal Artillery.

4.5 inch howitzers on the edge of Arras, April 1917. (IWM Q5142)

18-pdr guns in Arras Cemetery. (IWM Q6205)

compatriots further south. The second phase of artillery preparation in the Vimy area coincided with the beginning of the bombardment in 3rd Army, on 4 April.

The artillery pieces and ammunition necessary to feed them was available in numbers thus far never seen on the British front. For 3rd Army and that part of 1st Army involved (Canadian and part of I Corps) there were some 1,404 18-pounders and 450 4.5" howitzers available; these two types making up the Royal Field Artillery brigades in both divisions and corps. According to Farndale, heavy artillery was made up of: 258 60-pounders; 364 6" howitzers; 124 8" howitzers, 148 9.2" howitzers; 17 12" howitzers; eight 15" howitzers; 40 6" guns; two 9.2" guns and two 12" guns; a total of 2,817 guns or howitzers. Ammunition was also at an all-time high with, for example, 300 rounds per gun allowed in the first two days for 18-pounders.[17] An analysis of how these weapons were distributed amongst the attacking formations is given in the table below:[18]

	18lb	4.5" How	60lb	6" How	8" How	9.2" How	12" How	15" How	6" Gun	9.2" Gun	12" Gun
Can. Corps	546	174	104	144	40	56	4	3	16	0	0
XVII Corps	324	108	60	92	32	34	6	2	2	0	0
VI Corps	216	72	36	64	20	24	0	1	6	1	0
VII Corps	342	114	48	72	28	36	8	2	2	1	1

The table clearly calls into question the balance of the allocation of artillery resources. By not being fully involved in the offensive 1st Army had the resources to assemble a large artillery contingent to support its four attacking divisions. The 3rd Army, on the other hand, although having a large allocation of artillery had to split the effort between its three army corps, which it did in an interesting manner. XVII and VI Corps had similar frontage and objectives with, as will be seen, three divisions attacking with one to pass through. Why then, was the northern of the two corps, namely XVII, provided with almost 50 percent more artillery of all kinds? With a distant objective of Monchy-le-Preux, two substantial ridges to overcome before achieving that goal and forming the centre of the major effort towards Cambrai, surely a more balanced allocation was required. VII Corps had a larger frontage but more significantly almost the whole of its front was facing either the complex on Telegraph Hill known as the Harp or the formidable Hindenburg Line defences. The wire protecting the Harp, similar to the older parts of the line further north, although strong, was not comparable with what had been placed in front of the Hindenburg Line. If there was to be any chance of the divisions of this Corps being successful in getting through the double stretches of dense wire, sufficient resources would be required. A further imbalance was in the allocation of ammunition, or more correctly, fuses. Horne, an artilleryman by training and inclination, knew from experience the results of wire being insufficiently cut and fully appreciated the increased effectiveness that the No. 106 fuse would bring to that task. He requisitioned as many of the new fuses as he could for the appropriate guns in his command. As far as the evidence from artillery diaries can be interrogated, there were insufficient fuses to allow all wire cutting to be done by the medium-heavies of all the corps. It is also clear that in some units of 3rd Army the task of wire cutting had been allocated to 18-pounders using shrapnel in, what had become

17   Farndale, General Sir Martin, *History of the Royal Regiment of Artillery, Western Front 1914-18*, (London: Royal Artillery Institution, 1998), p. 165.
18   Totals for each type of gun, taken by adding up the batteries as given in Falls do not correspond with Farndale's figures but are close enough to adequately highlight the difference between corps.

the traditional manner. It is quite remarkable that the very area where distance to the German lines was at its greatest, namely in front of VII Corps in the south, the 18-pounders should have retained the task of wire cutting; bearing in mind that it is at extreme range that they lose most of the limited effectiveness they may have had.

In the Canadian sector the early start of the bombardment, even though limited to half the available batteries, soon began to make itself felt. The narrow nature of the ridge meant that lines were closer together than would normally be the case. Therefore, although there were thousands of yards of trench lines to cover, a greater proportion of the rounds landing in the area were effective in one way or another. Forward units were also tasked with using trench mortars to ensure that repairs to trench and wire was a most difficult exercise for the Germans. The men in those front trenches were also under considerable strain and is summed up in a report on 8 April by Major Anton Maier (*Bayerische R.I.R. 3* on 6 April) with these chilling last lines:

12 inch howitzer. (IWM Q7247)

As a result, each company spends ten days on the positions; under constant fire and without a break. When this is coupled to the need to counter the daily enemy raids, both large and small, by day and night, it amounts to a commitment which leaves anything on the Somme or at Verdun in the shade; not, perhaps, in terms of casualties, but certainly in the demands it makes on the battle worthiness of the troops.[19]

This period of time contrasts strongly with the other end of the line. In the Wancourt area the Germans were able to make substantial changes to their front line units during the same period. A detailed account in *Reserve Infanterie Regiment 84*'s history of the relief of the line south of the Cojeul stream in the Hindenburg Line provides a clear impression that the entire process was carried out with little or no disturbance from the British.[20] They even had the opportunity to make good some of the deficiencies that they found in the line after taking it over. This regimental history is certainly not full of the usual complaints about being under intense pressure from the bombardment and none of the usual comments about not being able to get food and water to the men at the front.

In the Air

The first large scale industrialised war brings to mind the domination of the battlefield by machine guns, artillery and increasingly the tank. It was, however, in the air where the most dramatic developments were taking place. It is astounding to think that only a matter of 11 years before the start of the war did man first take to the air in powered flight. What at first seemed a fairly subservient role to complement the cavalry in their reconnaissance role very quickly developed into much more. The stagnation of the conflict into trench warfare and the subsequent lack of ability to observe the enemy and its movements gave rise to what, throughout the war, was the major function of the fledgling Royal Flying Corps, that of observation. With artillery moving to an almost completely indirect firing role and the difficulty of forward observers to manage to get their guns registered on a particular target, the air branch became an indispensable arm within the fighting forces of all sides. In order to assault an enemy position its defences had to be known, in as much detail as possible. A glance at any trench map produced from 1915 onwards will provide ample evidence of the work of the R.F.C. Accurate mapping is not normally done ground survey. If that is impossible then the only alternative is to photograph the land from the air and use the prints obtained to map the land. That was the primary role of the R.F.C. and most (bombing the enemy being an exception) other facets of the air arm arose out of that key function. The more famous element of the air war, the battle between planes which became known as a dogfight, arose out of the wish to destroy the enemy's observation aircraft, or to protect one's own. What became known as scouts were sent up to carry out this task and obviously what often developed was a battle between scouts of both sides. The other part of the role of observation was to become the eyes of the artillery. Registering the fall of shell onto a certain position had previously been done by sight, a Forward Observation Officer being tasked with the role. The obvious limitations of this meant that more and more reliance was placed on a combination of using maps to gauge where a unit should aim its fire but then aircraft communicating the fall of shot so that accuracy could be gained – termed registering the guns. Wireless technology also allowed this activity to

---

19   Quoted in Sheldon, *The German Army on Vimy Ridge,* p. 270.
20   Speck, Justicz Inspector William, *Das Königlich Preußische Reserve-Infantrie-Regiment 84*, pp. 172-174. All through the 7 and 8 April the relief of forward companies was occurring in stark contrast to further north, especially Vimy Ridge, where all contact with forward companies had been lost.

BE2e. (Author)

be carried out. A one-way set could be carried in an aircraft and by using Morse code a message could be returned to the artillery battery from the air above the target. Codes were very simple, the methods seemingly crude today, but they were reasonably effective in bringing the battery fire down onto a particular point.

The Royal Flying Corps were actively carrying out these tasks all through the desperately cold winter months of 1916 and 1917, suffering severely in their open cockpits.

Not only the weather conditions deteriorated as autumn 1916 moved into winter. In the early days of the Somme operations the British pilots found they could dominate the skies even though still flying variants of aircraft first introduced in 1914. The BE2 variants had, up to that point, more than held their own along with the DH2 single seat pusher along with the FE2b 2-seater multipurpose aircraft.

As summer turned into autumn, there appeared a new German aircraft, the Albatross DI, closely followed by the improved DII. Supremacy in the air slowly moved towards the Germans and with new models some way off for the British the situation became serious to say the least. Arguments in the UK about who should control aircraft manufacturing carried on well into late 1916 which did nothing to speed the development and delivery of new machines. In January 1917 Haig was already indicating that it was doubtful that the RFC would be ready for an offensive by 1 April.[21] In a letter to Robertson on 15 February Haig lays out an even gloomier picture of the state of the air services with a bland statement underlined in the original:

> Our fighting machines will almost certainly be inferior in number and quite certainly in performance to those of the enemy.[22]

---

21   TNA: CAB 24/6 G.T. 59, Haig refers to this meeting although the minutes do not record the discussion for security reasons.
22   TNA: CAB 24/6 G.T. 59.

Albatross DII. (Author)

In command of the R.F.C. was Maj-Gen. Hugh Trenchard. Originally in the army and invalided home from Nigeria, he learned to fly and in 1913 became assistant commandant of the Central Flying School, Upavon, Wiltshire. In 1915, he assumed command in France of the Royal Flying Corps and became known for an aggressive policy of taking the fight to the Germans in their air space, an early understanding of the power of air superiority. The situation was clearly totally unacceptable to the man to be made responsible for creating that superiority over Arras. "You are asking me to fight the battle this year with the same machines as I fought it last year. We shall be hopelessly outclassed, and something must be done."[23]

New machines would not be arriving in time and therefore Trenchard was forced to begin the whole campaign at a disadvantage. Work began during the winter months whenever the weather allowed, with German lines around Arras being constantly photographed and thereby mapped in order to aid the eventual planning of the offensive. Unfortunately for the British, recently arrived to take over *Jasta 11*,[24] stationed at La Brayelles, just west of Douai, was a young man, who had recently become holder of the *Pour le Mérit*[25] and soon to be celebrated well beyond the air fraternity – Rittmeister Manfred von Richthofen. He found his new unit less than efficient but soon, under his very able leadership, turned them into a formidable group of airmen.

This deadly combination of better aircraft and a new, aggressive leader of a local German scout unit meant the beginning of a difficult time for the British airmen and casualties began to rise. Not only this enemy unit began to trouble the British as nearby was also *Jasta Boelcke* containing other 'aces' such as Werner Voss and Erwin Böhme. It was in fact Voss who shot down a young pilot and his observer on 19 March, thus being able to claim his 'Blue Max'.[26] The pilot was Captain Elred Bowyer-Bower, his plane crashing near Croisilles where the Germans buried the two unfortunate crew members. Coincidentally, one of the Royal Engineer units following up the withdrawal a few days later was commanded by Captain Thomas Bowyer-Bower, the young pilot's father. Presuming

23   Quoted in Boyle, A., *Trenchard: Man of Vision*, (London: Collins, 1962), p. 209.
24   Short for *Jagdstaffeln* or 'hunting squadrons'.
25   The military class of one of Germany's highest awards, pilots being awarded it after 16 'kills' in early 1917, although this figure increased as the war went on. Often referred to as the 'Blue Max', due to its blue colour and (reputedly) because one of its first recipients was the ace Max Immelmann.
26   Hart, Peter, *Bloody April*, (London: Cassell, 2006), p. 92. Much of the information in the description of the role of the RFC in the offensive is taken from this excellent account of the air campaign in early 1917.

his son had probably crashed somewhere in the vicinity he desperately searched for the plane and upon finding it discovered the two graves nearby marked 'Two unknown Captains of the Flying Corps'. Ordering the exhumation of the bodies the remains were eventually buried in a nearby newly created cemetery in Mory, a very rare occasion of a father burying his son on the battlefield.[27]

Trenchard remained resolute throughout and continued to push his crews hard to gain the information that was so vital to the preparations. One element that had escaped the R.F.C., probably as a result of its loss of superiority and the distance behind the front lines, was the construction of the Hindenburg Line. Once its existence was properly noted in January 1917 though, the crews very bravely (it was in places 20 miles behind the front, a very long way for early air crews) made photographic reconnaissance flights along its length.[28] This was more information than Nivelle received as his air forces were not well equipped for such work and the new line was even further in the rear of the present positions.

Casualties continued to mount and this was having an effect on training in the United Kingdom which became shorter and shorter in a rush to get pilots to France as well as more dangerous to those in training.[29] This generally showed itself in less and less experienced pilots and observers arriving at the forward squadrons. A reform in training techniques was underway in Britain; however, just as with the new aircraft which would win back the skies for the British, this came too late for the battles of April and May 1917. A useful method of comparing losses is given in the War Office publication after the war, that of 'hours flown per casualty (killed and missing), Western Front'. During the Somme campaign in July to September 1916 when the British had some measure of air superiority this figure averaged 245 hours per casualty. This figure had dropped to 166 with the arrival of the Albatross scout. The figure for March 1917 was 101 hours per casualty, the worst of the whole war bar one month and that was about to happen. In other words, compared to the Somme the British pilots were suffering two and a half the casualties in March compared to the first months on the Somme the previous year. Worse was yet to come.

The opposing air forces for the offensive were, approximately, 365 aircraft available to the British and Canadians, of which 120 were single-seat scouts. These were organised within Brig-Gen. Shephard's I Brigade, Maj-Gen. Higgins' III Brigade and Lt-Col. Newall's 9th Wing (a GHQ unit, at Field Marshal Haig's disposal.) A brigade would have a *Corps Wing* and an *Army Wing*, both of four or five squadrons, each of which would have about 18 to 24 aircraft; also a *Balloon Wing*. The role of the Corp Wing was to assist troops on the ground whilst the Army Wing would carry out orders from the army commander such as air fighting, long range reconnaissance and strategic bombing.

The I Brigade was attached to 1st Army with No. 16 Squadron (24 × B.E.2e, f & g) of First (Corps) Wing being attached to the Canadian Corps and No. 2 Squadron (B.E.2c, d & e) attached to 1st Corps. All four squadrons of Tenth (Army) Wing in I Brigade (No.8 (Naval) with Sopwith Triplanes, No. 40 with Nieuport Scouts, No. 25 with F.E.2b & d and No. 43 with Sopwith 1½ Strutters) were given tasks for the attack. The first two with their single seat aircraft had the role of offensive patrol and attacks on kite balloons whilst the latter with their two seater aircraft were to protect the artillery aircraft and undertake medium and long distance reconnaissance.[30]

---

27   The story is described by N. Franks in 'A Father's Love', *Over the Front*, Vol. 10, No.2, 1995, pp. 162-164. Thomas and his observer Lt. Eric Elgey lie side by side in Mory Abbey Cemetery.

28   Hooton, E.R., *War Over the Trenches*, (Hersham: Ian Allan, 2010), p. 70. Working had been seen as early as November 1916 but this was interpreted at first as a switch line and named the Cojeul Switch.

29   Between 30th Sept. 1916 and 1 March 1917, 139 pilots or observers were killed overseas whilst 83 were killed at home. See *Statistics of the Military Effort of the British Empire During the Great War 1914-1920*, (War Office: 1922), p. 504.

30   Jones, H. A. *The War in the Air Volume 3*, (Oxford: Clarendon Press, 1931), p. 332.

The III Brigade was naturally allocated to 3rd Army. Its Twelfth (Corps) Wing allocated one squadron to each of the attacking corps plus the reserve corps (XVIII). XVII Corps had No. 13 Squadron with its B.E.2c, d & e aircraft, VI Corps had No.12 Squadron with B.E.2 e's, VII Corps had No. 8 Squadron with B.E.2c, d & e's and XVIII Corps had No. 59 Squadron with R.E.8's. No. 35 Squadron (with Armstrong Whitworth F.K.8 aircraft) was specially attached to III Brigade to work with the Cavalry Corps). Thirteenth (Army) Wing of III Brigade had five squadrons. No. 6 (Naval), No. 29 and No. 60 Squadrons, all of which flew Nieuport Scouts were used for offensive patrols. No. 11 Squadron with F.E.2 b's was for reconnaissance, photography and night bombing whilst No. 48 Squadron used its Bristol Fighters for fighter-reconnaissance.

To oppose this force, the Germans could muster approximately 195 aircraft of all kinds.[31] This advantage in numbers was, unfortunately, almost cancelled out by the superiority of the German Albatross scout. Also, the defensive nature of the German approach meant that whilst many of the British aircraft were attempting to carry out a myriad of tasks they could not afford to retreat from, the German pilots had one aim and one only, that of bringing down the British observers. Artillery observation, already well underway in preparation for the beginning of the preliminary bombardment, intensified in the 1st Army sector before that further south due to the earlier start to the programme. The last days of March and the first of April saw RFC observers over and behind Vimy Ridge observing the fall of shot and correcting when required. The weather was quite simply appalling with snow and hail making flying extremely difficult as well as hindering visibility. The job had to be done, however, and so crew flew as often as possible in support. Various headquarters were also constantly appealing for more photographs as well as support for the artillery. 4 April then saw the beginning of the general bombardment all across the planned offensive front and the pressure of the squadrons was racked up yet another notch. Also being brought into effect was Trenchard's dictum that the skies must be cleared of German aircraft. That meant RFC scouts patrolling deep into German lines to actively prevent their German equivalents from interfering with observations over their front lines. The vagaries of chance of course brought some of the worse weather so far on that day and therefore observation was not what it could have been. Better weather on the 5th and the aggressive actions of the British Scouts meant that many of the observation flights of all kinds could carry out their missions successfully. Also entering the fray were a handful of new machines that Trenchard had held back for the offensive. One of these was the Bristol Fighter with its forward firing Vickers machine gun and a Lewis gun for the observer. Unfortunately, tactics had not evolved to use this more advanced machine efficiently and it was given to a relatively inexperienced squadron leading to results that were not good at this stage although later in the year the aircraft proved its worth. The DH4 bomber also made an appearance and its speed meant that the few missions it flew were successful at hitting railway installations in the German rear areas. It also carried out photographing missions, a vast improvement over the Sopwith 1½ Strutter, BE2e, and FE2d that had been literally shot out of the sky in large numbers over the previous few days. Indeed, losses were rising alarmingly and morale suffering accordingly. Both machines, decent pilots and even observers to man the rear Lewis guns were becoming scarce and it required help from the French in supplying a squadron of Nieuports. The situation was extremely serious though:

> We became used to losing two out of five planes or three out of eight, and there were occasions when we wondered how any of us got back at all. Often the planes we got back were not usable any more. We began to run out of replacement planes, and at one time, in a desperate effort to keep the squadron up to strength, Headquarters tried to fill our gaps by calling on

---

31   Hart, Peter, *Bloody* April, p. 120.

the French for some superannuated Nieuport two-seaters – which at least gave us something to laugh at, because the Nieuports only had two and a half hours' fuel and couldn't even keep up with the Sopwiths. It was, however, the extent of our crew losses that became crippling and eventually notorious.[32]

Although the officer quoted above eventually returned home having complained a little too hard and to a very senior officer, his view was not a false one. Trenchard knew though that to fail in the tasks set to the RFC would most likely result in thousands of more casualties on the ground when batteries were not silenced or strongpoints unidentified.

Other help came to the RFC in the shape of the Royal Naval Air Service and their nimble Sopwith triplanes which arrived with No. 8 (Naval) Squadron in early April. In addition, 56 Squadron arrived which were not only equipped with the SE5 Scout but also included a hand-picked set of pilots, some new but some with experience. Unfortunately, the SE5 arrived with some design faults which 56 Squadron sorted out themselves but not before some time had passed. The 8 April arrived as the last day to identify targets and dislocate as much of the German artillery as possible. Almost everything was thrown into the air in a final effort to aid the men attacking the next morning. That did not mean, however, that the task was complete. Far from it, the 9th would bring the next phase in the work of the men in their flying machines.

Tanks

When tanks first appeared on the Somme battlefield in September 1916 they caused extreme consternation in the German forces but in the indomitable Teutonic way they immediately set out to find solutions to this new fiendish weapon of the British. In the meantime, the relative success of this new fighting machine at Flers the previous year would, one would think, result in both lessons being learned but also the immediate mass production of the vehicles. For the attacking infantry and cavalry units awaiting their moment on the front at Arras, however, that is not what occurred. It had been immediately identified that the tanks used on the Somme, the Mk I, was too slow and mechanically unreliable and improvements were quickly devised but unfortunately not so rapidly deployed. The intent was there as on 26 September 1916 a provisional order for 1,000 tanks was made, confirmed on 14 October by the Ministry of Munitions. Production at 20 per week to begin on 12 November with an increase to 40 per week once 50 had been made. Then an important statement; "Improvements in design and armament should be introduced as found possible without hampering output as above."[33]

At a meeting on 23 November things seemed to be moving along fairly well when it was reported that 70 Mk I tanks were in France, 50 Mk II with a slightly improved design would be ready for delivery and by 7 February, 50 Mk III with more slight improvements, delivered. Finally, from 7 February to the end of May the much improved Mk IV would be produced at 20 per week. This all seemed to tie in with a meeting the same day which included Haig at which it was stated that; "Tanks are required in as large numbers as possible", and "It is important to get as many as possible before May."[34] On 6 February all seemed to be well with the Ministry of Munitions saying that 100 Mk II and III had been delivered and that during March 120 Mark IV will be produced. Of the former 50 were to be given for training in the UK with 50 going to France. Then on 28 February the ministry dropped its bombshell; no Mk IVs were going to be produced during

---

32   Captain Frank Courtney, 45 Squadron, RFC, quoted in Hart, Peter, *Bloody* April, p. 141.
33   TNA: CAB 24/7 War Papers GT Series, GT 109, 'Memo on the Output of Tanks'.
34   TNA, CAB 24/7.

A captured Mk II male tank. (*Bundesarchiv*, Bild 146-1984-059-07A/CC-BY-SA 3.0)

March.[35] The reason for the memo from the War Office from which these figures are derived is to point out that optimistic estimates are extremely unhelpful to planning – an understatement at best. What they do show though is that intent cannot always be turned into reality and that the forces attacking in April were not going to be blessed with the numbers of tanks they thought and none with any kind of real improvement in quality from the previous campaign.

Tanks of all marks were of either male or female variety. The male being fitted with 57mm Hotchkiss 6-pounder naval guns in the two sponsons, one on each side of the tank, the female having Vickers machine guns in place of the 6-pounders. Both had additional machine guns, initially these were Hotchkiss but increasingly these were replaced by Lewis guns.

The actual number of tanks available to 1st Brigade Heavy Branch for the offensive were 10 Mk I, 25 Mk II and III delivered to France and 25 Mk II and III training tanks taking from Woolwich Centre. The allocation from the north was as follows:

1st Army – Canadian Corps:	8 Tanks
3rd Army – XVII Corps:	8 Tanks
3rd Army – VI Corps:	16 Tanks
3rd Army – VII Corps:	16 Tanks
5th Army	12 Tanks

It will be seen that not only were the limited numbers available spread across the whole front but within the corps even smaller 'penny packets' were created. With no reserve to call on the breaking down of any number of machines that were already known to be unreliable and early models of

---

35 TNA, CAB 24/7.

tank, was going to be detrimental to any action. Moreover, the training tanks were built using mild steel plate as they were only ever meant to be; "Clambering around the training ranges in Dorset."[36] Not surprisingly then the plans in 1st and 3rd Armies for the use of tanks made them subsidiary to the main attack, not part of it. In every case they were to be following the infantry, not leading them. What was clearly evident is that nobody particularly felt that tanks were going to have any major influence on the outcome of the offensive.

Support Troops

Most modern warfare narratives concentrate on fighting troops, and seldom is the work of the myriad of combatants who, whilst maybe not directly contributing to the success or not of a campaign, are vital and without whom much depends. Very early in the war it was recognised that tasks requiring labour of one kind or another was going to outstrip the resources of the army. Initially the French were going to be responsible for such activity but as the conflict developed it was clear that this arrangement was not going to be feasible in the future. The Royal Engineer companies originally allocated to fighting units were simply overwhelmed by the requirements of trench warfare. The result for a great deal of the war was the use of fighting troops to carry out many of the tasks, the result being an obvious loss of recuperation time and training when out of the line and a consequent lowering of morale. During 1915 and 1916 the problem was addressed by the creation of a number of different additional units, under the overall command of the Royal Engineers. One of the most important of these units to divisions was the pioneer battalion, by this point in the war each division having its own. Not being front line troops they are sadly neglected in many histories but their role in creation and maintenance of trenches, creation of dugouts, repairing of roads or actually creating them was often as vital an activity as any other in the army. Other very important units outside the divisional structure constitute a formidable list of activities (not exhaustive, simply to give an impression of the range of requirements behind the front): Field Survey Companies (maps, observation, sound ranging), Tunnelling Companies, Special Companies (poison gas), Railway and Light Railway Companies, Tramway Companies, Electrical and Mechanical Companies, Pontoon Parks (bridging) and even Forestry Companies. A new element of the British Army came into being in February 1917, the Labour Corps, incorporating many of the other labour units that had been formed outside the usual Army and Corps structure, all of which up to this point had been within the Royal Engineers or Army Service Corps.

For Maj-Gen E. R. Kenyon, Chief Engineer of 3rd Army, all of these units were vital in carrying out the enormous task of preparing for the offensive. His planning began long before that of almost any other section in the army as the logistical requirements would be enormous. His plans included a number of road routes to the front to augment existing ones to move material from railheads to the advanced positions. In addition, material for five miles of slab or plank road to be readied at the end of each of these routes. This was to facilitate the construction of a temporary extension to the route over newly won ground to allow supplies to be got forward whilst more permanent roads were being constructed. Water mains would be constructed plus the required infrastructure to get water nearer to the front line troops. The latter consisted of over 100 motor vehicles in a water tank company with an additional 45 in a petrol tank company. Vast supplies of stone, timber, road metal and other R.E. stores were demanded; however, ammunition took priority and the situation by late March was not ideal. On 27 March only about five-eighths of the required stone and 10 percent of the road metal was available.[37] The consequences of not being

---

36   Campbell, Christy, *Band of Brigands*, (London: Harper Perennial, 2007), p. 267.
37   Falls, *Military Operations, France and Belgium 1917 Vol. 1*, p. 191.

able to rapidly repair roads in previously German territory can be easily imagined. Ironically the German withdrawal provided better approach roads in the evacuated areas than those behind the original British front line. Although there was some deliberate damage this could be easily repaired and on the whole roads were in good condition.

Within a division, as well as the infantry, artillery and engineers there were a number of other units making up the Order of Battle. The Royal Army Medical Corps (R.A.M.C.) provided three Field Ambulance units (one per brigade) to each division, providing the initial facilities for treating and evacuating casualties once they had been processed at the Regimental Aid Post (R.A.P.) where an R.A.M.C. team attached to the battalion had initially dealt with the wounded. The R.A.P. had no holding facility and therefore walking wounded would be sent back to the Advanced Dressing Station (A.D.S.), set up by the Field Ambulance. More serious cases would be collected, usually by stretcher, by R.A.M.C. men and taken back to the A.D.S. A Field Ambulance was normally organised as an H.Q. Company and two others. Each of the other companies would create one A.D.S. with the H.Q. creating a Main Dressing Station (M.D.S.) about a mile behind. Again the A.D.S. was not a holding facility whereas the M.D.S. could do this for a limited number of men and for a limited time. By this stage in the war the M.D.S. would also have the capacity for life saving surgery. The chain next led to a Casualty Clearing Station (C.C.S.), usually under Corps command, well behind the lines, with something like seven medical officers plus other R.A.M.C. staff and also a number of women belonging to Queen Alexandra's Imperial Military Nursing Service (Q.A.I.M.N.S.). A C.C.S. would normally hold a man for a maximum of around four weeks, either returning a man to the U.K. for convalescence, moving on to a hospital or returning to his unit. Most positions that were held by a C.C.S. can be readily identified today by a large C.W.G.C. cemetery in the vicinity.[38] The Army Service Corps also had a number of units, the largest of which was the divisional train which, with over 300 men and over 100 wagons and providing the ability to move supplies for the division, was usually organised in four companies. Other A.S.C. units, field bakeries and butcheries would be responsible for providing bread and meat to the regiments where the responsibility for feeding men in the First World War lay. Finally, divisions would have a mobile veterinary section, reflecting the horse drawn nature of vehicles in the war.

Raids

In 1914, once the opposing forces had settled into their trenches, very quickly the idea of a raid, a small scale attack, was taken up by local commanders. Harking back to earlier periods of warfare, the snatching of one of the enemy or simply disrupting the opposition by invading their space in a short-term flurry of destruction was regarded as very advantageous on a number of counts. Taking prisoners was, of course, both useful for gathering intelligence and reducing morale in the opposite camp. Add to this the effect of the sudden onslaught on your lines of armed men bent on destruction and mayhem and you are engaged in the act of creating dominance over an otherwise static battlefield.

Thus as early as 1914 emerged in war diaries reports of units dispatching small parties of men into the opposing trenches. The practice spread until it was seen as an essential element of a unit's period of duty at the front. Some accounts would have it that the Canadians were the inventors of the trench raid in 1915 but a short perusal of British war diaries in 1914 shows that not to be true. In preparation for any major offensive, patrolling and raiding took on even more importance.

---

38   Duisans British Military Cemetery, Etrun, not far from Arras is a good example of this, being the area occu-
     pied by 8th, 19th and 41st C.C.S. during 1917.

Intelligence gathering was vital to aid careful planning and the said dominance over the field of battle was crucial to help men achieve success when they 'went over'. Similarly, the side expecting to be attacked required information just as much, especially details such as timing and direction of attack. It was not difficult at this stage in the war to spot preparations for a major offensive, especially when you held the high ground, so the where was often known; what was more difficult to ascertain was the when.

Formations along the prospective April attack area carried out a number of raids in the months building up to the actual day. None were more aggressive in their raiding that the Canadians on Vimy Ridge. The British, whilst on Vimy Ridge, had of course carried out raids, often in conjunction with the ongoing underground struggle. The Canadians, however, upon their arrival, moved the whole process up a gear. Raids became more common but more than that, from December onwards they became much larger affairs in terms of forces involved and resources committed. For example, a raid on 13 February by units of the Canadian 4th Division was made up of a force of over 800 men, taken from four different battalions, backed by a full-scale artillery bombardment of the trenches being raided.[39] This is far removed from the image many have of the midnight raid by black-faced men sneaking over No Man's Land to strike at the opposite trench. Both sides lost heavily in the raid but the capture of 52 Germans could be seen as a significant result for the Canadians. It certainly shook the Germans.[40] That the same units involved here were carrying out their own raids only a few days afterwards involving 70 or so men gives ample evidence as to the intensity of such activity at this juncture.[41] The division was not finished with mounting large raids; however, one planned for an earlier date but actually taking place in the early morning of 1 March was so large that the word raid is scarcely sufficient.[42] Elements of four battalions, 54th, 72nd, 73rd and 75th Canadian Battalions took part, a total of approximately 1600 men. Most significant about this raid was that gas was to be used to enable the men to get over No Man's Land and into the German trenches. Gas released from cylinders was to be used which is the cause for the delay in the date of the attack as favourable winds had to be awaited. An overly high expectations of the effect of the release of gas, reminiscent of those following the pre-1 July 1916 bombardment on the Somme, that troops would simply walk over to the opposing trenches, was evident in planning. Training behind the lines on the role of units did not take place as it had for earlier raids and severe concerns of those commanders whose battalions would form the attacking force were overruled. The result was an unmitigated disaster. Only the first of two gas discharges was made due to a change in wind direction and all the evidence points to this first cloud having extremely little effect on the defending troops. The war diaries of all four units involved mention the fact that the troops manning the German front line seemed not to have suffered at all. Canadian losses ran at around 200 in each unit involved and for very little return. One remarkable result of the raid was a truce on 2 March, initiated by the Germans, which allowed many of the Canadian dead to

---

39   Library and Archives, Canada, war diaries – 44th Canadian Infantry Battalion, RG9, Militia and Defence, Series III-D-3 Volume 4939, Reel T-10745 File: 435.

40   See Sheldon, *The German Army on Vimy Ridge* pp. 233-235 for a detailed account of the reaction of local German commanders although he has the numbers of Canadians involved at a much lower number basing his figure on the statement of a captured Canadian sergeant; thus he regards the raid as a failure based upon mistaken percentage of losses.

41   Library & Archives, Canada, war diaries: 44th Canadian Infantry Battalion, RG9, Militia and Defence, Series III-D-3 Volume 4939, Reel T-10745 File: 435; 46th Canadian Infantry Battalion, RG9, Militia and Defence, Series III-D-3, Volume 4939, Reel T-10745, File: 436; 47th Canadian Infantry Battalion, RG9, Militia and Defence, Series III-D-3 Volume 4940, Reel T-10746/7, File 438 and 50th Infantry Battalion, RG9, Militia and Defence, Series III-D-3Volume 4941, File 441.

42   The Germans actually regarded the attack as a genuine attempt to take the high ground and hold it.

be taken back to their own lines from No Man's Land.[43] How much this disaster may have had a negative effect upon the performance of 4th Division in the subsequent offensive will be discussed when those events are covered.

Raids were not confined to Vimy Ridge, however, with many British units involved in constant raiding further south along the line. Another reason for a great deal of raiding in the British sector in March was to ascertain whether the German withdrawal was continuing or were the trenches opposite held in strength. An example of such a raid is that carried out by 11th Royal Scots of 9th (Scottish) Division on 21 March. As in the Canadian enterprises, this was not designed as a stealth raid but one consisting of over two companies of men (approximately 200 in total) and timed for 3pm in the afternoon with an attending artillery barrage to support the attack. Due to a delay in artillery support the raid began at 3.30pm and immediately met with problems getting into the opposing trenches because of the volume of fire the Germans were able to bring on the Scotsmen. Some prisoners were taken and it was estimated that somewhere in the region of 100 German casualties caused; however, it was at a cost of around 80 Royal Scot casualties. It is interesting looking through the reports on the raid in the war diaries. The hand-written report by 11th Scots O.C. Lt Col Croft was felt by Brigadier Marshall (his brigade commander) to be written in an overly 'disappointed' manner and his subsequent report to the divisional commander is worded somewhat differently. At the end of his report he states; "The casualties are regrettable, but it was recognised that the Brigade was out to fight and not to carry out a carefully prepared raid; nor were the casualties all on one side."[44]

The information obtained was probably the same as that obtained on 5 April by a two platoon size raid (around 60 men) carried out by C Company, 13th Royal Scots of 15th (Scottish) Division. It managed to cause disruption and casualties plus bring back prisoners at the cost of four wounded.[45] Overall then it might be said that the escalation of the raid into small actions at company strength or more was effective in disrupting the opposition and inflicting casualties, but at the cost of substantial losses to the raiders.

43   See Sheldon, *The German Army on Vimy Ridge* p. 239 for the German description of events. Canadian unit diaries differ somewhat in that 54th Battalion records 3 March as the date for the truce and one battalion actually refer to a man being shot dead whilst trying to retrieve his comrades.

44   TNA: WO 95/1774 War Diary of 11th Royal Scots Regiment.

45   TNA: WO 95/1946 War Diary of 13th Royal Scots Regiment.

5

Plan of Attack

But 'twas not winter –
rather a season of bliss unchangeable,
awakened from farm and church where it had lain
safe under tile and thatch for ages since
this England, Old already, was called Merry.

The Manor Farm

Canadian Corps (see colour map)

The role to be played by 1st Army, and in particular the Canadian Corps, was, as described earlier in the general background to the offensive, that of taking and holding Vimy Ridge. One only has to stand for a few moments near the Canadian Memorial on Hill 145 to realise the importance this position had with regard to the success or otherwise of the whole offensive. Any advance south of the ridge would be made untenable by the continuing occupation of this high ground by the Germans. The Canadian Corps divisions were aligned from north to south in reverse number order, 4th Division in the north down to 1st Division in the south. There was also the British 5th Division allocated to Byng as a reserve to be used as he required.

The Black Line was to be taken in 35 minutes, this in most cases being about 700 yards of advance. After 40 minutes consolidation, the advance was then to be made onto the Red Line. This meant a further advance of about 400 yards for 1st and 2nd Divisions, 3rd Division to be on the line of the ridge and 4th Division to be down the slope on the far side in order to capture the German 2nd line. This Red Line was to be the day's final objective for the northern two divisions (apart from the very right of 3rd Division). 1st and 2nd Divisions were to advance further onto the Blue Line; this point to be reached by the 5 hour 20-minute mark. Finally, for the day was the Brown Line, this should be reached by 7 hours 48 minutes after Zero Hour.

The 4th Division had, as its main objective, Hill 145. It was to attack on a two brigade front with a brigade holding back on the first day but subsequently to attack further north to take the area of high ground North West of Givenchy-en-Gohelle called the Pimple. Thus, as can be seen on the map, the Red Line creates a flank facing northwards. This line was to be the divisional final objective for the day, a much shorter distance than for any other unit, a few hundred metres in places, but still a formidable task as it was clear that the Germans would put all their efforts into regaining the high point. The 12th Brigade was allocated the left flank of the attack, the 73rd (one of the Royal Highlanders of Canada Battalions) to form the northwards facing line. In the centre was 72nd (Seaforth Highlanders) Battalion and the right 38th (Ottawa) Battalion. 78th (Winnipeg Grenadiers) Battalion was directed to pass through the 38th on the right, as the Brigade objective was furthest on this flank. 11th Brigade was to the right with two battalions in front; on the left 87th (Canadian Grenadier Guards) Battalion and to its right 102nd ((Central Ontario) Battalion. The support battalions, due to pass through were, left, 75th (Central Ontario) and right 54th (Central Ontario) Battalions.

The 3rd Division also attacked with two brigades. The area it was to attack was one of the most difficult in terms of terrain as it was very broken by the many craters created by the underground warfare of the previous two years. It was also to clear the ridge up to where it falls away steeply in La Folie Wood. On the left was 7th Brigade with, from left to right: 42nd Battalion (5th Royal Highlanders of Canada), Princess Patricia's Canadian Light Infantry and the Royal Canadian Regiment. To the right 8th Brigade with, from left to right: 4th, 2nd and 1st Canadian Mounted Rifles. Units on its far right were to be the first to move beyond the Red Line and to take the Blue Line.

A glance at the map will tell you the difficulties to be faced by 2nd Division. Not only was the village of Thelus in its path, it had a substantial distance to cover to the Brown Line and on an ever increasing front. To deal with this the divisional plan was to attack on a two brigade front with the Red Line as their objective, after taking this position the two supporting brigades would come through to take the Blue and Brown Lines. This would take the division through Thelus and to the edge of Farbus. In more detail, the initial attack was to be on the left by 5th Brigade with 26th (New Brunswick) Battalion left and 24th (Victoria Rifles) right; 25th Battalion taking over at the Black Line to attack the Red Line. Right of this was to be 4th Brigade with 19th (Central Ontario) Battalion left, 18th (Western Ontario) Battalion right and 21st (Eastern Ontario) Battalion coming through. Once the Red Line was taken on the left the British 13th Brigade of British 5th Division was to come through to take the Brown Line above the village of Vimy. This was to be carried out by 2nd King's Own Scottish Borderers on the left and the 1st Royal West Kents on the right.[1] Passing through the Red Line on the right was to be 6th Canadian Brigade. It was to attack from the Red Line to the intermediate Blue Line with three battalions from left to right: 29th Battalion, 28th (North West) Battalion and 31st (Alberta) Battalion. From there the attack would go on further to the Brown Line with 29th Battalion continuing on the left and the brigade support, 27th (City of Winnipeg) Battalion on the right.

Although 1st Division had even more distance to cover than its left hand neighbour it benefitted from having a narrowing front as it advanced. It was thus able to put three battalions of its two leading brigades in the attack to the Red Line and then pass its third brigade through to finish the advance to the Blue and Brown Lines. 3rd Brigade led the attack on the left with, from left to right: 16th, 14th and 15th Battalions. 2nd Brigade was on the right with, again from left to right: 10th, 7th and 5th Battalions. These battalions were to take both the Black and Red Lines. Passing through them all was to be 1st Brigade with an advance to the Blue Line of, from left to right: 4th, 3rd and 1st Battalions. Both 4th and 3rd Battalions were then tasked with going on from the Blue Line to the Brown Line on the southern edge of Farbus.

XVII Corps

The XVII Corps was to attack on a three division front up to the Brown Line with the novel idea of passing a whole division through for the task of capturing the Green Line. The divisions in the front line were from left to right, 51st (Highland) Division, 34th Division and 9th (Scottish) Division. 4th Division was tasked with passing through at the Brown Line.

The 51st Division, situated on the right flank of the Canadian attack, faced a number of complicated tasks. On the left the German line swung around to face south around the 'Labyrinth', the

---

1   This was originally part of 6th Canadian Brigade's objectives, but it was recognised prior to the offensive that the frontage was too long and that additional troops were required; thus the insertion of a British brigade. See Library and Archives, Canada, war diaries 6th Canadian Infantry Brigade, Militia and Defence RG9, Militia and Defence, Series III-D-3, Volume 4889, Reel T-10685 File : 264-265, Operational Orders.

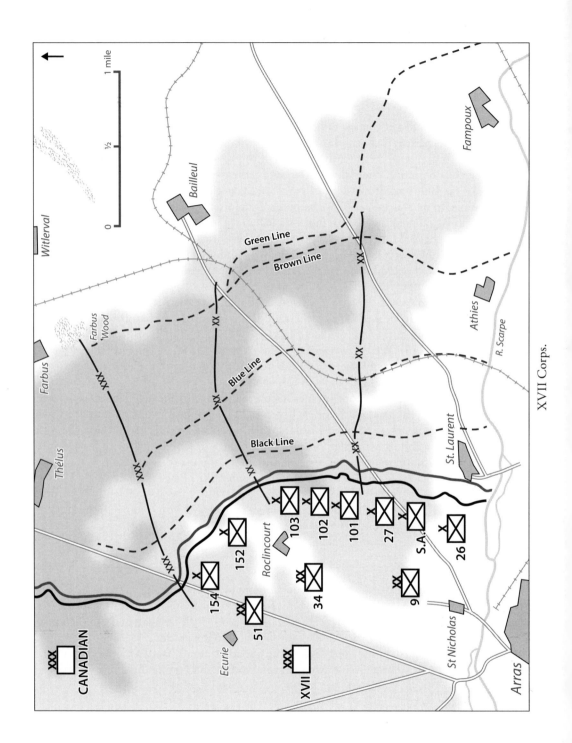

aptly named concentration of trenches made notorious from the French attacks of 1915. On the left the 154th Brigade had the problem of seizing this area of trenches and then continuing their general attack in a north easterly direction. They allocated one company of the 4th Seaforth Highlanders for the northward attack, the remainder attacking alongside the 9th Royal Scots. They were to take the Black Line and also a small extension to join up with the Canadian Red Line. Coming through the Seaforths to take the Blue and Brown Lines were to be 4th Gordon Highlanders and similarly through the Royal Scots were to be 7th Argyll & Sutherland Highlanders. Timing was a little awkward for the Gordons as the Canadian Blue Line was slightly in advance of the Scots and thus they would have to swing up to link with this line. 152nd Brigade, on the right, had 6th Seaforth Highlanders on the left and 6th Gordon Highlanders to their right. 5th Seaforths were to follow their brother regiment with 8th Argyll & Sutherland Highlanders going through the Gordons; both of these regiments to perform the same task as those in 154th Brigade. Then, with both brigades established on the Brown Line, 153rd Brigade would be tasked with taking the Green Line. In this arrangement, Major-General G.M. Harper, commanding, had decided against the instructions of the corps commander, Lieut.-General Sir Charles Fergusson. Fergusson laid down that each division should attack on a three brigade front. The reason he gave being that there would then be unified command throughout the depth of the advance. He gave his assent, however, to Harper's alternative plan. That the plans for the division did not quite turn out as Harper hoped and how much this could have been due to his decision will be discussed later.

Next in the line of attack was 34th Division. It would, as asked, attack with all three brigades in line. The major objective for the division was the Pont du Jour Line (see map) which constituted the Brown Line with the Green Line a few hundred yards beyond. To take up the left of the attack was the task of the 103rd (Tyneside Irish) Brigade. The 25th (on the left) and 24th (on the right) Northumberland Fusiliers were to take the Black and Blue Lines with the 27th and 26th N.F. respectively coming through to take the Brown and Green Lines. In the centre was the 102nd (Tyneside Scottish) Brigade. From the left the 22nd N.F. and the 21st N.F. being the assaulting battalions with the 23rd and 20th respectively behind with the same task as their sister battalions of 103rd Brigade. Finally, on the right was 101st Brigade with the heights of Pont du Jour in its sights. 11th Suffolk Regiment with 10th Lincolnshire Regiment coming through on the left and 16th Royal Scots with its sister battalion the 15th coming through to go to the Brown Line and beyond.

The 9th (Scottish) Division also had all three brigades up front and was to attack with the River Scarpe forming its right flank. This formation had a novel problem of having the Brown Line as its final objective but then to allow a whole division, the 4th, to pass through and advance to the Green Line. This final line was far in advance of that of its northerly neighbours where it constituted a mere few hundred yards. Although brigade sized units had been tasked with passing through forward troops in the past this was an experiment, never before planned into a major action. On the left, 27th Brigade was organised with 6th Kings Own Scottish Borderers (left) and 12th Royal Scots (right) to take the Black Line; 11th Royal Scots and 9th Scottish Rifles respectively to take the Blue. Which units were to make the final move to the Brown Line was to be decided on the spot, to make use of whichever units were strongest at the point in time. This was an interesting decision by the brigade commander Br.-General Maxwell, a sign that some general officers were beginning to realise the advantages of flexibility in planning. In the centre the South African Brigade had the more normal arrangement with 4th (left) and 3rd (right) South African Infantry to take the Black and Blue Lines; 2nd and 1st South African Infantry respectively to move onto the Brown. Aside the Scarpe, the 26th Brigade had another variety on the assault with 8th Black Watch (left) and 7th Seaforth Highlanders forming the attack battalions to take the Black Line. They were then to move onto the Blue with two companies of 10th Argyll & Sutherland Highlanders in support. The whole of the Argylls were then to move onto the

Brown Line. 5th Cameron Highlanders were kept in reserve to be used as and when required. 9th Division was indeed blessed with a commander who gave his brigades freedom to form their own plans according to local circumstances and brigade commanders capable enough to make these decisions intelligently.

The 4th Division had the very demanding role of following behind 9th Division, awaiting the moment when the Brown Line was seized and being ready, on time for the artillery plan, to advance through and carry on the attack to the Green Line some 3,000 yards distant. This distance moved the Green Line to one encompassing Hyderabad Redoubt in the north, Fampoux, then across the river Monchy-le-Preux and Guémappe. Two brigades were to cover the divisional part of this plan, with major objectives being Hyderabad Redoubt and the taking of the village of Fampoux. For this two brigades were allocated, 11th on the left and 12th on the right. 11th Brigade had the Redoubt as a focus whilst 12th Brigade was to take the village. Each had three battalions in the assault. For 11th Brigade, from left to right, were: 1st East Lancashire Regiment, 1st Hampshire Regiment and 1st Somerset Light Infantry. To take the Redoubt at the far end of the advance 1st Rifle Brigade were tasked with coming through. The others whilst 1st East Lancs formed a north facing flank due to the nature of the Green Line (see map). 12th Brigade also had three battalions in the line, from left to right: 2nd Essex Regiment, 2nd Lancashire Fusiliers and 1st Kings Own Regiment. The 2nd Duke of Wellington's Regiment was tasked with passing through to specifically take Fampoux, allowing the other regiments to move onto the Green Line itself. The plan was ambitious, leading if successful, to an advance of over 3½ miles.

VI Corps

This corps was also to attack on a three division front with its initial objective being the village of Feuchy and the Wancourt–Feuchy line, about 3,500 yards away. These were from left to right: 15th, 12th and 3rd Divisions. The plan also, as north of the Scarpe, included the passing through of a fourth division, the 37th, to take the Green Line which was even more ambitiously placed to take in the villages of Monchy-le-Preux and Guémappe.

The 15th Division put two brigades up front in order to take the Black and Blue Lines with a 3rd to then pass through to take the W-F Line. On the left of the attack with their flank on the river was 45th Brigade. The far left of this brigade, with the instructions to clear Blangy were 13th Royal Scots. In the centre 11th Argyll & Sutherland Highlanders and on the right 7th Royal Scots Fusiliers had the task of clearing the area north of the main railway line from Arras. On a narrower front 44th Brigade, south of the railway, attacked with only two battalions up, on the left 9th Black Watch and the right 8th/10th Gordon Highlanders. East of the Blue Line next to the river was marshy and difficult ground and therefore it was felt that the brigade passing through would not have too wide a frontage with three battalions up. It was to attack with 7th/8th King's Own Scottish Borderers left, 10th Scottish Rifles in the centre and 12th Highland Infantry on the right. They had the task of securing the Brown Line just beyond Feuchy.

The 12th Division had a similar task to that of 15th Division with its southern boundary being formed by the Arras–Cambrai road. Although again attacking on a two brigade front with the third coming through this division opted for a different approach with two battalions tasked with taking the Black Line in each brigade, two other coming through to take the Blue. Finally, the third brigade to move thorough the others and take the Blue Line which was again the Wancourt–Feuchy line. The left brigade was to be the 36th with 7th Royal Sussex Regiment on its left flank and 11th Middlesex on the right. Passing through to take the next line were to be, respectively, 8th and 9th Royal Fusiliers. 37th Brigade was to be next in line with 7th East Surreys (left) and 6th Queens (right) forming the initial attacking troops and 6th Royal West Kents and 6th Buffs respectively coming through. Once the Blue Line was secure 35th Brigade was to be passed

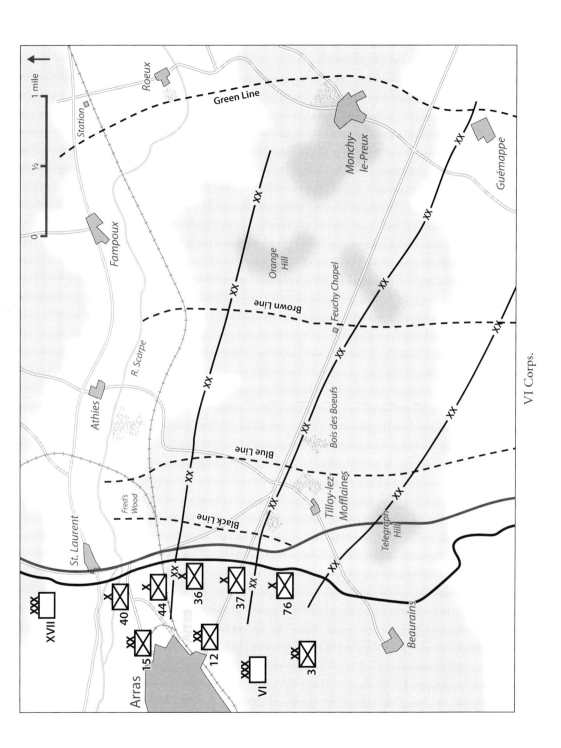

through to advance to the Brown Line. Four battalions were to constitute this force being from left to right: 5th Royal Berkshire Regiment, 9th Essex Regiment and along the Cambrai Road, 7th Norfolk Regiment and 7th Suffolk Regiment. The latter was tasked with crossing over the road somewhat in order to capture Feuchy Chapel and the Brown Line in the centre of Chapel Hill.

On the other side of the Arras – Cambrai road, the vagaries of the German line gave 3rd Division a bit of a headache when devising its plan of attack. In early March the German front line swung around, continuing to surround Arras. The retreat, however, led to the new front line swinging the other way in a south-easterly direction for a while until, on the south-western edge of the village of Tilloy-les-Mofflaines, it regained its generally southerly path. It was thus planned to bring the Black Line, once it had crossed in front of the village, across the German front line and to effectively end it there. The outcome for 3rd Division was that the Black Line was only an objective across half of its frontage. Only the first four trenches and then Devil's Wood in front of Tilloy had to be taken for the Black Line to be reached. This task was given to the Gordon Highlanders of 76th Brigade for the first phase and 10th Royal Welsh Fusiliers were to take the wood and therefore the Black Line. These were the only units of the division that were to attack at 5.30am. At 7.30am it was planned for 9th Brigade, with one battalion of 76th Brigade attached, to pass through to take the Blue Line. 13th King's (Liverpool) Regiment on the left and 12th West Yorkshire Regiment on the right were given the task of taking Tilloy village and just beyond to the Blue Line. To their right 4th Royal Fusiliers were to take the first two trench lines of the Harp, the front of the redoubt and the central trench called The String. Following on behind them, 2nd Suffolk Regiment, attached from 76th Brigade were to pass through and advance to the Blue Line just beyond the rear trench of the Harp.

VII Corps

The VII Corps assault plan must be examined more carefully than the others, as it comprises several elements that are not straightforward and should be kept mind in relation to the narrative. First, unlike the previous narratives, I will review all of the general divisional objectives as they are very interdependent and need to be seen together. The two left divisions of VII Corps, 14th (Light) and 56th had, as per Operational Orders, the Brown Line as their objectives. The 56th Division, on the right of these two divisions, had an additional task however and was instructed:

> During the advance from the Blue to the Brown Line [the division] should have a reserve of strength, so that there may be troops available on that [right] flank to assist the advance of the 30th Division by taking the trenches included in the latter's objective in flank and reverse.[2]

This assistance would be vital, as 30th Division had not only to attack the Hindenburg Line in front of it, in a north-easterly direction but then to advance to the Green Line, linking up with the VI Corps troops on its left, eventually to be facing east. On its right one brigade of 21st Division was to carry out a similar manoeuvre to complete the east facing Green Line to its junction with the existing British front line. Other important elements at a divisional level were the timing of the attacks. A glance at map will highlight the fact that the Black Line is, as mentioned above, already the British Front Line, thus the two-hour delay for 14th and 56th Divisions. Similarly, the left brigade of 30th Division also still has a Blue Line to reach. As it does not have any German lines to cross before that line, however, its start time is set at 11.45am with instructions not to pass the Blue Line (the Hénin – Neuville Vitasse road) until 12.06pm so as not to fall under their own barrage

---

2   Falls, *Military Operations, France and Belgium 1917 Vol. 1*, Appendices, p. 95.

and to match the progress of 56th Division on its left. Then, further south on the map you can see that the Black and Blue Lines are both on the British front line. This means that to conform to advances all along the line the right brigade of 30th Division was not to leave its assembly trenches until 3.06pm or in the case of the right battalion 3.07pm. By the time you reach the assembly trenches of 21st Division all bar the Green Line are concurrent and thus that division had a start time of 4.15pm. There is one additional instruction given by 21st Division to the attacking brigade and is found within its Operational Orders; "64th Inf. Bde. will not attack the enemy's position where it is found that the gaps in the wire are not passable."[3] The brigade commander was also possibly told that the attack should only go in if it is clear that the left brigade of 30th Division had been successful in taking certain trenches which would then threaten the flank and rear of the Germans in front of him.[4]

The 14th Division's attack on the Harp was to be led by 42nd Brigade on the left and 43rd Brigade right. 42nd Brigade had the Harp as its main objective next to 3rd Division; 9th Kings Royal Rifle Corps (left) and 5th Oxford & Buckinghamshire Regiment (right) were to capture the front line and String on the Harp, with 5th Shropshire Light Infantry passing through to take the rear and Brown Line. The boundary to 3rd Division then begins to come in from the left at this point (see map) and therefore it was only 43rd Brigade who had the task of pushing on towards the Brown Line. This also was to attack with two battalions in line, 10th Durham Light Infantry (left) and 6th King's Own Yorkshire Light Infantry (right), who had the task of taking all the German trenches to the Blue Line. It was the task of 9th Rifle Brigade (left) and 6th Somerset Light Infantry (right) to pass through and advance to the Brown Line. It was this brigade that was the only one of 14th Division to have to take elements of the new Hindenburg Line as it was attached here to the southern trenches of the Harp.

The 56th Division planned to clear the village of Neuville Vitasse by assaulting at an angle to the main defences, generally attacking the northern edge of the village and moving through to the other side. They would then have to wheel slightly left to attack the Hindenburg Line itself. 168th Brigade on the left had the task of taking the outlying Pine Lane Trench and then moving onto the Hindenburg Line itself about 500 yards further back. To do this 12th London Regiment (The Rangers) would attack on the left, 13th London Regiment (Kensington) on the right. The 14th London (London Scottish) had the task of passing through and advancing to the Brown Line. This plan sounds in order until it is observed that the Blue Line is just behind the village, leaving the two lines of the Hindenburg system to the one supporting battalion moving up afterwards. It is not difficult to see how this could lead to possible confusion with those troops of 14th Division to the left who were to be in the second line of the Hindenburg trenches after the first phase. On the right of the division was to be 167th Brigade with 8th Middlesex left and 3rd London Regiment right. Once these battalions had cleared the village to the trenches just beyond it, 1st London Regiment's task was to then move beyond to take the Hindenburg Line and sunken road behind. Only then were 7th Middlesex Regiment to move on and take the Brown Line on the Wancourt – Feuchy line. Although the final section of the Brown Line was quite narrow for the division the decision to only allocate two battalions to this second phase was surprising given that they had the two lines of the Hindenburg system to go through. The narrowness of the objective could have been solved by both remaining two battalions of each brigade being given the task of taking the Hindenburg Line with one of each receiving the order to move further to the Brown Line once the two trenches had been taken.

---

3   TNA: WO 95/2132 21st Division General Staff War Diary, Appendix E.
4   This is claimed by the brigade commander in an after-action report. This assertion is not substantiated in the relevant brigade diary.

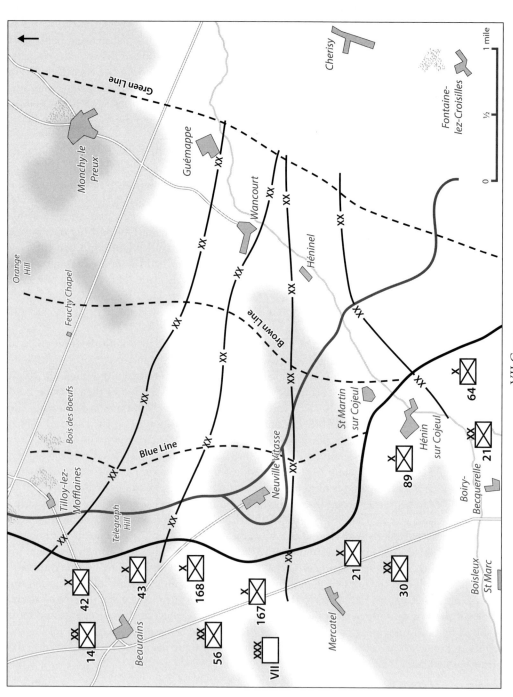

Maj-Gen. J.S.M. Shea commanding 30th Division had what must have been quite a rarity in any divisional commander's experience of an attack with two brigades, the fact that one was not due to attack until much later than the other. His left brigade, 21st Brigade has both a partially defended Blue Line and then the Brown Line to take whilst his right brigade, 89th Brigade was already on the Brown Line. The fateful decision was made to delay the attack of 21st Brigade, with 18th King's Liverpool Regiment left and 2nd Wiltshire Regiment on the right. That they could not attack at the same time as 56th Division, taking the Hénin-sur-Cojeul–Neuville Vitasse Road as the Blue Line and then attack from there later must remain a mystery. As it was they were condemned to a 2,500 yards advance. Being on the Brown Line it was not going to be until late afternoon that 20th King's Liverpool on the left and 19th King's Liverpool on the right were to attack the Hindenburg Line directly before wheeling right to form a flank facing eastwards on the Green Line. They had 2nd Bedford Regiment in support and 17th King's Liverpool on carrying and 'mopping up' duties. The decision to delay the attack of 21st Brigade is even more unfathomable when it is noted that 2nd Bedfords were tasked with taking St.-Martin-sur-Cojeul during the early hours of 9 April. This would mean that the attacking battalions would have the eastern edge of the village as their assaulting position. So on the one hand Maj-Gen. Shea did not allow an early forward movement to narrow the distance to be attacked and then on the other hand accepted 89th Brigade doing just that.

The final attacking unit in the south was one brigade of 21st Division. Br-Gen. Headlam's 64th Brigade were ordered to take the Hindenburg Line in front, block that line to the east and then form the southernmost flank behind, again facing east. Given the enormity of the task Headlam put three battalions into the attack, from left to right, 9th King's Own Yorkshire Regiment, 15th Durham Light Infantry and 1st East Yorkshire Regiment. They also had over 1,000 yards to cross before reaching the German wire but no attempt was planned to create a more advanced jumping off point. The 10th K.O.Y.L.I. were the battalion left to be in support. The remainder of the division was to continue to hold the British front line to the south.

The die was set, Operational Orders disseminated and worked upon over the preceding days. Training had been meticulously carried out over reconstructions of the trench systems being faced on the first day and units down to platoon briefed as to their task on the day. At points all the way down the line men moved into position, either in specially dug assault trenches or actually out in no man's land awaiting the time to rise and follow the barrage into what might be their final day.

6

Morning Success at the Blue Line

The flowers left thick at nightfall in the wood
this Eastertide call into mind the men,
now far from home, who, with their sweethearts, should
have gathered them and will do never again.

In Memoriam (Easter 1915)

Even before the designated beginning of the offensive at 5.30am a machine gun barrage commenced with 1½ minutes remaining before Zero Hour. Then promptly on the half hour the enormous artillery barrage erupted all along the line from the northern end of Vimy Ridge down to the Tilloy-les-Mofflaines area, as did a number of mines. Instructions to all troops had been very clear, get up with and stay as close as possible behind the barrage. The weather was cold with sleet in the air and would get no better during what was to come.

Canadian Corps

4th Canadian Division, 12th Canadian Infantry Brigade

Having the relatively straightforward task of securing the German front line and creating the left flank of the whole attack, 73rd Canadian (Royal Highlanders) Battalion had allocated two companies, A and C to the job. These promptly moved out of the assembly trenches as soon as the barrage began and the mines in Gunner and Kennedy Craters had detonated. As soon as the barrage moved off the German front line the Royal Highlanders were immediately behind and had little problem taking the trench; the time reported being 5.37am. A bombing attack behind Kennedy Crater had to be repulsed; otherwise the men could begin the process of blocking Cluny and Clucas trenches as well as the front line trench to the north. This trench was devoid of any Germans so this action could be undertaken with few problems. Major Stanley, who was in overall charge of the action, was slightly wounded and went back but otherwise at this stage in the day the battalion had carried out its task and was now left with ensuring that the left flank remained secure.[1] This flank attack was the only one at this stage to have elements of the German *16th Bavarian Division*, part of *Gruppe Souchez* opposite to it. The left flank of this division was held by *B.I.R. 11* and although the whole division had been subject to intense bombardment in the run up to the offensive it was the blowing of the mines that was the first indication of the attack for the regiment. What remained of the defenders after the bombardment and mine explosions were unable to hold back the Canadians until the third line. By which point, of course the objective had

---

1   Library & Archives, Canada, war diaries – 73rd Canadian Infantry Battalion, Militia and Defence, RG9, Militia and Defence, Series III-D-3 Volume 4943, Reel T-10750 File 451.

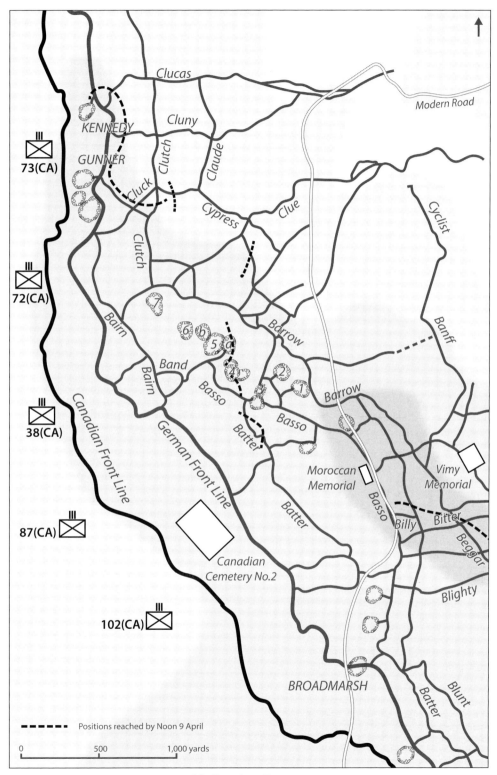

4th Canadian Division.

been reached and therefore attacks ceased. The German accounts mistakenly regarded this as the defenders causing the attack to falter.[2]

The 72nd (Seaforth Highlanders) Canadian Battalion, forming the centre of 12th Brigade, was another regiment with a proud attachment to their Scottish formation, after a group of Vancouver citizens with Scottish decent formed the unit as the Seaforth Highlanders of Canada in 1910 and became affiliated to the famous Scottish unit in 1912. Their task was a little more ambitious than that of the unit on their left in that they had to go beyond the German front line and form the elbow of the flank guard by taking and holding the communication trench between Gunner Crater and Clutch Trench. They then had the task of pushing down Cluck Trench to the junction with Claude and then further into Clue, these trenches then forming the northern face of the flank guard. They could then link with 78th Regiment when they had taken Cyclist and Banff Trenches. The plan began to unravel soon after the front trench was taken. Clutch Trench was then taken and a post established down Cluck Trench by Lt. McLennon opposite Claude. Lt Vickers was supposed to push down in support of McLennon but reported that he couldn't and instead bombed down Clutch as far as Cluny. There he and his men came under their own artillery barrage but that is not surprising as this was beyond the planned northern edge of the attack. The unit diary merely says that Cluck could not be cleared "owing to the impossibility of following the trench."[3]

It is clear that the Germans were not subdued in this area at all and were able to hold 72nd Battalion. This was the Fischer Sector of the front and was held by *Reserve Infanterie Regiment 261* of *79th Reserve-Infanterie-Division*. The German defenders fought fiercely and inflicted heavy casualties on the Seaforths even if claims they make in their regimental history to holding the whole of their front line trench do not seem to be correct.[4] The book also talks of a breakthrough to the north and troops flooding south behind them which is certainly somewhat overstating the position of the two companies of 73rd Canadian Regiment which had neither the intention nor the men to spare to turn south. The truth of much of Dieterich's book is, unfortunately, placed in doubt after he claims that the front line held all day, which it quite evidently did not.

They did, however, stop the breakthrough to the rear trenches of the ridge. The Black Line was not reached at the appointed time which left the units on the right of the 72nd with an open flank. Another factor in the lack of success of the Canadians could lie in the period of time previous to the attack. It should be recalled that the 72nd were involved in the disastrous 1 March raid and 130 replacements for losses in this and previous actions only arrived on the day of the attack and could obviously not be included. The result was that according to the unit diary[5] the attack was undertaken by 13 officers and 249 other ranks; worse than half strength! The task they were given was not in the least straightforward and being asked to carry out such a task with so few men was unfortunate to say the least. The men certainly gave their all as casualties amounted to 202, including all bar one of the officers who took part; a staggering 77 percent casualty rate. Thus it could be said that the decision to mount large scale and costly raids directly led to eventual problems in the actual offensive.

The role of 38th Canadian Battalion, with its men mainly from the Ottawa region, was to strike out of the Mandora trenches and take the chain of craters running across their front. This collection of craters was the one formed around the old front lines before the attack of the Germans the previous year had moved the line somewhat downhill. By creating strongpoints, a little beyond

2   Berhmann & Brandt, *Die Osterschlacht bei Arras 1917 I. Teil*, p. 134.
3   Library and Archives, Canada, war diaries – 72nd Canadian Infantry Battalion, Militia and Defence, RG9, Militia and Defence, Series III-D-3 Volume 4942, Reel T-10749-10750 File 450.
4   Dieterich, Gen.Lt. a.D., *Die 79. Reserve Division in der Schlacht auf der Vimy Höhe April 1917* (Raumburg/Magdeburg: Eigenverlag 1927), pp. 14-15.
5   Library and Archives, Canada, war diaries – 72nd Canadian Infantry Battalion.

these craters (see map below), the follow through attack of the 78th Canadian Battalion could be supported to enable the Red Line to be reached. The leading elements of A and D companies in the first wave were able to take the German front line trench with little or no problem. Although resistance became stronger the follow up companies were able to get through Bairn and Band Trenches and by 6.05 a signal station was set up in No. 6 Crater. It was thought at this point that all the craters had been taken and that impression was passed back to Brigade H.Q.; although it was pointed out that although all seemed good on the left there had been no report from the right. In actual fact at this point the area around craters 1 to 4 had not been taken and strong resistance was stopping the men in their tracks.

One officer in the leading waves was Captain Thain MacDowell who, with his two runners became separated from the main body at one point. Undeterred he and the two men then overcame 2 machine guns and then came across a large dugout containing 2 German officers with 75

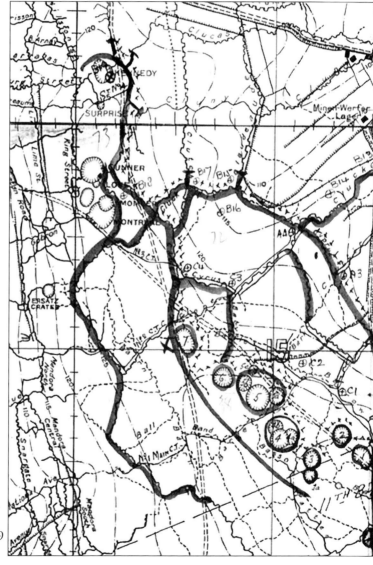

No. 1 to No. 7 Craters – The lines marked on the map are objectives for the day. (War diaries of 12th Canadian Infantry Brigade, RG9, Militia and Defence, Series III-D-3, Volume 4907, Reel T-10699 File: 326)

men. By conning the Germans into believing he was part of a larger force MacDowell was able to capture all the men. For his actions he was awarded the VC, his two runners[6] being awarded the DCM:

> For most conspicuous bravery and indomitable resolution in face of heavy machine gun and shell fire. By his initiative and courage this officer, with the assistance of two runners, was enabled in the face of great difficulties, to capture two machine guns, besides two officers and seventy-five men. Although wounded in the hand, he continued for five days to hold the position gained, in spite of heavy shell fire, until eventually relieved by his battalion. By his bravery and prompt action he undoubtedly succeeded in rounding up a very strong enemy machine post.[7]

The 78th Battalion is introduced at this point as they were, in this early phase before the pause in the barrage, supposed to be advancing behind the 38th and preparing to move on towards the Red line at 6.40am when the barrage recommenced. For this to happen however the area around the craters had to be secure. The companies of the 78th left Vincent Tunnel (D Coy was in nearby dugouts) and successfully moved over the first German trenches. Forward movement seems to have been possible on the left and therefore parties of the 78th were able to begin moving towards their first objective, the Black Line in Cyprus Trench. This advance was, however, done with both flanks in the air which caused some considerable concern to Lt. Col. James Kirkcaldy D.S.O., commanding the battalion. As Cluck Trench had not been cleared by 72nd Battalion there was a gap on the left of Kirkcaldy's men. As A and B companies consolidated as best they could on the Black Line the follow up companies moved forward. With no flank cover and intense resistance these companies could only set up scattered outposts beyond Cyprus Trench and therefore the Red Line was not reached as a fully manned and coherent defensive trench. The causes behind

Captain Thain MacDowell.
(University of Toronto)

---

6   Privates James T. Kobus and Arthur James Hay.
7   *London Gazette*, no.30122, 8 June 1917. His reports back during the 9th make for excellent reading and can be seen in Appendix IV. After praising the quality of the cigars and Perrier Water, especially enchanting is his invitation to Ken to come up for tea at the end of the third report. MacDowell, who had already been awarded the DSO on the Somme the previous year, was promoted Major after Vimy and survived the war.

the problems he found on his right will become evident when the first attacks of 11th Canadian Brigade are described.

4th Canadian Division, 11th Canadian Infantry Brigade

The events surrounding Br. Gen. V.W. Odlum's brigade in the first few hours of the day are shrouded in somewhat of a mystery. What is clear is that the attack went badly wrong. When 87th (Canadian Grenadier Guards) Battalion went into the attack from assault trenches about 150 yards from the German front line they were met by a hail of machine gun and rifle fire, stopping them in their tracks. The unit diary states that although held on their right, men in the centre and left did make it through to their objective which was the second line, Batter Trench. The British Official History makes short shrift of the battalion's attack, stating failure all the way across its front; making a strongpoint responsible for the carnage. No mention of a strongpoint is made in any of the Canadian diaries, for the assault itself, nor the preparatory bombardment. The Official History also lays the blame for their survival and effectiveness of this point on the decision not to bombard it further to a report on 7 April that it was intact, having been repaired; a decision it says was made by the infantry who wanted to make use of it. Nicholson goes further in blaming the commander of the 87th, Major H. LeR. Shaw for the decision. He bases this on the 4th Divisional diary where, in Appendix B (author unknown) is the following:

> Trench destruction by the Heavy Artillery was excellent, and only in one place was a portion of trench allowed to remain, and that by the desire of the Infantry, who proposed to use it afterwards. This was a mistake, which should not have been allowed to occur.[8]

Note it does not name the commander of 'the Infantry' castigated. It then, a page later, says that either the barrage did not cover this point or the infantry didn't keep up with the barrage. It seems to be trying overly hard to find reasons for the failure of the attack. The strongpoint created by Falls[9] has its origins in communication with the brigade commander whilst writing the Official History. I have failed to find the actual material sent to Falls, there is nothing in his correspondence files held at the National Archives from Odlum. However, in his work on the subject, Andrew Godefroy, in looking at Odlum's private papers found a note by him in the margin of a draft chapter:

> This section of trench was directly opposite and commanded at 400 yards range the exit of the British tunnel (Tottenham) under the Zouave Valley leading up to the brigade front. It had been destroyed earlier in the bombardment but air photographs taken on 11 [must be March, not 7 April as Falls notes] showed it again intact. Requests were made for the heavy artillery to destroy this position on the 8th [clearly April] but in compliance with the wishes of Brig. General Odlum who hoped to make it his headquarters during the advance, the bombardment was not carried out.[10]

8   Library and Archives, Canada, war diaries – 4th Canadian Infantry Division, RG9, Militia and Defence, Series III-D-3, Volume 4859, Reel T-1938 File: 159, Appendix B.
9   Falls, *Military Operations, France and Belgium 1917 Vol. 1*, p. 328.
10   Quoted in Andrew Godefroy, 4th Canadian Division: The Trenches Should Never be Saved in Hayes, *et al* (eds) *Vimy Ridge, A Canadian Reassessment*, Godefroy is uncertain whether this is a draft for the British or Canadian Official History, but the chapter number in the reference clearly makes it the former.

Stories clearly differ across the different sources. Shaw, as a possible culprit or at least a witness, is a mystery who disappears almost completely from history when replaced as battalion commander in May. There is then this one note from more than 20 years after the event claiming a higher authority decision but that has absolutely no contemporary supporting evidence. Furthermore, the dates in the British Official History do not correspond with the probable source of his information. Odlum's stated desire to make it a Brigade Headquarters also makes little sense. It is a matter of a few hundred yards from the Canadian front line with all the facilities required for an H.Q.; why move everything a small distance forward? It is as much of a mess as the assault itself which will now be pieced together and described as fully as possible. As already mentioned the German accounts of this section of the battle are difficult to accept as they give the impression of little or no Canadian progress until troops poured from around the flanks, an observation that can be dismissed. This difficulty will be come across again later in the day.

What is known is that 11th Brigade, in these first minutes of the attack, ran into severe difficulties. The Canadian Grenadier Guards were only partially getting into or through the German front line and the lack of clarity over the reasons why creates its own difficulties when trying to follow what comes next. The unit diaries of both the battalion[11] and the brigade[12] give no indication of total failure. As time progresses though, it becomes clear that elements that have reached the second line, Batter Trench are few in number and that casualties have been heavy. Also leadership is now a problem. Of the three initial waves only one lieutenant and a sergeant remain alive or unwounded and they are both on the left. Lt. Hannaford had managed to get forward to the area of Crater 4 where Batter and Basso trench meet with 15 men to form a strongpoint. Of the other officers most had not even reached the German front line. On the right all the first three waves of platoon leaders of C Company, Capt. Law, Lt. Planche and Lt. Simmons were lying wounded and as Major Ross rose to lead out the 4th wave of D company behind them he was almost immediately shot dead. In the centre Lt. Rooke and Major Joy were both killed and Lt Yonkles wounded. Again as D Company rose to follow in the centre Capt. Sare was killed. The lead platoon commander on the left, Lt Taylor was also killed. D Company's leader on this flank, Lt Sinclair, was wounded early, later dying of his wounds. The battalion had decided on an unusual pattern for the assault. Each of the first three waves was made up of one platoon from each of companies A to C, whilst three platoons of D Company made up the 4th Wave. This meant that each company had three different objectives depending upon the platoon a man was in. With only N.C.O. leadership and heavy losses, even if through the front line, this will have left confusion and thus the pockets of men remaining would essentially be ineffective in making good their area to facilitate the unit following up.

On the right of the 87th, the 102nd (Central Ontario) Battalion had fared better with early reports coming in via returning wounded officers that first the front line and then the second line had been successfully taken. It seems that this initial phase on this flank of the attack was having success. The battalion had made its objectives on the Black Line holding the line Beggar – Bitter – Billy. Casualties, especially amongst officers were heavy as a report back at 8.10am made clear when it reported:

> No officers, however, were to be seen anywhere; all were either killed, wounded or missing. Lt R.A. Stalker was reported in the first category; Major Brydon and Lt Wilson in the third. In

---

11   Library and Archives, Canada, war diaries – 87th Canadian Infantry Battalion, RG9, Militia and Defence, Series III-D-3, Volume 4944, Reel T-10752, File: 455.

12   Library and Archives, Canada, war diaries – 11th Canadian Infantry Brigade, RG9, Militia and Defence, Series III-D-3, Volume 4904, Reel T-10696, File: 315.

the meantime, the Battalion was under the active command of C.S.M. Russell, J. of "C" Coy while Sgt.Georgeson D.S. was maintaining a platoon in a section of Broadmarsh Crater.[13]

Thus at this early point in the attack although objectives had been met the situation was all but safe on the right of the brigade. To the left of them only scattered parties of men were holding small sections of the terrain they should have commanded to enable the supporting two battalions to push on and take the higher ground ahead. The heroic defence of 3rd, 9th and 11th Companies of *Reserve-Infanterie-Regiment 261* was the real reason for the problems faced as they fought desperately against these scattered groups of Canadians.

The 75th (Central Ontario) Battalion were due to move behind the 87th to go through and capture the final objective for the day, which at this point was still the Red Line, as were the 54th (Central Ontario) through the 102nd. The failures in front of them meant that all of the orders that the 75th had for that morning could quickly be forgotten. The unit diary is suspiciously quiet over the actions at this time, quickly moving onto events later in the day. It is most likely that they, like the 87th before them, attempted to progress over the German front line defences only to take heavy casualties. It was the role of 54th Battalion to follow through 102nd Battalion and the success of that latter unit allowed the 54th to make good progress. They got some elements across Beggar Trench, the Black Line but they became under increasingly heavy fire from flank and rear due to 75th Battalion not having got forward. So much so that as the barrage moved further on after 7.05am it left the 54th no other recourse than to fall back onto the Black Line and help the 102nd to consolidate there. The 54th went into the attack 350 strong, all ranks;[14] yet another depleted battalion having taken severe losses in 1 March trench raid. Again it could be argued that their inability to hold onto the summit area of Hill 145 was to some extent one of a depleted force not having the means to cope with their left flank being open.

3rd Canadian Division, 7th Canadian Brigade (see colour map for 3rd Canadian Division action)

The divisional plan of a two brigade frontage with three battalions up front for both brigades meant that it was a single battalion's responsibility to take both the Initial Black Line and then the Red Line ahead. This was facilitated in all cases of 7th Brigade by a two company front with the second two companies passing through at the Black Line (called by the units the Intermediate Line). The 7th Brigade had a very packed crater field in front of it stretching from the Longfellow chain on the left down to Commons Crater on the right. Their initial objective for this first phase was a line from the junction of Artillerie Weg and Farthing Trench northwards to just before where Blunt Trench meets Beggar Trench. Here it was to link up with 102nd Battalion.

The left battalion for the attack was the 42nd (Royal Highlanders of Canada) Battalion, affiliated with and taking the name of the famous Black Watch of Scotland. It was to attack from assembly and outpost trenches in the Longfellow Group of craters down Royal to Grange; the area easily seen today from the visitors centre in the park, looking towards the memorial. A and C companies formed the attacking troops, debauching from the security of the Grange tunnels into their allotted assault positions at 4.00am. At 5.30am they moved through the crater line, following the barrage without much resistance and moved quickly on to clear all the way up to

---

13   Library and Archives, Canada, war diaries – 102nd Canadian Infantry, RG9, Militia and Defence, Series
      III-D-3, Volume 4944, Reel T-10752, File: 456.
14   Library and Archives, Canada, war diaries – 54th Canadian Infantry, RG9, Militia and Defence, Series
      III-D-3, Volume 4942, Reel T-10748-10749, File: 445.

their objective in Beggar trench.[15] The only blot on this otherwise pristine copybook was that no contact had been made with any troops of 4th Division on the left, Beggar Trench not containing any of their troops as should have been the case. From the German perspective the area is now in Sector Zollern, defended by *Reserve-Infantrie-Regiment 262*. Unfortunately, again little is gained from the divisional history[16] as it claims the front line was destroyed by exploding mines, of which there were none and claims that it held the 3rd line until "enemy masses came upon them from the flank and rear",[17] which can be similarly dismissed. The preparatory artillery bombardment, in combination with an effective creeping barrage, gave little chance to the forward troops and the Black Line was taken in good time. The companies following through reached the Red Line, Lt McIntyre reporting back that he had even been to the bottom of La Folie Ridge and had not met the enemy; however, it was accompanied by other messages at this point giving a warning back to H.Q. that there were problems on their left.

In 7th Brigade's centre was Princess Patricia's Canadian Light Infantry, not surprisingly usually shortened to PPCLI; named after HRH Princess Patricia of Connaught,[18] one of Queen Victoria's granddaughters and a unit still in existence today. Their objective in the first 35-minute spell was Famine Trench. No 1 Coy attacked on the right with No 3 Coy on the left; the men will have advanced over the craters that can be viewed in the memorial park today. It is again clear that Famine Trench was taken timely and with relatively few casualties. At the same time the other two companies were advancing so as to be ready to move on further after the 40-minute delay in the movement of the barrage. The regimental history is rightly very proud of the action but is also quick to appreciate the role of the artillery in the success:

> The German front and support lines were in turn rapidly taken, the defences having been well-nigh obliterated by the bombardment and the Bavarians [sic] stunned beyond the power to resist. Nos. 1 and 3 Companies moved steadily and rapidly forward to the first objective. The ground was very difficult, but most of the obstacles were created by the terrible efficiency of the British and Canadian Siege Batteries. Occasionally the complete obliteration of a trench so destroyed landmarks that troops ran into their own barrage, but by 6 a.m. every unit of the Brigade was on the first objective-line and Lieutenant Haggard of No. 1 Company reported both attacking companies of the Patricias in position, few casualties, and the taking of a number of prisoners of the 262nd Regiment. Some slight opposition was met in Famine Trench itself, but this was quickly cleared and all four companies tumbled in. The action had opened with brilliant success.[19]

Once the artillery lifted again the remaining two companies, 2 and 4, moved swiftly onto the Red Line, in this case Britt Weg Trench as far as the junction with Staubwasserweg. Lt. Lownsbrough, commanding 4 Company reported few casualties whereas Lt. Tenbrocke of 2 Company said

---

15   Library and Archives, Canada, war diaries – 42nd Canadian Infantry, RG9, Militia and Defence, Series III-D-3, Volume 4938, Reel T-10743, File: 433.

16   Dieterich, Genlta. D., *Die 79. Reserve Division in der Schlacht auf der Vimy Höhe*, p. 13, apart from the two wombat mines further south which may have been taken for major mine explosions when recollected later. These will not have destroyed a great deal of front line.

17   Gentla, *Die 79. Reserve Division in der Schlacht auf der Vimy Höhe*, p. 13.

18   Her father was Governor-General of Canada at the time of formation, thus the connection.

19   Hodder-Williams, Ralph, *Princess Patricia's Light Infantry 1914-1919*, (London: Hodder & Stoughton Ltd., 1923), p. 218.

"casualties pretty strong"[20] although enemy resistance had been weak. The right battalion was the Royal Canadian Regiment, the only pre-war regular unit of the Canadian army, although by this stage of the war many of the men fighting will have been replacements arriving over the past year or so. Protected by being in the Grange tunnels they emerged to take up their positions, a task completed without incident by 3.40am. C and D Companies were in the observation trenches on the northern lip of Birkin Crater to Vernon Crater, their task being the Black Line. A and B Companies in a new trench 30 yards behind, tasked with moving through the initial companies to take the Red Line. The Black Line, for the assaulting companies comprised of Famine and Feather Trenches. As the troops moved out at 5.30am it was clear that the artillery preparation had again been systematic and effective:

> On all sides, evidence was seen of the crushing barrage and of the weeks of intensive shelling that had preceded it. At many points the enemy trench system had ceased to exist, and the German dead lay everywhere in the ruins of the positions they had held.[21]

The two lead companies had few problems taking what remained of the front trenches and established themselves in good time on the Black Line. Here they consolidated and awaited the support companies and the next phase of the attack. This second phase was also a total success but with considerably more casualties due to a strongpoint and snipers in La Folie Wood with the two attacking companies reduced to one or two officers and about 60 men each. Attempted counter attacks by elements of *R.I.R. 262* were broken up by rapid artillery fire and men began to dig in.

3rd Canadian Division, 8th Canadian Brigade

The units constituting 8th Brigade were Canadian Mounted Rifles (CMR), all of which had converted to infantry battalions in early 1916. They all had, as did their neighbouring brigade to the north, complex crater fields in front of them. Today it is in the area of forest still within the Park to the south of the visitor's area but not normally accessible. Within this wood are the remains of two wombat craters, actually trenches created by 702nd Tunnelling Company, 15 ft. deep and 35ft. wide, blown to create instant communication trenches across no man's land. The Black Line for all three battalions attacking in the brigade was the *Zwischen Stellung*.

4th CMR formed the left flank of the attack, choosing as its formation four waves of one company each with increasing distance to cover. Major Gale's A Company was first away to take the German front line system with B Company, under Lt. Hart, following behind to then attack and secure the *Zwischen Stellung*. Both of these companies, following the barrage closely, found their task straightforward with few casualties, the *Zwischen Stellung* being almost unrecognisable after the bombardment. German artillery was fairly heavy at this stage, flares from *Zwischen Stellung* calling down a barrage onto their own front line and Flapper Trench. In the next phase the remaining two companies were able to take Fickle Trench (C Company) and then reach the ridge (D Company) and consolidate that position as the final one for the day. D company had a problem as their O.C. Major MacKenzie was wounded at the outset but the company was ably led to their objective by Lieutenant Butson. One unfortunate incident was when Major Menzies, O.C. of C Company assisted Lieutenant Pierce in covering a gap that had formed on their left.

20   Library and Archives, Canada, war diaries – PPLI, RG9, Militia and Defence, Series III-D-3, Volume 4912, Reel T-10703, File: 347.
21   Fetherstonhaugh, R.C., *The Royal Canadian Regiment 1883–1933*, (Uckfield: Naval & Military Press reprint of 1936 edition), p. 279.

After the success of the attack these two officers were shaking hands when Pierce was shot through the head.[22]

The story was a similar one for 2nd CMR attacking in the brigade centre. With the same formation, B Company under Lt (acting Major) Cameron taking the front line without a problem and following through, C Company under Major Godfrey consolidating on the *Zwischen Stellung* by the end of the first phase. It was reported back at this stage that Fickle Trench was in such an obliterated state that the *Zwischen Stellung* would be better for creating a defensive line. Soon afterwards the follow up troops had cleared La Folie Farm, now a heap of rubble, and a front line trench was begun on the final objective. A large number of prisoners were taken, many from the western end of the Prinz Arnolf Graben.

One difference reported by 1st CMR on the right of the brigade was that, although both the front German systems and the *Zwischen Stellung* were taken with little opposition, German artillery fire was heavy and considerable casualties were caused. The trenches were almost non-existent, as was wire and most of the dugouts had been destroyed. One peculiarity on this stretch of front was the Schwaben Tunnel connecting Flapper Trench with the *Zwischen Stellung*. This was built to provide covered approaches to the front lines and had a number of dugouts leading to the communication trench *Prinz Arnolf Graben*. After D company had taken the front lines, one platoon of C company went through the tunnel to clear dugouts but found the whole complex deserted and most of the dugouts blown in. The rest moved through to take the Black Line, with the other two companies following up to await the next phase. These found virtually no opposition in the next phase, finding trenches almost obliterated and dugouts empty or full of water. Thus they were also able to dig a front line trench and be well in control by mid-morning. They make no reference, however, to being in touch with troops to their right or taking the northern parts of Bois de Bonval which, according to the plan, they should have done. The boundary between Canadian 3rd and 2nd Divisions on maps in the diaries[23] clearly shows the boundary running through the centre of the wood, SW to NE. The final objective for the left flank of 2nd Division was the Blue Line running east of the wood. This means that 1st CMR should have been tasked with taking the northern part of the wood and forming a line on the east end of it with Canadian 2nd Division. The situation maps in their diary clearly show them at 5.00pm not in the wood at all and in the Red Line facing South East. This mistake would leave the left flank of British 13th Brigade open as will be seen.

In front of Canadian 3rd Division were men of *R.I.R. 262* but also *R.I.R. 263* of *79th Reserve Division*. *R.I.R. 263*, commanded by *Oberstleutnant* von Behr, had suffered badly in the preliminary bombardment and it was not long before they were being pressed back through their lines. Every time an attempt to counter was made, for example by Vizefeldwebel Borcherding with all the reserves he could put together, it was too late to save the situation and many fell as a result.[24] The remnants of the regiment made their way back into Vimy and also to the railway line in order to create a new line there. What they were not to know at this point was that Canadian 3rd Division had no intention of advancing further and had reached their objectives for the day. German accounts mention a counter attack by *Oberleutnant* von Richthofen winning some ground back on the Canadian 3rd Division front, but there is no evidence of either this attack or loss of ground in Canadian accounts.

22   Bennett, Captain S.G. M.C., *The 4th Canadian Mounted Rifles*, (Toronto: Murray, 1926), pp. 53-54.
23   Library and Archives, Canada, war diaries H.Q. 3rd Canadian Division, RG9, Militia and Defence, Series III-D-3, Volume 4853, Reel T-1934, File: 139.
24   Berhmann & Brandt, *Die Osterschlacht bei Arras 1917*, p. 36.

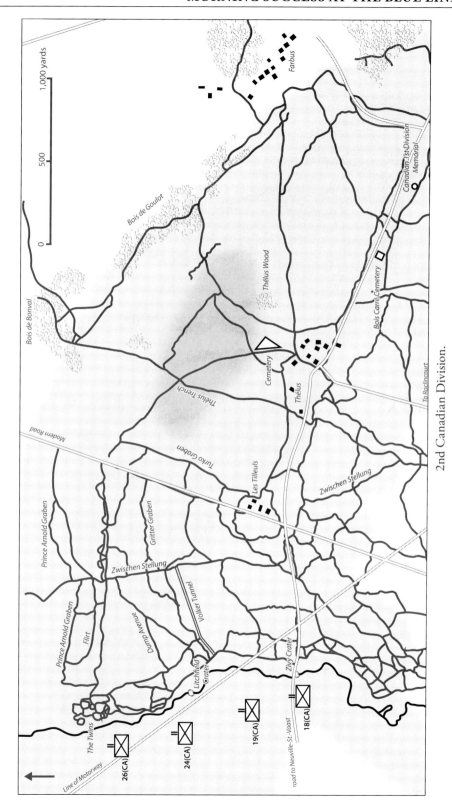

2nd Canadian Division.

2nd Canadian Division, 5th Canadian Brigade

This division had what was arguably the most challenging of the Canadian Corps tasks on the 9th April when you look at the distance that they were set to reach the Brown Line, for they now had that more advanced position as an objective. Not only that, but in front of the final objective on the right lay the village of Thélus with the attendant problems of clearing such a location. As outlined earlier in the section on planning, this initial assault was to be by two brigades to take the Black and Red Lines with a further two brigades to continue the attack. At the early stage therefore only the 5th Brigade on the left and 4th Brigade on the right is being considered. However, when we have reached the Red Line the attack is continued by the British 13th Brigade on the left and Canadian 6th Brigade on the right to reach the Blue Line.

Attacking the Black Line for 5th Brigade were 26th (New Brunswick) Canadian Battalion on the left, who were to take the *Zwischen Stellung* between its junctions with Flirt Trench in the north to the junction with the southern fork of *Gritter Graben* in the south. "A" and "C" Companies did this with only relatively slight casualties, with "D" in support and the battalion spent the remainder of the day digging in and forming the trench into a defensive line. On the right, 24th (Victoria Rifles) Canadian Regiment also had little difficulty taking the first German lines with its "B" and "D" Companies, but as these companies moved on with "C" company in support, they found resistance in the *Zwischen Stellung* on its front fairly strong and it was with casualties of around 225 including two officers killed that this was taken. A platoon from "A" Company with supporting sections from 22nd Canadian Battalion also cleared Volker Tunnel, another of the covered approaches to the German front lines. It was the case for both battalions that German artillery in this sector was "comparatively feeble."[25] Its area of attack can be seen today if you visit Lichfield Crater Cemetery and look up the slope above the lane you have driven on. The final objective for the brigade was the Red Line running along *Turko Graben*.[26] This was entrusted to 25th Battalion (Nova Scotia Rifles) which moved up behind the leading battalions to pass through; suffering casualties through artillery[27] as by this time the Germans were managing to bring down fire on the area. Attacking on time at 6.45am they were able to take the Red Line by around 8.00am after some "hard fighting",[28] mainly with unsubdued machine gun posts. They were able to take eight machine guns, six trench mortars and quite remarkably two 77mm field guns in this relatively forward area.

2nd Canadian Division, 13th Brigade (attached from British 5th Division)

Once Canadian 25th Battalion had secured the Red Line, it was the task of the British 13th Brigade, 'borrowed' from 5th Division, to pass through and take the Blue Line, which for this area was still the final objective. The two assaulting battalions, 2nd King's Own Scottish Borders (KOSB) on the left and 1st Royal West Kent Regiment on the right, left their assembly trenches at 7.20am and moved forward. The KOSB moved on a one company front in the order 'A', 'B' 'C' and 'D using artillery formation in sections but suffered "A considerable number of casualties"

---

25   Library and Archives, Canada, war diaries – 24th Canadian Infantry Battalion, RG9, Militia and Defence, Series III-D-3, Volume 4932, Reel T-10733, File: 414.

26   Lies about 100 metres east of the Main road towards Vimy after passing the main road junction near Thelus.

27   Clements, Captain Robert (ed), *Merry Hell, The Story of the 25th Battalion 1914-19*, (Toronto: University of Toronto Press, 2012), p. 168. The War Diary plays this down, but Clements (who was present) specifically mentions heavy casualties in this advance.

28   Library and Archives, Canada, war diaries – 25th Canadian Infantry Battalion, RG9, Militia and Defence, Series III-D-3, Volume 4933, Reel T-10735, File: 417.

during this period.[29] The Royal West Kents had a better experience, complaining only of the heavy going underfoot caused by the mud and previous bombardment, suffering few casualties. The first objective for both battalions was Thelus Trench which they rushed (the second company of the KOSB having moved up alongside by now) when the barrage moved off it at 8.35am. Casualties were light in carrying out this task except on the left where unsubdued German elements in the north of Bois de Bonval caused some loss to the KOSB. The diaries are critical of the Canadians to the north here and it does seem that orders for the latter were not as they should have been. The attack continued with elements of the KOSB pushing into the south of Bois de Bonval. Meanwhile the main force moved into the northern part of Bois de Goulot, capturing 200 prisoners, four machine guns and two 8 inch howitzers, causing other Germans to flee, many of whom were shot as they did so.[30] In the meantime the West Kents had been clearing the disconnected lengths of trench lines that occupied the space between Thelus Trench and the woods with little opposition. The 3rd Company of both battalions now moved up to complete the clearance of Bois de Goulot and secure the Blue Line.

2nd Canadian Division, 4th Canadian Brigade

4th Brigade's Headquarters was in Zivy Crater, a spot that is now a cemetery and can be visited near to the village of Neuville-St.-Vaast. It is one of two unusual burial places[31] as it is in essence a mass burial site for 53 men, five of whom were unidentified and the others commemorated on a wall on one side of the crater. The left battalion of this assaulting brigade was 19th (Central Ontario) Canadian Battalion. It and its neighbouring unit the 18th (Western Ontario) Canadian Battalion chose the formation of three companies (B, C and A) across its front, a platoon in each wave with "A" Company providing a platoon behind each of the other companies. As far as could be determined, 19th Battalion had little difficulty in reaching the Black Line and was in place at the appointed time along the *Zwischen Stellung* to the north of the Neuville to Les Tilleuls road. 18th Battalion also had little problem taking the first German lines but then met stiff resistance from the complex of trenches south of Les Tilleuls. Here the *Zwischen Stellung* bent back south of Les Tilleuls and in fact formed the Red Line for the battalion. In this intermediate set of trenches, a surviving machine gun post caused considerable casualties before being dealt with in most heroic fashion by Lance Sergeant Sifton of "C" company:

> For most conspicuous bravery and devotion to duty. During the attack in enemy trenches Sjt. Sifton's company was held up by machine gun fire which inflicted many casualties. Having located the gun he charged it single-handed, killing all the crew. A small enemy party advanced down the trench, but he succeeded keeping these off till our men had gained the position. In carrying out this gallant act he was killed, but his conspicuous valour undoubtedly saved many lives and contributed largely to the success of the operation.[32]

The 27 year old Ellis Wellwood Siften was born in Wallacetown, Ontario and having enlisted in October 1914 was soon found to be excellent soldier material, thus the rank. He is buried in Lichfield Crater Cemetery where his name can be found on the wall. Sadly, it seems he was shot by

---

29   TNA WO 95/1552 War Diary of 2nd King's Own Scottish Borderers, 9/4/17.
30   TNA WO 95/1552.
31   The other, not far away at Lichfield Crater, is almost astride the 9 April frontine on the edge of the Vimy Ridge Memorial Park. The site can be approached from Neuville-St.-Vaast, although not a good road.
32   *London Gazette*, 8 June 1917, p. 5704.

one of the wounded German soldiers he left in his wake holding off the German party advancing down the trench. Once this machine gun was out of action the battalion were able to man the Black Line, in this case *Zwolfer Graben*.

The next stage, the Red Line, meant the taking of the hamlet of Les Tilleuls and the trenches *Turko Graben* to the north of the road into Thélus and the *Zwischen Stellung* to the south. This was to be undertaken by 21st (Eastern Ontario) Canadian Battalion. Having waited in a variety of locations until the Black Line was reported taken, the four companies reorganised in line, each having a strength of three platoons with the remainder in transport lines. Then at 6.30am they moved through the Black Line to take the Red. Casualties were caused by a number of machine guns that had not been subdued, especially on the front of C Company. Half an hour after reaching the objective a large cave was discovered in Les Tilleuls from which six officers and 100 men of the *Bayerisches R.I.R. 3* were persuaded to come out after a few bombs were thrown down an entrance.[33] Casualties were 10 Officers and 250 OR at this point, demonstrating that although the wire was well cut and the artillery barrage effective a small number of surviving machine guns can cause a great deal of damage. As well as the usual machine guns and trench mortars the battalion also captured a field gun in the hamlet. The 21st spent the remainder of the day consolidating the position although in moving Battalion Headquarters forward from Zivy Cave they did lose their C.O., Lieut. Colonel Jones DSO who was wounded and taken back. Command fell to Major H. Pense who moved forward to Olmer House, which must have been a surviving (at least in part) building in Les Tilleuls.[34]

2nd Canadian Division, 6th Canadian Brigade

The difficult task of taking Thelus village, the Blue Line beyond and finally the Brown Line in front of Farbus was left to the 6th Canadian Brigade. For this task it was decided that three battalions should move through 4th Canadian Brigade and assault the Blue Line; from left to right 29th, 28th and 31st Battalions. The Brigade Headquarters had been established in Zivy Cave during the afternoon of the 8th. All three battalions advanced at 8.05am, eventually reaching the Red Line around 9.00am where they all deployed about 100 yards in advance of that line to await the lifting of the barrage. This occurred at 9.35am and all went forward into the attack. On the left, A and B Company of the 29th (Vancouver) Battalion "captured THELUS LINE without opposition"[35] As they moved on, according to the War Diary, retreating Germans were shot at from the hip by both riflemen and Lewis gunners. Continuing forward they occupied the sunken road north of Thélus and, "Most casualties up to this time were caused by 'shorts' from our own barrage."[36] Trenches just behind the Blue Line were occupied with outposts on the actual line to await the next phase as this battalion was also due to make the final advance to the Brown Line. Casualties are notably light by this stage being one officer killed, four wounded and a total of 48 other ranks wounded.

---

33 This was the right flank regiment of the *1st Bavarian Reserve Division*, holding the line down to near Roclincourt. This large cave was called *Felsenkeller* by the Germans and the main account of fighting here is in the *R.I.R. 263* history; Heinicke, Lt. d.Res. a.D., Karl &Bethge, Lt. d.Res. a.D., Bruno, *Das Reserve-Infantrie-Regiment Nr. 263 in Ost und West,* (Oldenburg: Stalling, 1926), p. 117. It could be that there were some Bavarians also in the cave as it lay on the boundary between them and the 263rd, thus the mistake by the Canadians over whom they had captured.

34 Library and Archives, Canada, war diaries – 21st Canadian Infantry Battalion, RG9, Militia and Defence, Series III-D-3, Volume 4930, Reel T-10731, File: 410.

35 Library and Archives, Canada, war diaries – 29th Canadian Infantry, RG9, Militia and Defence, Series III-D-3, Volume 4936, Reel T-10740-10741, File: 427.

36 Volume 4936, Reel T-10740-10741, File: 427.

The story was similar for the 28th (Northwest) Battalion in the centre whose task included taking some of the northern elements of the village of Thélus. This they managed again with relatively few casualties although a little more than the 29th Battalion with one officer wounded, 11 O.R. killed and 33 wounded. Finally, on the right for 31st (Alberta) Battalion the main problem again seems to have been artillery "shorts" which caused the men to have to retire to the Red Line, only moving forward again when the barrage lifted at 9.35am. A, B and C Companies succeeded in clearing Thélus with D Company passing through to take the Blue Line beyond. They were joined on the left by B Company to make sure of the final line for the battalion. The German after-action report, written by a Major von Poschinger,[37] acting for the missing C.O. of *Bayerische R.I.R. 3*, holding this sector, clearly shows that the forward German companies were simply overwhelmed; contact having being lost with all those units.

1st Canadian Division, 3rd Canadian Brigade

Although the division's task on 9 April encompassed the longest distance it was on a narrowing front and therefore the two brigade frontage could be used in the same way as with 2nd Division with one brigade going through. It fell to 3rd Brigade to form the left of the attack, their target for the Black Line being *Zwolfer Stellung* the other side of the Lille – Arras road south of Les Tilleuls. The 16th (Canadian Scottish) Battalion were on the left, led throughout the advance by Pipe Major James Groat playing "We will take the Good Old Way" along with five other pipers. Groat would, by the end of the war, have won the DCM, MM and bar. On a two company front, Number 3 Company under Captain Scroggie on the left and Number 4 Company under Captain Tupper the right. The other companies were in support. Their frontage corresponds today with the area to the south of the new road complex near Zivy Crater Cemetery; attacking across the motorway towards the south of Thelus. The ground in front of them was heavily crated from months of underground warfare but both companies were successful in taking the Black Line on time, digging in to prepare for the next phase. Casualties had been, however, fairly heavy due to a number of machine guns on their front. For capturing first one in the German front lines and then another shortly afterwards Private William J. Milne was awarded the Victoria Cross:

> For most conspicuous bravery and devotion to duty in attack. On approaching the first objective, Pte. Milne observed an enemy machine gun firing on our advancing troops. Crawling on hands and knees, he succeeded in reaching the gun, killing the crew with bombs, and capturing the gun. On the line re-forming, he again located a machine gun in the support line, and stalking the second gun as he had done the first, he succeeded in putting the crew out of action and capturing the gun. His wonderful bravery and resource on these two occasions undoubtedly saved the lives of many of his comrades. Pte. Milne was killed shortly after capturing the second gun.[38]

Scottish-born William (he emigrated from Scotland to Canada in 1910) was, according to one source, buried nearby; however, either the grave was subsequently lost or he was in fact never found and is therefore commemorated on the Vimy Ridge Memorial to the Missing. In the centre was the 14th (Royal Montreal) Battalion, again on a two company front with No. 4 Company left and No. 3 Company right. It was this latter company who suffered badly from strong opposition, including four machine guns. Lt. Davidson managed to clear one gun whilst on the left Company Sgt-Maj.

---

37   Quoted in Sheldon, *The German Army on Vimy Ridge,* p. 284.
38   *London Gazette*, no.30122, 8 June 1917.

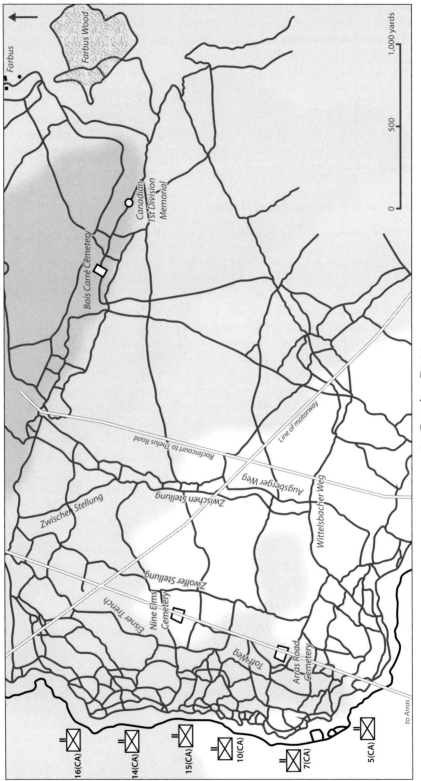

1st Canadian Division.

Hurley bayoneted the 3-man crew of another.[39] The last line before the road, Eisener Trench gave stubborn resistance but once overcome the Black Line on *Zwolfer Stellung* fell more easily. Right of the line was 15th (48th Highlanders of Canada) Battalion. They met with slightly less opposition in this early phase with an early message back to Brigade H.Q. of "Beautiful Get Away."[40] They were at the Black Line shortly after the time allocated and set about consolidating whilst awaiting the next phase. The German artillery response had been light all along the brigade front with stubborn machine gun crews being the main problem met by the advancing troops. From the rather sparse reports that all three units give in their diaries it seems that the next stage of the advance, from the Black Line across to the Red Line in *Zwischen Stellung* was far less problematical to that of the first phase of the attack. Resistance seems to have lessened and all three units were in position in good time and making the Red Line secure for the further advance of 1st Brigade.

1st Canadian Division, 2nd Canadian Brigade

The instruction to battalions was to attack on a two company frontage, each company having a two platoon frontage. The first two companies were to take the Black Line and the remaining two to move through to take the Red Line. The attack would then be handed over to 1st Canadian Brigade. The 10th Canadian Infantry Battalion (Canadians) formed the left wing of the attack by 2nd Brigade. Getting off promptly with the barrage, the leading companies reported German artillery response to be weak but machine gun and rifle fire to be very strong, this in spite of being impressed with their own artillery. This heavy defensive fire caused many casualties so that, by the time the battalion had reached *Toff Weg*, that is, not yet at the Black Line, casualties were already three officers killed and 10 wounded plus 85 O.R. killed and 238 wounded. The Black Line in *Zwolfer Stellung* was taken with the assistance of the third and fourth waves (C and B Companies) but by this stage, with the Red Line still to take, these two companies had only one unwounded officer between them. Major Critchley was therefore sent forward to take control of these two companies to take them to the Red Line. Attacking whilst firing from the hip, both companies managed to reach the Red Line which, as was the case farther north, were on the *Zwischen Stellung*. The 7th Canadian Battalion (1st British Columbia) had an inauspicious start with one enemy machine gun opening fire from a support trench prior to the barrage lift, and killing No 4 Company's commander Capt. C.L. Harris.[41] With a similar experience to the battalion on their left, the first trenches were taken easily but always under fire from the rear German support trenches. A glance at the map will show four lines of German trenches to be overcome before the Black Line in *Zwolfer Stellung* can be attacked. It was moving through this area where casualties were taken, including from one of their own guns that dropped short all the way to the Red Line.[42] The two companies tasked to capture the Red Line in *Zwischen Stellung* found it difficult going, resorting to bombing through communication trenches to avoid the heavy fire. Casualties were such that No 1 Company, that had taken the Black Line were ordered up to support, a company from the reserve battalion (8th Canadian Battalion (90th Winnipeg Rifles)) moving up to replace

---

39   Library and Archives, Canada, war diaries – 14th Canadian Infantry Battalion, RG9, Militia and Defence, Series III-D-3, Volume 4951, Reel T-10767, File: 478.

40   Library and Archives, Canada, war diaries – 3rd Canadian Brigade, RG9, Militia and Defence, Series III-D-3, Volume 4877, Reel T-10674, File: 223.

41   Claude Llewellyn Harris, as were many Canadians fighting this day, was originally British, born in Wakefield. He is buried in Arras Rd. Cemetery, not far from where he fell.

42   Library and Archives, Canada, war diaries 7th Canadian Battalion, RG9, Militia and Defence, Series III-D-3, Volume 4917, Reel T-10709, File: 366.

it.[43] Casualties are only reported from Zero until the next morning but the majority of the seven officers and 336 OR must have been in this early phase. Again a heavy price was paid to take the Red Line. 5th Canadian Infantry Battalion (Western Cavalry) who also went under the affectionate name of 'Tuxford's Dandys' after their first commanding officer,[44] formed the right flank of the whole Canadian Corps initial attack. They had a similarly torrid time in the early stages after easily storming the German front line trench. A number of German machine guns caused substantial casualties and one particularly difficult nest was in *Wittelsbacher Weg* and an attempt to bomb down this trench was made. Eventually the position was taken after A and B companies stormed *Wittelsbacher Weg* drawing all the fire enabling the other two companies to move forward towards. The same German trench was then used in order to attack towards the Red Line in Augsberger Trench as attacking across the open ground would have caused even greater casualties. This was successful and the Red Line was taken. Casualties, as with the other units in the 2nd Brigade had been heavy, estimated in the diary at 14 officers and 350 O.R. with five officers killed. The cause to this fairly severe loss to the Canadians was the fight put up by *Bayerische R.I.R. 1* which seems to have been able to make a withdrawal to the *Zwischen Stellung* without severe loss and there put up further resistance, as described above. Only the loss of this line further north where *Bayerische R.I.R. 3* had been unable to hold on caused a further withdrawal. There were attempts by *Bayerische R.I.R. 1* to take back ground but this was disrupted by the standing artillery barrage of the Canadians.[45]

1st Canadian Division, 1st Canadian Brigade

The brigade objective was the Brown Line south of Farbus and in Farbus Wood itself. On the left, 4th Canadian Infantry Battalion (Central Ontario) began its move in artillery formation to the Red Line in good time, arriving there between 8.00am and 9.00am, only losing four casualties on its way up. A and C Companies formed up as the initial attacking wave with B and D behind. The barrage lifted for the advance at slightly different times, 9.55am on the left and 10.05am on the right and the attacking companies were piped over the Red Line by pipers of the 16th Battalion who held the line. The Blue Line was reached and consolidated with moderate casualties, contrasting quite starkly with the experiences of the two brigades taking the Red Line.[46] In the centre, 3rd Canadian Infantry Battalion (Toronto Regiment) began to move forward towards the Red Line at 7.30am. Casualties were not heavy moving up to the Red Line, although A Company did lose its OC, Maj. W.E. Curry[47] to shellfire. At 10.05am the men moved forward and by 11.00am the Blue Line had been taken although there was some delay due to the required wheeling of the barrage slightly to the left. Again casualties were light although it was reported that the Blue Line was being heavily shelled for a while.[48] On the extreme right of the Canadian advance was 1st Canadian Infantry Battalion (Western Ontario). B and C companies, leading off the advance had some difficulty reaching the Red Line in *Zwischen Stellung*, being held up for a while because of

43   Library and Archives, Canada, war diaries 7th Canadian Battalion.
44   Now Brig. Gen. G.S. Tuxford was now commanding 3rd Brigade a little to the north. A Welshman who emigrated to Canada in the 1890s.
45   Schacky, Siegmund Frh. Von, *Das K.B. Reserve-Infanterie-Regiment Nr. 1,* (München: Bayerische Kriegsarchiv, 1924), p. 52.
46   Library and Archives, Canada, war diaries 4th Canadian Battalion, RG9, Militia and Defence, Series III-D-3, Volume 4915, Reel T-10707, File: 360.
47   Toronto born and a pre-war regular, Maj. Walter Curry is buried in Ecoivres Military Cemetery.
48   Library and Archives, Canada, war diaries 3rd Canadian Battalion, RG9, Militia and Defence, Series III-D-3, Volume 4914, Reel T-10706-10707, File: 357.

the difficulties that the leading battalions in the attack were having. They did manage to form up in good time though for the advance to the Blue Line, which, in a similar manner to their neighbouring battalions they reached with light casualties. This location they then begin to consolidate as they were not to be part of the final advance to the Brown Line later in the day.

51st (Highland) Division, 154th Brigade

The 51st Division was part of the Territorial Force, disembarking in France as a whole in early May 1915. By April 1917 it had gained a reputation as a hard fighting formation. Its constituent units were all the traditional highland regiments with long histories such as: the Seaforth Highlanders from Fort George, near Inverness; the Gordon Highlanders from Aberdeen and the Argyll and Sutherland Highlanders with Stirling Castle as its base.

The attack alongside the Canadians was complicated somewhat by the German salient between the two Corps. This had its apex on the Lens-Arras Road and meant that for a short length the attack had to be northwards as opposed to the general eastward direction. In order to encompass this, five platoons of the 4th Seaforth Highlanders[49] were given the task of clearing the front of the salient and creating a left flank to allow the Canadians to advance across them and meet up with the rest of the Highlanders in the Black Line. This task was allotted to No 3 Company and one platoon of No 1 Company. They succeeded in this but only after a hard fight as some of the Germans in the area had escaped the barrage and were encountered in the communication trenches. Only after the Canadians had gone across their rear did all German resistance cease. It cost the Seaforths two officers and 11 men killed. The remainder of the battalion had the task of advancing to the Black Line which they did in three waves, three platoons of No 1 Company in the first, four platoons of No. 2 and No. 4 companies in the second and the same in the third wave. For the Seaforths this line constituted Law and Leg Trenches plus a small section of *Wittelsbacher Weg* to connect up with the Canadians at its junction with *Bereitschaft Stellung*. The front line was taken by the initial wave without casualties but then the second wave came under machine gun fire and all the officers in No. 4 Company became casualties, stalling the advance. Movement was restarted by Capt. Will who led his company forward to join the second wave. This combined force was then able to take the Black Line. Moving up behind the Seaforths were the 4th Gordon Highlanders,[50] who had tasked B and D Companies to take the Blue Line. The timings for taking this line were complicated by the fact that the Canadian Blue Line finished on the border between the Canadians and the Scottish in different places. This meant that the Gordons had an additional area to take to keep pace with those on their left. First of all, D Company suffered from the German barrage and then both companies were held up by machine gun and rifle fire; B Company managing to get to the extended Blue Line first and make contact with the Canadians. The difficulties were such that at 9.35am it was decided to send up A and C Companies to support the leading two and then to prepare to make their final advance to the Brown Line later. This they did, setting off at 10.00am and soon the Blue Line was fully taken and consolidated.

On the right of the Brigade the initial attack was to be by the 9th Royal Scots[51] with the Black Line as their objective, which in their case was *Poser Weg*. The objective was taken with little mention of difficulties in the unit diary but casualties of two officers and 69 OR killed plus nine officers (1 later dying of his wounds) and 138 OR wounded with 27 missing, demonstrates that the task was not so straightforward. Apart from providing carrying parties for the advanced units

---

49   TNA: WO 95/2888 War Diaries of the 4th Seaforth Highland Regiment.
50   TNA: WO 95/2886 War Diaries of the 4th Gordon Highland Regiment.
51   TNA: WO95/2887 War Diaries of the 1/9th Royal Scots Regiment.

during the day the battalion remained consolidating the Black Line. Moving through to take the remaining objectives for the day were the 7th Argyll & Sutherland Highlanders. In actual fact the diary of the 7th Argyll & Sutherland Highlanders mentions that the Royal Scots did not succeed in taking the Black Line by the time, 7.10am, that their own troops advanced and they had to give aid to finally completing the task.[52] The result was that the leading two companies, A & B, lost the barrage and only with considerable difficulty from machine gun fire did they manage to take the Blue Line. C & D Companies, following up for the next phase, had to assist in the final clearing of the Blue Line which for this unit was Bolt and Bond Trenches down to the Roclincourt road. Clearly the first phase for 154 Brigade had not gone as smoothly as they would have liked, but they were in position in time to await the lifting of the standing barrage for the next phase; though the two companies of both leading battalions had both had to fight in the taking of the Blue Line.

Responsible for the difficult time being experienced by the highlanders was *Bayerische R.I.R. 2*. In particular, the forward companies 7 and 8 seem to have given a good account of themselves in the fight to the Black Line, with a number of machine guns reported to have fought to the end. The 8th company alone lost 41 killed in this first hour of fighting. The German Official History describes the five machine guns and their battle to hold the Scots back in this first phase.[53] Clearly the loss of the barrage was costing the 154th Brigade dear as it had to battle these German opponents who had been able to come out of their deep dugouts and man their heavy weapons before the Scotsmen could get to them.

51st (Highland) Division, 152nd Brigade

On the left of the brigade 1/6th Seaforth Highlanders adopted a three company front (B left, A centre and B right) with two platoons from each tasked with the first two German trench lines and then two platoons, one each from B and D companies, were to finish in the Black Line; here that line was Natil Trench. At 5.30am, as the barrage commenced, the men left the assembly trenches to advance with it. An interesting comment in the War Diary here is that some of the men felt the barrage to be weaker than that at Beaumont Hamel and were disappointed in it.[54] Another interesting comment and evidence of how units had learned from bitter experience concerned what happened next. When the barrage left the German front line the Seaforths rushed up to it but remained on the parapet firing into the trench. They had previously experienced the dangers of jumping straight into a trench and being fired upon from dugouts. "This was found to be a most effective means of gaining the mastery [sic] over the enemy in occupation of the trench."[55] Although this first wave suffered few casualties when the advance continued to the second and third lines, machine gun and rifle fire caused more men to fall. In fact, the Black Line took some considerable time to clear completely and only one officer of the two companies there remained unwounded, 2nd Lt C.L. Read. Casualties were heavy, being four officers and 142 OR killed plus five officers and 176 OR wounded; two men were missing. The 1/5th Seaforth Highlanders followed closely on the heels of their sister regiment with the triple task of first taking what was called the New Black Line which was the extra trench line of Nut and Strelitzer Weg which it was felt had to be added; then the Blue Line and then finally the Brown Line. Two platoons (nos. 5 & 13) were given the task of taking the New Black Line but first they lost the officer in charge whilst

52   TNA: WO95/2886 War Diaries of the 1/7th Argyll & Sutherland Highlanders.
53   Berhmann & Brandt, *Die Osterschlacht bei Arras 1917*, pp. 73-74. Machine Guns; Bethman, Daniel, Lützov, Hindenburg and Blücher. The naming of their guns and crews clearly showing the importance attached to them.
54   TNA WO 95/2867 War Diaries of the 1/6th Seaforth Highland Battalion.
55   TNA WO 95/2867.

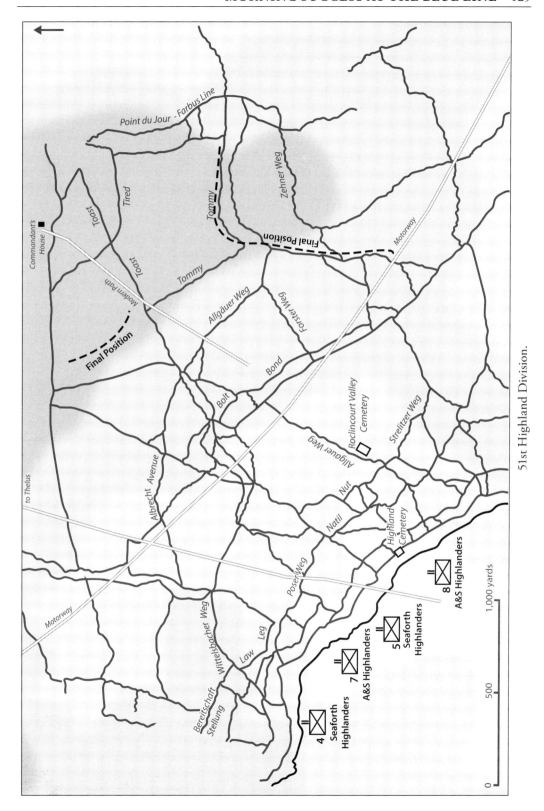

51st Highland Division.

in No Man's Land, then to be held up at the Black Line (where of course the 6th Seaforths were already having problems) and finally taking heavy casualties capturing machine guns in the New Black Line. A and C Companies were tasked with taking the Blue Line but soon became embroiled with the fighting for the Black, A Company losing 90 casualties so that it was mainly C Company that eventually was able to move on the Blue Line. All of the delay meant that the Blue Line was only taken at 2.15pm., well after the barrage was to move forward and the attack on the Brown Line to commence. Certainly on its left 152nd Brigade was in trouble.

The right battalion for the first phase of initial attack was 6th Gordon Highlanders. Attacking with D Company on the right (with two platoons of A Company) and B Company on the left they took the three lines of German trenches but only after a still fight with substantial casualties although their report to Brigade does not reflect the losses using the phrase "trenches quickly and effectively cleared".[56] Actual losses including those dying of wounds amounted to five officers and 75 OR killed plus three officers and 175 wounded with six missing. Following behind were the 8th Argyll & Sutherland Highlanders with, as on their left, two platoons tasked with the New Black Line. This unit experienced similar difficulties to those on the left except that the New Black Line was taken as planned according to the report back to Brigade. Things then began to go badly wrong as the troops designated to take the Blue Line set off from the New Black Line. The officer commanding this wave had been wounded and when it was held up by machine gun fire about half way to the Blue Line the officer remaining in command decided to withdraw to the New Black Line. He is heavily criticised in the after-battle report to Brigade,[57] nothing being mentioned in the unit diary which is very meagre in its description of events.[58] The barrage was lost and the story became a similar one of the Blue Line eventually being taken but only with the support of the companies allocated to eventually take the Brown Line beyond. No time is given for when the Blue Line was eventually taken but it is likely, as was the case to their left, to have been into the afternoon.

The 152nd Brigade was to be supported by four tanks of 7 Company of C Battalion, Heavy Machine Gun Corps. All four managed to get to the start line but the poor condition of the ground meant that all bellied on or around the Black Line and none were able to give any assistance at all. The same German defenders who had caused so much delay and problems for the 154th Brigade were active here. *Bayerische R.I.R. 2*, as reported above, gave an excellent account of themselves and was responsible for the delays inflicted on both brigades. Although eventually pushed back during the morning, *R.I.R. 2* had managed to draw in more and more of the two brigades follow up troops into the fray, thus weakening them for the final afternoon push to the Brown Line.

Thus on both flanks of the 152nd Brigade the advance had been stalled for periods of time and the supporting troops sucked into the battle for the Black and Blue Lines. If the chronology is followed strictly then at the end of this chapter the brigade is not as yet in the Blue Line, with serious consequences when the narrative is moved forward to the afternoon advance on the Brown Line. One notable incident, which contributed to the delays on this front, was the explosion of a *Minenwerfer* store within the area of the 8th Argylls causing some casualties, confusion and creating a large crater. Sgt. Ross of the 1/5th Seaforths witnessed the explosion and the consequent emergence and surrender of six Germans who he determined caused the blast and were subsequently killed by his men.[59]

56   TNA: WO 95/2862 War Diaries of 152nd Infantry Brigade, report by 1/6th Gordon Highlanders on operations 9 April 1917.

57   TNA: WO95/2862 War Diaries of 152nd Infantry Brigade, report by 1/8th Gordon Highlanders.

58   TNA: WO95/2865 War Diaries of 1/8th Argyll & Sutherland Highlanders.

59   TNA: WO 95/2862 War Diaries of 152nd Infantry Brigade, report by 1/5th Seaforth Highlanders on operations 9 April 1917; The relevant German histories, unfortunately, shed no further light on this incident, only

34th Division, 103rd Brigade (Tyneside Irish)

The 34th Division was originally formed as 41st Division, part of 5th New Army, an element of the Kitchener recruiting campaign in 1914 discussed earlier.[60] Renumbered 34 in 1915 after the reorganisation of the New Army formations, it was formed of many 'Pals Battalions' from the North East of England with one brigade each of Tyneside Scottish and Tyneside Irish with the third made up of service battalions from Edinburgh, Grimsby and Cambridgeshire. Arriving on the Western Front in early 1916, its introduction to the war was in front of La Boisselle on the first day of the Battle of the Somme, suffering some of the worst casualties of the whole of 1 July. Reconstituted by April 1917, having spent most of the winter in a relatively quiet area near to Armentières, complete with entertainment from 'The Chequers', the divisional theatrical group. This included two French female entertainers, much to the consternation of higher command. In February the division was moved to 3rd Army and made the move south to the Arras area, as the unit history puts it, "The holiday was over."[61] Attacking on a three brigade front, each with all four battalions involved in the phases of the attack to the Brown Line there was no reserve left to Maj.-Gen Nicholson, commanding.

On the left, with 51st (Highland) Division on their flank was 103rd (Tyneside Irish) Brigade. The job of getting to the Blue Line on the left of the brigade fell to 25th Northumberland Fusilier Battalion (2nd Tyneside Irish). A and B Companies took the first trenches being led forward by 2nd Lt. J.K. Murphy and Lt J.F. Huntley respectively. C and D Companies continue the attack on the Black Line; however, at that point neither company had an officer still on his feet, all being either killed or wounded. Confusion then reigned as the 8th Argyll & Sutherland Highlanders on their left veered across the front of A and B Company as they began the assault on the Blue Line as the barrage lifted. The *Mittel Weg* became a mix of both battalions with a machine gun on the left causing most of the problems. Finally, they were sorted out and an advance to the Blue Line possible, mostly on the right where a small depression hid A Company, supported by C Company, as they made their way forward, from the machine gun fire coming from *Zehner Weg* and Pump Trench. When in the Blue Line, these 80 men led by 2nd Lt. J.G. Kirkup and 2nd Lt. J. Snee worked their way left to take as much of the line as possible allocated to the battalion. On the left a mixed group of Tyneside Irish and Highlanders attempted to silence the machine guns in *Zehner Weg*. This was made possible by the actions of CSM R.E. Forster of the 25th who was awarded a bar to his DCM for his leadership at this point.[62] Another machine gun holding up the advance was well hidden and Lt. Huntley with Lance Corporal Thomas Bryan went out to locate it. Huntley was killed trying to find the gun but Bryan went on and silenced both the weapon and its team, being awarded the Victoria Cross:

> For most conspicuous bravery during an attack. Although wounded, this Non-commissioned Officer went forward alone, with a view to silencing a machine gun which was inflicting much damage. He worked up most skilfully along a communication trench, approached the gun from behind, disabled it and killed two of the team as they were abandoning the gun.
>
> As this machine gun had been a serious obstacle in the advance to the second objective, the

---

that in other German narratives, on other parts of the front, the order is often given to blow up dugouts when having to retire.

60   See Chapter 4.

61   Shakespear, Lt. Col. J., *The Thirty Fourth Division*, (Uckfield: Naval & Military Press Reprint, 2010), p. 90.

62   TNA: WO 95/2467 War Diaries of 103rd (Tyneside Irish) Brigade.

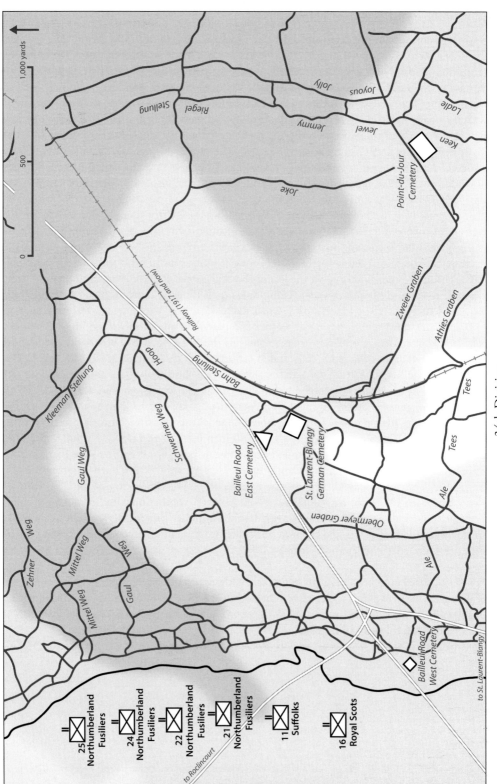

34th Division.

results obtained by Lance Corporal Bryan's gallant action were far-reaching.[63]

When the unit designated for the next phase, that of taking the Brown Line, 27th Northumberland Fusiliers (4th Tyneside Irish) had joined in the fight, the Blue Line could finally be consolidated. All of this had taken time and as already described earlier it is now beyond the point at which the barrage moved on.[64] As well as L/C Bryan, the Tyneside Irish were to be awarded a further Victoria Cross when Private Ernest Sykes of the 27th Battalion, during the fight to get into the Blue Line, bravely helped the wounded lying out under fire.

> For most conspicuous bravery and devotion to duty when his battalion in attack was held up about 350 yards in advance of our lines by intense fire from front and flank, and suffered heavy casualties. Private Sykes, despite this heavy fire, went forward and brought back four wounded – he made a fifth journey and remained out under conditions which appeared to be certain death, until he had bandaged all those who were too badly wounded to be moved. These gallant actions, performed under incessant machine-gun and rifle fire, showed an utter contempt of danger.[65]

On the right of the 25th was a sister battalion, the 24th Northumberland Fusiliers (1st Tyneside Irish). There is nothing in the unit diary to help put together events with any clarity but it is clear from other sources that although the Black Line was taken with few problems, moving towards the Blue Line was extremely difficult with casualties being heavy from the same machine guns that caused the 25th advance to stall. Here again, only support from the battalion coming from behind, the 26th (3rd Tyneside Irish) enabled the Blue Line to be fully taken and that occurred only in the afternoon, well behind schedule.[66]

Yet again it was the machine guns of *Bayerische R.I.R. 2* which caused the Tyneside Irish so much grief. This unit had, almost single-handedly, managed to disrupt the advance to the Blue Line of both the right flank of 51st Division and the left flank of 34th Division, a perfect example of the power of a resilient defence by a few machine guns and the men around them, unsubdued by the barrage.

34th Division, 102nd Brigade (Tyneside Scottish)

Taking the left flank of the attack was 22nd Northumberland Fusiliers (3rd Tyneside Scottish) with A and B Companies in front with C and D Companies forming the support for going through to the Blue Line. Both lines were taken promptly, the Blue Line by 8.30am and troops reported that the barrage was very effective with little opposition from the Germans. For this battalion the Black Line was Rod Trench, the Blue Line a section of *Kleeman Stellung*. Individual acts of bravery were recorded even if the unit War Diary is brief in the extreme. As resistance stiffened towards the Blue Line CSM John Duffy and Sergeant Joseph Glendinning were responsible for the taking a large number of German prisoners and later both awarded the DCM. Although on their right the 21st Northumberland Fusiliers (2nd Tyneside Scottish) reached the Black Line with similar ease their

---

63 *Supplement to the London Gazette*, 8 June 1917, p. 5704. Bryan was 35 at the time of his action, survived the war and died in South Yorkshire in 1945.

64 TNA: WO 95/2467 War Diaries of 25th Battalion Northumberland Fusiliers.

65 *Supplement to the London Gazette*, 8 June 1917, p. 5704. Sykes too survived the war although wounds suffered in Gallipoli almost removed him from active service before this action and he was discharged in May 1918. He died in Huddersfield in 1949.

66 TNA: WO 95/2467 War Diaries of 103rd (Tyneside Irish) Brigade.

next phase towards the Blue Line took longer, it only being finally taken at 11.00am with some considerable loss to officers.[67] However, the brigade could report that, with some time to spare, the assault on the Brown Line could commence as required when the barrage lifted at 12.34pm.

34th Division, 101st Brigade

The 11th Suffolk Regiment on the left had *Mittelberger Graben* as its initial Black Line objective and this it took with C and A Companies, the former reporting slight casualties, the latter actually saying they had none so far. There was a little confusion in the Black Line but the companies pushed on and were able to cross the valley despite some uncut wire and get into the railway cutting and beyond where they were to set up the Blue Line. The area they advanced through is now that upon which can today be found Bailleul Road East Cemetery. Some indication of the condition that the German soldiers were in can be seen in the report that Battalion H.Q. with its runners and pigeon man was able to hold 20 prisoners without any problems, despite the close proximity of many German grenades and rifles. At 9.30am Battalion H.Q. was able to move up to the Blue Line. By now B and D Companies had been able to push out beyond the railway cutting and were digging in 50 yards in front. 16th Royal Scots Regiment (2nd Edinburgh)[68] with two platoons each of A and B Companies in front, the remaining platoons following behind, had a similar experience to the Suffolks, the Black Line, now *Obermayer Graben* being taken with ease. The first three German lines were taken by 5.40, C and D Companies having provided the moppers up. Reports made by the attacking troops told of trenches having being demolished and "wire shattered by our artillery."[69] At 7.36am the attack continued with the companies somewhat disorganised but able to move forward, finding the valley less covered in wire than they expected. They were now moving up to the Bois de la Maison Blanche, which today houses the St. Laurent-Blangy German Cemetery, with the railway cutting behind which was the Blue Line. According to their diary they were able to take and consolidate the railway cutting without a great deal of trouble, capturing a large number of Germans and freeing Captain A.C. Cowan who was lying wounded in a German dugout. 11th Royal Scots of 9th Division on their right complain of this flank being open for some time and that C Company of that unit had to assist in the removal of a German machine gun[70] therefore possibly the whole exercise had been a little more difficult than the 16th claim. The Scots then pushed outposts beyond the line as protection to await the next phase.[71]

As midday approached, 34th Division have had mixed fortunes. Whilst on the left there have been considerable problems and troops from 103rd Brigade were still trying to move into and consolidate the Blue Line, the brigades further south were established in that line and awaiting the reserve battalions to move up and take up the battle by advancing to the Brown Line. The greater success of the southern two brigades was against the *Bayerische I.R.4.*, the right hand unit of the *14th Bavarian Infanterie-Division*. An eye witness report by a Major Hoderlein, the unit commander and the only evidence available to the German Official History, makes it clear that the

67   Sheen, John & Stewart, Graham, *Tyneside Scottish*, (Barnsley: Pen & Sword, 1999), pp. 141-142; TNA: WO 95/2462 War Diaries of 21st Battalion Northumberland Fusiliers; TNA: WO95/2463 War Diaries of 22nd Battalion Northumberland Fusiliers.

68   Unofficially known as 'McCrae's Battalion' as Sir George McCrae was active in raising the Edinburgh-based which at its conception comprised of at least 30 professional footballers, 13 from Heart of Midlothian, of which McCrae was a director.

69   TNA: WO95/2458 War Diaries of 16th Royal Scots.

70   TNA: WO 95/1773 War Diaries of 11th Royal Scots.

71   TNA: WO 95/2458 War Diaries of 16th Royal Scots.

overwhelming British artillery with little support from their own, resulted in being pushed back relentlessly to the railway line. Hoderlein mentions tanks, but the 4 vehicles of 7 Company allocated to the 34th Division were in action further south in the 9th Division area. He also mentions his reserve battalion being in Douai, a remarkably long way back for what should have represented his counter attack unit and subsequently of no use during the morning.[72]

9th (Scottish) Division, 27th Brigade (Lowland)

Formed in 1914 as part of the K1 element of Kitchener's New Army, until mid-1916 this was a homogeneous Scottish Division. However, 28th Brigade was broken up in May of that year and replaced by the South African Brigade, which became an integral part of the 9th until 1918. With a reputation for hard fighting first at Loos, then the Ypres Salient and finally on the Somme, notably at Delville Wood which has been enshrined by the South Africans in the shape of their memorial situated there, this was fast becoming one of the best fighting units on the Western Front. Since moving to 3rd Army in November 1916 the division had a change of leader after General Furse left to take up the post of Master-General of the Ordnance. Replacing him was the former commander of the South African Brigade, Major-General H.T. Lukin. Soon afterwards the division took over the line from the Scarp northwards to Roclincourt where they settled into the normal trench life of intermittent 'hates', trench raids but also the opportunity to train those that had replaced losses on the Somme. Firstly though, the division had to deepen the trenches as they had previously been occupied by the 35th 'Bantam' Division and were, "too shallow for people of ordinary stature".[73]

The 27th Brigade, on the left of the 9th Division attack, had similar ground to cover as the units on their left, that is, the Bois de la Maison Blanche and the railway beyond. To do this they had two battalions up with the other two coming through to take the Blue Line which again was the railway. The 6th Kings Own Scottish Borderers waited for Zero Hour in and around Claude and Clarence Craters.[74] At the start of the barrage at 5.30am they moved out into No Man's Land but suffered severely from the barrage falling short. By 6.04am though, in spite of these losses, the Black Line in Obermeyer Trench had been taken. This trench had been so badly damaged that many men overshot it and pressed on into the sunken road beyond. This was noted by brigade in their after-battle report;

> Evidence points to the fact that the impetus of the assault caused our men to outpace the barrage and an examination of our dead up to the first objective gave convincing proof of this.[75]

Another problem caused by the cutting up of the ground making identification of trenches difficult, was that the moppers up missed some of the dugouts which had not been destroyed. This led to one German machine gun in *Liller Graben* being overlooked and causing casualties to the Seaforth pioneers[76] who silenced it after taking casualties. At 7.30am the 11th Royal Scots Regiment passed through the Borderers to advance on the Blue Line. It is clear from the diary that the men were at the Black Line for some time before they moved off which;

---

72 Berhmann & Brandt, *Die Osterschlacht bei Arras 1917*, pp. 98-99.
73 Ewing John, *The History of the Ninth (Scottish) Division 1914-1919*, (London: John Murray, 1921), p. 176.
74 These are the only remaining remnants of all the mining activity in this area of the front. They can be seen today as the two mounds covered in undergrowth near to Bailleul Road West Cemetery.
75 TNA: WO95/1769 War Diaries of 27th Brigade.
76 The 9th Seaforth Highland Regiment, divisional pioneers since 1915. Formed in Fort George, August 1914.

Severely tried the patience of the men who in some cases could not be prevented from running into it [the barrage] and also it did not appear to me to particularly assist because the moment it lifted a hostile m.g. raked my left flank which was rather in the air owing to the absence of the 34th Division at this point.[77]

The said machine gun was dealt with by rifle grenade and the Blue Line in the cutting was reached although again, the diary complains of having to work to the north to make contact with 34th Division.[78] Similar to those units on their left a line was pushed out beyond the railway but not without difficulty as German artillery began to shell the cutting after their aircraft had flown over spotting where they were. The units were thus in a narrow band between their own barrage in front and the German one behind. On the right of the brigade 12th Royal Scots Regiment had a tragic incident almost immediately after they jumped off at 5.30 from their assembly trenches. Only yards from their own front line, commanding officer Lt. Col. Thorne was hit by shellfire and died soon afterwards in a shell hole. The question must be raised as to why he was there in the first place.[79] Going on close, again at times too close, to the barrage, the Black Line in *Obermeyer Weg* was taken, Major Hay taking command of the battalion. The battalion then went into support of 9th Cameronians (Scottish Rifles) Battalion, following them in their advance on the Blue Line, mopping up as they went, during which time they also lost their Regimental Sergeant Major, Donald McKay, wounded. When the Blue Line was reached by 8.30am, casualties to that point were around 180 killed and wounded. A and B Companies of the 9th Cameronians had gone with the initial attacks as "moppers-up" for 12th Royal Scots and then the remaining two companies moved up to the Black Line. The advance to the Blue Line was made by A and B companies in waves with C company moving up Alz trench, D Company in reserve. The railway was duly taken with again advanced posts being put out beyond the cutting.[80]

9th (Scottish) Division, South African Brigade

The centre of the attack for 9th Division was given to the South African Brigade. Again the decision here was to use two battalions to the Black and Blue Lines with the others in support and then to swap roles to the Brown Line. During the night both lead battalions moved two platoons of the lead companies out into No Man's Land to take up assault positions in shell holes and other holes created by engineers the night before. The brigade advance was on each side of the new dual carriageway heading towards Gavrelle and the A1 motorway although it is still possible to follow the attack on each side. The 4th South African Regiment formed the left of the initial attack and it was reported that some men were again too quick in advancing and were caught in their own barrage. Nevertheless, the Black Line in Tree and Trap Trenches was reached by D and C Companies without too many casualties, the German barrage being weak and only a small amount of opposition. The other two companies, having being involved in mopping up, moved off when the barrage lifted to advance to the Blue Line. Increased machine gun and rifle fire made this element of the advance more difficult and yet more casualties were caused by moving into the barrage before it had moved on. Using good platoon tactics, however, Lewis guns laid down covering fire whilst the others moved in; the German gunners were found to be dead upon arrival of the attacking troops. 2nd Lt. Momson, commanding B Company, reported at 8.45am

---

77   TNA: WO95/1773 War Diaries of 11th Royal Scots.
78   TNA: WO95/1773 War Diaries of 11th Royal Scots.
79   Thorne is buried in St Nicholas British Cemetery in Arras.
80   TNA: WO95/1776 War Diaries of 9th Cameronians (Scottish Rifles).

that he was in the railway cutting which was still the Blue Line at this point. He also said that casualties had been heavy and he was at around 60 men strength but had sent back 100 prisoners and his men were all digging in about 60 yards east of the cutting. With 243 casualties altogether the battalion was now in position but weak as it was down to 350 officers and men.[81] A and D Companies of the 3rd South African Regiment lost considerably in the first advance to the Black Line, which was now Wish Trench, in spite of the good artillery barrage, two officers being killed and eight wounded in this first phase. As soon as the Black Line was secure next two companies, B and C moved into the sunken lane west of the German trench and awaited the lift of the barrage. At 7.15am they moved past the Black Line to the ground in front to then attack at 7.30am. Casualties were heavy as machine guns and rifles opened up and it required men of the other companies to make up numbers and support as they advanced. The Blue Line was taken in good time and work commenced on consolidation and Lewis gun parties pushed out beyond as far as they could towards the protective barrage; some 200 prisoners being sent back to the rear. A number of men of the neighbouring Black Watch unit, who had lost their officers, were found at this point mingled amongst the South Africans and as there seemed to be some problems on the right Captain Vivian ordered them to work down the cutting which they did with some success.[82]

Opposing both the northern elements of 9th Division during the morning was the *Bayerische I.R. 25* of *14th Bavarian Division*. Little was ever heard again of the men of the 1st Battalion of *B.I.R. 25* in the first three lines and very soon the support battalion, the 2nd, found itself fighting to try and retain the second line, the railway. The divisional history tells of a brave fight for this line, delaying the British somewhat, but what they recount is, in fact, the pause between the taking of the Black Line and the advance to the Blue. Then it relates a sudden massive artillery strike, the beginning of the next phase to the Blue Line, and British troops breaking into the railway line and men having to rush back towards the main second line in the rear.[83]

9th (Scottish) Division, 26th Brigade (Highland)

The account of the action by 26th Brigade has an opening paragraph that it is worth quoting here as it does give an excellent example of how successful the day was seen at this level:

> Owing to the fact that the whole attack from Zero to the moment that the 4th Division passed through the 9th Division was carried out exactly to the timetable previously arranged, there is very little comment to make on the whole operation.[84]

The brigade attacked on a two battalion front with 8th Black Watch Regiment (Royal Highlanders) on the left to advance north of the village of St. Laurent-Blangy whilst the 7th Seaforth Regiment had the complicated task of taking the majority of the village. B and C Companies of the Black Watch led off and were successful although there was a tendency to veer off to the left. The reports

81 TNA: WO95/1777 War Diaries of South African Brigade; TNA WO95/1785 War Diaries of 4th South African Regiment.

82 TNA: WO95/1777 War Diaries of South African Brigade; TNA: WO95/1784 War Diaries of 3rd South African Regiment.

83 Berhmann & Brandt, *Die Osterschlacht bei Arras 1917,* pp. 110-111. Interestingly the German Official History makes little use of the *Bayerische I.R. 25's* Official History; Braun, Maj. a.D., Heinrich, *Das K.B. 25 Infanterie-Regiment,* (München: Verlag Bayerisches Kriegsarchiv, 1926). It is not difficult to see why as most of the description in this book is laying blame on neighbouring units, not uncommon in unit histories, or writes of hours of resistance when this was not the case.

84 TNA: WO95/1762 War Diaries of 26th Brigade.

9th Division.

were that the four German lines were strongly held but that the barrage meant that resistance was weak. Around 150 prisoners were taken, including a battalion commander, with losses of around 60 for the two companies. Lt. Pelham Burn was killed by shellfire from the first companies; 2nd Lt. Mann was mortally wounded as A and D companies followed up in artillery formation, dying the next day.[85] These latter companies moved off punctually at 7.36am but were thrown into confusion with their own barrage falling short, causing casualties. Another problem they faced was machine gun fire coming from the other side of the River Scarpe, from as yet untaken positions over there. 2nd Lt. Ross and many men were killed or became casualties, causing these companies as well to veer northwards, away from the river. The Blue Line, still the railway cutting, was entered at the northern end and by bombing down the whole line was cleared, casualties being on the whole, however, heavy; A company only having 25 men remaining, D Company, 50 men. Only Captain Shepherd and Lt. Austin were left unwounded from the officers of these two companies. Men from the other two companies were therefore sent up to assist in consolidating the Blue Line whilst the 10th Argyll & Sutherland Highlanders, who had been following close behind, moved through to prepare for the next phase.[86] D company of the 7th Seaforth Highlanders attacked on the left of the battalion over the ground just north of the village. They reported a rapid advance to the Black Line, following the barrage closely and meeting little or no opposition. One problem they did have was with the strong emplacement known as Parrot's Beak which they had been trying in vain to destroy for some weeks before the assault because of the command it had over No Man's Land to north and south.[87] 2nd Lt. Adamson, commanding the left platoon was killed here before the emplacement could be cleared. The company took somewhere between 200 and 250 prisoners commenting amusingly in its diary that, "A receipt for one batch of 14 officers and 90 O.R. was obtained."[88] C Company on the right in front of the village got to the third German line without meeting any opposing troops at all. By pushing troops through the village, dealing quickly with the small amount of resistance from rifles and bombs led to the Germans realising they were surrounded and many then surrendered. The island[89] formed by the river and the offshoot formed to house a lock for boats was thought to be clear; however, later on Germans were observed there holding up the attack south of the river. Some men of this company under 2nd Lt. Brash moved down across the bridge and attacking from the rear forced the Germans out, capturing 20 of them. Casualties up to the Black Line had been light so far amounting to the one officer and 14 O.R. killed with two officers and 39 O.R. wounded. In following up the initial attack A Company also suffered from the fire from the Parrot's Beak position, losing three of its four officers wounded. It also realised that the Black Watch, having veered northwards had left a gap in the line and so a platoon was ordered to cover the gap, which it did, dealing with a number of dugouts around Legh Trench. When they got across the cemetery they were able to move back southwards, now being in touch with their neighbours. The whole of A company then reorganised in preparation for moving on towards the Blue Line. This proved fine until a barrage just before Hervin Farm plus sniping from that location held up the advance. Soon afterwards, the sniping having been dealt with, the advance could continue. Welcome help was received from a tank which had stopped just

85   2nd Lt. A.J. Mann is buried in Aubigny Communal Cemetery Extension. 30th, 42nd and 1st Canadian Casualty Clearing Stations were in Aubigny at this time.
86   TNA: WO95/1766 War Diaries of the Black Watch (Royal Highlanders).
87   The entire area discussed here lies on and around the present road passing through the modern St. Laurent-Blangy and then the road extending up the hill towards Roclincourt after the roundabout.
88   TNA: WO95/1765 War Diaries of the 7th Seaforth Highlanders.
89   This still exists as an island although not easy to spot as such. It now houses on one side of the road, the aquatic centre for canoeing for which St. Laurent-Blangy is now quite well-known.

west of the railway bridge. This had lost its officer[90] as he led the tank forward but an officer of the Seaforths, 2nd Lt. Rees, having come up from Battalion H.Q. to report on the situation, was directing its fire. This helped in the final taking of the Blue Line, here the railway embankment south of the railway bridge, B Company mopping up behind them. Losses for A Company, as well as the three wounded officers early in the morning, were 11 O.R. killed, two wounded later dying of wounds, 28 wounded and one missing.[91]

The third and southernmost of the German units of *14th Bavarian Division*, opposing 9th Division at this point, was *Bayerische I.R. 8.* Both the German Official History and the regimental history are full of the brave stand made by their men under difficult conditions. The regimental history mentions the tanks, which as has been seen, were effective in some manner but it also mentions of flamethrowers which the British Army did not possess at this time. The German official account expands on this exaggeration by describing the screams of men hit by great jets of burning oil. Thus the remainder of what is described in these accounts must be read carefully.[92] In reality the whole of the *14th Bavarian Division* had not had a good morning and its placement of the reserve battalions for each regiment[93] was very poor as none of them could intervene until the situation had almost got out of control.

With a number of operational hiccups here and there, 9th Division, as a whole, was successful in obtaining its objectives on the Blue Line. Casualties had been heavy for some units but there was general praise for the effectiveness of the smoke being mixed amongst the artillery barrage. Divisional H.Q. now had to decide how losses might affect the further advance to the Brown Line and how plans could be altered to accommodate the weakness of some of the units in the line.

15th (Scottish) Division, 45th Brigade

Like its northern Scottish neighbour, the 15th (Scottish) Division was also quickly achieving a reputation as a very effective fighting unit. Formed in September 1914 as part of the K2 element of Kitchener's new force, it was again, as was 9th (Scottish), bloodied at Loos and then had its turn on the Somme. Spending six months on this front, all the way into the New Year of 1917 they finally moved to 3rd Army and thus northwards in early February after a short period of rest and recuperation.

With its left on the River Scarpe, 45th Brigade, as did both attacking brigades, had two battalions up but in this case Brig.-Gen. Allgood had also attached two companies of the 13th Royal Scots Regiment to cover the trenches that neighboured the river for a while until the Black Line is reached. Allocated to this task were A and C Companies of the Scots. The latter of these companies had already been in the very trenches they were attacking a mere five days before having carried out a very successful raid. Under the command of Capt. J.A. Turner the 180 men or so of these two companies moved swiftly onto the Black Line, the only problems being for the 4th Wave clearing some of the buildings of the village south of the river and also from the island that has already been described in the 7th Seaforth's account. That said, even though cut off, the last remnants of German opposition in the village did not cease until mid-morning, showing the decision to use the two companies as very wise. It seems, when orders are examined, that neither unit

---

90 This was 2nd Lt. W.D. Tarbet, originally a Seaforth Highlander himself. Having fought his way to the Blue Line, because this was a railway embankment he had got out of his tank to reconnoitre the area. Unfortunately, his grave was subsequently lost and he is commemorated on the Arras Memorial.

91 TNA: WO95/1765 War Diaries of the 7th Seaforth Highlanders.

92 Berhmann & Brandt, *Die Osterschlacht bei Arras 1917,* pp. 96-98; Götz, August, *Das K.B. 8 Infanterie-Regiment, Großherzog Friedrich II von Baden,* (München: Verlag Bayerisches Kriegsarchiv, 1926), p. 28.

93 *3rd Bayerische I.R. 4, 3rd Bayerische I.R. 25* and *1st Bayerische I.R. 8.*

15th Division Morning.

on each side of the river was given the island to clear and thus it became a problem to both. At 10.00am these companies reported the island clear but of course by then the 7th Seaforths had dealt with the garrison. Capt. Turner then settled his men who had moved directly to the Black Line to support the centre attack on the Blue Line.[94] This centre attack was to be made by 11th Argyll & Sutherland Highlanders Regiment. Their diary makes light work of both the advance to the Black Line and the subsequent taking of the Blue Line, sighting just a small problem in Blangy Wood and, "Being temporarily held up at the Railway Triangle".[95] Fortunately, the 6/7th Royal Scots Fusiliers Regiment[96] are more forthcoming about the action. They describe how the leading companies, A and D, make good progress over the first four trench systems meeting little opposition and then settled into positions east of Fred's Wood. It then became clear that opposition in the embankments of the Railway Triangle had caused the attack to falter. It seems from reports that the leading companies, now B and C, had not reached the embankments when the barrage lifted and thus the defenders had time to react to the attack and man their positions. The C.O. of the 6/7th only had this confirmed as the morning moved on and so it was as late as 11.40am before the brigade decided to renew the barrage on the Triangle from 11.55am to 12.05pm. It was around this time that a tank then appeared. This was Tank Number 788, crew C47 of C Company, 1st Brigade, Tank Corps with 2nd Lt. Chas Weber. His after-battle report shows that although he knew the attacking troops were being held up he did not realise what a difference he had made. All kinds of delays meant that it was 9.30am before Tank 788, named *Lusitania*, could make it lumbering way over the old German Trenches. They caught the troops up as they were held up in front of the Blue Line. Discharging their 6 pdr. gun at machine gun posts and moving forward led to the German defenders in the Triangle area either surrendering or, as the 6/7th Royal Scots Fusilier diary notes, "Retiring hastily down Feuchy Lane, some of them throwing away their equipment."[97] This is not the last occasion that the Lieutenant will feature as he and his tank appear again in the afternoon.[98] The action of the tank and good use of stokes mortars on the defenders allowed the Blue Line to be finally entered around 12.30pm.

The German defenders of *11th Division* in front of 45th Brigade were made up of *Grenadier Regiment Nr. 10's* 2nd, 4th Companies of 1st Battalion plus 9th and 11th companies of the 3rd Battalion. The preliminary bombardment had meant that many of the forward positions had been isolated for some days and casualties were fairly heavy. Nevertheless, the 2 companies north of the river, 2nd and 4th were the ones that put up the resistance that caused some of the problems in St. Lauren-Blangy that have been described. The regimental history[99] gives the usual reason of the flank units giving way as the cause for their retreat but as has been seen it was more the strength of numbers that pushed the defenders back eventually. Reserves from 10th Company plus some engineers were rushed to the area of the railway where the line had been more easily broken. It was here along the railway line that these reserves held the British up until Weber's tank intervened. As the morning passed it was clear to the Regimental Commander, Major von Rode that the first lines

94   TNA: WO95/1946 War Diaries of the 13th Royal Scots.

95   TNA: WO95/1944 War Diaries of the 11th Argyll & Sutherland Highlanders.

96   The 6th and 7th Royal Scots Fusiliers were formed in Ayr in August 1914 as part of K1, being firstly part of 9th (Scottish) Division. They amalgamated in May 1916, becoming the 6/7th Battalion and joined 15th (Scottish) Division.

97   TNA: WO95/1947 War Diaries of the 6/7th Royal Scots Fusiliers.

98   KCLMA Fuller/1/4/1, Summary of tank operations 1 Bde Heavy Branch, 9 Apr–3 May 17.

99   Schütz *Generalmajor* a.D., Wilhelm v. & Hochbaum *Leutnant, Das Grenadier-Regiment König Friedrich Wilhelm II (1. Schlesisches) Nr. 10,* (Oldenburg: Stalling, 1924), 186, Hochbaum was Adjutant of the regiment, eventually a General in the Second World War, dying in 1955 a Soviet prisoner of war.

were lost and that he had to pull back to the second line, 1st Battalion north and 3rd Battalion south of the river.

15th (Scottish) Division, 44th Brigade

The 9th Black Watch (Royal Highlanders) formed the left battalion of this brigade attack. As with their neighbours to the north the initial taking of the Black Line was without serious incident and on time. Moving forward though proved as difficult as to their left and any advance was held up, again until the arrival of Weber with Tank 788, after which the Blue Line was taken and consolidation commenced.[100] The Blue Line at this point is Observation Ridge, an important landmark to take if troops are to be pushed on further towards the next ridge of Orange Hill. The Germans had fortified the ridge with a number of redoubts on the slope in front plus on the heights themselves and the delay cause on the left of the ridge by the Railway Triangle was going to have consequences for the remainder of the day. At the time of writing you can walk up onto the ridge today and see what a commanding position it holds with clear views over the British lines all the way into the centre of Arras. Right of the Black Watch and tasked with, alongside 12th Division to their right, taking Observation Ridge and the Blue Line, were the 8th/10th Gordon Highlanders.[101] With A and B Companies leading the battalion got off to a good start, officers having to hold men back from advancing too fast into their own barrage. After taking the Black Line the two remaining companies advanced up Observation Ridge but were held up both by the Railway Triangle and a redoubt on their right. This was Hart Work and was the responsibility of the neighbouring units on the right. However, those units were seen veering south to avoid the machine guns within and therefore Captain Martin, O.C. A Company decided to send two parties under himself and 2nd Lt. Hay to attack the redoubt. This was a success although unfortunately both officers were killed in the action.[102] The unit diary is then very clear that as well as the clearance of this redoubt it was the arrival of Tank 788 which allowed them to regain the initiative and move onto the ridge and take the Blue Line. Finally, at around 12.10pm the Blue Line was taken but this was the time that 46th Brigade were supposed to be passing through and attacking the Brown Line and therefore a serious delay had been put on proceedings.[103]

The sector attacked by 44th Brigade was defended by men of the *R.I.R. 51*. Despite the fact that resistance stiffened after the Black Line had been taken, their regimental history is a difficult one to take at face value. They give times for the 3rd line of the forward positions eventually falling much later than was the case. Also they complain of their right flank being lost due to the withdrawal of *Grenadier Regiment 10*, the same complaint as that unit made about their left flank. What is clear is that the forward companies were overwhelmed although the unit history is loath

100 TNA: WO95/1937 War Diaries of the 9th Black Watch (Royal Highlanders). A poignant story of one of the officers mortally wounded in this phase can be found in Reid, Walter, *To Arras 1917*, (East Linton: Tuckwell. 2003), pp. 157-168), the officer being the 20-year-old Captain Ernest Reid.

101 The 8th Gordon Highlanders were formed August 1914 as part of K1 and initially were in 9th (Scottish) Division. 10th Gordon Highlanders were formed September 1914 and when the 8th were transferred to 15th (Scottish) Division in May 1916 the two battalions were amalgamated to form the 8th/10th Battalion.

102 Capt. John Martin MC was awarded his MC for his part in a raid on the Butte de Warlencourt in January of 1917. He was from Edinburgh and was originally buried in Blangy Military Cemetery but this cemetery was closed in 1924 to allow industry to rebuild there and he was moved to Cabaret Rouge British Cemetery near Souchez. 2nd Lt. Alfred Hay, attached to the battalion from 3rd Battalion Gordon Highlanders, from Tarves, Aberdeenshire, has papers that originally show him concentrated from an isolated grave to Feuchy Chapel British Cemetery; however, none of the men on the concentration form seem to have made it there, they and Alfred now being commemorated on the Arras Memorial.

103 TNA: WO95/1937 War Diaries of the 8th/10th Gordon Highlanders.

to admit the fact. What seems more truthful are the accounts of holding out a little further back which is where the redoubts on Observation Hill were situated. One report, by Reserve *Leutnant* Bindseil of 9th Company has a particularly interesting section where he describes watching the attack unfold below him:

> The enemy creeping barrage – there was little answer from our own artillery, the guns had probably been put out of action by gas shells – moved slowly towards us and then beyond without halting over our trench for long. Losses from artillery fire were at this point light.[104]

This seems to confirm the impression from the British diaries that the barrage was lost on Observation Hill and that only a long-winded fight outmanoeuvring the redoubts led to the surrender of their occupants. Although the claim in the unit history where Reserve *Leutnant* Schlensog says that; "We felt that we remained undefeated",[105] is an exaggeration, the *R.I.R. 51* clearly caused enough of a problem to ensure that Monchy-le-Preux was not going to fall on this day.

At this stage then, the 15th (Scottish) Division could be generally pleased with the situation. Both initial lines had been taken; however, the delay caused was holding up 46th Brigade and it has to be remembered that according to the plans 37th Division were yet to pass through to take the Green Line. The divisional history[106] gives all kinds of reasons for breaking the deadlock of the Railway Triangle none of which, bar the extra artillery barrage, are reflected in the unit diaries. The main reason that the Blue Line was achieved, even if at a later time than planned, 2nd Lt. Weber's tank, is not mentioned at all in the volume.

12th (Eastern) Division, 36th Brigade

Another New Army division, the 12th was created as part of K1 in August 1914 from volunteers in Eastern Command and therefore throughout the war had a distinctive London and East Counties composition. Arriving a little later than other units at Loos it nevertheless saw a lot of action there and eventually spent considerable time around the notorious Hohenzollern Redoubt. Again not involved in the first 1 July attacks on the Somme, the division was in action the next day against the fortress village of Ovillers. Further fighting was interrupted by a short spell with 3rd Army near Arras in late August and September before returning to the Somme in October; finally being relieved and sent back to 3rd Army in late October. This was the first of the divisions to be able to make use of the accommodation provided by the caves beneath the Arras – Cambrai road described in an earlier chapter. The divisional diary makes special mention of the fact that the men could not only be protected from German artillery but also that it, "Allowed them real rest and enabled the attack to be commenced with physically fresh men."[107]

On the left, the 7th Royal Sussex Regiment. The Black Line did not follow any particular trench line system in front of Observation Ridge and therefore instructions were to take and consolidate first Guildford and then Hertford Trenches, pushing out to the junction of these when the barrage lifted. The unit diary reports this being done with relative ease by A and B Companies to Guildford Trench and then D Company taking Hertford Trench, C company acting as moppers

---

104 Quoted in; Nollau, *Oberstleutnant* a.D., Herbert, *Geschichte des Königlich Preußischen 4. Niederschlesischen Infanterie-Regiments Nr. 51*, (Berlin: Kolck, 1931), p. 168.

105 Nollau, *Geschichte des Königlich Preußischen Infanterie-Regiments Nr. 51*, p. 168.

106 Stewart & Buchan, *The Fifteenth (Scottish) Division 1914-1919*, pp. 119-120.

107 TNA: WO95/1824 War Diaries of the Headquarters of 12th (Eastern) Division.

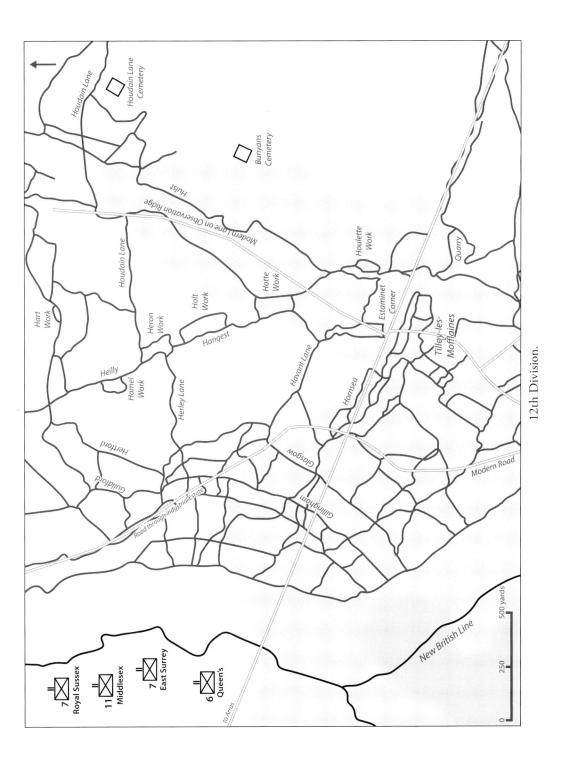

12th Division.

up. Following through the Royal Sussex were 8th Battalion Royal Fusiliers but they were almost immediately held up in front of Hamel Work. They managed to work around the flanks of this but time was pressing and according to the brigade diary the barrage was by now 400 yards ahead.[108] Mention is made of working with 8th/10th Gordons to clear Hart Work which was heard about above. Then Hem Trench was taken and the unit began to consolidate this line which is behind the crest of the ridge.[109] Casualties were: one officer mortally wounded,[110] four others wounded, 42 O.R. killed or died of wounds, 117 wounded and seven missing. The actual Blue Line is the trench ahead, Hulst Trench and the brigade diary speaks of units advancing towards that and coming under fire and subsequently retiring out of sight.[111] Whilst this may have seemed a sensible move to the units involved it would obviously have repercussions for the units tasked with advancing to the Brown Line. 11th Middlesex Regiment on the right of the brigade similarly made light work of taking the initial trenches and were consolidating in Hertford Trench in good time with, "wonderfully slight"[112] casualties. Many of those killed, including Sgt. Hunter,[113] were of the H.Q. detail when the German dugout they had taken over blew up. This and several other explosions meant that the remaining German dugouts were avoided leading to many of the units complaining of the conditions in the night to come.[114] Two Officers were lost killed in the attack, 2nd Lt. Wright and Sinclair, around 100 other casualties.[115] Coming up behind the Middlesex were 9th Royal Fusiliers. Their diary would have us believe that the operation was carried out perfectly smoothly, however from the brigade diary it is clear that the 9th had as much trouble as their sister battalion to the left, this time in front of Heron and Holt Work, both of which took some time to take. Again the two diaries, battalion and brigade disagree over the outcome, battalion claiming they reached their objectives, brigade saying they had retired behind the crest and were not on the Blue Line.[116] Again it was *I.R. 51* in front of 36th Brigade and the evidence from both sides seems to point towards the barrage having been lost and as a consequence the Blue Line not fully taken in time for the afternoon's action.

12th (Eastern) Division, 37th Brigade

A glance at the trench map of the area just north of the Arras – Cambrai road will show that this brigade had five or even six trench lines to pass before it could claim the Black Line. The left battalion for this task was the 7th East Surrey Regiment and in the after-action report in their unit diary they talk of it, "being carried off like a parade".[117] The Black Line being taken in good time but coming under serious fire from Hangest Trench, about half way from the Black Line to the

---

108 TNA: WO95/1854 War Diaries of 36th Brigade.

109 TNA: WO95/1857 War Diaries of 8th Battalion Royal Fusiliers.

110 2nd Lt. Gervase Maude from London died later that day and is buried in Duisans British Cemetery near Etrun, the site of 8th Casualty Clearing Station.

111 TNA: WO95/1854 War Diaries of 36th Brigade.

112 TNA: WO95/1854 War Diaries of 36th Brigade.

113 Sgt. Hunter and probably many others of the 20 killed by the explosion have no known grave and are commemorated on the Arras memorial.

114 A report by *Oberartz* Dr. Wolff in Nollau, *Oberstleutnant* a.D., Herbert, *Geschichte des Königlich Preußischen 4. Niederschlesischen Infanterie-Regiments Nr. 51*, p. 173 mentions being interrogated over the blowing of bunkers, which he laughed off, saying they had no time for such work. He was, however, ordered to search a number of other bunkers at revolver point.

115 TNA: WO95/1856 War Diaries of 11th Middlesex Regiment.

116 TNA: WO95/1854 War Diaries of 36th Brigade; TNA: WO95/1857 War Diaries of 9th Battalion Royal Fusiliers.

117 TNA: WO95/1862 War Diaries of 7th East Surrey Regiment.

Blue. His platoon, suffering casualties as it dug in, was too much for Sgt Harry Cator of 7th East Surreys and in spite of it being beyond the objective of his unit he took it in hand to deal with the problem for which he was awarded the V.C.

> For most conspicuous duty and devotion to duty. Whilst consolidating the first-line captured system his platoon suffered severe casualties from hostile machine gun and rifle fire. In full view of the enemy and under heavy fire Sgt Cator with one man advanced across the open to attack the hostile machine gun. The man accompanying him was killed after going a short distance, but Sgt Cator continued on, and picking up a Lewis gun and some drums on his way, succeeded in reaching the northern end of the hostile trench. Meanwhile one of our bombing parties was seen to be held up by a machine gun. Sgt Cator took up a position from which he sighted this gun, and killed the entire team and the officer, whose papers he brought in. He continued to hold that end of the trench with the Lewis gun with such effect that the bombing squad was enabled to work along, the result being that 100 prisoners and five machine guns were captured.[118]

This personal action was of great assistance to the unit following through the East Surreys, 6th Queens Own (Royal West Kent) Regiment. Their diary would not have you believe there were problems though, as it states the taking and consolidating of the Blue Line as being a straightforward task without difficulty. Suffering nine officer and 129 OR casualties shows that despite the barrage, resistance was present in some force at least.[119] The only officer killed was 2nd Lt. W.H. Proctor.[120] Adhering to the Arras – Cambrai Road and forming the right of the divisional assault was the 6th Queen's (Royal West Surrey) Regiment. The also had to reach the 6th German trench in order to capture their Black Line objective, Glasgow Trench. In doing so there were few losses, the diary claiming only four O.R. being killed although it says two officers were also lost, Capt. R.M. Clerk and 2nd Lt. E.H. Aspdenand 19 O.R. as missing. The CWGC actually records 19 O.R. as having died therefore it follows that many of the missing were clearly killed.[121] Moving through 6th Queen's to attack the Blue Line was 6th Buffs (East Kent) Regiment. C and D Companies led the way against significant opposition which had to be dealt with by flanking movements and machine guns that were sought out by rifle grenades. D Company on the left managed to get to and take Houlette Work but C Company, under fire from ruins at Estaminet Corner, had to deal with these nests of opposition first before moving on; the Blue Line being eventually taken.

Opposition to the attack of 37th Brigade was both the responsibility of the left elements of *I.R. 51* and the right of *Fusilier Regiment 38*. The latter had also complained bitterly about the condition of the trenches they only took over scant days before being attacked and again it is clear that the forward trenches, held by their 3rd Battalion, were simply overwhelmed, many of their occupants having been killed by the bombardment or found still in their dugouts. According to the German Official History, 9th Company of *Fusilier R. 38*, on the right and therefore defending against 37th Brigade held the first attack but this is not borne out by the successful taking of the Black Line, on time, that seemed to be the case. Although it is clear from British accounts that the advance to the Blue Line was strongly resisted, very soon both the 3rd Battalion and the 1st, that

---

118 *London Gazette*, 8 June 1917, p. 5704. Harry, already a holder of the Military Medal from an action on the Somme, survived the war, going back to his native Norwich, dying in 1966.

119 TNA: WO95/1861 War Diaries of 6th Queen's Own (Royal West Kent).

120 2nd Lt. William Proctor from Chepstow was originally in a field grave in the British trenches under the wrong name Porston, but thankfully when his remains were relocated to Feuchy Chapel British Cemetery in 1919 his proper name was verified.

121 TNA: WO95/1863 War Diaries of 6th Queen's (Royal West Surrey).

had been in support, were reduced to a mere skeleton of their original form as they retreated away from the northern part of Tilloy-les-Mofflaines.

Although 12th Division had succeeded in breaking the substantial defences in front of it, both in the German front lines, the strongpoints situated on the slopes of Observation Ridge and then the ridge itself, it had not been possible to keep to the timings given to the division. The divisional history states: "Owing to the strong resistance met with, the Blue Line had not been completely captured in the scheduled time."[122] On the other hand, with relatively few casualties and not a great deal of mention of serious problems in the unit diaries, it could be argued that there was maybe a lack of push and drive during the morning. It was thus left in question how 35th Brigade, with the task of advancing to the Brown Line in the afternoon, would be able to prepare the ground for 37th Division, waiting to carry the attack further later in the day.

3rd Division, 76th Brigade

A Regular Army division which was one of the four originally forming the B.E.F. when it first came to France in 1914, the 3rd had already seen action on almost all fronts in the Western European sphere and had also undergone many changes in its make up with regard to the battalions making up its compliment. One whole brigade had been exchanged in 1915, the 7th leaving and the 76th arriving. This latter brigade was part of the New Army and as there will have been few actual pre-war regular men remaining by this point in the war, making any distinction between this division and those alongside would be fatuous. No divisional history was ever written for the 3rd, maybe a reflection of its continual change in constituent units and therefore lack of a core upon which such things are built. The division had a tricky task as it straddled the point at which the old German pre-withdrawal front line finished and the new line, eventually but not immediately the Hindenburg Line, began. In addition, a change in direction of the line had placed problems before the planners, as outlined in an earlier chapter. One could say they had to 'turn the corner' so to speak.

The lead brigade, the 76th, was given the task of taking the Black Line, the last time this line would appear on the planner's maps. Here it only constituted a small piece of the German defences, the far side of Devil's Wood. The 1st Gordon Highlander Regiment had the privilege of leading the division into action at Zero Hour with the task of taking the first four lines of German Trenches in front of 'Devil's Wood'. It had in support one company of the 8th King's Own (Royal Lancaster) Regiment. This company had the misfortune to lose its officer commanding, on their way up to the assembly trenches, this was very unfortunate as the route was through tunnels for most of the way and the company had suffered no other casualties by this point. C and B Companies were chosen to form the first line with the others in support; the 8th King's Own forming a third line. With around 60 casualties Glasgow and Gateshead Trenches were taken and the company of 8th K.O.R.L. formed a flank facing south.[123] Coming through to take Devil's Wood[124] and the Black Line at the other side of it were the 10th Royal Welsh Fusiliers. Apart from casualties to one platoon, caused by a shell when exiting the Arras cellars, the Fusiliers took the wood and the Black Line without considerable opposition. They lost one officer in the wood, 2nd

---

122 Brumwell, P. Middleton, *The History of the 12th (Eastern) Division in the Great War*, (London: Nesbit & Sons, 1923), p. 101.

123 TNA: WO95/1435 War Diaries of 1st Gordon Highlanders.

124 The small remnant of Devil's Wood can be seen near the roundabout on the main Cambrai road in Tilloy adjacent to the agricultural school. Wartime traces can still be discerned of one looks carefully.

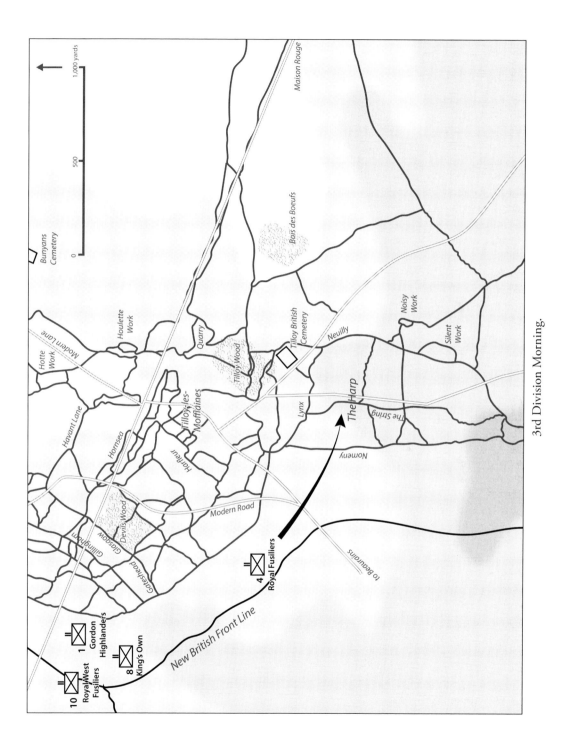

3rd Division Morning.

Lt. J.C.R. Edmunds-Davies, who was badly wounded and died later, and also their medical officer, Lt. E Evans, R.A.M.C., was hit by shellfire and killed whilst tending to the wounded.[125]

3rd Division, 9th Brigade

Moving up in columns of sections behind the leading two battalions the three assaulting units of 9th Brigade formed up in the Black Line and when the barrage lifted at 7.46am they moved out to attack the village of Tilloy-les-Mofflaines and get to the Blue Line positions the other side and, on the right, the northern element of the Harp. It was 13th Kings (Liverpool) Regiment's task to take the village and although getting to and taking Harfleur Trench was relatively straight forward; from then on it became a difficult fight with snipers hidden in Tilloy Wood. The wood itself was difficult to clear due to it being festooned with wire that had not been cut. Just beyond the wood was a quarry which again proved a difficult obstacle and was not easy to take and consolidate.[126] Two officers were killed in the process of clearing the village, quarry and wood, seven others wounded and about 170 other casualties. By 8.30am though the task was complete and the Blue Line was being consolidated with the capture of 19 officers and 449 men of the German defenders.[127]

In the centre, 12th West Yorkshire Regiment had a similar experience, meeting more serious opposition in the latter part of the advance but by employing bombers and Lewis gunners they overcame the resistance and were able to similarly consolidate on the Blue Line at 8.30am. The West Yorks also lost two officers killed, three wounded and around 144 other casualties.[128] The task of clearing the village might have been more straightforward had the level of support from tanks been what it should have. Ten tanks of 9 Company, C Battalion, 1st Brigade were allocated but five vehicles bogged down well before the start line. Of the others it looks as they did do some work around the village at various times although none of the infantry units admit their presence at this point. Certainly the after-battle report by 2nd Lt. S.O. Norman of C41 in Tank 780 is clear that he fired his 6 pdr into the village in support, although finding it difficult to progress across the ground south of Tilloy, ditching on a number of occasions.

The defence of Tilloy-les-Mofflaines was complicated for the German defenders as the boundary between *F.R. 38 and R.I.R 76* of *17th Reserve-Division* passed through the northern part of the village. This was not merely a battalion boundary but the divisional one. Thus the initial attack on Devil's Wood was against men of *F.R. 38* whereas later attacks into the village will have been resisted by men of *R.I.R. 76*. For once a German source from the latter unit is fairly accurate in describing the results of the morning attack. According to this source,[129] the greater part of 2nd Battalion in front and all but one company of 1st Battalion in support were wiped out. The German Official History is less secure in claiming that it was only the loss of Hill 94, which is on Observation Ridge, which caused the village to fall. The timings don't work here as the Blue Line was reached by 3rd Division in reasonably good time, before the eventual late arrival of 12th Division on the ridge. The typical German source reasoning that withdrawal was only caused by the flank giving way is again evident here.[130]

---

125 TNA: WO95/1436 War Diaries of 10th Royal Welsh Fusiliers.
126 Both the wood and quarry still exist and can be visited, the former in the modern chateaux park and the latter at the end of the village.
127 TNA: WO95/1429 War Diaries of 13th Kings (Liverpool).
128 TNA: WO95/1432 War Diaries of 12th West Yorkshire Regiment.
129 Vizefeldwebel Warnke, quoted in Sheldon, Jack, *The German Army in the Spring Offensives 1917*, (Barnsley: Pen & Sword, 2015), p. 98.
130 Berhmann & Brandt, *Die Osterschlacht bei Arras 1917 II. Teil* (Oldenburg: Stalling, 1929), p. 37.

The task of assaulting part of the Harp to the south of the village fell to 4th Royal Fusiliers. With W Company on the right and Z Company on the left in the normal two platoons up formation they attacked the Harp on time, moving within 75 yards of the British barrage and then at 7.34am when it moved on, attacked and took Nomeny Trench which forms the frontal element of the Harp complex. During the advance the leading companies had come under considerable shell fire, some its own according to the diary. Then when the right company swung to its left to conform to the change in direction caused by the alignment of the German front line trench, they came under fire from Nomeny Trench, which caused some considerable casualties. X and Y Companies in support were able to reinforce the now depleted and exhausted leading men and carry Lynx Trench and the String by around 8.10am.[131]

By this time the support battalion, the 2nd Suffolk Regiment,[132] had moved up to the String and was able to continue the attack to the far side of the Harp and capture Neuilly Trench and Noisy Work which completed the Blue Line. Seen beforehand as a tough nut to crack, the northern part of the Harp had succumbed fairly easily and the casualties for the Fusiliers of two officers and 37 OR killed with around seven officers and 160 wounded or missing, although relatively heavy were, for the level of success, within reason. The O.C. of X Company, Capt. A.E. Millson was severely wounded; the other officer lost was 2nd Lt. William Paddock, both men dying the same day.[133] The decision to allot an addition battalion in sending forward the Suffolks seems to have paid off; this unit losing one officer and 18 OR killed; two officers and 69 OR wounded with 12 missing.[134] Although some of the Fusiliers went forward with the Suffolks the task would possibly have been too much for the remaining men to carry out alone. One interesting discrepancy in the diaries is that the Royal Fusiliers state that one of the tanks allotted sat on Nomeny Trench but none were of real value due to the state of the ground. On the other hand, the Suffolk diary is clear that Tank 777[135] did useful work on the *eastern* side of the Harp. The Tank Corps diaries show three of the four tanks allotted to this sector doing some work on the Black Line, one Tank 582 being put out of action by bombs there, 776 and 777 going on towards the Blue Line, the former bellying at some point. Tank 777 is shown near to the Blue Line and being hit whilst ditched and set on fire. The narrative in the Tank Corps diary has it on the Noisy Work and that it had put several machine guns out of action. The two varying sources do seem to confirm that some good work was done by the tanks; maybe the Battalion H.Q. of the Royal Fusiliers was unaware of this when writing the day's events. This section of the Harp was also held by *R.I.R. 76* of *17th Reserve Division*, but there is little evidence in German sources of what happened to the defenders, most of the narrative covering the fight for the village.

The 3rd Division was thus securely on the Blue Line in very good time and could use the intervening period of the morning to consolidate and complete the task of clearing Tilloy-les-Mofflaines in which there were still some Germans holding out in the ruins and cellars. In this area the complete destruction of both the enemy wire to a greater or lesser extent is still heard and the demolishing of the forward German trenches; all of which allowing leading troops to make rapid progress with a reasonable level of casualties. It is also evident in all the reports that the creeping barrage was extremely effective and definitely allowed troops to get forward.

---

131 TNA: WO95/1431 War Diaries of 4th Royal Fusiliers.
132 Attached from 76th Brigade, 3rd Division.
133 TNA: WO95/1431 War Diaries of 4th Royal Fusiliers. Alvan Millson is buried in Beaurains Road Cemetery, William Paddock is in Duisans British Cemetery, Etrun.
134 TNA: WO95/1437 War Diaries of 2nd Suffolk Regiment.
135 KCLMA Fuller/1/4/1, Summary of tank operations 1 Bde Heavy Branch, 9 Apr–3 May 17. Tank 777 had crew C/24 led by 2nd Lt. P. Saillard.

The château in Tilloy-les-Mofflaines. (Author)

14th Division, 42nd Brigade

The 14th (Light) Division was formed as part of the K1 New Army in August 1914, first of all as 8th Division but as it became possible to create an extra Regular division that was given the number and so 14th Division was born. It moved to the Western Front quite early, fighting at the dreadful Hooge sector and in battles on the Somme in 1916. The nomenclature 'Light' was primarily because of the unit make-up of regiments with light infantry lineage from an era when that made a difference, e.g. Rifles and Durham Light Infantry, Somerset Light Infantry, King's Own Yorkshire Light Infantry amongst others. It did not mean any difference in equipment or appearance in this age of industrial warfare.

The British Official History succinctly puts the task of this division as "particularly formidable".[136] The Harp had been forming even when the German Front line was further west and even though not part of the Hindenburg Line was still a potentially difficult nut to crack. The Black Line was actually the British front line at this point so there was a delay before the division was to attack. It must have been with a combination of apprehension but also delight that the initial excellent progress of 3rd Division on the left was followed. That allowed 9th Brigade, as has been seen, to be ready to move forward with the two brigades of 14th Division at the allotted time of 7.34am. This was important as it would have been especially difficult for 42nd Brigade on the divisional right to have attacked the Harp without it being a coordinated attack from both divisions.

---

136 Falls, *Military Operations, France and Belgium 1917 Vol. 1*, p. 210.

14th Division Morning.

On the left, 9th King's Royal Rifle Corps had the 'String' as its objective, attacking with the usual two company front, each with two platoons in each wave, in this case B Company of the left A Company of the right. D Company advanced behind with instructions to mop-up the German front line trench and C Company behind them in support. The initial advance did not go well. Clearly there were some unsubdued German machine guns as casualties mounted quickly. In A Company all four officers and three of the four sergeants were hit before reaching the German front line, Lt G.M.C. Leech later dying of his wounds. In B Company Capt. A.E. Dent, commanding, and 2nd Lt E.R. Clarke were both killed as well as 2nd Lt R.B. van Praagh of C Company. Remarkably, the men went on and were able to take the front line, advancing beyond and lay down under the barrage to wait for the next lift. With C Company joining in support the next attack went in to take the String. Again unfortunately machine gun fire was heavy and the wire was not well cut, a deadly combination at any point. Lt H. Stewart, commanding C Company, and 2nd Lt. R. Cook of the same company were killed here. More fortunately two groups of men had advanced along the two communication trenches on each side of the advance and obtain entrance to the String in that manner. Observing the way a small group of B Company had managed to use the communication trenches, more men of C Company were sent the same way. By working down the String they were able to clear the snipers and two machine guns and meet the small group of A Company at the other end. The unit is, at this point in the diary, extremely critical of the tanks, saying that if they had got here where they should be the wire and machine guns would have been dealt with. You feel the effect the losses sustained had in the tone of the writing in the diary. This passed up to brigade who wrote, "The failure of the tanks for the second time in the experience of the Brigade."[137] Their job done, the men of the K.R.R.C. began to clear the dugouts and consolidate the line.[138]

The right of the brigade was led by 5th Oxford and Buckinghamshire Light Infantry Regiment. Although they do not go into great detail about the assault with casualties of five officers and 45 O.R. killed, eight officers and 116 O.R. wounded plus 11 missing it must have been a similarly difficult exercise even with the excellent barrage. They do mention the use of Lewis guns and rifle grenades therefore some element of platoon tactics must have been employed in the taking of the 'String'. The Brigade was not as yet though on its objective, the Blue Line, which was at the back of the Harp complex and down Pole Trench. What happened here with the 5th King's Shropshire Light Infantry Regiment was quite remarkable in its audacity, but is not remarked upon in any of the diaries nor the Official History. A glance at the map will show you that by attacking through the leading battalions of the brigade, into the southern elements of the Harp and then pushing with two companies to the eastern edge of complex and two companies to Pole Trench they were in effect working down, from the north, the beginnings of the Hindenburg Line. Luckily the account in the diary is written by the O.C. of C Company, the right flanking company of the battalion. This allows a close examination of how this attack from the flank of the German lines played out:

> At this time there were two tanks just in front of assembly trenches, and two just behind, the condition of the ground seemed to make their progress very slow and in my line of advance I saw nothing more of them, and they played no part in the operations. The enemy barrage which appeared to be fairly heavy was drawn through the crest of Telegraph Hill immediately west of Telegraph Work. At this point the attacking line also came under heavy machine-gun fire from the direction of Neully Trench and Tilloy. Slight resistance was encountered in

---

137 TNA: WO95/1898 War Diaries of 42nd Brigade.
138 TNA: WO95/1900 War Diaries of 9th Kings Royal Rifle Corps.

Telegraph Hill Trench, and Head Lane, but this was immediately overcome and my company captured between 50-75 prisoners here. No resistance was offered in Pole Trench, but enemy fired a machine gun from Nouvion Lane. On a patrol being sent forward, the enemy abandoned Nouvion Lane and ran to the rear, but were shot down by our Lewis-gun fire. One enemy machine gun was captured. The D.L.I, [Durham Light Infantry] of the 43rd Brigade had converged slightly into my area, but I occupied a part of Pole Trench and had established communication with the D.L.I. on my right by 8.45 a.m. Germans in dug-outs were cleared out by 9.10 a.m., and work was forthwith started in consolidating the line. I captured and consolidated this line with the remnants of A, B and C Companies. D Company had meantime obtained their objective in Silent Work, and by 10 a.m. communication had been established with the Suffolks on their left and the Ox. and Bucks Light Infantry in the String and Negrine Trench.[139]

It is difficult to reconcile the differing accounts of the infantry and the Heavy Branch with regard to tank performance on Telegraph Hill. What is clear is that the ground was not suitable for tanks, borne out by the lack of arrival of five out of 10 allocated and the eventual bellying of three more somewhere on the hill. The tank diary gives a detailed account of the remaining tanks helping out on the German front line trench and also further into the complex of trenches. All the infantry accounts mention the absence of any tank support at all. If the German accounts of *R.I.R. 76* are to be believed the tanks did make a significant impression on the defenders. It is, however, a common theme in German histories to place great emphasis on the role of tanks in any kind of defeat. If the truth lay somewhere in-between, then although some support was forthcoming, in truth this was an infantry affair and lessons to be learned in trying to involve poor quality tanks that could not cope with the conditions resulting in being not effective in any real sense.

It seems to have been 6th Company of *R.I.R. 76* that made life difficult within The Harp itself but in the end the remnants of the whole of II Battalion of the regiment amounted to 25 men and 2 officers and thus the whole position was lost.[140]

14th Division, 43rd Brigade

The two leading battalions of 43rd Brigade, 10th Durham Light Infantry Regiment on the left and 6th King's Own Yorkshire Light Infantry on the right, had a slightly complicated manoeuvre in that the first German trench was to be attacked in a south Easterly direction but then the men had to wheel slightly to the left to continue the attack. Although suffering a little from rifle and Machine gun fire from Nice Trench, 10th D.L.I., once this obstacle was taken, moved swiftly to the Blue Line in Pole Trench down to Dog Lane. In this advance the comment is that, "The enemy was chiefly in his dugouts waiting to surrender."[141] The line was consolidated but disconcertingly it became clear that Telegraph Hill Trench further south had not been attacked leaving the right flank very exposed. Machine guns were set up to take this area in enfilade and thus although German firing continued it was not effective against the Durham men.

On the right, 6th K.O.Y.L.I had the northern element of Pine Trench as an initial objective and then the triangular redoubt known as Fir Alley. The former caused no particular problem but the latter was still heavily wired and for the first time in our journey from the north uncut wire in the initial stages of an attack is reported. The K.O.Y.L.I War Diary also mentions men

139 TNA: WO95/1898 War Diaries of 5th King's Shropshire Light Infantry.
140 Berhmann & Brandt, *Die Osterschlacht bei Arras 1917 II. Teil*, p. 37.
141 TNA: WO95/1908 War Diaries of 10th Durham Light Infantry.

on the previous evening out at the German front line cutting wire. Clearly here the preparatory bombardment had not been as effective as that seen on Telegraph Hill and beyond to the north. Luckily for the Yorkshiremen there were three tanks on hand and with their help the redoubt was overcome. Leaving two platoons in Fir Alley the rest of the battalion advanced on Telegraph Hill Trench, they also commenting upon the fact that their right flank was not being covered by the neighbouring division. By around 8.40am Telegraph Hill Trench was taken and by 8.50am the trench beyond as well. A party had to bomb down Telegraph Hill Trench for about 100 yards though and create a block due to there being no contact with the unit from 56th Division that should have been on the right.[142]

The defenders for the majority of 43rd Brigade's attack also belonged to *Reserve-Infanterie-Division 17* but this time it was men of *I.R. 162*. The 5th and 6th Companies on the right claim to have held the attack until tanks further south broke through but this doesn't really tally with events (especially 10th D.L.I. diary comments quoted above and the time that the brigade reached the Blue Line). What the account in *I.R. 162's* history does make clear, though, is the clearly important role the few tanks that did make it through had to the success of the attack. However, the claim that tanks breaking through to the north before turning south to take the regiment in flank can be discounted.[143]

At this point in the day then, 14th Division was very pleased with the progress made thus far. Despite a few problems with wire in places, mostly on the right, all their units were on the Blue Line with casualties generally being far less that those experienced in previous campaigns. The barrage had been excellent and units following up were in good time for the next phase in the afternoon. The only worrying aspect of the morning was that there was not any secure contact with 56th Division on their right. Where were they and how long before they would be up to protect the right when the attack on the Brown Line was due?

56th (1st London) Division, 168th Brigade

The 56th (London) Division, a Territorial Force unit, had a rather disrupted initial deployment in the war, its units being mostly used in an independent role when sent to France. It was not until early 1916 that it was decided to reconstitute the division and subsequently it concentrated in France during February that year. Its first major engagement was not a happy one, being one of the two divisions attacking in the diversionary effort at Gommecourt. Here it suffered heavily in what many modern commentators see as a pointless and costly diversionary attack to the 1st day of the Somme to the south.

Before describing the start of the 168th Brigade attack, the reader must recall the last assault preparations described in a previous chapter. It was reported that a patrol inspected the wire in front of the left flank of this brigade's initial objective of Pine Lane and found the wire to the virtually untouched. Also that the trench, when the patrol was able to inspect it, was found to be in good condition "with a duckboard in place".[144] When it is recalled that in many instances further north the experience of attacking troops was that the front line trench was totally destroyed and almost unrecognisable and that the wire was non-existent the question is raised, why not here? The problems that attacking units faced, described hereafter, have to be considered within that context

---

142 TNA: WO95/1906 War Diaries of 6th King's Own Yorkshire Light Infantry.

143 Dziobek, Otto, *Geschichte des Infanterie-Regiments Lübeck (3. Hanseatisches) Nr. 162*, (Oldenburg: Stalling, 1922), p. 204.

144 TNA: WO95/2954 War Diaries of 12th London Regiment (The Rangers).

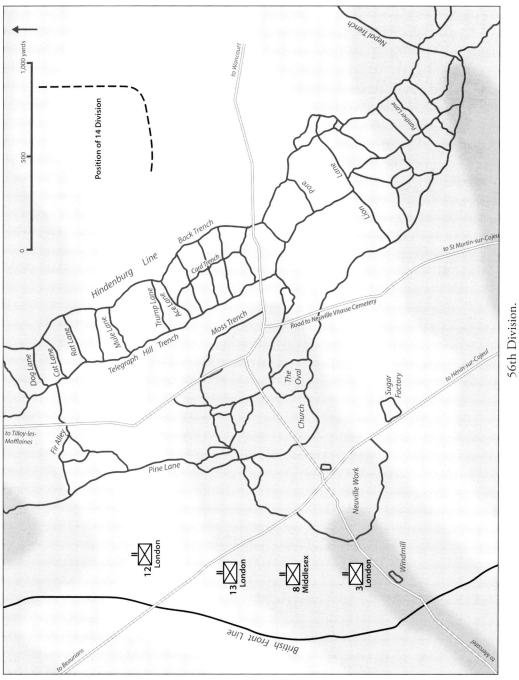

56th Division.

by the reader. A more detailed analysis of why that should be the case will be postponed until after the narrative of the whole battle is complete.

On the far left of 168th Brigade was the 1/12th (County of London) Battalion (The Rangers). In front of the battalion was Pine Lane and to ensure that the configuration of the line did not put the brigade at a disadvantage the attack was timed for 7.45am, a few minutes after those of 14th Division.[145] The Rangers attacked with B Company on the left, A Company on the right. Both companies came under heavy machine gun fire as they attempted to find a way through the wire. Casualties were mounting until two events broke the deadlock. 2nd Lieutenant Cunningham of 'B' Company led his platoon through a small gap in the wire that he had found. Fighting through the Pine Lane Trench, they managed to kill the machine gun team that had inflicted heavy casualties on the Rangers. Also a tank, spotting the difficulties the companies faced moved down along the wire, flattening it. With no gap in front of them A Company had suffered very badly, Company Commander, Captain Barrett being the only officer left on his feet in Pine Lane along with 50 surviving men. He found he had no sergeants or corporals in the group.[146] With the aid of C Company coming through in support the battalion managed to get to the Blue Line in the Sunken Lane. By this point A Company was under the command of L. Cpl. Drew. It is somewhat uncertain what was happening on the flank between the Rangers and the 6th K.O.Y.L.I. on their left. The Rangers say that D Company had to form a flank in that direction until the neighbouring battalion had got through the wire but as has been seen; as far as the Yorkshire Regiment was concerned they couldn't see the Rangers as they advanced. Looking over the operation orders of the two units, the 6th K.O.Y.L.I. had Telegraph Hill Trench as an objective and was to work outwards until linking up with the Rangers. The latter did not have Telegraph Hill Trench in their area, the boundary being where that trench meets the Sunken Lane. There was clearly a lack of sufficient liaison between the two units before the attack although luckily it did not lead to any major problems. There was clearly a gap between the two units as they advanced caused by the awkward direction of assault being an oblique angle to Pine Lane and the Hindenburg Line. 2nd Lt Peebles was the only officer fatality that day[147] although casualties were heavy with Capt. Perkins being the only officer in the Blue Line at 9.30am when it was being consolidated.[148]

The right assault battalion was the 1/13th (County of London) Battalion (Princess Louise's Kensington). They had the northern part of the village of Neuville Vitasse to attack and then to take Moss Trench on the far side of it as their Blue Line objective. Fortunately for the men of A and C Companies in the lead, 2nd Lt. Mortlock and a small body of D Company had managed to cut three lanes through the generally uncut wire the night before. Thus, when they attacked at 7.45am they were able to break through into the village and take their section of it by 8.20am and by 10.00am were reporting their presence in Moss Trench and in touch with the Rangers.[149] B Company, coming up into the village was directed to help the 8th Middlesex on the right as they were having some difficulties clearing the place. Casualties of five officers and 123 O.R.

---

145 A glance at the map and the actual ground shows that this delay does not make sense and is another example of questionable decision making at the planning stage.

146 The Company Sergeant Major, Charlie Clark, perished with many of his men on the wire. There is a very poignant set of headstones in London Cemetery, only a few hundred yards from the action, consisting of CSM Clark at the head of the row and many of the men of his company by his side, in death as they were in life.

147 Peebles is buried in nearby London Cemetery.

148 TNA: WO95/2954 War Diaries of 12th London Regiment (The Rangers); TNA: WO95/2951 War Diaries of H.Q. 168th Brigade.

149 Bailey, Sgt. O.F. and Hollier, Sgt. H.M., *'The Kensingtons': 13th London Battalion*, (Uckfield: Naval & Military reprint of 1935 edition), p. 112; TNA: WO95/2955 War Diaries of 13th London Regiment (Kensington).

were regarded as "slight in view of what was undoubtedly the most successful day's fighting the battalion had had since coming to France."[150]

56th (1st London) Division, 167th Brigade

167th Brigade had the rather complex task of taking the main part of the village of Neuville Vitasse. The task was made more complicated by the salient nature of the German positions with the windmill on the road to Mercatel being yet another strongpoint. The strongpoint at the windmill had to be removed and then the area of the village west of the Arras Road before a general wheel to the left to take the rest of the built up area to the Blue Line beyond and the Sugar Factory on the right.

Taking the left of this task was the 1/8th Middlesex Regiment, who were to brush the left flank of the salient, take the trenches in the main part of the village and dig in beyond The Oval. On a one company front with C Company leading the way at 7.45am, everything started well with the German front line being taken with few problems. As A Company took over, however, resistance became more difficult to overcome and a combination of machine gun fire and uncut wire held them up for some considerable time. They found a nest of machine guns in the village and only by careful flanking movements were they able to cause the small garrison to surrender, taking 68 prisoners and four machine guns in the process. It was now 11.00am but they could finally move out of the village on the far side and consolidate the Blue Line around The Oval.[151]

In front of the centre of the salient built around the village was the windmill. A previous failure to remove the forward strongpoint before 9 April meant that 1/3rd (City of London) Battalion (Royal Fusiliers) had to extend their attacking waves by two platoons in order that the mill could be attacked. They did this by allocating the reserve, B Company, to the task. In addition, a tank of No 10 Company, D Battalion, Heavy Brigade was allocated the role of assisting in the taking of the mill. When the attack went in at 7.45am C Company succeeded in taking Neuville Work without too much problem whilst the two platoons of B Company with the clearly threatening presence of the tank, which German sources say fired thorough the embrasure, forced the surrender of the mill, killing nine of the occupiers and capturing the remaining four.[152] D Company passed through the leading men and was successful in taking the next set of trenches and finally A Company attacked towards the Blue Line. The 1/3rd's diary says that apart from some machine gun fire from the left there was little opposition. What is a little disconcerting being that in the diary it says A Company attacked the Blue Line with two map coordinates given that would have put the company around 300 yards behind where the Blue Line was supposed to be and leaving out a small area of trenches just in front of the foremost trenches of the Hindenburg Line. That possible error will be returned to when the story is taken up later in the afternoon.

The two brigades of 56th Division had, as their opponents, almost exclusively the men of *I.R. 163's*, also of *17th Reserve Division*. 3rd Company under *Leutnant* Thüden was holding the forward lines including the mill and here they were either killed or taken prisoner, the second time in the space of six months that the company had been destroyed. The front line in the village was held by 11th Company which, after some fighting had to give way but a number of posts in the village did hold out for a while. Meanwhile in the northern area of the regiment the initial success of 8th and 7th companies at holding the British attack was broken by tanks flattening the wire and aiding

---

150   Bailey, Sgt. O.F. and Hollier, Sgt. H.M., *'The Kensingtons'*, p. 112.
151   TNA: WO95/295 War Diaries of 1/8th Middlesex Regiment; TNA: WO95/2947 War Diaries of H.Q. 167th Brigade.
152   Paland, Wolfgang, *Die Abenteuer des Musketiers Albert Krentel*, (Norderstedt: Books on Demand, 2015), p. 187.

12. - NEUVILLE-VITASSE (P.-de-C.) - La Fabrique

Neuville Vitasse Sugar
Factory. (Author)

2. - NEUVILLE-VITASSE (P.-de-C.). - Le Moulin

The mill near Neuville
Vitasse. (Author)

the attacking British in taking both trenches of the Hindenburg Line, held at this point by 12th Company. The support companies, 2nd and 4th now fought to hold onto the Hindenburg Line behind Neuville Vitasse, 2nd Company establishing a northern flank.[153]

At this point 56th Division must have been mightily pleased with its morning achievements. In spite of the difficulties caused by uncut wire and unsuppressed defenders in places, they had reached the Blue Line in good time to allow for following up troops to carry on with the advance to the Brown Line in the afternoon. Casualties had on the whole been light, only on the left of any significance. What must have weighed on Maj.-Gen Hull's mind though at this point was that the main Hindenburg Line had still to be assaulted in the later phase.

As the morning drew to a close the general situation could be described as a very positive one. It certainly was at 3rd Army Headquarters where congratulation messages were sent out to all corps commanders. The failure of 4th Canadian Division to take the highest point on Vimy Ridge was an irritation in the north but not one which threatened success in the major area of thrust, that of the units either side of the River Scarpe. The success of the other three Canadian divisions in securing the majority of the ridge, especially that area flanking 3rd Army, meant that the left flank of XVII Corps was secure. It was not clear, however, at corps or even divisional level, what was happening on Point du Jour with some confused messages about open flanks. The 4th British Division had been ordered up and all seemed ready for the next phase where for the first time a division would be pushed through another whilst in place. South of the Scarpe had also seen success although a report from 15th Division that it had timed the attack on the Brown Line for 2.00pm must have worried Corps H.Q. somewhat, given that this was late, and 37th Division were still to pass through on the part of that experiment. Would they still have time to fulfil their role? VII Corps had fulfilled its role fully at this point with a major obstacle overcome and troops actually through and almost behind the northern extremities of the Hindenburg Line. It was now in the positions required to finish their role for the day in securing the southern flank of VI Corps in its thrust to the East, the Brown Line and beyond to the Green. The right hand units of VII Corps, 30th and 21st Divisions, were now also about to enter the fray.

The Royal Flying Corps was met from the outset by the foul weather but gallantly put as many machines in the air as possible, although many bombing raids were cancelled. The primary tasks carried out were those of artillery spotting and reporting progress of the troops. Although the former seems to have been successful in terms of outcome the latter was less so. The Official History is very complimentary in its description of the efforts of Nos. 12, 13 and 16 Squadrons in reporting the movement of troops for the whole day.[154] In reality, many of the reports included in the corps diaries are vague and at times simply wrong and did not add a great deal to the information reaching the rear lines.

---

153 Paland, *Die Abenteuer des Musketiers Albert Krentel*, p. 187.
154 Jones, H. A. *The War in the Air, Volume 3*, p. 344.

7

The Unravelling

All was foretold me; naught
could I foresee;
but I learnt how the wind would sound
after these things should be
The New House

A reminder first of all about the plan and how time and the artillery fitted into it. This is important, as the effectiveness of being with the barrage has been demonstrated and how opposition was most subdued when troops were fully up with the exploding chaos in front of them. The next phase of the assault, which would take units to the Brown Line and possibly beyond had a timing of Zero + 6 hours 40 minutes. As Zero is taken as the initial attacks on the Black Line, a quick calculation has that time as 12.10pm. As the plan had occupation of the Blue Line by Zero + 3 hours there was a built-in pause of well over three hours. It has already been seen that this, in one or two cases, was not a long enough space of time after delays in the initial attacks. It is now the time to see how that begins to take its toll on the units following through.

Canadian Corps

Events on Vimy Ridge can be taken as a whole as, for the greater length of the line, the day's objectives had been taken and so it is mainly a story of digging in and a look at the reaction of the Germans. Only on Hill 145 and to the South, where the Brown Line was still to be taken, is there narrative of real interest. In 3rd Canadian Division areas the rest of the day was spent in consolidating, reconnaissance and watching out for German counter attacks. Only on the left of 3rd Division was there little time to rest as they had the open flank to the north and were at the start of the afternoon having to form a flank in Blunt Trench from the Red Line. The question was, when was 4th Division going to attack again and take Hill 145?

At the same time the orders were coming from the headquarters of *Reserve-Division 79* for a counter attack against the Canadians. This would involve the divisional reserve, namely *I/R.I.R. 262* but also *II/I.R. 118 and III/R.I.R. 34* which were underway from the rear. This attack was originally times for 3.00pm but then delayed until 5.00pm. Which side would succeed in attacking first?

Early in the afternoon it was decided to use two companies of 85th Canadian Infantry (Nova Scotia Highlanders) Battalion to attack again to clear the Germans off the high ground. A major complication and cause of difficulty for this exercise was the isolated pockets of Canadian troops of a variety of battalions who had established posts on and beyond the German front line. In order to keep some semblance of order to the attacks, given the presence of other units already forward it was decided to put the left company, in this case C Company under Capt. Crowell, under the command of the 87th Battalion and the right, D Company under Capt. Anderson, under command of 102nd Battalion. Only while meetings between officers of the various regiments were taking place was this idea abandoned and the two companies were to be under their own command. Meanwhile the afternoon was passing and eventually a start time of 6.45pm was decided upon with a short barrage of 12 minutes planned. Also earlier in the afternoon, at 2.00pm, two companies of 46th Canadian Infantry (South Saskatchewan) Battalion had been called forward from reserve and told to clear up the situation in Craters 1 to 7 as 1,2 and 3 were still thought to be in German hands and contact with 11th Brigade on the left was unclear. At 5.45pm A and B Company of the 46th advanced and although everything was unclear for some time messages eventually came back (the last at 1.45am the next day) that this operation had been successful. As troops of the 85th Battalion emerged from the left exit of Tottenham Tunnel to prepare for the attack a message came through from 11th Brigade that there was to be no barrage. The C.O. of the 85th, deciding it would be folly to attempt to change orders at this stage, waited to see if the men could get forward without the artillery. At 6.45pm they attacked and although coming under machine gun fire the attack was successful, taking Batter Trench and clearing it of all the remaining opposition. The officer commanding the attack, Capt. Anderson, pressed on beyond the objective and took hold of Basso Trench. This solid presence of a substantial body of men finally brought a halt to much of the sniping and machine gun fire from Hill 145 therefore as the day concluded; although the high point was not in the actual hands of the Canadians they had consolidated sufficiently to feel it was almost in their hands.

The German plan to counter attack had been overtaken by events. In the end the reserves had either to simply fill the line following the Canadian taking of the heights or to be pushed further south to help counter the advances of 1st and 2nd Canadian Divisions and to try and recapture Farbus and the area around. Thus it was that there were few, if any, extra men to hold back the Canadians at the end of the day. This left the isolated men of 1st to 4th Companies of *R.I.R. 261* with a hopeless task of trying to hold against the final Canadian attack and post by post men were either killed or forced to surrender.

This narrative now jumps southwards to pick up the story of 6th Canadian Infantry Brigade of 2nd Division as they wait on the Blue Line. Of the three battalions that had taken the Blue Line one, the 29th on the left was to continue onwards to take the Brown. Although this was timed for 12.26pm it was not until 1.30pm that the troops, D Company, could move forward. They did so close under the barrage and took hold of the trenches on the near edge of and in the centre of, Bois de la Ville with outposts on the Brown Line running along the north-eastern edge.[1] On their right the whole of 27th Canadian Infantry (City of Winnipeg) Battalion had come through the lines during the morning losing some casualties to shellfire. The barrage lifted at 12.42pm[2] and they followed into the German lines, A, B and C Companies all attacking and taking the gun pits that lined the Bois de la Ville. These companies consolidated a little up the slope from Farbus but D Company, coming up behind moved through into the village, all the way to the railway line. Finding their own barrage falling in this area they moved back but established three platoon strength outposts quite a way beyond the Brown Line. Joining into the attack, after gaining permission, was Bandsman 'Paddy' Smith, who played the regimental march on his piccolo as he went in with the leading waves. Unfortunately, he was killed at the objective and any grave subsequently lost and therefore he is commemorated on the Vimy Memorial. The remainder of the day was spent consolidating the line and avoiding sniper fire that was persistent. There was

---

1   Library and Archives, Canada, war diaries – 29th Canadian Infantry Battalion.
2   There are some strange timings reported for this final phase of the day. It seems that in places the ones given in original orders were not completely adhered to; however, this does not seem to have had any adverse effect upon any of the attacks on the Brown Line. What must be identified though is that timings for the barrage seem to have been adjusted – something that seemed to be impossible on many other areas of the front this day.

a plan at one point for D Company to attack the railway embankment where it had been seen that Germans were collecting but this was cancelled.[3]

On the right of 6th Brigade, 1st Canadian Division had been left successfully digging in on the Blue Line. Of the three initial attacking battalions it was the task of 3rd and 4th Battalions to continue the attack to the Brown Line. On the left 4th Battalion moved off at 12.26pm and was followed closely by B and D Companies, C Company mopping up. The advance moved forward steadily, C Company mopping up in Bois Carré; the wire being found uncut bit it was cleared under covering fire of the Colt Machine Gun Section that had been sent up with the attack. Whilst waiting for the barrage to move on Lt. Harrison and Lt Salsbury moved through the barrage and found the gun pits in Farbus Wood evacuated.[4] They chalked the battalion's name on the guns and returned. When the barrage moved further on towards the railway Farbus Wood was then occupied, including the already 'claimed' battery position; "The German retirement from this battery position was so hasty that the officers [sic] lunch was left ready on the table in their dugout. It was of course promptly consumed."[5] German rifle fire began to die down as the afternoon wore on and the remainder of the day was spent consolidating the position on the high ground and calling down artillery on any German movement that looked as if it could be preparations for a counter attack.[6] Also at 12.26pm 3rd Battalion moved off under the barrage towards its objectives on the Brown Line. Their own artillery was described as, "very heavy and seems to be very effective".[7] By just after 2.00pm the Brown Line had been taken although the news from D Company on the right was disturbing as they could not make contact with the Scots of 51st Highland Division. B Company was therefore ordered to form a flank along the sunken road that goes south east from The Commandant's House. Similar to 4th Battalion, they were able to push through Farbus Wood and thus have complete control over the lower ground in front of them. As evening approached and some possible counter attack scares had been seen off with artillery the remaining worry, "is that our flank is left absolutely in the air."[8] The battalions estimated casualties for the day were said to be around the 150.

The possible counter attacks consisted of units of *1st Bavarian Reserve Division, R.I.R. 263* and also part of *I/R.I.R. 225* and the first reports were that they were making progress but then around 9 it became clear that this was false and that artillery had prevented any kind of coordinated attack, confirming the Canadian reports.

By the end of the day then it could be said to have been one of major achievement. To all intents and purposes the Germans had been thrown off Vimy Ridge by the combined forces of all four Canadian divisions. Yes, there remained work to be done the next morning on Hill 145 but Canadian Corps could announce to everyone that the job had been more or less done and the Ridge taken. It would never, in this war, be in German hands again.

51st (Highland) Division

The question to be answered now, having seen the actions of 1st Canadian Brigade, is why their flank was open. The morning had left the division on their right, 51st Division, on the Blue Line

---

3   Library & Archives, Canada, war diaries 27th Canadian Battalion RG 9, Militia and Defence, Series III-D-3, Volume 4935, Reel T-10738-10739 File: 423.

4   The emplacements for these guns can still be seen in the woods if you follow a track into what is now called Bois de Berthonval.

5   Library and Archives, Canada, war diaries, 4th Canadian Battalion.

6   Library and Archives, Canada, war diaries, 4th Canadian Battalion.

7   Library and Archives, Canada, war diaries, 3rd Canadian Battalion.

8   Library and Archives, Canada, war diaries, 3rd Canadian Battalion.

and readying themselves for the next phase in the afternoon. What happened? On the left of the division A and C Companies of the 4th Gordon Highlanders had already had to intervene and support the rest of the battalion in taking the Blue Line. Their diary then talks of the fact that as soon as they left the Blue Line to advance to the Brown, all bar one platoon lost direction and veered off to the right; it gives as an explanation for this that 7th Argyll & Sutherland Highlanders were responsible for direction! "They [7th A. S. H.] lost direction however and pushed on to ZEHNER WEG (in 152nd Brig. Area) C Coy and three platoons of A Company following."[9] The diary of 7th Argylls is a picture of innocence. It describes C & D Companies helping out in taking the Blue Line and then at the appointed time moving off further. It then mentions that 152nd Brigade on their right was held up before the Blue Line and that there was heavy machine gun fire from *Zehner Weg*. It goes on; "They swung round attacked & captured three lines of trenches."[10] As they eventually ended up facing south in Tommy Trench it must mean they took Allgauer Trench, then the portion of Tommy Trench that has a north west/south east orientation, swung round and took the other portion of Tommy Trench, proudly proclaimed all the captures they had made, but of course they were not in the Brown Line. Touch was made with 152nd Brigade, the line consolidated and even a claim that patrols were "pushed out to near the railway".[11] An astonishing assertion when they were not even up to the Brown Line. The only acknowledgment of their mistake is in the diary for the next day when they say that patrols found "our Brown Line objectives to be strongly held by the enemy".[12] Nowhere do they acknowledge that things had not gone well. Evidence that they really did think they were in the correct position is to be found in the divisional diary which has reports at 6.30pm that 154th Brigade are on the Brown Line and in touch with the Canadians. All the reports talk of the platoon that had held direction and were in the Brown Line alongside the Canadians. If this had really been the case, why were the Canadians so adamant that they had no contact with the Scots? The divisional after-battle report blandly states the troops lost direction and were in the wrong trench and that nobody was aware of the situation until first light on the next day. What forms of liaison with the Canadians on their left had been set up? Surely at a divisional level the Canadians should have been saying "where are you" to 51st Division. There is no evidence in any papers of this being the case. This can be seen as a prime example of poor inter-unit liaison communication at this point in the war. This was an inter-Army boundary which actually makes it even more important that some kind of system should have been in place. Fault on the slopes of the ridge must lay with 4th Gordon Highlanders. To say that a neighbouring unit is responsible for direction is very wrong. Visibility is never mentioned as a problem, in spite of the weather being a mix of sleet and rain. The Canadians on their right are on higher ground and it would not have been difficult, had the units been cohesive, to keep with them. There is no mention of casualties to the two companies before they move on towards the Brown Line, already having had to fight at the Blue. If they had substantial officer casualties that would have made the final task that much more difficult, but it is not clear where and when casualties occurred. Even more damning for the Gordons is the experience of Lt. MacNaughton who, in command of two sub-sections of 153rd Machine Gun Company, managed to not only stay in the correct direction but get his guns all the way to the Brown Line. He even made contact with the Canadians and walked down the German trench some distance without meeting anyone. He only had to withdraw the next morning when he

---

9   TNA: WO95/2886 War Diaries of the 4th Gordon Highlanders.
10   TNA: WO95/2886 War Diaries of the 1/7th Argyll & Sutherland Highlanders.
11   TNA: WO95/2886 War Diaries of the 1/7th Argyll & Sutherland Highlanders.
12   TNA: WO95/2886 War Diaries of the 1/7th Argyll & Sutherland Highlanders.

found Germans had re-entered the trench and were nearby.[13] These will have been men of *Bayerisches I.R. 2* who, having been forced into a rapid retreat towards Bailleul then found that they could, as part of *1st Bavarian Reserve Division's* attempt to counter attack, simply move into the trenches of the Point du Jour Line.

If the reader recalls, the 1/5th Seaforth Highlanders, having had to add its second two companies to the fight for the Blue Line had only obtained that line by 2.15pm. So there were now two depleted companies, already well behind schedule, with the daunting task of going onto the Brown Line. The diary is very clear about what happened next. They moved forward and took *Regiments Weg* and that was it. The troops stopped at that trench line, with no mention of any attempt to get further forward, they set about consolidating where they were. In his report the C.O. Lt Col. Scott makes no mention of any attempt to get further forward or why he stopped where he was.[14] Nor is there any comment by division that day questioning the position and asking why the attack was not pushed on. The clue as to the decision comes in the report by 1/8th Argyll & Sutherland Highlanders on the right. They had also not managed to gain the Blue Line at the appointed time and when advancing towards the Brown found fire from Elect Trench to be heavy; "It was impossible to get on during daylight, as the ground was absolutely open, and the barrage irretrievably lost."[15] Why then, with such a delay, was there not a rescheduling of the barrage? The above is the only comment in all the diaries about the barrage which clearly began its forward movement again at 12.10pm, as scheduled, moved over the ground between the Blue Line and the Brown Line and beyond by sometime after 1.30pm. By the time either of the forward battalions of the 152nd Brigade left the Blue Line it was long gone. The answer lies in the communications received by Brigade H.Q. during the morning. At 11.45am, "Blue Line apparently captured". 12 noon, "Blue Line appears to be held by 5th Sea. Hrs. & 8th A&S Hrs."[16] Only at 2.51pm is a message seen that the Blue Line is definitely captured. The over-optimistic reports about the Blue Line had not led to anyone questioning that the men were going to be able to move forward with the barrage when it began. However, "apparently" and "appears to be" also did not lead anyone to send out men to confirm the reports, a serious error.

The day finished then with 51st Division having gained ground but not to where it was planned to be. The O.C. of 51st Division, Maj.-Gen Harper had, as was seen in a previous chapter, made the decision to go against Corps orders and attack with two brigades, each with an extra battalion from the remaining brigade. Only eight battalions were used in the assault, the two attached from 153rd Brigade were never used. The remaining two from that brigade, due to move forward and take the Green Line, never moved, even though it was reported that the Brown Line was taken.[17] Harper's decision had gone badly wrong with a smaller number of troops failing to take the Black Line in good enough time, leading to losing the barrage attacking the Blue Line and eventually to no barrage whatsoever for the attack on the Brown Line with already weakened and exhausted troops.

---

13   Falls, *Military Operations, France and Belgium 1917 Vol. 1*, p. 236.

14   TNA: WO95/2862 War Diaries of 152nd Infantry Brigade, report by 1/5th Seaforth Highlanders on operations 9 April 1917.

15   TNA: WO95/2862 War Diaries of 152nd Infantry Brigade, report by 1/8th Argyll & Sutherland Highlanders on operations 9 April 1917.

16   TNA: WO95/2862 War Diaries of 152nd Infantry Brigade.

17   There is absolutely no mention of these two battalions in the brigade or divisional diaries for the first day. With the Divisional H.Q. informed that the Brown Line was secures, why were these units not sent forward?

34th Division

On the left of 34th Division, the Tyneside Irish were in a similar position to the Scots on their left. They had not managed to take the Blue Line until well into the afternoon and in spite of urgent orders from Brigade H.Q. that the leading troops, whatever unit they belong to, should advance with the barrage, it was not until 1.30pm that any move was made. By this time the barrage was gone and the result was inevitable; the troops of 27th and 26th Northumberland Fusiliers (4th and 3rd Tyneside Irish) barely left the trenches of the Blue Line before coming under heavy machine gun and rifle fire and subsequently returned forthwith to their starting point. Brigade H.Q. quickly came to the conclusion that only a properly formed (i.e. with artillery cooperation) attack on the Brown Line had any hope of succeeding.[18]

The Tyneside Scottish were in a much better position to the right of the Irish. The 21st and 22nd Northumberland Fusiliers (2nd and 3rd Tyneside Scottish) had managed, against strong opposition to gain the Blue Line with sufficient time for the following up battalions to come up and form up for the assault on the Brown Line. On the left the 23rd Northumberland Fusiliers (4th Tyneside Scottish) were able to move at 8.00am up to the Blue Line in artillery formation with very few casualties, a distinct contrast to the experiences of their Irish counterparts. Shaking out into line for the further advance the 23rd then found their own barrage rather scattered, a good example of how much more difficult a creeping barrage was at more extreme ranges; some of their own men being hit. They also could see that their left flank was in the air due to the failure of the Tyneside Irish to get forward. This, however, did not halt the battalion which simply kept on going. The next problem was that the wire in front of the first set of trenches (referred to as the Western Brown Line in the unit diary) was think and uncut. Bravely weathering the sniping that was still prevalent, Capt. T.E. Heron MC calmly cut a lane through the wire, the gap and his fine example allowing the men to get into these first trenches with relative ease. The Germans, however, were not about to give up the eastern Brown Line as easily. In addition, the barrage had moved on, giving the defenders a little time to reorganise. Small unit tactics got the 23rd near to the line which they then rushed with the bayonet. Capt. Heron, 2nd Lt. S. C. Kerridge and 2nd Lt. F Ashworth were all wounded, the latter succumbing to his wounds later.[19]

On the right, 20th Northumberland Fusiliers (1st Tyneside Scottish) had a similar experience, gaining both of the Brown Line trenches but not without fairly substantial total casualties of 289 all ranks, around a 50 percent casualty rate.[20] 2nd Lt. Jack Lakeman was wounded in the head almost immediately, later dying in hospital at Le Touquet with his parents by his side.[21]

The 101st Brigade was left in control of the Blue Line and awaiting the troops to come through. On the left these were men of the 10th Lincolnshire Regiment, the 'Grimsby Chums'. The battalion were only ordered to move off at 9.30am, strange when it has already been noted that the Tynesiders moved at 8.00am. Due to this relatively late start and the extremely muddy conditions it was a battle simply to keep up to time. An interesting note in the unit diary here is that in advancing to the Blue Line they were able to pick their way through the German barrage because it always fell in exactly the same spot. Managing to reach the Blue Line shortly before noon the Chums just had time to form up and make ready to advance at 12.16pm. Concerned about their right where there seemed to be only a small number of 15th Royal Scots, the Chums advanced under their barrage, veering a little to their right because of this apparent gap. They reached the Joke Line 30 minutes later without encountering too much opposition; however, they did then

18   TNA: WO95/2467 War Diaries of 103rd (Tyneside Irish) Brigade.
19   TNA: WO95/2463 War Diaries of 23rd Northumberland Fusiliers (4th Tyneside Scottish).
20   TNA: WO95/2462 War Diaries of 20th Northumberland Fusiliers (1st Tyneside Scottish).
21   Sheen & Stewart, *Tyneside Scottish*, p. 142.

come under fire from a gun battery not far away to their front. The wire in front of the Brown Line, here Jemmy Trench, was found to be uncut and there was considerable delay while lanes were cut. Fortunately, there was not a great deal of opposition at this point, only sniping, therefore with some casualties but not serious, the first of the two trenches could be taken. The barrage had moved on and the leading companies very mixed but the second line, and thus the Pont du Jour position, was taken "without any serious opposition".[22] Moving beyond the second trench line the Chums established themselves on the lane from that line down to the main Arras –Gavrelle road, thus being the first unit along the line to reach the Green Line as laid out in orders. The question now to be asked was what had happened to the 15th Royal Scots Regiment on the right? The Operational Orders for the brigade are quite clear that the 15th Royal Scots were the "right rear" battalion of the assault, the equivalent of the 10th Lincolns on the left. When, however, you read the unit diary of the Scots,[23] it talks of the Lincolns being the reserve unit and that it was the Royal Scots' duty to support the attacks on the Black and Blue Lines. During the morning this is what they did, so that by lunchtime and on the Blue Line they had a mere 100 or so men remaining to assault the Brown Line. This is why the Lincolns were so perplexed as to the small numbers of Scots to their right. Fortunately, most of the serious work in moving forward to the Pont du Jour Line was done by the Lincolns and eventually the 15th Royal Scots formed a strongpoint on the right, around the area of the road, linking with 9th Division next to them. Reading the diaries, it is clear that the C.O. of the 15th Royal Scots either did not fully understand, or chose to ignore, the Operational Orders he had from brigade. The latter is more likely. Had there been greater German resistance on the Brown Line where the wire was uncut could have made this course of action a very costly one for the division, especially for the Lincolns.

It was somewhat fortunate, therefore, that the scattering of the *Bayerische I.R. 4* in the early attacks and the reserves being too far away meant that the Brown Line was thinly held by the remnants of this Bavarian regiment. Had one of the reserve battalions been on hand and up onto the Point du Jour before the afternoon it is very likely that the whole of the 34th Division would have failed to make the Brown Line

As the day closed, 34th Division was in the unhealthy position of being in two sections with a vast hole between them. With its left flank so uncovered the Tyneside Scottish were forced to push out blocks in the Brown Line trenches. More seriously, there was an opportunity for German counter attacks to exploit the gap behind 102nd Brigade. This threat never materialised but remained ever present throughout the night until it could be closed the next day. It seems clear that the eyes of the *1st Bavarian Reserve Division* were fixed on the Vimy heights and it was towards those and the dug in Canadians that their attempts to form for a counter attack were concentrated. Had they noticed the gap between 1st and 3rd Army and been able to move into it, the result would have been a very serious situation indeed.

The decision to attack three brigades across and committing all 12 battalions to a task with no reserve had led to a mix of success and failure. Success where the initial attacks had gone well but failure where the support units suffered from being pulled into early actions to then be without the strength to progress to the final objective. Communications also were lacking in that a bombardment programme could not be altered even though it was clear by mid-morning that the Tyneside Irish were not going to be up to time for the afternoon phase. With no barrage to support the outcome was a forgone conclusion. The importance of the success in taking at least the southern part of the Point Du Jour high ground can be measured though by the fact that the important

22   TNA: WO95/2457 War Diaries of 10th Lincolnshire Regiment.
23   TNA: WO95/2457 War Diaries of 15th Royals Scottish Regiment.

manoeuvre to the south, passing 4th Division through, could be undertaken with a secure left flank.

9th (Scottish) Division

Having reached the Blue Line successfully, the two battalions of 27th Brigade, 11th Royal Scots on the left and 9th Scottish Rifles on the right, then had the task of moving onto the Brown Line. The brigade diary very succinctly describes what follows:

> The attack was a procession, and happily so for the heavy wire protecting the Brown Line was untouched. Passage through it was either cut, or affected through gaps of the enemy's making.[24]

A party of 6th K.O.S.B., clearly following up the successful march in support, were seen to rush a German machine gun post and demolish their breakfast. The Brown Line was taken and posts pushed out beyond; eight machine guns that had come forward in support were installed. Here the diary becomes critical in the wait that was now forced upon them by the battery timetable and that of 4th Division which was to pass through. They had no complaints about the barrage so far, bar for one gun falling short continually. What they now saw, however, was that the Germans were so disorganised that pushing onto the Green Line immediately would have been very effective.

> I confess to a very strong inclination, almost amounting to decision, to push my Brigade through the Brown Line protective barrage in order to seize the Green Line, thereby denying the enemy the two hours respite allowed by the programme.[25]

The aggressive Brigadier F.A. Maxwell, commanding 27th Brigade, made a very bold statement regarding the idea of standing protective barrages in that they, "Kill initiative and exploitation."[26] This opinion is worth bearing in mind when the use of artillery is discussed later. The brigade was to withdraw once 4th Division has passed through but Maxwell decided to keep his troops on the Brown Line for a while longer when he heard from 11th Brigade in 4th Division that they were "uneasy".[27] In fact, the German reserve battalion, *I/Bayersiche I.R. 8* was just getting below the Point du Jour heights as the British appeared above. It might not have been the walk over that Maxwell imagined. On the other hand, had 27th Brigade disrupted the German reserve battalion as it marched in and given the chaotic state of the hostile artillery and reserves a long way off, the question of the standing barrage remains.

Although the attacking units of the South African Brigade had suffered something like 50 percent casualties in taking the Blue Line, their task was done. The 1st and 2nd South African Regiments were tasked with taking the Brown Line and they advanced on time and with a good protective barrage. They also found the wire uncut but with little opposition they were able to progress by using the gaps the Germans had left. About 30 prisoners were taken and by three o'clock the South Africans had been relieved by troops of 4th Division and retired to the Black Line. Both battalions with casualties of around 90 of all ranks must have felt that this was a job well done with relatively little cost. The comment was made, however, that had there been more

---

24   TNA: WO95/1769 War Diaries of 27th Brigade.
25   TNA: WO95/1769.
26   TNA: WO95/1769.
27   TNA: WO95/1769.

opposition where the wire was uncut casualties would have been heavy as a subsequence.[28] Major Symmes of 2nd Battalion was one of the more senior fatalities.[29]

The two battalions tasked by 26th Brigade for the subsequent advance to the Brown Line had differing fortunes on their advance to the Blue Line. On the left, 5th Cameron Highlanders had a straightforward advance with few casualties, not being pulled into the fighting around St. Laurent-Blangy. On the right, 10th Argyll & Sutherland Highlandersfound themselves embroiled in the fighting as they advanced and subsequently were weakened as they reached the Blue Line. Notwithstanding their losses the 10th held pace with their stronger neighbours on the left as both advanced on the Brown Line against very little opposition. The 5th Camerons' diary passes the advance off with few words, the Argyll's merely commenting on the effectiveness of the barrage. The latter battalion stormed the village of Athies, described as fairly intact before the barrage rolled through it, walls collapsing in front of the men as they advanced behind the exploding shells. Both battalions consolidated the Brown Line and were subsequently relieved around 3.00pm by the support units of 4th Division as they came up. The other reserves of *14th Bavarian Division, III/Bayerische I.R. 25* and *III/Bayerische I.R. 4* were tasked with counter attacking but as they came up, in a rather scattered way, they simply met the advancing troops of their opponents and anything other than attempting to stem the tide became out of the question. The last remaining possibility for the Germans was *I.R. 31* of *18th Division* which started the day in Douai. It was all a question of how long they would take to get to the front after the first elements set off at around 11.00am.[30]

The 9th Division felt very satisfied with their day's work. All along the line after some hard initial fighting the Germans had in many cases ceased to put up a fight of any kind. Although there were cases of 4th Division troops advancing a little too quickly the challenge of passing a whole division through the advanced positions of another was working well. The only major criticism made by staff of 9th Division being that the advance could have been carried out more quickly; the rate of the advancing barrage deemed too slow and the pauses between each phase consequently stifling initiative and steady progression.

4th Division

One of the original regular divisions to arrive in France in August 1914[31] the unit had obviously by this stage in the war lost the vast majority of those initial troops. It had, on the other hand, had a fairly static composition with only a few changes in regiments within the brigades and therefore was a well-trained and experienced unit.

The question now was how successful could this division be in moving through the 9th Division and carrying the attack forward to the ambitious Green Line. The division moved forward from west of Arras during the early part of the assault to their assembly points. On a two brigade front, 11th Brigade left and 12th Brigade right, units began to move from thosepoints some hours after the initial assault, namely at 10.00am. The plan had said four hours after Zero but there was some delay, mentioned in the brigade diary as news was awaited that the Blue Line had been taken, a strange decision given that the time for messages to get back almost automatically built in an element of delay but reflecting the nervousness of command in what was a totally new

28   TNA: WO95/1777 War Diaries of South African Brigade.
29   Major Symmes, originally buried in the railway cutting, can now be found in Highland Cemetery, Roclincourt.
30   Berhmann & Brandt, *Die Osterschlacht bei Arras 1917 II. Teil*, p. 126.
31   4th Division disembarked in France after the other B.E.F. formations, but was in time for the majority of its units to take part on the Battle of Le Cateau on 23 August.

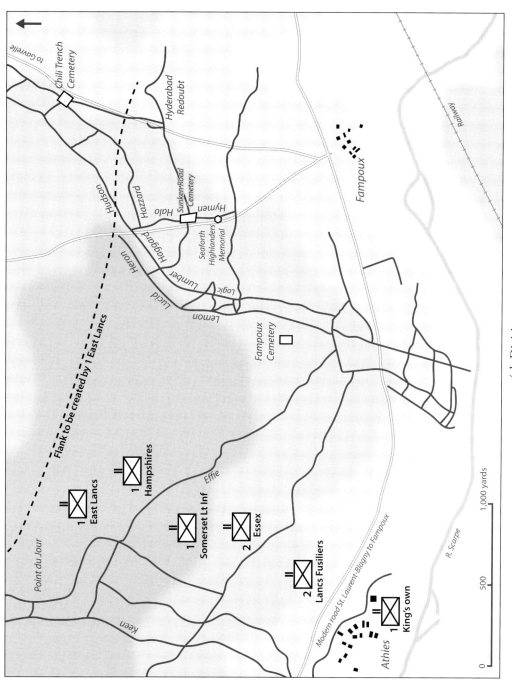

4th Division.

manoeuvre.[32] 1st Hampshire Regiment, on 11th Brigade's left, marched in column of route all the way to the Blue Line, waited there an hour and then moved in artillery formation to its assembly position just behind the Brown Line. One company was badly hit by a shell on its way up to the Blue Line suffering 17 casualties but otherwise the lack of any rifle or machine gun fire made it clear to the Hampshires that the Brown Line was safely in British hands. Following another hour wait, at 3.03pm, the battalion then began its move towards the Green Line, following the barrage closely. The Germans fled at this renewed attack and although the wire in front of the German Lines was uncut the lack of any real opposition or fire meant that men could cut gaps and get through. Trenches taken by the battalion at this point were Heron and Hudson in the front line with Haggard and Hazzard behind. The leading companies were in their positions between 3.50pm and 4.05pm. Losses in this attack amounted to three officers wounded and six O.R. as casualties. In fact, for the whole day (bearing in mind the 17 on the way up) casualties amounted to four officers wounded, 12 O.R. killed and 47 wounded.[33] This advance was, of course, not matched by anything from the division on their left. It was the task of the supporting regiment, 1st East Lancashire, to create and hold a northern flank. The very wet but good-humoured men of the East Lancs were cheered up as they moved forward through the northern outskirts of Arras by the sight of so many German prisoners passing back so early in the battle. In their diary the delay until 10.00am to move forward is excused by the possible need to support 34th Division if they had such a need. These various time comments are difficult to clarify as operation orders do not exist in 4th Division and 11th Brigade diaries; however, 12th Brigade orders are in their diary and they have a timetable that has movement from assembly points at 10.00am so it seems that the later start may have been part of the plan anyway. What is clear though from 4th Division diaries is that they awaited Corps command to move forward which came at 10.00am. So the timetables so exactly laid out in orders in fact came down to decisions from above. The unit diary describes the move forward as "more like a route march than moving up close behind the front assaulting troops."[34] When they were up to the railway embankment, however, casualties were taken with shellfire killing a number and wounding others. Up to this point the units had noticed no more than 20 dead on the field of both sides; regarded as remarkable when the strength of the positions was considered. Next stop was Keen trench to await the next move forward. There was a long communication trench running from Point Du Jour towards Fampoux, Effie Trench and when the battalion moved forward at 3.10pm D Company were tasked with making this line secure as support whilst A & B Companies were to move to the flank and begin to dig a trench to protect the left flank of the divisional assault; all companies moving in artillery formation. As A Company crested the ridge on the right of the battalion front to begin digging in, a battery of German guns was seen still in position. This was charged by Lt Charney and his No. 4 Platoon and despite taking casualties from a shell landing in their midst, the guns were captured. The company completed digging in by around 6.30pm having suffered approximately 26 casualties. B Company had a similar experience on the left, suffering casualties as they completed the digging of their section of the flanking trench, the company commander, Lt. P.E. Argyle being killed. At around 4.45pm one platoon was almost entirely wiped out when a shell landed amongst them. Then soon afterwards, whilst visiting B Company, the battalion C.O., Lt.-Col C.J. Burke, his orderly and a substantial number of the platoon in the area were killed by a shell.[35] In spite of these losses the

---

32   TNA: WO95/1791 War Diaries of 11th Brigade.

33   TNA: WO95/1495 War Diaries of 1st Hampshire Regiment.

34   TNA: WO95/1498 War Diaries of 1st East Lancashire Regiment.

35   Lt.-Col. Charles James Burke came out to France in August of 1914 in command of No. 2 Squadron, Royal Flying Corps and was actually 2nd Battalion Royal Irish Regiment attached to the East Lancs. Originally buried with others in a plot near Effie Trench, he is now in Point Du Jour Cemetery nearby.

job of digging in was completed by reserve platoons moving up. The remainder of the day was spent consolidating both Effie Trench and the new line running west to east joining the Green Line of 34th Division with that of the rest of 11th Brigade.[36] On the right of 11th Brigade were the 1st Battalion Somerset Light Infantry whose task was to take the trench system of Lemon, Lucid, Logic and Lumber and also to then support 1st Rifle Brigade who were to pass through and take the Hyderabad Redoubt which lay beyond. The Somersets had a similar experience to others in the area, moving up through the various positions to eventually reach the Brown Line in very good time. They also found the wire uncut in front of the first German line and had to force their way through but covering fire seemed to be the last straw for many Germans who surrendered or ran back, coming under Lewis gun fire as they did so. By the time it came to take the second of the German lines all resistance had ceased except for German artillery who continued to fire from the Gavrelle direction. The battalion had lost two officers killed and 50 other ranks killed or wounded, again relatively light losses for what had been gained.[37] The 1st Rifle Brigade had set off from the Brown Line 25 minutes after the Somersets having had no problems up to then advancing from Arras. They did suffer some casualties from artillery fire when they had to get through the uncut wire, where the Somersets had only been able to cut some paths, so bunching clearly led to more problems. B Company was dropped off at the sunken road where they cleared Hymen and Halo trenches. The other assaulting companies, C and A, then attacked Hyderabad Redoubt. The wire was again uncut but there were two gaps that allowed troops to rush the German position. No. 11 Platoon preceded their rush on the position by kicking a football into the German trenches. The position was taken but putting outposts out and consolidation was hampered by sniping and machine gun fire from the Gavrelle – Rœux road. This became so bad that the outposts were brought in and the consolidation was limited to the redoubt itself with blocks being put out in the communication trenches running north and east from there. As the light faded the Germans did launch a counter attack from the direction of Gavrelle but this was beaten off. The Germans then dug in, forming a semi-circle around the redoubt about 200 to 400 yards away. Casualties, mainly from artillery being targeted on the redoubt were two officers killed with four wounded and 123 O.R. in total.[38]

12th Brigade was tasked with advancing the right flank and gain the Green Line from Hyderabad Redoubt down to the river, to the east of the village of Fampoux. They advanced to the Brown Line behind 9th Division, complaining that a delay in front of them at the Blue Line meant that casualties were incurred whilst waiting in the open behind the line.[39] It is difficult to determine the correctness of this statement. 9th Division advanced with the barrage towards the Brown Line and therefore it is difficult to see how they could have been tardy in their timings,

It is more likely that 12th Brigade troops, in their eagerness to advance, gained the back of the Blue Line too early and therefore had to wait. On the left, 2nd Essex Regiment, having marched to the original front line then took up artillery formation and advanced to the Blue Line which, after a short wait to allow the formation ahead to get on, they crossed at 1.10pm. Reaching the Brown Line at around 2.10pm they deployed into waves and fixed bayonets for the attack. Promptly at 3.10 the attack started with the unit diary emphasising that, "hostile artillery was NIL [capitals in the original]." After capturing four 5.9" guns and a 77mm gun the troops reached the wire, as elsewhere uncut, at 3.40pm. Three men were killed by two machine guns although most other

36   TNA: WO95/1498 War Diaries of 1st East Lancashire Regiment.
37   Majendie D.S.O., Major V.H.B., *A History of the 1st Battalion Somerset Light Infantry – 1 July 1916 to the end of the War,* (Taunton: Goodman & Son, Phoenix Press, 1921), pp. 32-34.
38   TNA: WO95/1496 War Diaries of 1st Rifle Brigade.
39   TNA: WO95/1502 War Diaries of 12th Brigade Headquarters.

Feuchy after the offensive. (IWM Q5200)

Germans were seen running away. Good cooperative work with Lewis gunners advancing firing from the hip silenced the machine guns and the battalion could enter and clear the German lines. The advance to the Green Line could then begin at 4.10pm and the sunken road up to Hyderabad Redoubt was successfully taken. With only 11 OR killed, 63 wounded and four missing plus one wounded officer this can clearly be seen as a very successful attack. The 2nd Lancashire Fusiliers were to the right of the Essex men and when their unit diary for the day is read it is clear that by this point almost all serious opposition up to the Green Line had ceased. Very few casualties were experienced by the Lancashires as they moved up to the Brown Line and similarly it seems that the taking of the Green Line led to similarly low losses. 13 guns and around 50 prisoners were taken and only when patrols were pushed out beyond the sunken road were German machine guns and serious opposition encountered. This forced the unit to dig their Green Line trench just beyond the road and not further to the east. Total casualties for the day were two officers wounded, eight O.R. killed or died of wounds, one OR missing and 53 wounded.[40] One point made in the Lancashire's diary was reflected also in that of the right battalion of the brigade, the 1st King's Own (Royal Lancaster) Regiment. Both comment on the enormous morale boost that was created by the arrival of large numbers of German prisoners as the men awaited their move to the front. St-Lauren-Blangy was clearly still the target of shelling as, unlike the units north of them, the King's Own suffered quite a number of casualties, 43 all told, including two officers killed, whilst passing through the village. They then moved to behind 9th Division, catching them up for a time, before

---

40   TNA: WO95/1507 War Diaries of 2nd Lancashire Fusiliers.

halting in Athies at 1.35pm. Advancing then to the German 4th Line with very little opposition they captured 60 to 70 troops and seven guns. Their role at an end for the day, they dug in to the west edge of Fampoux and became the brigade reserve.[41] This then left the actual taking of the village to the 2nd West Riding Regiment. Leaving Arras at 10.45am the West Ridings reached the Blue Line at 2.40pm and remained there a while during the 9th Division assault. Passing through the King's Own they took the village without a great deal of problem although there was heavy machine gunfire from the southern banks of the Scarpe. Some Germans also had to be bombed out of some of the houses in the village. The brigade War Diary complains that there were some problems in the village due to their own heavy artillery but interestingly the unit diary makes no mention of it. What both agree upon, however, is that further progress was not possible due to machine gun fire from the front. The West Riding diary is clear that, "Further advance without artillery preparation was impracticable."[42] With casualties of one officer and six O.R. killed, six officers and 16 OR wounded with two OR missing and a relatively intact battalion just behind in reserve, it was not for lack of numbers that a further advance was not attempted. The divisional diary tells of machine guns being brought up and installed in the upper stories of some of the house in Fampoux, then firing with good effect on the Germans both in front of them and to the south of the river; also of five Stokes mortars brought forward, but out of range of suitable targets. Given this level of possible support for an attack the question could be raised as to the possibilities of an advance even without full artillery fire. They were at present in the sunken road that would become infamous over the next days and even weeks of the offensive.

It is only when German sources are investigated that it becomes clear what a precarious position the defenders were in by the end of the day in front of 4th Division. It will be recalled that the last possible unit to get up that day, *I.R. 31*, was underway. The time to get forward meant that the first units of that regiment began to appear on the front at around the same time as 4th Division began their attack. The straightforward nature of their advance can then be understood but also the fact that all the plans of *I.R. 31* to counter attack came to naught. They were then told to man the 3rd positions but these were exactly the ones now occupied by the British. *II/I.R. 31* was ordered to side step to the north and ensure that a connection with *1st Bavarian Reserve-Division* had been made, not easy in the rapidly fading light. By the end of the day all three battalions of *I.R. 31* were in the line, each with just one company in reserve, covering almost one and a half kilometres of front. The opposition mentioned by the British units in front of them was that thin, but they did not realise the fact.

Given their objectives for the day 4th Division must have been very satisfied with the position as darkness approached. All the objectives had been reached and all of their units were in good shape, casualties being relatively light and one brigade in reserve that had moved up to the Brown Line without doing anything else than act as carriers during the day. With three or four hours of light remaining was there not an option for an even bolder move and to continue the attack? It shall be seen in the next chapter that the only difference the next day, when further attacks were made, is that the Germans had had the whole night and morning to recover, bring up reserves and make the task even more difficult. The only instructions received from XVII Corps Headquarters during the day were firstly to have a brigade support 9th Division in taking the Brown Line which was not required and nothing then until one was received at 12.50am the next morning saying, "All Divisions will push onto GREEN Line on tenth and consolidate those positions which give

---

41   TNA: WO95/1506 War Diaries of King's Own (Royal Lancaster).
42   TNA: WO95/1508 War Diaries of 2nd West Riding Regiment; TNA: WO95/1446 War Diaries of General Staff, 4th Division.

best observation."[43] Thus, with only one German regiment in front, rapidly digging themselves in as they were not in a previously formed position, 4th Division received no morning orders.

15th (Scottish) Division

The timetable was not being adhered to in this sector and when 46th Brigade were ready to advance at 11.10am to the Blue Line they were ordered to halt. The order got through to all the battalions bar the 11th Highland Light Infantry who continued. The order to advance came at 12.15pm to attack from the Blue Line at 2.00pm with an altered artillery plan; at least here the delay did not mean an advance without artillery support.[44] On the left, 7/8th King's Own Scottish Borderers reached the Blue Line at 1.50pm and went into the attack at 2.00pm as with the new schedule to take the village of Feuchy and then onwards to take the double line of trenches which rested on the forward slopes of Orange Hill and constituted the Brown Line. The attack went well until coming up against Feuchy Redoubt where the British artillery was still firing and remained doing so for 20 minutes, thus holding up the attack. Some sniping from the railway bridge was dealt with by 2nd Lt. Strachan with four other men, capturing 17 Germans in the process. Finally, the redoubt and the whole village was successfully taken and the Brown Line reached at 4.45pm against virtually no opposition. No Germans were seen forward of the line either and outposts 200 yards in front of the line were established. Interestingly the unit diary states these outposts were to, "assist the cavalry to cut through."[45] A strange comment with another infantry division supposed to be following close behind. In the centre of the brigade push was 10th Cameronians (Scottish Rifles) whose advance towards the Brown Line was held up as they did not wish to get ahead of the Borderers on their left, held up in front of Feuchy Redoubt. They did get down into Battery Valley, taking a gun there that had been held up in the mud and then a battery of guns with 29 prisoners as they moved beyond the valley into the sunken road to the east. When they saw the Borderers advancing through the village they moved on again. D and B Companies moved down the road into the village and helped the Borderers clear it whilst A and C Companies, keeping parallel with those in the village, moved into the Brown Line by around 4.00pm. Not a great deal of opposition was met although there was machine gun fire from the south east. Consolidation of the eastern support line started at once although patrols couldn't be sent out further due to the British barrage still coming down around 400 yards to the east. Recall that on the right, 12th Highland Light Infantry had not received the communication to delay the advance to the Blue Line and therefore they became caught up in the fight for that line, losing some casualties in the process. They only received the order not to advance after the leading two companies (A and B) had already begun to advance. After getting a message to them the only thing they could do was to take whatever cover they could and sit out the British rearranged barrage as it passed over them. During their eventual advance on Battery Valley they came under fire from three batteries at very close range. This point blank fire caused heavy casualties until rifle and Lewis gun fire removed the problem. Especially effective in this action was Lt. Cummeford and eventually nine field guns were captured. The battalion then reorganised in Battery Valley in order to continue onto the Brown Line. This they did with the help of a tank which made crossing the uncut wire easier and dealt with some troublesome machine guns.[46] This was the very hardworking 2nd Lt

---

43 TNA: WO95/1446 War Diaries of General Staff, 4th Division.
44 TNA: WO95/1950 War Diaries of 46th Brigade.
45 TNA: WO95/1953 War Diaries of 7/8th King's Own Scottish Borderers.
46 TNA: WO95/1952 War Diaries of 12th Highland Light Infantry.

The medals and headstone of just two of
the men killed on 9 April 1917.

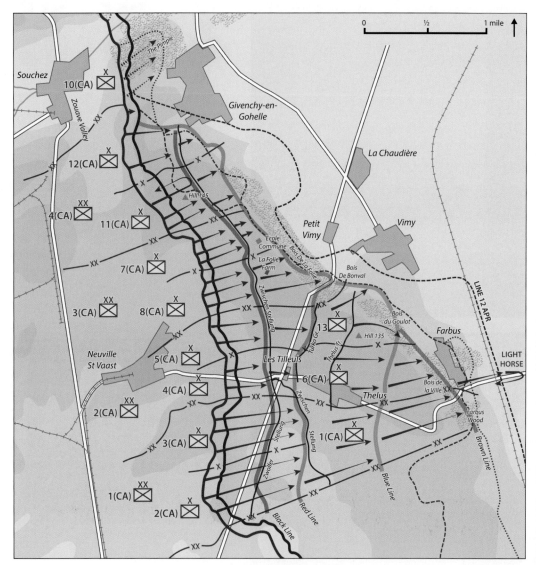

1st Army objective lines for 9 April.

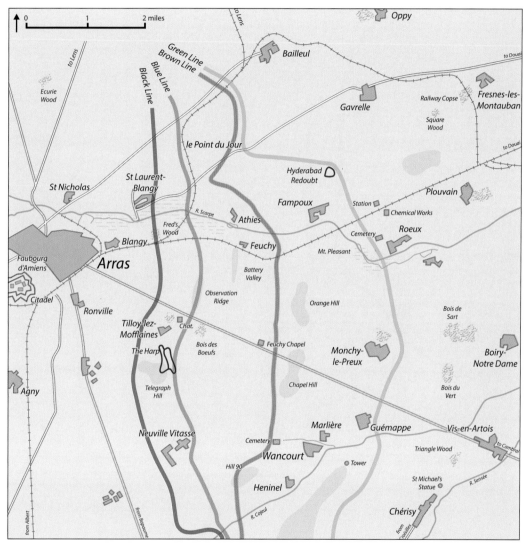

3rd Army objective lines for 9 April.

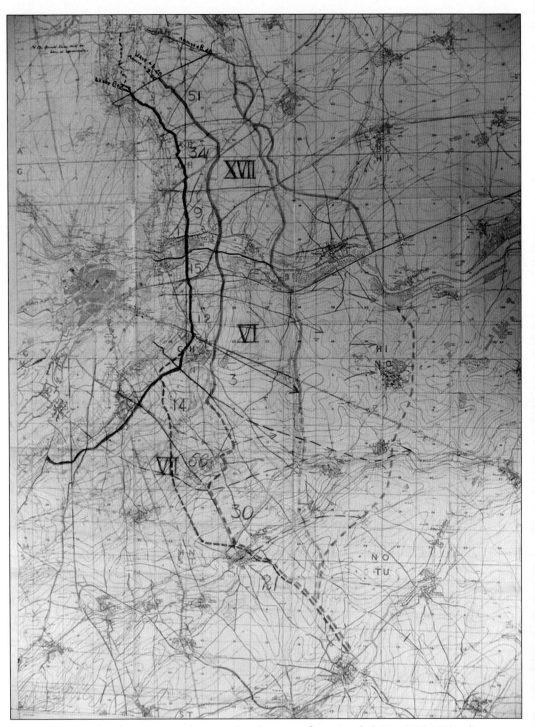

Original 3rd Army map showing the objectives for 9 April. (TNA WO158/224)

The Basilica and Ablain-St.-Nazaire French Military Cemetery on the heights of the Notre Dame de Lorette. (Author)

The British and French cemeteries at La Targette, near Neuville–St.-Vaast. (Author)

The headstone of the 14 year old German soldier Paul Mauk, mortally wounded on the Lorette Ridge. (Author)

The grave of Ferdinand Kulfanek, one of the Czech soldiers killed assaulting Vimy Ridge at the commemoration of the 100th Anniversary at the Czech Memorial and Cemetery near Souchez. (Author)

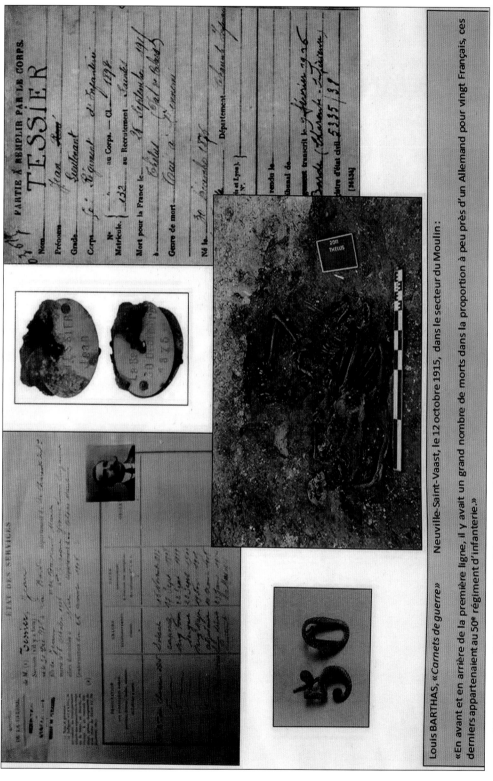

Louis BARTHAS, «Carnets de guerre»   Neuville-Saint-Vaast, le 12 octobre 1915, dans le secteur du Moulin:

«En avant et en arrière de la première ligne, il y avait un grand nombre de morts dans la proportion à peu près d'un Allemand pour vingt Français, ces derniers appartenaient au 50e régiment d'infanterie.»

The remains of Lieutenant Jean Tessier were found during an archaeological dig at the mill near Zivy Crater in 2015. (Author)

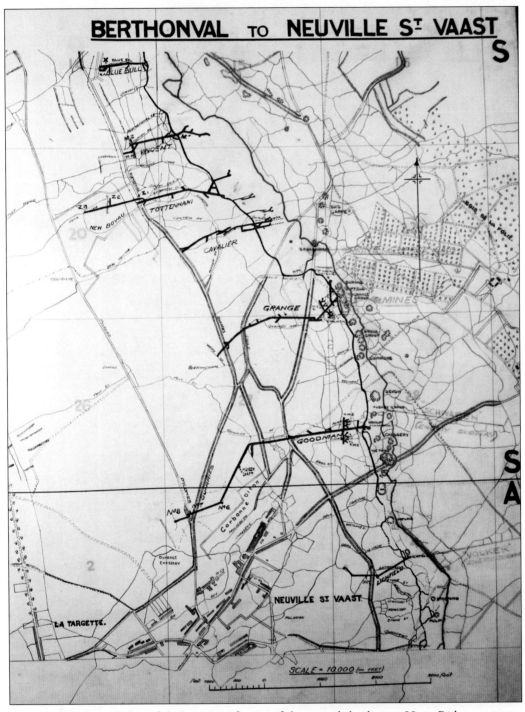

An original plan of the location of some of the tunnels leading to Vimy Ridge.
(TNA: WO153/914 Mining First Army Scheme 1917)

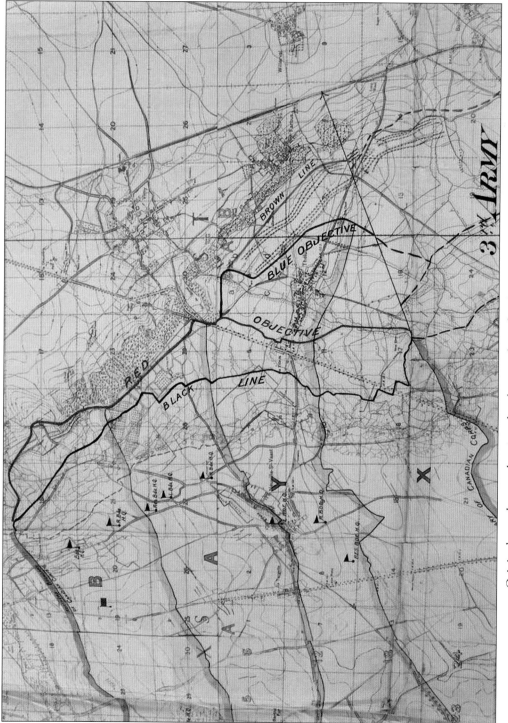

Original trench map showing the objective lines for the Canadian Corps. (Author)

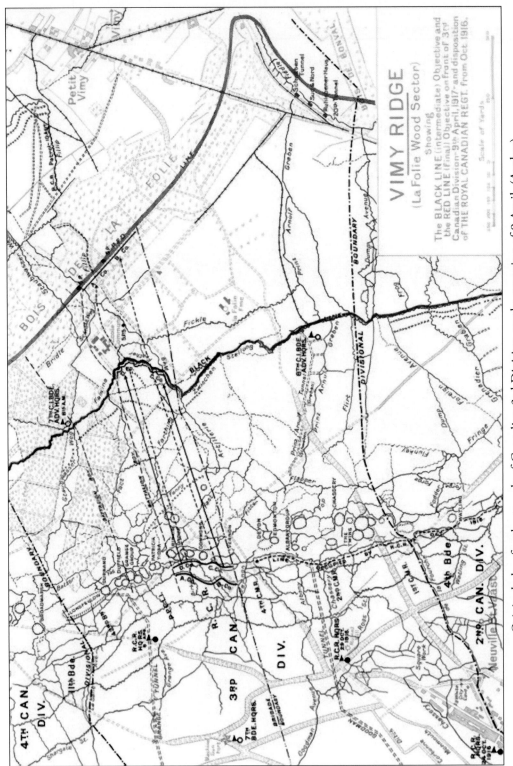

Original plan for the assault of Canadian 3rd Division on the morning of 9 April. (Author)

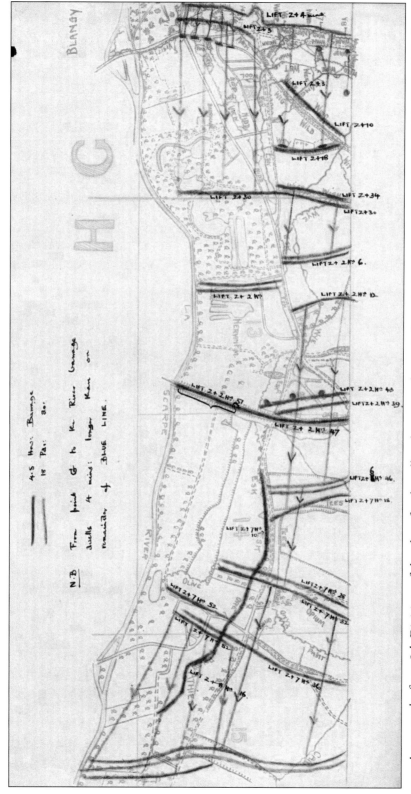

An example, from 9th Division, of the plans for the rolling barrage to be carried out during the attack on 9 April. (TNA: WO95/1672)

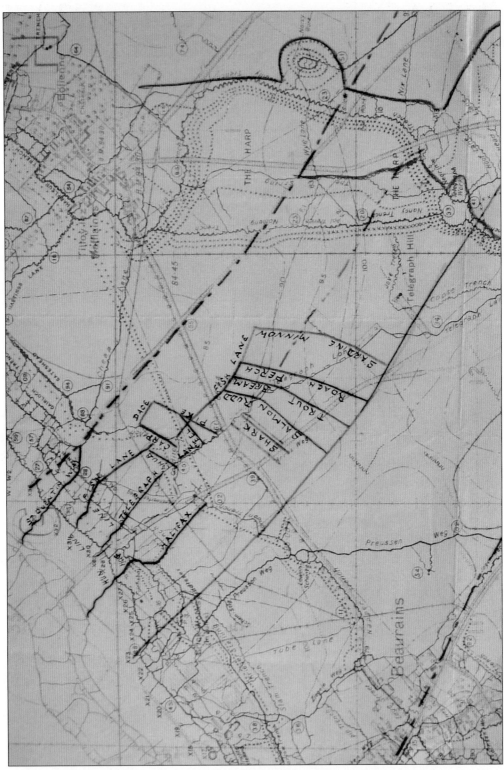

An original trench map showing the creation of new trenches for the attack following the withdrawal of the Germans in late March. (TNA: WO95/1869)

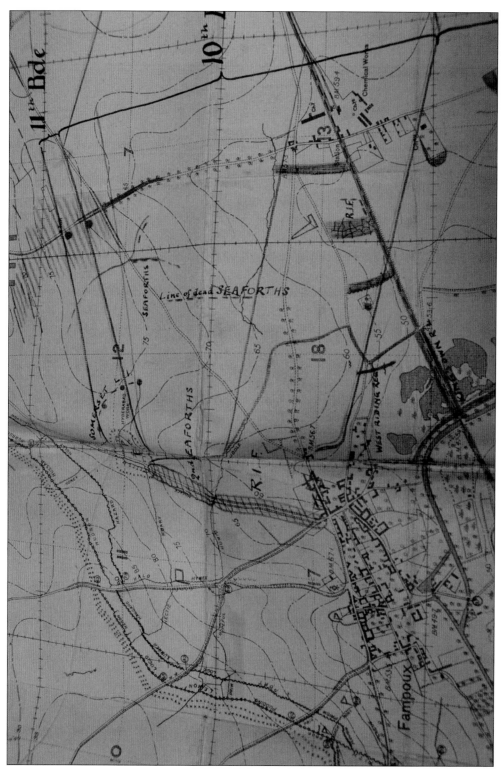

A trench map with the chilling addition of the 'Line of dead Seaforths' after the attack on 11 April. (TNA: WO95/1491)

The vast German cemetery near to Neuville-St.-Vaast with 44,843 men buried here. (Author)

Chas Weber and his crew again. Having helped the division at the Railway Triangle, 788 then followed the railway to the arch at Feuchy sitting there a while before he, "went back up slope to see what had become of our infantry, found them on top and gave them the green disc signal."[47] Seeing many abandoned guns in the valley (the infantry having gone through by then as he had to sort out the magneto that had troubled them all morning), 2nd Lt Weber then found a place where he could get over the slope and proceeded to the Brown Line where, as observed by the Highland Light Infantry, he drove along the wire and deal with any enemy that he could see. After observing the 15th Division battalions safely digging in on the Brown Line, Weber could see that the line to the south was not occupied by British troops. Heading down this line, "doing as much damage as possible,"[48] short of fuel he was aiming for Feuchy Chapel when, in Weber's words, a Colonel asked him to go back and deal with a trench. Doing all he could at the trench and within 10 yards of the wire the magneto finally gave out and the crew had to abandon the tank. So ended probably one of the most effective individual tank operations of the day, Weber being quite rightly awarded the MC for his actions. The tank was hit by a shell some time the next day and burned out.[49]

The 15th Division were thus in the Brown Line but it was late afternoon, the timetable was askew and, what was worse, it was clear that to the south events had gone even more astray. The German reserves of 5th and 6th Companies of *G.R. 10* were already in the *Monchy-Riegel* (the Brown Line for the British) and were being reinforced by further companies of that regiment, a company of *I.R. 51* and two companies of pioneers, all rushing forward in an attempt to stop any breakthrough. It is very clear in the German Official History that *I.R. 51* was on its last legs at this point and losing the Monchy-Riegel, casualties reaching 50 percent for the four companies involved. Weber's tank gets a special mention of being the main cause of *I.R. 51* having to give up their position.[50] The last immediately available German reserves had been committed and any further push beyond the Brown Line at this point in time would have meant the collapse of the whole of the German 2nd line, the *Monchy-Riegel*.

12th Division

It was the 35th Brigade's task to move through and take the Brown Line. That this was not going to be as straight forward as planned was quickly evident as the 5th Royal Berkshire Regiment moved up on the left of the brigade after orders were given at 10.30am. They came under machine gun fire from Heron Work as they moved up, an area they would have expected to have been taken by this point. This halted the battalion for three quarters of an hour and so at 11.45am the advance could begin again with one of their platoons working around Heron Work and finally ending its resistance. It was thus at 12.45pm that the first companies went over Observation Ridge and advanced down into Battery Valley. Here they faced, as the units north of them did, batteries of guns firing over open sights at them. With a combination of short rushes and rifle fire these guns were overcome. An incredible total of four 4.2" howitzers and eighteen 77mm guns were claimed by the battalion after the advance. The divisional history tells of some of these guns being turned on the enemy but the unit makes no mention of this. Indeed, being already behind schedule it

47   KCLMA Fuller/1/4/1, Summary of tank operations 1 Bde Heavy Branch, 9 Apr–3 May 17; Lt.-Col. J. Stewart, D.S.O. & John Buchan, *The Fifteenth (Scottish) Division 1914-1919*.

48   Summary of tank operations 1 Bde Heavy Branch, 9 Apr–3 May 17; Lt.-Col. J. Stewart, D.S.O. & John Buchan, *The Fifteenth (Scottish) Division 1914-1919*.

49   Summary of tank operations 1 Bde Heavy Branch, 9 Apr–3 May 17. The Fifteenth (Scottish) Division 1914-1919, again makes no mention of any tank assistance.

50   Behrmann & Brandt, *Die Osterschlacht bei Arras 1917 II. Teil*, p. 21 and p. 32.

would have been folly to have wasted more time doing such a thing. The Berkshires had lost the barrage as it was 2.30pm when they assembled for an attack on the Brown Line and no change in the timings of the barrage had been made. Given that 15th Division had had similar difficulties in moving onto Observation Ridge and had subsequently delayed the barrage it is difficult to understand why this had not been done by 12th Division. The result was that the Berkshires reached a position well short of the wire, gaining the level of the road across their front before being halted by rifle and machine gun fire. Of course at this time the delayed attack by 15th Division on their left meant that this flank was also open. It could have been that it was someone from this battalion that asked tank commander Weber for assistance but no mention can be found in the diaries to substantiate this. The result was that the battalion stopped completely, even though they must have seen the troops on their left getting to the Brown Line later and then beyond that line when elements of 37th Division came up. The comment in the diary is clear:

> It was evident that a frontal attack was impracticable, especially as information showed that the BROWN LINE had not been captured on left or right flanks. These approximate positions were maintained until nightfall.[51]

In other words, no further attempt was made to gain the Brown Line, even following movement forward on their left and the arrival of units of 37th Division. It seems there was no attempt to bring back the barrage at any point. That failure doomed the follow up division to also fail and thus not only was an advance to the Green Line impossible but time would be required the next day to take the Brown Line. Berkshire casualties are only given for the five days, 9 to 13 April and are two officers killed with four wounded, five O.R. killed and 92 wounded. Most will be from 9 April as the battalion, after taking the Brown Line on 10 April was not further employed in this date range.

Having spent a few hours in London Cave after moving up the 9th Essex Regiment moved out at Zero Hour to advance which they did with hardly any casualties. Moving forward at 10.20am to the attack they came under heavy machine gun fire from Hotte Work which had not yet been subdued. After being held up in a similar way to the Berkshires on their left, smart action by 2nd Lt. Barker, leading his platoon around the flank, forced the occupants to surrender and the advance could continue. The Essex then, on broaching Observation Ridge, had the batteries below then to contend with. Again progress was slowed by having to bring Lewis guns to bear on these nine guns which, with their crews, were finally captured. The unit diary then goes on to say that their own barrage delayed further movement but this must be a mistake as they, like the Berkshires, had lost the barrage long ago. It seems from brigade diary entries, that one gun was firing short and thus gave the impression that the barrage was still active.[52] They did, however, come under fire from the German line in front of them. C Company, under 2nd Lt. Brown had its right on the Arras-Cambrai road and progressed by short rushes until they were able to rush and take Feuchy Chapel Redoubt. A Company, with some of D Company, worked their way up Tilloy Lane trench as far as Chapel Road. Although 2nd Lt. Peters did try with a party of men to work further up the trench they were stopped at the wire and eventually, after a number of casualties were taken, were forced to create a block and stop there. B Company on the left had a very similar experience to that of the Berkshires and were stopped at the road. No further attempts were made by the battalion, the time

51   TNA: WO95/1850 War Diaries of 5th Royal Berkshire Regiment.
52   TNA: WO95/1848 War Diaries of H.Q. 35th Brigade.

now being 5.00pm. The Essex's casualties for the day were one officer killed and four wounded, 37 O.R. killed or died of wounds and 124 wounded.[53]

On the right of the brigade the plan was for the 7th Norfolk Regiment to advance beyond the Blue Line and take ground up to and including the position called Maison Rouge on the trench map. They would then allow 7th Suffolk Regiment to pass through towards Feuchy Chapel. The first problems again arose for the battalion when they had cleared the original front lines and found the Blue Line not taken, considerable casualties then being taken whilst assisting in the final taking of the position. From that point the advance met little opposition and many prisoners were taken along with 11 field guns, although casualties for this little action did amount to two officers and 21 O.R. killed plus two officers and 135 O.R. wounded; evidence of the difficult fighting around the Blue Line.[54] Unfortunately, only the brigade diary is of any use for discovering the experience of the 7th Suffolk Regiment as their diary is missing the commanding officer's report which the manuscript states should have been attached. Advancing from Maison Rouge at around 1.35pm instead of 12.55pm meant no more barrage in support and thus the uncut wire experienced all along the line at this distance proved too much as German machine guns and snipers made the cutting of it by hand virtually impossible.[55] Thus the whole advance was again brought to a standstill short of the Brown Line.

Examination of German sources provides an indication of the seriousness of losing the pace of the attack. The units that fell back to the Monchy-Riegel, or Brown Line, were the *"Trümmer"*[56] of *I/I.R. 38, III/I.R. 38 and I/R.I.R. 76*, but during the afternoon these remnants were relieved by the fresh *III/R.I.R. 76* from the divisional reserve. Also appearing in the line as the afternoon progressed were further divisional reserves from *17th Division*, namely *III/I.R. 162* and *II/I.R. 163*. Thus these fresh troops brought the advance of 12th Division to a halt. These fresh reserves would, as was the case in the north, have run head on into the attack of 12th Division, had it kept to time. They would have been left in the open on Orange Hill and there would have been an excellent chance for 37th Division to continue the attack to the east. As the evening approached yet more fresh German reserves arrived in the area north of the Arras–Cambrai road in the shape of *I/R.I.R. 99*, part of *220th Division*, closely followed by *I/R.I.R. 55* from the same division with two more battalions from *26th Division* approaching.[57]

By the end of the day then it became clear that 12th Division had not created the platform from which 37th Division could spring and move on to take Monchy-le-Preux and the remainder of the Green Line. Communication with Brigade and Divisional Headquarters does not seem to have been a problem and therefore the question has to be asked as to why the barrage was not adjusted, as it was by 15th Division, to allow the afternoon attacks, however late, to have some chance of success. The divisional diary has a clear description of events and admits that the troops were behind schedule and that the Blue Line was not finally cleared until 1.05pm. Meanwhile the barrage had begun to move forward, as planned at 12.10pm and was therefore, in the aspect of the attacking infantry, a complete waste. The diary goes on to criticise the decision that the Commander Royal Artillery of 12th Division should then go to 37th Division for the latter phase. It makes no mention of timings for this change and it is unclear why this should have

53   TNA: WO95/1851 War Diaries of 9th Essex Regiment.
54   TNA: WO95/1853 War Diaries of 7th Norfolk Regiment.
55   TNA: WO95/1848 War Diaries of H.Q. 35th Brigade.
56   Berhmann & Brandt, *Die Osterschlacht bei Arras 1917 II. Teil*, p. 25; literally 'ruins'.
57   Berhmann & Brandt, *Die Osterschlacht bei Arras 1917 II. Teil*, p. 33.

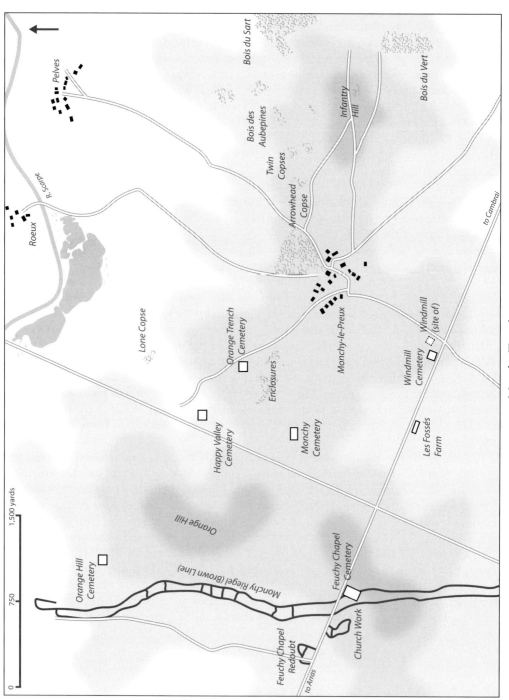

Monchy Trench.

disrupted any alteration in the artillery plan.[58] Also criticised is the fact that the headquarters of the two divisions were not in the same place but again no reason can be seen as to why this should have resulted in the lack of flexibility in the artillery plan to adjust to circumstances.[59] What seems to have happened is that the division tried to hold to original timings, in the face of mounting evidence of delay with the result that the Brown Line was not taken that day. The artillery is quite clear in its diary that it knew that there had been a delay, even to the point that one of its batteries did not move forward on time. It never received any instruction to delay the beginning of the barrage movement at 12.10pm and in fact worked hard to have all the batteries in place to carry it out. It began on time and the simple statement in the diary is that the infantry did not keep up.[60]

37th Division

The 37th Division was tasked, in the same manner as 4th Division, with passing through elements of both 15th and 12th Divisions and continuing the attack to the east. The failure of 12th Division to establish itself on the Brown Line doomed the majority of this plan from the outset. The division, plus VI Corps mounted troops were at their control points on the western fringes of Arras, from St Nicholas around to the citadel area. At 9.15am being told, "the situation on the Blue Line being sufficiently clear,"[61] they moved forward through the city to arrive at the British front line trenches at around 11.30am. Further orders meant a move forward to the Black Line at 12.30pm for troops of the 111th Brigade on the left and 112th Brigade on the right. At 3.00pm it was then ordered that 111th Brigade should follow up 15th Division and 112th Brigade should do the same behind 12th Division, 63rd Brigade moving behind as far as Battery Valley where it would form the divisional reserve. At 4.21pm a telegram was received from 12th Division stating, quite correctly, that Chapel Work was taken but also and very wrongly that Church Work was also in British hands. This led 37th Divisional Command to put plans in motion to move forward for a 7.00pm attack on Monchy-le-Preux, by this stage in the afternoon a nonsense. By 6.37pm the information was that 15th Division had reached the Brown Line but that the position of 12th and 3rd Division was unclear. The leading brigades moved forward but in both cases they stopped at the sunken road line held by 12th Division.[62] This is where the actions of 111th Brigade are not without reproach and seemingly somewhat incomprehensible. The brigade had been ordered to follow 15th Division and as such should have been able to gain the Brown Line, currently held by that division. This they evidently failed to do as they simply halted, probably too far south, on the Feuchy-Feuchy Chapel lane, stopped by fire from the Brown Line.[63] What makes this seem worse is that when elements of 63rd Brigade are sent forward at 7.35pm, namely the 8th Somerset Light Infantry and the 8th Lincolnshire Regiment, they move through the Brown Line and onto Orange Hill, establishing a line there and reporting no sign of 111th Brigade.[64] Also, the corps mounted troops, the Northamptonshire Yeomanry, had worked their way along the river and

---

58   In fact, the artillery diaries time this at sometime around 5.00pm, by which time the situation was not under control anymore; TNA: WO95/1832 War Diaries of C.R.A. 12th Division.

59   TNA: WO95/1824 War Diaries of H.Q. 12th Division.

60   TNA: WO95/1832 War Diaries of C.R.A. 12th Division.

61   TNA: WO95/2513 War Diaries of H.Q. 37th Division.

62   TNA: WO95/2513 War Diaries of H.Q. 37th Division.

63   TNA: WO95/2531 War Diaries of H.Q. 111th Brigade. Cyril Falls, in the British Official History, states the order to follow 15th Division correctly but adds that the brigade was in the 12th Division area and it being too late to affect a change. Clear fault lies in the leadership within this brigade.

64   TNA: WO95/2528 War Diaries of 63rd Brigade.

successfully moving through 15th Division on the Brown Line at Feuchy, continued onwards to not only secure the river crossing south of the village but also the railway crossing further east. Later they linked with elements of the 8th Lincolnshires who had moved down the sunken road which reaches the bridge. Following the line taken by 15th Division out of Battery Valley should not pose a problem as you have both the valley and railway line on the left as a guide. This clear navigational handrail was clearly not used and subsequently the possibility of a whole brigade passing through the Brown Line and moving to form a continuous line with 4th Division north of the river was missed.[65]

3rd Division

3rd Division had experienced a reasonably successful morning, given that the Harp was considered a formidable obstacle and that was now behind them. The 8th Brigade were to follow up this early success and as such had moved up during the morning without any problems until they had to move through Tilloy-les-Mofflaines at which point the as yet unsubdued snipers caused some problems. The left of the two assault battalions, 7th King's Own Shropshire Light Infantry, were ordered to move around the northern side of the village. As they did so, many Germans then ran from the village back towards the quarry and the Bois des Boeufs which were both then cleared with 126 prisoners taken. They also captured four howitzers and a heavy gun of some kind behind the wood. The 2nd Royal Scots Regiment had also advanced on the brigade right without much problem until about 600 yards from the Brown Line. So far so good and although behind time both units were in good shape for the final attack, "All this had somewhat delayed the advance."[66] At this point, however, in front of the Brown Line they came under significant machine gun fire from both flanks, especially from Chapel and Church Works. All the diaries point to this as being the reason for the advance to stall at this point. They also realised that the left flank was completely open as 12th Division had not moved up with them as has already been seen. The brigade reserve battalion, 1st Royal Scottish Fusiliers were ordered up to from a left flank along the Arras–Cambrai road. If, however, they had been up to time, the barrage would have still been on the Brown Line and fire should have been subdued by it. The 'slight delay' moving through Tilloy may have been a root cause of the problems they now faced. None of the diaries[67] mention losing the barrage but then how was the German opposition so clearly without pressure when the leading battalions advanced? Not only is it obvious that the barrage had moved on but with no advance from 12th Division (they were even further behind) the machine guns at both Chapel and Church Works had only the 8th Brigade units to fire at. The presence of the support battalion, the 8th East Yorkshires was to no avail and therefore it was decided to order, at 5.30pm a re-bombardment of the Brown Line, to continue until 6.45pm and then at 7.00pm for the two battalions of 76th Brigade allocated to support 8th Brigade to attack. These two battalions, 1st Gordons and 8th Kings Own Royal Lancaster received these orders at 6.35pm and 6.50pm respectively, resulting in the attack being carried out initially by the Gordons alone, a fact not mentioned in any of the higher echelon diaries.[68] In fact they even state that the attack by both battalions failed when in

---

65 The relevant map in British Official History does not record the outstanding work of the Northamptonshire Yeomanry or that of the 8th Lincolns in linking up at the river. The line of their achievements should run northwards to Feuchy and not extend back to the Brown Line.
66 TNA: WO95/1378 War Diaries of H.Q. 3rd Division.
67 TNA: WO95/1378 War Diaries of H.Q. 3rd Division; TNA: WO95/1417 War Diaries of H.Q. 8th Brigade; TNA: WO95/1423 War Diaries of 2nd Royal Scots; TNA: WO95/1421 War Diaries of 7th Shropshire Light Infantry.
68 TNA: WO95/1435 War Diaries of 1st Gordon Highlanders.

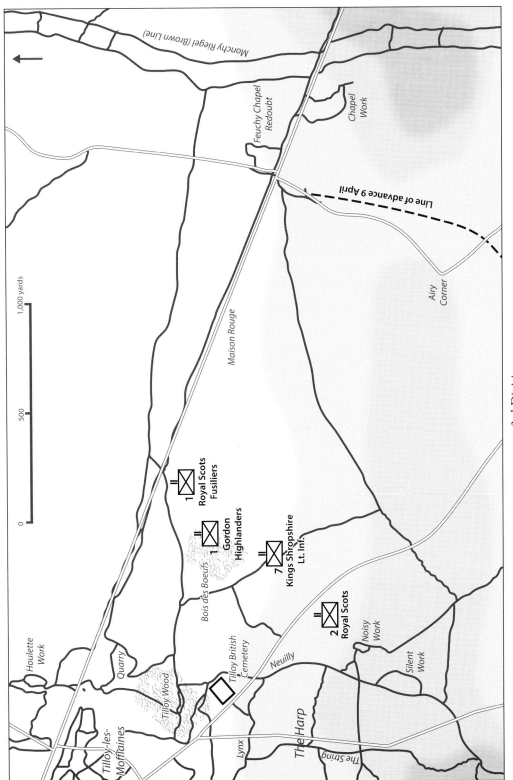

Monchy Riegel (Brown Line)

Feuchy Chapel
Redoubt

Chapel
Work

Line of advance 9 April

Airy
Corner

1,000 yards

500

0

Maison Rouge

Royal Scots
Fusiliers

1

Gordon
Highlanders

1

Kings Shropshire
Lt. Inf.

7

Royal Scots

2

Bois des Boeufs

Houlette
Work

Quarry

Tilloy Wood

Tilloy British
Cemetery

Neuilly

Noisy
Work

Silent
Work

Tilloy-les-
Mofflaines

Lynx

The Harp

The String

3rd Division.

fact by the time the 8th K.O.R.L. had covered the over one mile to even get to the attack line all that remained were scattered men of all the battalions, including those of the Gordons who had failed in their attack; the K.O.R.L. never even attacked.[69] The 8th Brigade diary also states that the bombardment was weak and ineffective, "hardly any of the shells falling in the enemy's wire."[70] Further evidence of the loss of adequate artillery support is that the 3rd and reserve battalions of *R.I.R. 76* were able to relief the wreck of the units that had retreated into the Monchy-Riegel. It was these fresh troops with others of *17th Division*, taking control of Feuchy Chapel and Chapel Hill that were the cause of the halt of 3rd Division, just as they were to 12th Division to the north. Thus it was that the arrival of elements of a few reserve battalions that was able to bring the attack of two divisions to a halt.

The Brown Line was, yet again, at this point not achieved without it being easy to ascertain why this was done so successfully further north and not here. It has already been seen that the wire in lines further back was also uncut north of the Scarpe but when units were up to the barrage this did not prove an insurmountable problem. South of the river this does not seem to have been the case. In the case of 12th Division, the Blue Line proved a delaying factor, in 3rd Division's some delay caused by the village of Tilloy-les-Mofflaines. It has proved impossible to find an adequate reason for why the attack on the Brown Line did not begin on time. The lengthy time lapse between the timings for the Blue and Brown Line should have been sufficient as none of the units in the morning complain of being seriously delayed. Already at 3.00pm, it can be clearly seen that things were not going well, however, in all the higher echelon diaries, including the Commander Royal Artillery for the 3rd Division, there is a communication gap between around that time and 5.00pm when, finally, the decision is made to re-bombard the Brown Line. The lack of prompt orders and the late arrival of such to battalions is going to become a common thread in the coming days.

14th Division

The 14th Division was in a relatively good position with, however, concerns over their right flank which seemed somewhat open. On the left the situation was straightforward for 42nd Brigade that had only to secure a trench line just in front of the Blue Line and allow 3rd Division to pass in front of them. The angle of attack meant that only 43rd Brigade were to actually attack the Brown Line. For 42nd Brigade, only 9th Rifle Brigade were to move forward and this they did, suffering only 11 casualties in carrying out their task. 6th Somerset Light Infantry had the task for 43rd Brigade of taking the Brown Line which they began to do promptly at 12.30pm closely behind the barrage as it crept forward. The first distraction was having to send two platoons to their left as the Rifle Brigade had not yet cleared high ground there. Eventually, having mopped up a machine gun and 30 Germans some of the Rifle Brigade arrived to relieve them and they could join the rest of the battalion. In the meantime, the two remaining companies in the attack, advancing in spite of finding no troops on either flank, got to within 600 yards of their objective. Heavy machine gun fire from the south first slowed (thereby losing the barrage) and then halted the leading waves at this point and they were forced back to a new German trench not marked on the maps. Support then seemed to come from the right at this juncture with a company of 14th London (London Scottish) of 56th Division coming up and mixing with their own men. They were then suddenly withdrawn, leaving this flank completely open and as such a southern facing flank had to be created. This was done with the help of some of 6th Duke of Cornwall Light Infantry, the brigade

---

69   TNA: WO95/1436 War Diaries of 8th King's Own Royal Lancaster Regiment.
70   TNA: WO95/1417 War Diaries of H.Q. 8th Brigade.

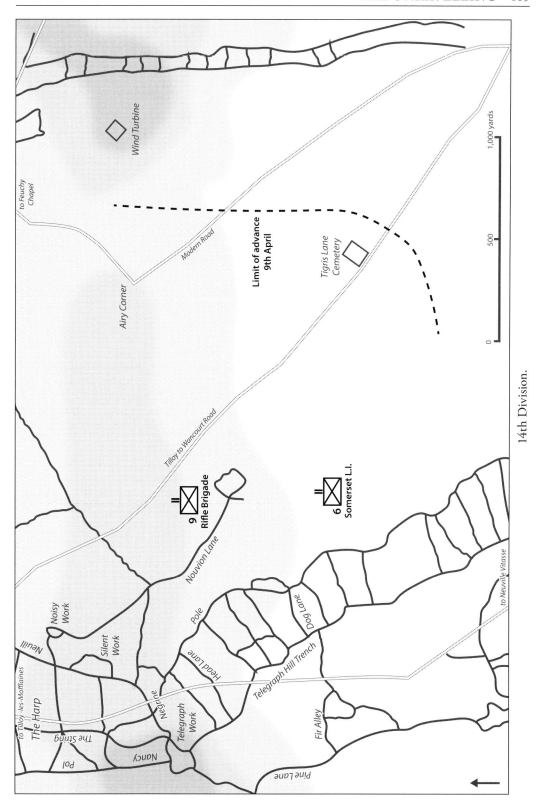

14th Division.

reserve battalion that had arrived in support.[71] The first of the difficulties faced by 56th Division in the morning have already been noted. The renewed attack planned for 7.00pm, as described above, had even less chance of success here in 14th Division. They faced having Germans well in their rear in any advance, even had they the necessary troops to carry it out. 6th D.C.L.I. were put under the orders of the C.O. of the Somersets but all the arrangements were very late and as such went seriously astray. The D.C.L.I. companies arrived too late to follow the barrage and instructions to the leading companies in the front of the Somersets arrived at 6.55pm. Little progress was made with severe machine gun fire coming again from the south, almost in the rear of troops attempting to attack. Night came with troops digging in where they were, well short of the Brown Line.[72] This Brown Line was now occupied by elements of the German immediate reserves. The *III/R.I.R. 76* had moved into the area north of Feuchy Chapel with *II/I.R. 163* putting two companies into the line to the south. Also east of Neuville Vitasse, *R.I.R. 31* was able to put its reserve companies into the area between the village and the Monchy-Riegel and it was these troops that were able to both protect the Brown Line and at the same time be a danger to the flank of 14th Division as they were not directly attacked by 56th Division.[73]

The narrowing of the 14th Division's objective and the resultant allocation, as per the original plan, of only one battalion, left the leading troops severely undermanned to deal with the prevailing situation. Although the brigade reserve was available this was only sufficient to create a flank to the south. The renewed attack at 7.00pm was an abject example of how far the British Army still had to go in its ability to plan quickly and decisively when in action. It was already clear at 14th Divisional Headquarters during the afternoon that their right was going to be completely unprotected but nowhere in any of the communications with Corps was the question asked about possible use of the divisional reserve brigade in supporting 56th Division. Instead a new assault using already tired troops was finally decided upon too late to have any real chance of success. Communication was clearly a problem and on examining the brigade diary it is clear that inexperience and in some cases incompetence were to blame, it really does read like a comedy of errors. Wires on the power buzzers[74] were wrongly connected, in one instance the apparatus and the operator had been left half way with no orders and so it goes on. There were clearly many lessons still to be learned if rapid reaction to events was to be forthcoming.

56th Division

After recovering from a possible difficult start in the morning 56th Division had managed to reach its Blue Line objectives with sufficient time to follow up in the afternoon. The three battalions tasked with moving the advance forward in the afternoon had all began to move up but on the left 14th London (London Scottish) Regiment, found the going heavy and after passing through the lines of the Kensingtons and Rangers reached the area to assault too late to "benefit from our artillery barrage."[75] This lateness is not mentioned anywhere except in the battalion diary but had the consequence that the companies on the centre and right found it very difficult to even get into the front line of the Hindenburg positions in front of them. Only on the left did a company get through all three lines and into the area beyond. It was this body of men who were to meet

---

71 TNA: WO95/1909 War Diaries of 6th Somerset Light Infantry.
72 TNA: WO95/1909 War Diaries of 6th Somerset Light Infantry.
73 Behrmann & Brandt, *Die Osterschlacht bei Arras 1917 II. Teil,* p. 50.
74 A power buzzer, utilised to pass simple messages back, in Morse and usually pre-arranged codes, was an apparatus that used ground induction to send a signal, therefore no wires were required but the enemy could listen in.
75 TNA: WO95/2956 War Diaries of 14th London (London Scottish).

the Somersets of 14th Division. However, seeing none of the remainder of his battalion by his side the company commander decided to withdraw back to Telegraph Hill Trench and thus the disappearing act in the eyes of the Somersets. The diary speaks of this company being north of the Neuville Vitasse to Feuchy Road. In that case they were successful in getting through because that area of the Hindenburg Line was in 14th Division area and was part of the Blue Line objectives, that is to say, already taken. At this point there was no attempt, once in the line, to bomb down to the south to aid those trying to get in. Nobody seems to have thought of that possibility at this point or in assaulting the German lines from the rear.[76] To the right 1st London (Royal Fusiliers) had not only to take the Hindenburg Line but in front of that remained the Neuville Vitasse Trench. They managed to take this trench and Telegraph Hill Trench but due to a loss in direction and bunching this was not as far as Lion Lane and was some distance from where the London Scots were in the line. They were also now very low in numbers and could go no further. It had also only been eventually fully taken with the assistance of two companies of the 7th Middlesex Regiment, the unit originally tasked with going through and onto the Brown Line. It was planned to go on and take the rear line of the German positions but this failed due to heavy fire from the right. The reason for this fire became clear when word came from 21st Brigade to their right that they had not been able to take the front line and were digging in further back. Upon learning of this, the decision was made to consolidate the Telegraph Hill Trench in the first instance and create a block where Lion Lane joined it. In fact, a block had to be created in both Neuville and Telegraph Hill Trenches and it was further north than Lion Trench, in fact in a line from Pore Trench.[77] What is remarkable is that remaining elements of *I.R. 163* and those of *R.I.R. 31* were able to hold 56th Division back. As has been seen, support companies of *R.I.R. 31* could be deployed against the flank of 14th Division because they were not required in the Hindenburg Line. It was a matter of a few companies of Germans that stood between 14th and 56th Divisions and the Brown Line; no other reserves were expected until the next day.[78]

As the day drew to a close then 56th Division had succeeded in clearing Neuville Vitasse village and had a foothold in the first trenches of the Hindenburg Line but was woefully short of the Brown Line, leaving 14th Division on its left very open to attack from the south. During the day only six of its battalions had been involved in the action with a whole brigade remaining in reserve. Given the combination of tasks; taking a village and then a newly created and strong line beyond, the question has to be raised as to whether sufficient force had been allocated for the task, or whether there had been sufficient drive behind the actions of the division. Usually such failure to take an objective, such as seen in the afternoon, is accompanied by a large casualty list. Casualties for the division, for the whole day, were at around the 850 mark, relatively low at a divisional level for a major offensive.

30th Division

The 30th Division was relatively new to the conflict, being part of K5 and spending most of 1915 training and waiting for equipment before finally arriving in France during November. Taking part in the Battle of the Somme they showed what a New Army unit could do by storming Montauban on the first day, the only real success experienced by the British that day. After being involved in the taking of Trones Wood they were then back in the line for the Battle of the Transloy Ridges in October.

---

76   TNA: WO95/2956 War Diaries of 14th London (London Scottish).
77   TNA: WO95/2950 War Diaries of 7th Middlesex.
78   Behrmann & Brandt, *Die Osterschlacht bei Arras 1917 II. Teil*, pp. 50-51.

30th and 21st Divisions.

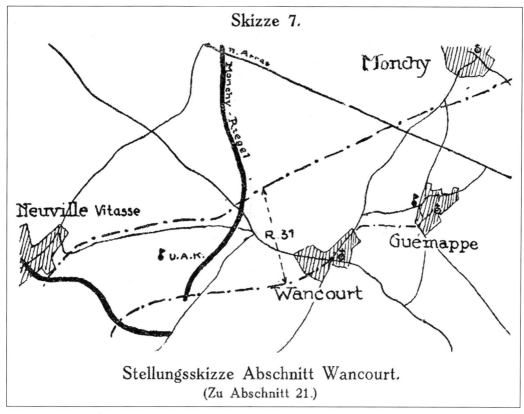

German map of Wancourt and vicinity; Förster, Sigismund von, *Das Reserve-Infanterie-Regiment Nr. 31*. (Oldenburg: Stalling, 1921)

As already seen in the planning section, very unusually the division had completely different start times for its brigades. The 21st Brigade on the left had start times to coincide with the second phase of the attacks of 56th Division, in other words the attack on the Brown Line. However, it also had a great deal of ground to cover before reaching the Blue Line. It was decided not to move up to the Blue Line well before the attack as at this point it was the Neuville Vitasse-Hénin sur Cojeul road and in full view of the Germans. The idea being to move at such a time to get to the German front line just as the barrage was about to lift at 12.10pm. This was therefore timed at 11.38am, giving just over half an hour. On the brigade front were 18th King's Liverpool Regiment on the left and 2nd Wiltshire Regiment on the right; 19th Manchester Regiment were in support but further behind than usual "because of the nature of the task."[79] Having to deploy from artillery formation because of fire from the strongpoint on the Blue Line they were able to take the position, capturing two machine guns without such a delay as to make them late for the barrage. Unfortunately, as well as coming under considerable enemy artillery fire, they also found damaged wire, but "still a most efficient obstacle."[80]

79   TNA: WO95/2311 War Diaries of H.Q. 30th Division.
80   TNA: WO95/2311 War Diaries of H.Q. 30th Division.

This was critical as has already been mentioned, the wire in front of the Hindenburg Line being both wide and dense. No way could be found through which drove both attacking units back into the sunken road connecting Neuville Vitasse and St.-Martin-sur-Cojeul. They could do no more that day other than consolidate that line. Opposing the brigade was 3rd Company of *R.I.R. 31*. It is with a single sentence that the German Official History dismisses the attack of 21st Brigade namely, "At the same time [as they were holding back the flank attacks down the Hindenburg Line] Lt. Siegel was able to throw back a frontal assault against his company, whereby Lt v. R. Kraushaupt was wounded."[81] In other words, due to the uncut wire a company of Germans was able to repulse two battalions of British infantry.

In the meantime, 19th Manchesters had been ordered to attempt to enter the line at Lion Lane as they had been informed that 56th Division was there; they were then to bomb down the trench. As has been seen that was not the case and the Manchesters could not get into the line until the early hours of the next morning. 89th Brigade on the right of 30th Division had the later start time of 1.55pm as the Black and Blue Line coincided for them and in any case they had already pushed forward, as has been described, into the village of St.-Martin-sur-Cojeul before zero hour; thus they were almost already on the Brown Line. At 1.30pm, the O.C. of 89th Brigade was given conflicting accounts of the success or not of the units to his left. On the one hand observers thought they saw men entering the German front line but on the other a report from their C.O. of 2nd Wiltshires stated that he had been "held up and sustained heavy casualties."[82] Nevertheless, the brigade attacked with 20th King's Own Liverpool Regiment on the left and their sister battalion the 19th on the right. The timings of the advance were to coincide with the lifting of the barrage off the German front line at 4.13pm. The 19th KLR War Diary noted the men were "cheerful and in the best of spirits." As they advanced both battalions came very quickly under heavy artillery and machine gun fire from a clearly unsuppressed enemy. In a similar experience to that of their fellow units to the left, they endured heavy fire until, reaching the wire; they found it uncut with no way through the thick bands. Retreating a few hundred yards men began to dig in as best they could or find shelter in shell holes. In the early hours of the morning the group commanders of the two artillery groups had commented that they did not feel the front wire was sufficiently cut and asked for more heavy artillery to be used on it. By 12.00pm they were "much more satisfied with the state of the wire."[83] How much more wrong could they have been? Unlike the section of German line opposite 21st Brigade, which lay just beyond a rise and was difficult to observe, the line east of St.-Martin-sur-Cojeul would have been in clear sight.[84] Such a comment from the artillery is difficult to understand and could be regarded as reprehensible. Between 5.00pm and 6.00pm it became clear to the brigade that no one had succeeded in entering the German lines. Another bombardment was therefore arranged but this entailed bringing the troops back somewhat as they were too near the lines to be shelled. Both battalions therefore retired to lines further back, the 19th Liverpool to the south side of the Cojeul stream where they were less overlooked by the Germans. In these positions the men settled for the night.[85] The attack was made against *III/ R.I.R. 86* who, although they lost their forward outpost from 10th Company, brought everything

---

81   Behrmann & Brandt, *Die Osterschlacht bei Arras 1917 II. Teil*, p. 51.

82   TNA: WO95/2332 War Diaries of H.Q. 89th Brigade.

83   TNA: WO95/2332 War Diaries of H.Q. 89th Brigade.

84   Standing on the eastern edge of St.-Martin-sur-Cojeul today, the German Line lay this side of the new railway embankment as it crosses the road to Héninel, left to right, thus in plain sight. Further to the right the wire will have passed over the present railway/motorway but if you climb up into the fields on the other side to where the wire would have been the view back to the British lines is clear. A short walk further on takes one into 21st Brigade area behind the slope.

85   TNA: WO95/2332 War Diaries of H.Q. 89th Brigade.

they could to bear on the attacking British troops and were thus able to stop them. Apart from strengthening the right flank with elements of a further company and putting *II/R.I.R. 86* into the *Monchy-Riegel*, both moves because of the loss of Neuville Vitasse, the regiment did not have to do any more on this first day.[86]

The afternoon had thus been a disappointment for 30th Division through no particular fault of their own. It was clearly a failure to both create any possibility of getting through two thick bands of wire and in any real way subdue the German garrison of the front line. The diary of 89th Brigade is in no way critical of the artillery, thanking them for their close support and stating that it was no surprise, at the distance they had to shoot, that wire cutting had proved difficult.[87] The question to be raised, however, is not that of the range for field artillery but why were heavies using a No. 106 fuse not available for some of the most strongly wired part of the whole line to be attacked?

21st Division

The plans only required one brigade of this division to take part in the attack, namely 64th Brigade. In front of them, on the high ground above Wancourt, lay the Hindenburg Line with its thick, strong belts of wire, its concrete emplacements and deep bunkers protecting the defenders; a formidable challenge to the men of the brigade. Assembling way back in assembly trenches along the road coming south east from the west end of St.-Martin-sur-Cojeul, the plan was to advance to get to the German front line at zero which was timed for 4.15pm. Br.-General H.R. Headlam (commanding 64th Brigade) had originally wanted to attack on a narrow front with two battalions but was overruled by Maj.-Gen 'Soarer' Campbell at Divisional H.Q., after Maj.-Gen Shea of 30th Division objected.[88]

All units set off at 3.54pm in order to get to the German line in time. They all moved in artillery formation and comment was passed as to the quality of the advance by all who saw it, congratulations being sent from the corps to the south. The formation was kept all the way to the wire because it had already been seen that there were but few gaps in the wire and those very narrow. Two machine gun teams and their weapons had crept forward during the night into the sunken lane nearer to the Germans and opened fire to support the attack. These men had been out under a mere 3-foot bank for 24 hours before the attack around 100 yards from the front line. According to Headlam it was the fire of these guns that "put the wind up"[89] the defenders so much it allowed his men to get into the German front line. On getting to the wire the fortunes of the different units varied dramatically. The 9th King's Own Yorkshire Light Infantry on the left were at first thought by observers to be through the wire but this was later seen to be wrong. Some poor gaps were in the first belt and some men got through to the space between the two belts but that was as far as they got.[90] Casualties were mounting from machine gun and rifle fire and the men found what shelter they could in shell holes. In the centre, 15th Durham Light Infantry Regiment found some

---

86   Behrmann & Brandt, *Die Osterschlacht bei Arras 1917 II. Teil*, pp. 52-53.
87   TNA: WO95/2332 War Diaries of H.Q. 89th Brigade.
88   TNA CAB45/116 Military: Western Front: Battles: Comments, Letters, Personal Accounts, Arras, letter to Falls from Headlam. In his letter to Falls, Headlam blames Shea for the 9th K.O.Y.L.I. having to attack at all, using the term, "pig-headedness".
89   TNA CAB 45/116 Military: Western Front: Battles: Comments, Letters, Personal Accounts, Arras, letter to Falls from Headlam.
90   TNA: WO95/2162 War Diaries of 9th King's Own Yorkshire L.I., *The History of the Regiment* (R.C. Bond, (Uckfield: Naval Military Press reprint, 2004), p. 868) has the men reaching the German front line, however, this is contradicted by all the consulted diaries.

gaps and one company, fully up with the barrage, actually got into the front line trench without a single casualty. The other company, with more difficulty, also entered the German front line. On the right, 1st East Yorkshire Regiment, with the help of Stokes mortars enlarging some of the narrower gaps, also managed to enter the line. The mortars on the right also managed to destroy a concrete emplacement but their commander, Capt. Piza, was subsequently killed.[91] After a quick exchange of views between the leading officers of both the Durhams and the East Yorks it was decided that further progress across to the support line was found impossible as the wire between was fully intact. Also, an attempt by the D.L.I. to bomb down the line to support the K.O.Y.L.I. failed due to a lack of bombs. The defenders of *R.I.R 84* reacted aggressively and soon bombing duels broke out on both flanks. The 10th K.O.Y.L.I., the reserve battalion was sent up as darkness fell to enter the German lines behind the D.L.I. and lend support, two companies doing this and the others digging a trench alongside the sunken lane in front of the wire. The 9th K.O.Y.L.I. were able to retreat to this sunken road although with casualties of 183 all ranks out of the 562 that attacked they were later brought back further. As night fell a tenuous hold on the Hindenburg Line remained but under increasing pressure from the defenders. A trench was dug from the sunken lane into the front line to allow ammunition, especially bombs, to be got forward as well as some food and drink for the men.[92]

Major Koller. His officially recorded death on 10 April is almost certainly an error. (Speck, Wilhelm, *Des Königlich Preußische Reserve-Infanterie-Regiment 84*)

The defenders opposing 64th Brigade were *II/R.I.R. 84, 18th Division*. The German Official History comments that the regiment threw back an assault earlier in the day, but this can be dismissed. Indeed, it is possible that a portion of 30th Division's attack was against *R.I.R. 84*. When the assault did come the initial success was against 7th and 8th Companies whereas 6th Company on the right were the defenders that held the front trench as the British tried to bomb down it, further right 5th Company were successful in opposing 9th K.O.Y.L.I. On the German left it was 7th Company of *R.I.R. 99* (part of the neighbouring *220th Division*) that had to be held back by the 1st East Yorkshires. The action had cost *R.I.R. 84* one important casualty, that of their commander Major Koller, as he attempted to find out what had happened to his 8th Company.[93]

The strength of the Hindenburg Line, as on 30th Division's front, proved too great for

---

91   Capt. Daniel Piza is commemorated on the Arras Memorial.

92   TNA: WO95/2162 War Diaries of 9th K.O.Y.L.I.; TNA: WO95/2161 War Diaries of 15th D.L.I.; TNA: WO95/2161 War Diaries of 1st East Yorks.

93   Behrmann & Brandt, *Die Osterschlacht bei Arras 1917 II. Teil*, pp. 54-55; Speck, William, *Des Königlich Preußische Reserve-Infanterie-Regiment 84*, (Zeulenroda: Sporn Verlag, 1937), pp. 177-180. Two pages of the battle description are given over to a eulogy for Major Koller who was regarded as a serious loss that day.

a single brigade of 21st Division in spite of excellent work by the men when a least some gaps had been made in the wire. Unable to move forward to the support line left the advanced men in a very precarious position with an aggressive and unsubdued enemy working constantly to throw them out. In the planning stage it was made clear to Headlam that his brigade was only to advance if their immediate neighbours in 30th Division had reached their objectives. This they had not done and his after-battle report makes interesting reading. This is the relevant paragraph in full:

> In the general plan of the battle a promise was given that the Brigade would not be called upon to advance until the troops on the left had seized and consolidated the NEPAL trench north of the COJEUL River and were ready to advance thence on HENINEL and WANCOURT simultaneously with the advance of the Brigade. It is unnecessary to point out here that this arrangement was vital to the success of my attack, since the defenders of such a position as I was called upon to attack could scarcely be expected to be dislodged unless they felt that by staying on in their position they would be captured by the advance of the troops on their flank and towards their line of retreat. *Circumstances arose however which made it necessary* [author emphasis] to make my attack in conformity with the advance of 30th Division on my left.[94]

The italicized section is handwritten and inserted to replace a section scribbled out which, as far as can be discerned, reads differently and seems to infer an assault ordered for reasons he was not made aware of. When it is remembered that the whole of the attack of VII Corps was at first felt to be inappropriate given the strength of the German defences, reversing a sensible instruction to await success on the left before attacking seems irresponsible and can only lay at Campbell's feet. No one else could have made such a decision in the time available. Headlam's whole report is carefully written but is clearly a criticism of the decision to attack at all. The Official History makes no mention of the caveat for the attack merely stating that capturing some element of the German front line was, "a remarkable feat of arms."[95]

So ended the most successful day the British Army had experienced since the Marne in 1914 and, given the size of the forces engaged it could be said since the beginning of the war. At last the German lines had not only been penetrated but broken and that to a distance never before experienced. Admittedly success had not been as great on all points along the line but in those where it was mostly sought, namely Vimy Ridge and the sections north and south of the Scarpe it would not be incorrect to say that the German defences were in disarray. The problem lay with exploitation and speed. The reserve cavalry was targeted at the attack south of the Scarpe but it was precisely here that progress had been slow and even the reserve division, the 37th couldn't get through to assault the Green Line. Cavalry had not been allocated to the attack north of the river where all the lines had been broken and there was open countryside ahead with little or no concerted opposition. The 12th Brigade diary is in no doubt that once the uncut wire in front of the German front position had been dealt with there was an opportunity for exploitation:

> On reaching the fourth system a considerable number of the enemy fled and, had a squadron of cavalry been available then a considerable number of the enemy would have been captured – and we would undoubtedly have been able to push our line further forward. During the night, however, more machine guns were brought up by the enemy and these made any advance impossible.[96]

94   TNA: WO95/2332 War Diaries of H.Q. 89th Brigade.
95   Falls, *Military Operations, France and Belgium 1917 Vol. 1*, p. 206.
96   TNA: WO95/1502 War Diaries of H.Q. 12th Brigade.

On the actual day the brigade commander, Br.-General Carton de Wiart, was said to have commented on the fact that the cavalry would not be available until the next day with; "Tomorrow will be too late."[97] In another instance, Lt.-Colonel Croft, C.O. of 11th Royal Scots had phoned his brigadier and when asked "Is cavalry good business?", replied, "Yes, ten thousand times yes, but it must be done now. Too late tomorrow."[98] In the afternoon 3rd Cavalry Division was stretched out from north of Tilloy-les-Mofflaines back to Arras and 2nd Cavalry Division similarly arranged south of the village but in the circumstances could not be deployed and therefore simply returned to bivouacs. Just one brigade in the hands of VI Corps and up with the movements of 4th Division could have possibly allowed an even more impressive advance. The stark difference between the advances possible north and south of the River Scarpe will be examined in more detailed later but for now the state of the wire and forward trenches in the descriptions above must be borne in mind when giving thought to the successes in the north and failures in the south. What is without doubt is that the British Army had finally experienced the taste of success. The question remained, what would they do with it?

Common themes throughout contemporary descriptions were that of poor German artillery response when the attack got underway, the excellence of the creeping barrage, poor performance by tanks and uncut wire. The comprehensive programme of counter-battery fire supported by the gallant pilots and observers of the Royal Flying Corps ensured a very different experience for men crossing No Man's Land when compared with July 1916. Advances in sound ranging, flash spotting plus direct observation meant the German batteries had a very hard time in responding to the S.O.S signals of their front line troops. The barrage placed in front of the advancing British, Canadian and South African troops, on the other hand, was of an excellent nature. Men moved as close to the barrage as they could and as long as its coat tails were held onto, progress through the German lines was good. Only where delays caused the barrage to be lost did the level of difficulty grow. This is clear testament to the considerable and lasting difficulty of advancing against an enemy allowed to recover from being under artillery fire. In the north even uncut wire was no obstacle as long as the barrage remained on the line being attacked. On the contrary, where the barrage was lost, without lanes through the wire advancing infantry was at the mercy of rifle and especially machine gun fire and was in many cases defeated, sometimes by as little as a company of Germans and a couple of supporting machine guns. The success of a small number of individual tanks has been described and certainly without their intervention some of the advances gained might have been more limited. What is clear is that their numbers were too small and too scattered and the crews operating machines not up to the job. Even the more successful crews battled as much against the mechanical inefficiencies of their vehicles and their willingness to 'belly', as against the enemy. As already mentioned, where wire was uncut the result could be as disastrous as that of 1 July 1916 attack. The lack of a wire obstacle in some areas of the German front line yet clear presence in others will be examined later but common was the fact that in the third and fourth German lines, nearly all the wire was uncut. This clearly demonstrated the continuing problems that British and Dominion artillery had in engaging wire at long distance.

Engineers and signalmen worked tirelessly from the earliest possible moment to prepare tracks and communication links behind the advancing troops. The weather, of course, did not help as the torn up ground that many of the troops found difficulty in walking over was not exactly the kind of terrain that lend itself to anything heavier than a man moving on wheels. The primary tool to be got forward as quickly as possible was of course the artillery. In many cases the lighter field artillery had begun to move forward during the day but if the momentum of the advance was to

---

97   Falls, *Military Operations, France and Belgium 1917 Vol. 1*, p. 237.
98   Falls, p. 237.

Cavalry passing through Arras. (IWM Q2825)

be maintained it fell upon elements of the heavier artillery to also get forward. This was to prove a momentous task and the severity of the undertaking must be kept in mind when delays and problems with artillery support are read in accounts of subsequent days. The combination of poor (in terms of temperature and precipitation) April weather and a week-long bombardment do not allow for rapid movement over the terrain advanced over, the mud of the area being of a particularly sticky composition.[99] Supplies were also a necessity for the forward troops and the road to Tilloy-les-Mofflaines from Arras was already in action for lorries by midnight.[100] Most of the time it was by pack transport that all the necessities to continue the fight were brought forward. The unenviable task of getting telephone wire forward to aid communication with advanced troops seems to have been not been carried out evenly across the front. It is clear from brigade and divisional diaries that in some cases (9th Division is a good example) news of events from the front were rapidly in the hands of the commanders in the rear. The best example of how different levels of communication had a profound effect upon events can be seen by comparing the actions and reactions of the two divisions side by side attacking Observation Hill, south of the Scarpe. Both 15th and 12th Divisions had met similar difficulties when moving forward from the Black Line. The 15th Division had, on two occasions, used good communications to alter its artillery plan, firstly at

99   The author has experienced this on many occasions, and can testify that 100 metres in muddy conditions
      leaves one exhausted and that without equipment, etc.
100 Falls, *Military Operations, France and Belgium 1917 Vol. 1,* p. 238.

the Railway Triangle and then again later on Observation Hill, pulling back the barrage to allow the Brown Line to be taken. Although it did not reach its final objectives for the day that could be put down to different reasons, not because the commanders were unaware of what was happening or could not communicate with the relevant arms. The 12th Division, on the other hand, seems to have been blind to events from the moment the Black Line was left. There are gaps in the diary entries of upwards of an hour where nothing seems to have been heard and certainly no attempt to change plans was forthcoming; the artillery simply stuck to its pre-attack fire plan and off the barrage went into the distance, leaving attacking troops floundering in its absence.

The Germans at the end of this first day were in almost total disarray. New tactics of manning the front line thinly and then counter attacking had been either ignored or reserves so far back that it was too late by the time they could get to the fighting. Local reserves had been used to plug holes in the defensive lines and there was little left to cope with further attacks and certainly no way could a counter attack at any point on the front be contemplated. Apart from a scattering of units from reserve divisions the line was still being held by those who had been present on the first day or their immediate reserves. A great deal of artillery had been lost and again, reserves of this important arm were only slowly approaching the battlefield. *Kronprinz* Rupprecht von Bayern, commander of *Heeresgruppe Kronprinz Rupprecht*[101] of which *6th Army* was a part, noted in his diary that "the first news was most worrying" and that the "bad news multiplied as the day passed and in the evening came the sad report that not only the Vimy heights had been lost but, even worse, that the third line at Fampoux had been broken."[102] The Army Group leader was even given to ponder the further prosecution of the war in his diary such was the news. He felt the success would revive any flagging determination in the Entente to prosecute the war to its bitter end, namely a German defeat.

---

101 Army Group Crown Prince Rupprecht.
102 Rupprecht, *Kronprinz* von Bayern, *Mein Kreigstagebuch, Zweiter Band*, p. 135.

8

The Day After

Desire of desire. And yet
life stayed on within my soul.
One night in sheltering from the wet
I quite forgot I could forget.
The Other

The long, complex and extremely detailed operation plans created by Army and then Corps staff officers and then translated into similarly long, complex and detailed operation plans at divisional level were for one purpose only, the assault on the German positions on Z day, in this case 9 April. Objective lines are given and all the necessary organisation and movement of troops and material, fire plans, timings and a whole plethora of miscellanea which can be examined in Appendix II. Nowhere in the plans is the next step contemplated. At an Army level broad brush plans such as:

> The Third Army will then capture the German defensive line which runs from Arras to Cambrai (the Hindenburg Line)[1] by attacking it in flank and rear, and will advance on Cambrai,[2]

are laid out but how they are to do this, where they are to aim towards over the next day and so on is not to be found. Nowhere in Corps orders is the above more than reiterated with no attempt to put flesh on those general instructions. Two and a half years of trench warfare had reduced planning to that of how to take that which is in front of you and if successful the lines for a given distance beyond. Thus divisional plans have instructions for one day and no more and also absolutely no freedom to go beyond those plans without Corps instructions.

Therefore, what was to happen on 10 April falls into two categories. The most straightforward and the one that many corps and divisional staff were at ease with, was that to be given to units that had not gained the first day's objectives. Staff officers had gained a great deal of experience of doing just this throughout 1915 and 1916. The second and much more complicated were to be those orders for units that did find themselves at the far end of the instructions given so far; that is, they had gained the objectives of Z Day and wanted to know quite simply 'what now?' A novel experience for many staff officers.

The more straightforward of the situations will be taken first, which, in the case of the Canadian Corps, was only applicable in the north where 4th Division had not fully taken Hill 145. Here in the early hours 85th and 75th Battalions had pushed men forward into Beggar and Bessy Trenches,

---

1   In actual fact the Hindenburg Line did not run to Cambrai, but approximately 7 miles to the south west of the town; so even this broad instruction would be difficult to follow the measuring of some unknown distance of the German defensive line and also Cambrai.
2   Falls, *Military Operations, France and Belgium 1917 Vol. 1 Appendices*, Appendix 30, p. 99.

taking a number of prisoners and thus establishing a good jumping off point for later that day. Later, in fact, didn't come until the afternoon. Brig.-General Odlum decided to have a look for himself at 3.00am and saw that it would require fresh troops to ensure that the full objectives were taken that day. The organising of this attack and the required artillery barrage to support it meant that it was afternoon[3] before the as yet unused 44th and 50th Battalions of 10th Brigade moved up in artillery formation towards the new Canadian front line on the hill. In the meantime, the remnants of 5th and 1st Companies of *R.I.R. 261* had, during the night, been pulled back below the ridge but during the morning they returned to the upper trenches. At 3.04pm the barrage opened on Banff Trench and when this intensified at 3.15pm the men of A and C Companies of the 50th Battalion on the left and C and D Companies of 44th Battalion on the right moved out to just behind it. After four minutes the barrage lifted and the men moved forward and occupied the German trenches after about half an hour of severe fighting. On the right D Company of the 44th had to clear parts of Bois de la Folie, in which they succeeded, causing heavy casualties on the retreating enemy. The last line for 4th Division had finally been taken but at considerable further cost as casualties for 50th Battalion alone amounted to 11 officers and 218 O.R.[4] One act of bravery during this attack was that of Private John Patterson of the 50th Battalion.

> For most conspicuous bravery in attack. When the advance of our troops was held up by an enemy machine-gun, which was inflicting serious casualties, Pte Pattison, with utter disregard for his own safety, sprang forward, and jumping from shell-hole to shell-hole, reached cover within thirty yards of the enemy gun. From this point, in face of heavy fire, he hurled bombs, killing and wounding some of the crew, then rushed forward, overcoming and bayoneting the surviving five gunners. His valour and initiative undoubtedly saved the situation and made possible the further advance to the objective.[5]

This advance also allowed 12th Brigade on the right to move forward and thus the whole of 9 April objectives for 4th Division were now established and consolidated. 47th Battalion later moved forward to relieve 44th and 50th Battalions as the latter were still tasked, as originally planned, with taking Hill 120, the Pimple. The German account reads a little differently with a claim that once lost, some of the upper trenches were retaken, but they then came under the fire of their own artillery. Although it is clear that the Canadians had the ridge in firm hands by the end of the day the German account does reinforce the fact that this was a hard battle. By now *79th Reserve-Infanterie-Division*, that had clearly fought most gallantly to hold Hill 145 was down to two thirds of its original strength.[6]

The only other movement on 10 April on the Canadian Corps front was in the evening when the British 13th Brigade was pulled out of the line to return to 5th Division in Corps reserve. 1st and 2nd Canadian Divisions adjusted their frontage to replace the line vacated by the British. German accounts mention a number of attacks by the Canadians around Farbus with the railway

---

3   The C.O. of 44th Battalion received orders at 11.00am.

4   Library & Archives, Canada, war diaries – 44th Canadian Infantry Battalion, RG9, Militia and Defence, Series III-D-3, Volume 4939, Reel T-10745, File: 435; war diaries – 50th Canadian Infantry Battalion, Militia and Defence, Volume 4941, File 441.

5   *London Gazette*, 2 August 1917, no.30215. Pattison unfortunately did not live to receive the VC as he was killed near Lens on 3 June 1917. He is buried in La Chaudière Military Cemetery, not that far from the action described above.

6   Behrmann & Brandt, *Die Osterschlacht bei Arras 1917 I. Teil*, p. 152.

line seemingly the goal but this is not confirmed by Canadian diaries.[7] Patrols were sent out by the Canadians which probably accounts for the comments.

The next unit down the line from the Canadians, 51st Highland Division, had the overnight task of sorting out where their units were. Even into the night, although it was known that 152nd Brigade had been stopped short of the Brown Line, it was still thought that 154th Brigade held that position. It seems that the repeated concerns expressed by the Canadian 1st Division that they had nobody on their right did not percolate to the Headquarters of 51st Division. That a platoon of the Gordon Highlanders had kept touch with the Canadians but then when finding themselves alone actually came out of the Brown Line to join the others in Tommy Trench really does raise the question of how such a mistake could be made and never realised. 152nd Brigade's instructions for the morning were simple and brief; take the Brown Line that you should have done the day before. These orders were given at midnight[8] and the attack, carried out by 1/5th Gordon Highlanders, went in at 5.00am. No barrage was to be put onto the German trenches, merely a defensive one beyond. It is interesting that both Elect Trench and then the Brown Line itself were taken in fairly quick time and that in the words of the unit diary, "with comparatively few casualties." It was found, however, that all the reports of 154th Brigade being in the Brown Line were false and Gordon Highlander's flank was in the air.[9] This prompt action of the brigade is the one positive that can be taken out of the two days for the division. The assumptions made about being in the Brown Line led 154th Brigade into giving no new orders and thus it was only when news filtered down that the position was not as they had thought were measures put in place. Buy this time 4th Gordon Highlanders and 7th Argyll & Sutherland Highlanders, realising their error had begun to try and take the Brown Line by attacking down the communication trenches Tommy, Toast and Tired. These attacks failed as the Germans had been given plenty of time to return to their trenches, it being clear from the reports of Lt MacNaughton that at one point they had retired from them. Not until 8.00pm was another attempt organised, this time trying to move down both left and right flanks but yet again, with the Germans back in depth, uncut wire in front and little or no artillery support, both attacks failed. The best that could be done was to create some outposts to at least connect the line with the Canadians around the Commandant's House and 152nd Brigade around Zehner Weg.[10] 51st Division H.Q. seems to have been blissfully unaware of what had been going on. Only at 1.50pm did they hear from 152nd Brigade that there was nobody to their north when they got into the Brown Line (they had already been there for over six hours, why only now report?). Shortly afterwards Brigadier General J.G.H. Hamilton DSO, O.C. 154th Brigade, himself reported to Maj.-Gen Harper that he was not holding the Brown Line but Tommy Trench. This cannot have been a very comfortable conversation. Hamilton told Harper that bombing attacks were underway to take the Brown Line but then, contrary to other reports, the divisional diary goes on to say; "This [the two o'clock attack] and a subsequent bombing attack failed to materialise." Thus no properly orchestrated attack was carried out on the 10th and the right flank of the Canadians was left uncovered the whole day. Hamilton remained O.C. of 154th Brigade until almost the end of the year before returning to the UK 'to rest'. It is perhaps most fortunate for the history of the 51st Division that, at the same time they were slowly sorting themselves out on the heights of the Point Du Jour, the

7   Berhmann & Brandt, *Die Osterschlacht bei Arras 1917 I. Teil*, p. 160.
8   The Operation Order for this attack talks of men of 154th Brigade being in the Brown Line and note has to be taken of this.
9   TNA: WO95/2881 War Diaries of 5th Gordon Highlanders; TNA WO95/2862 War Diaries of 152nd Brigade.
10   TNA: WO95/2884 War Diaries of 154th Brigade.

Germans were having to deal with their own problems. As dawn approached on the 10th it was clear that the retreat of all the elements of *Bayerische I.D. 14* had left a substantial gap between them (with the reserves of *I.R. 85* that had been given to them) and *I.R. 31* which, it will be recalled, had come up just at the right time into the third line between Roeux and Gavrelle. Thus, instead of counter attacking up onto the area held by the Scottish division the Germans were busy plugging holes in their own defences.[11]

The next unit down the line had a similar set of orders for the early hours of the 10th as they too had not reached the Brown Line. 103rd Brigade had, after severe losses and delays getting to the Blue Line, been unable to reach their objective and it was decided at Divisional H.Q. to pause and organise a more formal attack on the Brown Line for the next morning. Interestingly, a staff officer from Divisional H.Q. went forward to 103rd Brigade H.Q. to organise the details of the attack, Operational Orders for which had been written. Another remarkable detail is that 1/5th Gordon Highlanders, who it will be remembered were the sole unit of 51st Division to attack this day, were put under 103rd Brigade orders. In other words, they attacked because of an initiative of 34th Division, not their own. This aspect of the attack is glossed over in 51st Division diaries which merely state that the Gordons were attacking in line with 34th Division on their right. Three Companies of the divisional pioneers, the 18th Northumberland Fusiliers, were moved up to the Blue Line to enable the brigade to make the attack as strongly as possible. This was very necessary when the remaining strengths of the two battalions in the Blue Line are seen, namely the 26th N.F. at five officers and 120 men and the 27th N.F. at 17 officers and 270 men. Together just overhalf a battalion strength left. They attacked at 5.00am and quickly overcame some of the German outposts in Gaul Weg, only coming under sustained fire when approaching Maison de la Côte. By working around the flanks this strongpoint was also overcome, the defenders making off. Troops of 27th N.F., 4th Tyneside Irish, entered the Brown Line at 7.15am, "standing up and firing at enemy retreating down the hill and cheering lustily."[12] Their fellow 26th N.F. came up next to them at around 7.45am; however, both units were unable to move to and consolidate the Green Line owing to lack of men and active sniping from Bailleul although posts were established there and held all day until the evening. Each of the battalions was reinforced by a company of the pioneers from 18th N.F. On a number of occasions during the day it was seen that the Germans were preparing a counter attack against Maison de la Côte. Around 7.45 this attack developed out of Bailleul but a prompt response to S.O.S. calls by the artillery meant the Germans made little progress. On reporting this counter attack to Divisional H.Q., 11th Suffolk Regiment from 101st Brigade reserve were sent up but by the time they arrived the situation was well in hand.[13]

Continuing with taking the more straightforward requirements for 10 April the narrative has to spring southwards now into VI Corps. How plans for the successful remains of 34th Division and that of 4th Division adapt to their being in a position to exploit will be taken later.

It is a very interesting exercise to follow the telephone message log of the General Staff of VI Corps as events of the afternoon and evening of the 9th unfold. Although it is clear that telephone communication is in place between corps and divisions the information coming back from 15th and 12th Divisions is very sparse indeed. It is of such a meagre nature that when 3rd Army telephones at 5.35pm with the following instruction,

---

11   Berhmann & Brandt, *Die Osterschlacht bei Arras 1917 I. Teil*, p. 163.
12   Report from C.O. of 27th Northumberland Fusiliers, found in TNA: WO95/2464 War Diaries of 103rd Brigade.
13   TNA: WO95/2464 War Diaries of 103rd Brigade.

Army Commander takes great store by Corps taking Brown Line as soon as possible and pushing on towards the Green Line in order to let the cavalry through and in order to support the Corps that has gained HYDERABAD REDOUBT on the Green Line.[14]

the corps is in no position to reply with any kind of affirmation or indeed that the attack will not happen. It is thus not before 11.01pm that the order comes through from 3rd Army, now finally aware of the failure to take the Brown Line south of the Scarpe, to renew the attack on that line at 8.00am the next day. This is not an order that should have taken VI Corps by surprise but their first instructions to divisions to be ready for an attack in the morning only goes out after this order is received, that is at 11.17pm. Then at 3.00am the 8.00am start time is changed to 12.00 noon. That means that, unlike north of the Scarpe where the divisional commander of 34th Division, knowing he had not reached the previous day's objective, simply pushed on as soon as was possible, all of VI Corps simply sat and waited on orders. 15th and 12th Divisions make no attempt to take matters into their own hands even though they have clear orders that have not as yet been completed. Corps initially says 8.00am so orders are prepared for then but then subsequently it becomes 12.00 noon. As to the reason for this change in timing it is necessary to go beyond VI Corps and look at communications with VII Corps. Clearly VII Corps were in accordance with their neighbouring Corps in terms of the need for an 8.00am attack and this message was sent out to divisions. 56th Division received this message at 10.40pm but at 12.15am sent a message back saying an attack at 8.00am was "not possible".[15] At 1.10am they messaged again to say the division would be ready by noon.[16] The next couple of hours saw the whole of the attack for the day in both VII and VI Corps put back to noon from the earlier start time. The reasons given by 56th Division for the delay are that the situation needed to be cleared up on their front. By this they meant that they wanted to clear the rear of the Hindenburg Line behind Neuville Vitasse by bombing down from the north before any further assault. There is no record of this decision being questioned, it was merely accepted and the attack delayed. The result of this dubious decision making process was a morning spent by two of the three British Corps doing little or nothing whilst the Germans moved reserves closer and closer to the front.

To look at the negative effect of this decision a return to the northern element of VI Corps has to be made. The previous evening, because of the partial success of 15th Division in entering the Brown Line, elements of 37th Division had been able to make progress up onto Orange Hill. During the night, as well as making progress in bombing down the Brown Line, troops of 63rd Brigade had also secured most of the northern part of the crest of Orange Hill. As morning came more efforts were made in this area and one company of the 8th Somerset Light Infantry had progressed to the enclosures that can be seen north-west of Monchy-le-Preux. 37th Division wished to reinforce this advance using 111th Brigade with 112th Brigade supporting to the south. The latter, however, had been moved back to allow 12th Division to restart its attack on the Brown Line. This of course was now timed for noon and therefore it was not until after this time that they could do so. In the meantime, the Somersets, supported by 8th Lincolnshires had reached the outskirts of Monchy-le-Preux. 111th Brigade, with 13th Royal Fusiliers on the left and 10th Royal Fusiliers right, advanced around noon over Orange Hill and in the direction of Monchy. Both battalions came under considerable artillery fire which caused significant casualties. Added to this when they reached the enclosures and woodland they also came under rifle and machine gun fire. In the end the line of 8th Somersets, 13th Royal Fusiliers and then 10th Royal Fusiliers

---

14   TNA: WO95/770 General Staff H.Q. VI Corps.
15   TNA: WO95/2933 War Diaries of H.Q. 56th Division.
16   TNA: WO95/2933 War Diaries of H.Q. 56th Division.

could not make any more headway and all the leading troops were withdrawn a little.[17] The 37th Division diary makes a couple of interesting notes with regards to artillery here. Firstly, it claims that heavy artillery fire from the vicinity of Greenland Hill could not be countered due to the unknown position of 3rd Cavalry Brigade in that area. Also that all morning sufficient artillery could not aid the advance on Orange Hill as it had mostly been involved in the noon attack on the Brown Line. The former statement is difficult to confirm but the latter is a direct consequence of the delay imposed upon the morning attack. The said artillery could have had four more hours to move forward had the attack gone in at 8.00am. As it was it was 2.30pm before a proportion of those guns could be brought into action from more forward positions.[18] It was already clear to German commanders that their intention of counter attacking would not be possible, the news being so that "*Generalleutnant* von Schöler had decided to finally give up the attempt to take Hill 102 [the German name for Orange Hill] and connect with the remaining sections of *Res. Inf. Rgt. 76* in the *Monchy-Riegel*".[19] In fact the decision was also made that the *Monchy-Riegel* should be abandoned which puts into context the attack to be described below.[20]

The attack on the Brown Line in the Feuchy Chapel area was carried out by 35th Brigade of 12th Division plus six companies attached from 36th Brigade. These six companies, three from 11th Middlesex Regiment and three from 7th Royal Sussex Regiment, were attached to 5th Royal Berkshire Regiment. This reinforced battalion had the task of moving north to pass through the Brown Line where it had been taken and then swinging south to assist the attacking units north and south of the Cambrai Road. Only at 5.00am did the brigade commander learn of the postponement of the attack until noon, only just sufficient time to ensure all his units were aware. He also makes an interesting observation that he could see men of 37th Division on Orange Hill at around 7.30am moving around in the open without being fired upon. Then at 9.30am he received orders to attack Feuchy Chapel without delay. There is no record of where this came from but he of course replied that having changed orders to 12.00 he could not at that short notice change them. Artillery preparation for the coming attack did not seem to be happening to any large extent, the Brown Line not being bombarded at all, until the Artillery Group Commander joined the brigade commander and a change could be put in place. The most telling observation by the brigade commander in his diary entry is that of events after 12.00 when the attack began. He watched the Berkshires come around the back of the Brown Line from the north on Orange Hill; immediately noting that the Germans who had been digging in east of Feuchy Chapel withdrew. With this flanking manoeuvre the units attacking frontally, 9th Essex Regiment and 6th Sussex Regiment, were able to take the Brown Line easily and around 1.00pm they set about digging in as their particular task was now complete.[21] This success then allowed 112th Brigade from 37th Division to move through which they did led by 8th East Lancashire Regiment on the left and 6th Bedfordshire Regiment on the right. Both battalions advanced at a pace and soon reached Les Fossés Farm (as named on the trench maps, diary entries name it La Fosse Farm) where they were checked by fire from both flanks, especially from Monchy-le-Preux above them on the left. The Bedfords managed a little further but were pulled back before dark. Another attack was made at

---

17   TNA: WO95/2532 War Diaries of 10th & 13th Royal Fusiliers. The decision forced upon *Generalmajor* von Reuter of *17th Infanterie-Division* to abandon the Monchy-Riegel is why men were able to continue forward towards Monchy; Berhmann & Brandt, *Die Osterschlacht bei Arras 1917 II*, p. 62.
18   TNA: WO95/2513 War Diaries of H.Q. 37th Division.
19   Berhmann & Brandt, *Die Osterschlacht bei Arras 1917 II*, p. 61.
20   Behrmann, et al, p. 61.
21   TNA: WO95/1848 War Diaries of H.Q. 35th Brigade. The ease of taking the line and the visible retreat has already been mentioned as a consequence of taking Orange Hill; Behrmann & Brandt, *Die Osterschlacht bei Arras 1917 II*, p. 61.

7.30pm but the promised artillery support "never materialised"[22] and it thus made no progress. The success of the flanking movement, when eventually carried out, again emphasises the possibilities that were in place the previous day when a hole had been punched in the Brown Line and the opportunity to push units through that break were in place. The hastily prepared, bravely carried out, but ultimately useless attack in the evening is a foretaste of what is to come. In fact, the Germans had already identified that the Monchy-Riegel was no longer tenable and orders went out to *I.R. 51* at 3.30am on the morning of the 10th to withdraw onto the high ground about 700 metres west of the Monchy-le-Preux to Roeux road. The reasons for this increased opposition after the initial rush can be seen by two different German reinforcements of their front. Firstly, due to the attack on *R.I.R. 84* by 21st Division being held by its 2nd Battalion without a fear of a breakthrough, the reserve battalion, the 1st, was able to be placed in the Wancourt area as support for the retreating *17th R.I.D.* and secondly the first elements of *26th Infanterie-Division* from the reserve were beginning to arrive, namely the 1st and 2nd battalions of *Grenadier-Regiment 119*. During the afternoon these began to relieve the worn out units of *11th Infanterie-Division*, whose total casualties amounted to 105 officers and 3154 O.R.[23]

3rd Division south of the Arras-Cambrai Road also had the task of taking the Brown Line and was similarly delayed by orders to 12.00. These orders from Corps were to lead to the next failure to use the day properly. The delay has already been discussed but the wording of the orders led to the next failure. Order g545 goes out from Corps at 10.30am with the following key sentences;

> As soon as BROWN LINE is captured it will be consolidated.
> 37th Division will move and capture MONCHY as soon as it can pass the BROWN LINE.
> The 3rd and 15th Divisions will be prepared to move after 37th Division and to consolidate the GREEN LINE as follows.[24]

There then follows where that objective is to be found, namely the previously arranged Green Line. The 3rd Division allocates 8th Brigade, all four battalions in line for the attack at noon.[25] Instructions to the units are to take and consolidate the Brown Line, nothing more. The attack goes in with, according to the 7th King's Shropshire Regiment, poor artillery support with most of the shells falling behind the advancing infantry.[26] The line was easily taken and consolidation was carried out.[27] There followed nothing, no orders for a further advance nor can any reasons for them not being given be found in any of the divisional, brigade or unit diaries. 3rd Division had clearly interpreted the order for VI Corps as one to take the Brown Line and await 37th Division's taking of Monchy, in other words await further instructions. It has already been seen that the difficulties of taking Monchy and the area south of the village were exacerbated by fire from the south, in other words from Guémappe. This was precisely the place that should have been under attack

22 TNA: WO95/2536 War Diaries of H.Q. 112th Brigade; TNA WO95/2537 War Diaries of 8th East Lancashire. There are discrepancies in the various accounts for this attack over whether there was any artillery at all (brigade diary), that the artillery was due at 7.30 for half an hour and the attack was at 8.00pm (East Lancs Diary), or that the artillery lifted at 7.30 just as the East Lancs got the orders (Falls, *Military Operations, France and Belgium 1917 Vol. 1*). Whatever did actually happen, the attack failed, the German reserves were now firmly placed.

23 Berhmann & Brandt, *Die Osterschlacht bei Arras 1917 II*, p. 62.

24 TNA: WO95/770 War Diaries of H.Q. VI Corps.

25 1st Gordon Highlanders, 1st Royal Scots fusiliers, 7th King's Shropshire, and 8th East Yorkshire regiments.

26 TNA: WO95/1421 War Diaries of 7th King Shropshire.

27 The line being taken easily of course as the Germans had already decided upon a retreat, all a consequence of the taking of Orange Hill. This was *R.I.R. 76* retreating out of the Monchy-Riegel; Berhmann & Brandt, *Die Osterschlacht bei Arras 1917 II*, p. 63.

from 3rd Division. The whole day therefore passed by with the only action by 3rd Division being the taking of a line, with few casualties, that should have been taken the day before. An objective remained from their original orders for the 9th but that was deemed, without being questioned, to be superseded by the new orders from VI Corps and their unclear and unambitious content. The British Army was clearly still deep into the principle of top down command with little in the way of initiative at divisional level.

14th Division, having also dug in short of the Brown Line spent the morning reorganising the two lead battalions of 43rd Brigade, 6th Somersets and 6th Duke of Cornwall's L.I., into one composite battalion and preparing the remaining two battalions, 6th K.O.Y.L.I. and 10th D.L.I. (who it will be remembered formed the assault troops the previous day) for an attack at noon. Both the units complained that it was insufficient time to get up and therefore the attack was delayed until 12.25.[28] With the composite battalion providing fire support the leading battalions caught up with the artillery barrage and advanced. They saw 3rd Division matching with them to the left but no sign of 56th Division on their right. This led to coming under severe machine gun fire from the southern flank resulting in the 6th K.O.Y.L.I. on the right veering left. The K.O.Y.L.I. diary is clearly aggrieved by this; "no move, however, was made by this division [meaning the 56th] which left our flank entirely exposed."[29] Both unit lost direction, eventually reaching and getting into, intermingled, a small element of the Brown Line. When it was seen that an element of the Brown Line in the divisional area was not occupied the brigade ordered up the composite battalion. The C.O. of the Somersets, in command, ordered up the two composite companies of the D.C.L.I. who, after cutting the wire, entered the Brown Line.[30] After clearing some of the wire "in preparation for cavalry"[31] the brigade was finally relieved by 41st Brigade during the afternoon. As they relieved the 43rd Brigade, the 7th King's Royal Rifle Corps and 7th Rifle Brigade found that, contrary to their understanding, the whole of the Brown Line had not been taken. Only the first line was occupied in the southern section of the divisional area, the second line still being held by German troops. 7th K.R.R.C. on the right even had to clear some Germans out of the front trench as well. Both units found themselves under fire from Hill 90 to their south.[32] An attempt to get to this troublesome hill by 8th Rifle Brigade, coming up in support, was stopped by the wire on the Wancourt–Feuchy Line and the effort was abandoned.[33] There does not seem to have been a concerted effort by the K.R.R.C. to get into the 2nd German Line. Thus the division finished the day just about on the Brown Line but not comfortably and with no cover on their right. Again, no organised (that is with proper artillery support) attempt can be identified from sources that there was ever an intention to get beyond the Brown Line. An excuse for difficulties in getting into that line can be seen in the lack of flank cover south of the division but the tardiness in getting orders through to the units tasked with the noon attack (remembering it had all been delayed from earlier in the morning) is more difficult to excuse. As is the use of troops in the same brigade that had been used to assault the Germans the day before with a whole fresh brigade to hand. Only later was that brigade engaged and then only as a relief, with no plan to use it to get on and advance the

---

28   TNA: WO95/1906 War Diaries of 6th K.O.Y.L.I.; TNA WO95/1908 War Diaries of 10th D.L.I.
29   TNA: WO95/1906 War Diaries of 6th K.O.Y.L.I.
30   TNA: WO95/1904 War Diaries of H.Q. 43rd Brigade.
31   TNA: WO95/1904 War Diaries of H.Q. 43rd Brigade. A remarkable statement, but orders had been given as shall be seen for cavalry to advance.
32   TNA: WO95/1896 War Diaries of 7th K.R.R.C & 7th Rifle Brigade.
33   TNA: WO95/1904 War Diaries of H.Q. 43rd Brigade. Although the 8th R.B. diary makes no mention of an attempt to get to Hill 90, merely stating that it formed a defensive flank on the Neuville Vitasse – Wancourt road; TNA: WO95/1895 War Diaries of 8th Rifle Brigade.

line. For yet another division the day had passed with very little to show and increasing signs of Germans reinforcing their lines and preparing fresh ones in the rear.

56th Division had finished the day before with the success of having taken Neuville Vitasse but then the failure to break through the Hindenburg Line and swing partly right to take the Wancourt-Feuchy Line and onwards to Wancourt itself. It has already been see that possible opportunities to get behind the Germans in the Hindenburg Line had not been followed up, namely the excursion of a company of the London Scottish out towards the rear. Overnight the objective was to clear as much of the line southwards as possible by bombing. To this end the proposed attack at 8.00am the next morning was deemed not possible as "the situation was not likely to be cleared up before daybreak."[34] It is also very unclear what was meant by being "cleared up". How much was Major-General Hull hoping to achieve which eventually meant holding up the whole of VII and VI Corps the next morning? Basically the idea was to use 7th Middlesex and 4th London Regiment to clear the Hindenburg Line southwards to the junction with 30th Division at Lion Lane trench. Such an action could have been carried out without prejudicing any attack eastwards by fresh troops at 8.00am the next morning. The whole of the divisional attention seems to have switched to one of bombing down the Hindenburg Line with little thought to moving behind it and taking the Wancourt-Feuchy Line; surely a manoeuvre which would have forced the Germans out of that area of trench in any case. The companies of the *I/R.I.R. 31*, already in action the day before managed, despite dwindling numbers, to make the progress of the 56th Division a slow one down the trenches.[35] The actions of units in the afternoon are very difficult to follow as the descriptions given by the various diaries do not tally at all well and is good evidence of a lack of cohesive command on the day. All four battalions of 167th Brigade are described in the brigade diary as bombing down different elements of the German Lines. That this course of action required a delay until noon is extremely difficult to comprehend as it was basically a continuation of what was occurring through the night and in the early hours. The consequences of this approach by 167th Brigade (never questioned by the division) was that the Brown Line was not attacked until later. This explains why 14th Division found their flank in the air when attacking north of the 56th and why the Germans in the Wancourt-Feuchy Line could target them, so badly disrupting their assault. The 3rd London Regiment blandly reports moving to the attack at 3.00pm, hours behind any artillery support that had been organised to fall on the Brown Line. It is then clear that the battalion had no clear idea of where their boundary was to the north. The diary complains of 14th Division being too far away, when they were in fact by this time on their divisional boundary. Map references for the position of 3rd London do not hold any water either (one puts them in Nepal Trench) 8th Middlesex, on the other hand, state their attack started at 12.00 prompt but that it was held up by machine gun fire in front of Nepal Trench. Casualties amounted to 24 which does not seem to point to a sustained attempt to get at the Germans. 7th Middlesex diary talks of working in the trenches and then at 4.30pm being in a trench parallel to Nepal Trench. Only late in the afternoon at 5.30pm were units told to reform in the area behind the Hindenburg Line where the Wancourt-Feuchy Line, called Nepal Trench here was situated. Reports then came in from all units that Nepal Trench was held, all objectives taken. Slowly but surely as the evening wore on these reports were seen to be false. All the units seemed to be in an unknown trench in front of Nepal Trench, which was seen to be strongly held with all its uncut wire in front.[36] Two battalions of the brigade seem to have been

34   TNA: WO95/2933 War Diaries of H.Q. 56th Division.

35   Behrmann & Brandt, *Die Osterschlacht bei Arras 1917 II*, p. 67.

36   TNA: WO95/2947 War Diaries of H.Q. 167th Brigade; TNA WO95/2949 War Diaries of 1st & 3rd London Rgt; TNA WO95/2950 War Diaries of 7th & 8th Middlesex Rgt; Ward, Maj. D.H. Dudley,

engaged in a confused fight for the trenches of the Hindenburg Line with only partial and unco-ordinated attempts to break into Nepal Trench which was clearly the brigade objective. The other two engaged in two separate, in time, attempts to attack the Brown Line in Nepal Trench. There seems to have been little or no brigade command and control over these actions. Coordination of action seems to have been sorely lacking on 10 April in 56th Division. What the division also missed by not pressing behind the Hindenburg Line was the fact that the decision had already been made by the Germans to pull out of this line north of where it connected with Nepal Trench and *III/R.I.R. 86* had already pulled back. "Now Hauptman Schellins' [O.C. *I/R.I.R. 31*] left flank was open, and he only had the lack of awareness of the enemy to thank that this was not seen and used against him."[37]

The failure of 56th Division on its left led to a day of relative inactivity for 30th Division as well. They had the thick uncut wire of the Hindenburg Line in front of them and in spite of time being available to bring artillery down on this wire or bring trench mortars into action little progress in wire cutting was evident. One excuse the day before for finding the wire impregnable was the distance back that units were advancing from precluding the use of trench mortars for wire cutting. This reason could not now be used as the division held the sunken lane only a few hundred metres away from the German front line. No mention is made of any attempts to now use mortars. Patrols were sent out to ascertain whether the line in front was held or not. All afternoon comments are made about the front line being empty and more patrols being sent out but finding the wire a barrier no troops managed to get to the front line. Finally, at 10.30pm the divisional diary makes the simple statement that "Enemy is still in his trenches opposite us – lines strongly wired."[38] 90th Brigade had relieved the men of the 21st Brigade who had suffered in the attack the previous day so the troops in front of the Hindenburg Line immediately to the right of 56th Division who should, surely, have been benefitting from the work of 167th Brigade in bombing down the trenches, were fresh. The diary entry for 10 April of this brigade is beyond belief when the story of the day is known;

> An attack to be made in conjunction with 89th Inf. Brig. was cancelled owing to withdrawal of enemy from the immediate front.[39]

Therefore, a whole brigade, not as yet engaged, sat impotent in the sunken lane in front of the Hindenburg Line, whilst its neighbouring division spent the afternoon bombing the area in front of them. A unit tasked with helping out in the action of bombing down the German lines was "hampered by the presence of troops of other divisions in front of them."[40] Had all this been the result of a rushed situation where cooperation would have been more difficult it could be more readily understood. That a whole morning of inactivity passed by without any attempt by the two divisions to coordinate their actions or perhaps see the use of 90th Brigade to do the trench clearing whilst 167th Brigade concentrated on its task on the Brown Line, is difficult to understand. There is no evidence of any attempt by the two divisions to communicate with each other in any way. 89th Brigade diary gives as a reason for the attack on the Hindenburg Line being cancelled as the fact that the attack was dependent upon 56th Division taking Nepal Trench, which of course it didn't. As 89th Brigade still had the Hindenburg Line in front of it, with no troops bombing across

The Fifty Sixth Division, (Uckfield: Reprint Naval & Military Press, 2002), pp. 124-125. Ward simply writes of clearing the trenches of the Hindenburg Line with no comment on trying to take Nepal Trench.

37   Behrmann & Brandt, *Die Osterschlacht bei Arras 1917 II*, p. 67.
38   TNA: WO95/2311 War Diaries of H.Q. 30th Division.
39   TNA: WO95/2337 War Diaries of H.Q. 90th Brigade.
40   TNA: WO95/2337 War Diaries of H.Q. 90th Brigade.

its front, this can be appreciated as a sensible decision. At this point there were no new German reserves in the Monchy-Riegel and the German Official History is clear that it was only small groups of men holding the line that prevented any advance.[41] It speaks of the heroic efforts to hold the line without knowing, of course, that only a limited number of British units were in fact engaged. It is very questionable whether these exhausted and depleted units would have stood for long against a concerted and coordinated attack by 56th and 30th Divisions.

Men of 64th Brigade in 21st Division were desperately holding on in some of the front line of the Hindenburg Positions throughout the night, a communication trench having been dug to support the members of 10th K.O.Y.L.I., 1st East Yorks and 15th D.L.I. who were there. Even tea was brought up to the men but more importantly large quantities of bombs as that was the weapon being used at the trench blocks. These defensive actions continued all day especially on the left where the trench block held by 10th K.O.Y.L.I. came under intense pressure. For his part in defending this block for most of the day until he was finally killed Private Horace Waller was awarded the V.C.:

> For most conspicuous bravery when with a bombing section forming a block in the enemy line. A very violent counter-attack was made by the enemy on this post, and although five of the garrison were killed, Pte Waller continued for more than an hour to throw bombs, and finally succeeded in repulsing the attack. In the evening the enemy again counter-attacked the post, and all the garrison became casualties except for Pvt Waller, who although wounded later, continued to throw bombs for another half an hour, until he was killed. Throughout these attacks he showed the utmost valour, and it was due to his determination that the attacks on this important post were repulsed.[42]

During the day, success on the left was awaited before any extra offensive action was considered with 10th Yorkshire Regiment from 62nd Brigade being put at the disposal of the O.C. 63rd Brigade for this possible attack. Also Br.-Gen. Headlam had on more than one occasion instructed Lt.-Col. Postlethwaite of 10th K.O.Y.L.I. that he should counter attack with his two companies in the lane they were in, just in front of the German front line, should the German attack. This German attack came in at 7.00pm from the right of the brigade, against the 1st East Yorks. It was too much for them and they were forced out which in turn forced out the D.L.I. and K.O.Y.L.I. back to the support trench newly dug behind. The SOS call to the British artillery was answered but some fell short. This deterred Postlethwaite from immediately attacking and by the time Headlam wanted to order the counter attack Divisional H.Q. refused as some time had elapsed and the Germans had returned to the trench line in strength with machine guns.[43] The fact that this angered Headlam can be seen in his continuing to comment and his condemnation of Postlethwaite on the lack of a counter attack years later when writing to Falls, as part of the review of the Official History.[44] Waller's bravery was then eventually for nought as all the Hindenburg Line was back in the hands of its German defenders. The German Official History has this action

41   Berhmann & Brandt, *Die Osterschlacht bei Arras 1917 II*, pp. 67-69. Only later in the day did one company, the 9th, of *Reserve-Infanterie-Regiment 121*, belonging to *26th Reserve-Division*, join *I.R. 31* in the battle. The remainder of *III/R.I.R. 121* was held in reserve, only to be used in an extreme situation.

42   *The London Gazette*, 8 June 1917, no.30122. Pvt Waller's grave can be visited very close to where he died in Cojeul British Cemetery near to St.-Martin-sur-Cojeul. Originally from Batley Carr, a district of Dewsbury, his name can be found on war memorials in both these places.

43   TNA: WO95/2159 War Diaries of H.Q. 64th Brigade.

44   TNA: CAB45/116 Military: Western Front: Battles: Comments, Letters, Personal Accounts, Arras, letter to Headlam from Falls.

occurring in the early hours of the 10th with Stormtroopers of 8th Company *R.I.R 84* but this does not match in any way the account in the regimental history which correctly has the attack timed at 7.00pm. This more reliable source has the company involved as the 12th under the leadership of *Leutnant* Probst with *R.I.R. 99* on the German left assisting in throwing the British out of the line.[45]

Therefore, where there was no real need for orders other than a "complete the task you already have instructions for" type, the programme for 9 April had more or less been completed north of the River Scarpe but to the south progress had been sparse and the Brown Line was still elusive in places. The Green Line, final objective for the day before was, south of the river, far away and by now had some German reinforcements arriving between it and the British. North of the river though, the first day had left 4th Division on the Green Line and the reaction of British command to that situation must now be examined. The first instruction to 4th Division, as already related in the last chapter, was just after midnight and it was merely one of pushing onto the Green Line and consolidating, not one to stir the divisional commander to begin preparations for any major move. The next is received at 9.45am and tells the division to push patrols out "to regain touch with enemy."[46] Again, not a command that required any action as there was certainly contact with the enemy. Regardless of instructions, at 4.00am Major-General, GOC 4th Division, went forward to see his brigadiers and upon his return instructions were put together to renew the attack although to give the necessary time for this to be organised it was due for 3.00pm. The Maj.-General wanted the station, the Chemical Works and Roeux to be attacked and taken by 11th and 12th Brigades. Another set of orders arrived, however, at 1.25pm which put a stop to the preparations for that action. XVII Corps had decided to send in the cavalry and therefore the order read:

> 17th Corps ordered to support cavalry. 1st Cav. Bde. left ACQ about 11.30am and marches via FAMPOUX. 4th Dvn. Plus one 1 Inf. Bde. 9th Div. will support Cavalry and make good spur S.W. of PLOUVAIN – GREENLAND HILL – INN at I.7.2a 2.8 – HYDERABAD REDOUBT – POINT DU JOUR.[47]

Orders were immediately sent out to brigades by telephone to cancel the attack. 4th Division diary states that this arrived too late at 12th Brigade H.Q. and that 1st King's Own Royal Lancaster and 2nd West Riding regiments both attacked with losses. Smaller unit diaries paint a different picture in that neither brigade diary admits to receiving an order to attack except the one to support cavalry. Only 1st King's Own Lancasters describe an order to attack which they did at 2.30pm, losing heavily as soon as they left the shelter of Fampoux. They then received the cancellation order at 2.40pm and drew back to await the cavalry. All other units in both brigades describe no other action to that after the cavalry arrive. It seems that Lambton's wishes were not turned into action but subsequent events would seem to point towards that being a blessing.[48] That this attack was doomed without sufficient support and coordination was caused by the arrival overnight of various elements of *I/Grenadier-Regiment 119* into the line around Roeux with *II/G.R. 119* in support

---

45   Berhmann & Brandt, *Die Osterschlacht bei Arras 1917 II*, p. 73; Speck, Justiczinspector William, *Das Königlich Preußische Reserve-Infanterie-Regiment 84*, p. 181.
46   TNA: WO95/1446 War Diaries of H.Q. 4th Division.
47   TNA: WO95/1446 War Diaries of H.Q. 4th Division.
48   TNA: WO95/1491 War Diaries of H.Q. 11th Brigade; TNA: WO95/1502 War Diaries of H.Q. 12th Brigade; TNA: WO95/1506 War Diaries of 1st King's Own Lancaster Regt; TNA: WO95/1508 War Diaries of 2nd West Riding Rgt; TNA: WO95/1499 War Diaries of 1st Somerset Rgt; TNA: WO95/1495 War Diaries of 1st Hampshire Regiment.

nearby and finally *III/G.R. 119* held in Plouvain as *26th Infanterie-Division* reserve. No longer were the troops of 4th Division attacking exhausted and defeated units but fresh reserves who had been given the necessary time (a night and most of a day) to dig in and thus would require concerted effort to remove.[49]

When Brig.-General E. Makins, O.C. 1st Cavalry Brigade, arrived at the H.Q. of 12th Brigade in Athies he was not greeted with particularly welcome news. The attempt by the 1st King's Lancasters to advance was described and the situation generally with regards to the level of German opposition in front. Makins also talked to the COs of both the Lancasters and West Ridings and heard much the same message, sensibly deciding that no kind of action by the cavalry could do more than that already attempted by the infantry. After a small mounted effort north of the village, an attempt of dismounted men to get forward had failed and some casualties had been taken by shellfire, it was decided to pull the cavalry brigade back. Units of 11th Brigade did still push out patrols as requested. 1st Somerset L.I., promised artillery support did so only to find that no artillery fire materialised and the leading platoons were destroyed with only two men returning.[50] The 1st Hampshire, who had observed this, did try to put some men out but soon abandoned any further patrols. Throughout the whole of this confusion of action or in some cases inaction, there seems to have been almost no attempt to coordinate any kind of artillery support for any of the movements. In fact, this seems to have been the primary motive around the decision to employ cavalry. Lt.-General Fergusson had gone to General Allenby during the morning and said that there would not be sufficient artillery support to allow the infantry to advance. But he did feel that a rapid advance by cavalry would gain Greenland Hill. How, in 1917, two experienced generals could have come to such a decision is, to be frank, quite extraordinary. That this was only decided upon during the morning and thus delaying and in actual fact, cancelling any kind of possible action for the day is equally astonishing. An examination of the unit diary of 9th Division C.R.A. is illuminating in this respect. This division had, at its disposal for 9 April: 14th Brigade R.H.A. plus 23rd, 29th, 32nd, 50th, 51st and 52nd Brigades R.A. Movements during the day as each objective line was reached meant that by the end of the day 50th, 29th and 52nd Brigades had moved up to the British support line and 32nd Brigade had moved up 3,500 yards beyond the German Front Line. This meant at nightfall only 32nd Brigade remained in range. 14th R.H.A. and 23rd R.A. moved forward during the night.[51] In fact 51st Brigade had also moved up during the evening so in the morning 32nd and 51st Brigades were available, two out of seven brigades.[52] Although the 14th and 23rd had moved they did not seem to be available, not having registered on any targets.[53] Three brigades of artillery had been out of range since the afternoon of 9 April and yet remained in their positions throughout the next day. 50th Brigade only report moving again on the 11th.[54] A note must be taken here that the lack of an advance was not due to any adverse conditions, they were simply not ordered to move. Quite clearly, control over the artillery support required for a further advance on 10 April had fallen down completely.

49 Gemmingen-Guttenberg-Fürfeld Oberst Freiherr von, *Das Grenadier-Regiment Königin Olga (1 Württembergisches) Nr. 119 im Weltkrieg 1914-1918*, (Stuttgart: Belser, 1927), p. 119.
50 Majendie D.S.O., Major V.H.B., *A History of the 1st Battalion Somerset Light Infantry – 1 July 1916 to the end of the War*, p. 36.
51 TNA: WO95/1746 War Diaries of Commander Royal Artillery, 9th Division.
52 TNA: WO95/1752 War Diaries of 51st Brigade, Royal Artillery.
53 Falls, *Military Operations, France and Belgium 1917 Vol. 1*, p. 256.
54 TNA: WO95/1751 War Diaries of 50th Brigade, Royal Artillery.

The final act of the day in 4th Division area belongs to the Germans who, around 7.00pm mounted a counter attack which was broken up due to artillery and fire from the British lines. At least some artillery was available at this juncture when the SOS signals went up in the British Lines.[55]

The second day of the offensive had drawn to a close and any analysis of the outcomes can only result in a sense of disappointment and frustration. The excellent work on many parts of the front of the day before, the sacrifices of so many to ensure success and reach objectives, had been allowed to lay fallow for just the amount of time that the Germans required to make the succeeding days ones of pain and suffering. Where the task was a clear one, that of completing those set the previous day, delay in actually starting the operations was critical in ensuring the failure that ensued. Why 56th Division was allowed to force the delay across all of the southern area of the battlefield is a key question. As this decision crossed Corps boundaries then it lay at the feet of 3rd Army. Nowhere in any papers[56] can a reasoned argument be found as to why Allenby yielded to Maj.-Gen Hull's insistence that he could not start until noon. This was a prime example of the preoccupation with taking lines of trench when there existed a clear opportunity to get behind those very trenches and force the occupiers to retire. Hull asked and it seems to have been accepted without question. The following lack of cohesion in many of the attacks can therefore not be laid at the haste at which orders had to be issued. Many units were making ready to continue at 8.00am and thus had extra time to ensure a coordinated effort. This, as has been seen, was not always forthcoming, especially with regard to artillery support which was in many cases sadly lacking. There was clearly not as yet the clear communication necessary to ensure that the carefully laid out plans of 9 April which resulted in such good artillery support could be repeated. In many cases guns did not have to be moved as many remained in range so the constant mention by units of a poor barrage cannot be easily explained. In the case of VII Corps, when the attack finally went in, 167th Brigade seems to have lost control of what its battalions were doing, with one case of not even attacking with what barrage there was. This was in spite of having the whole morning to ensure orders were properly prepared and distributed. It has been seen how much the Germans were rapidly moving the reserves they had forward and that the distance some had to travel was considerable. The extra hours they were afforded can only be seen as catastrophic for the actions of the afternoon when combined with the disjointed approach of the British units. All the German sources make it clear that on the 10th only relatively small numbers of these reserves arrived but those that did, for example at Roeux, did not find it difficult to hold back the uncoordinated and unsupported efforts that were made. Where the success of the previous day had promised much for the dawning of a new one, the story was one of prevarication and lack of drive. 4th Division had little in the way of positive orders to work with, so that any possible continuation of forward movement was already condemned to the afternoon. Then, almost as an afterthought during the day the decision was made to move the cavalry forward, thus halting any possible action by the infantry. It required no more than a question of forward commanders as to the feasibility of this approach to condemn it to the rubbish bin. Decision making on the run was clearly not within the capabilities of commanders at this stage of the war. Later there was a ready excuse of not being able to get artillery forward to support further attacks. When the orders for forward movement are inspected, the usual excuse that can be seen in post war accounts of the difficulties in moving forward cannot be held as universally true. Some artillery brigades simply had no orders to move forward in at least

---

55   There is no mention of any attempt by *G.R. 119* or *I.R. 31* to attack in any German source, although the latter did push out patrols to ascertain how strongly Fampoux was held; these could have been mistaken as an attack; Berhmann & Brandt, *Die Osterschlacht bei Arras 1917 II*, p. 164.

56   This includes all Army and Corps papers and those of Allenby.

one divisional area. Where they did move it was at a pace that can only be described as leisurely. Nowhere in the diaries of the artillery units that moved late on the 9th or early on the 10th is any difficulty in moving forward described. One example of this seeming lack of drive can be seen in the papers of XIV Brigade R.H.A.[57] Under orders to move overnight to a forward position, which they did, they only began registering on new targets during the afternoon. Not a level of performance for a regiment trained for rapid fire and movement than can be applauded. As such then, they were missing from any possible artillery support the whole day having had little reported difficulty in moving forward. To conclude for now there is on the one hand no direct leadership to ensure existing orders are carried out promptly and on the other, where new orders are required, an inability to create a coherent set at all. The British Army clearly had a great deal yet to learn in creating an efficient command and control system.

---

57   TNA: WO 95/385/1.

9

Chasing Shadows

And I think that even if I could lose my deafness
the cuckoo's note would be drowned by the voice of my dead.

The Cuckoo

1st Army – Canadian Corps

To assist with the creation of a coherent commentary on the remaining days of the battle, the narrative will return to one which relates events on the Canadian front and then southwards and will in each case cover the remaining days per corps.

On the 1st Army front in the north there remained only one final objective for this first phase of the battle, the taking the hill to the north of the summit of Hill 145, known as the Pimple. It has already been seen that leaving this position out of the original plans had caused difficulties to the left of the Canadian 4th Division on the first day and in hindsight maybe this was a mistake. The plan, however, was to attack this position within 24 hours of the main assault, but only if 10th Canadian Brigade had not been committed. The requirement to use this brigade to complete the taking of Hill 145 therefore put the plans to assault the Pimple back 48 hours. Before that time the only real activity of the rest of the Canadian Corps was one of consolidation and alertness with regard to the possibility of German counter attacks. 1st Army had planned to continue the move forward on 10 April but, given the delay in assaulting the Pimple, and the need for adjoining divisions on the right to get forward, this move was delayed.

The orders for the capture of the Pimple were altered in date but not in substance. It was still to be carried out by 10th Canadian Brigade on the right, actually taking the hill and the spur within the Bois de Givenchy, with the British 73rd Brigade from 24th Division taking the Bois en Hache on the lower slopes of the Lorette Ridge. The Canadian attack was to be made by the already blooded 44th and 50th Battalions who had barely two days rest since being on Hill 145, plus a couple of companies of 46th Battalion.[1] This latter was an addition to the original orders to make up for losses of the 9th, allowing 50th Battalion to create two ad hoc companies, No. 1 and No. 2 for the attack on the Pimple with a narrower frontage.[2] The 73rd Brigade attack was to be carried out by 9th Royal Sussex Regiment on the left with 2nd Leinster Regiment[3] on the right.

Changing orders on the evening of 9 April meant a prolonged stint in the front line for 13th Middlesex, now not to be relieved until the night of the 10th and 11th by 12th Royal Fusiliers. All of this was to allow the two assault battalions to move up during the 11th and assemble

---

1   Library and Archives, Canada, wardiaries 46th Canadian Battalion, RG9, Militia and Defence, Series III-D-3, Volume 4939, Reel T-10745, File: 436.

2   Library and Archives, Canada, war diaries 50th Canadian Battalion, RG9, Militia and Defence, Series III-D-3, Volume 4941, Reel T-10747-10748, File: 441.

3   An interesting coincidence is that the Prince of Wales Leinster Regiment was designated Royal Canadians, having been originally raised in Canada as the 100th Foot, and had that nation on its right flank for this attack.

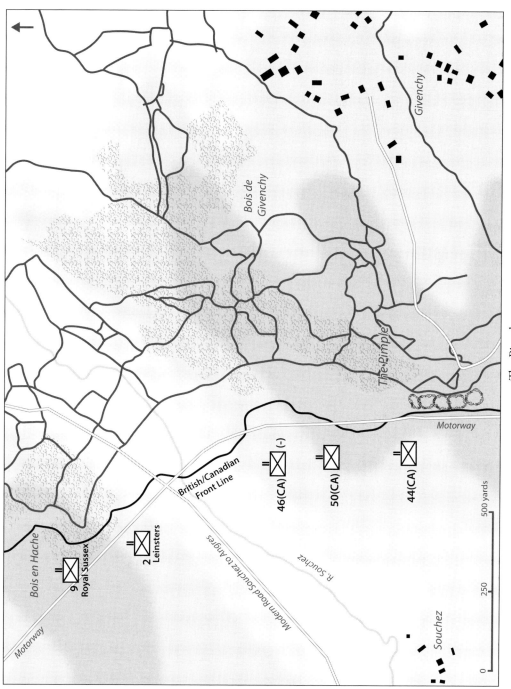

The Pimple.

during the night. This they had done by 4.00am on the 12th and both battalions reported beyond their own wire by 4.35am with 25 minutes to go. These developments occurred during a severe snowstorm, luckily for the British and Canadian troops, blowing directly into the faces of the Germans. A combination of the weather and the recent heavy bombardment of the area, however, created a major obstacle to the attacking troops. No Man's Land had been reduced to a mixture of water filled shell holes with the mud around them two to three feet deep. For all the troops that advanced that morning the blizzard was a Godsend as they struggled through the morass. Reducing visibility to 20 or 30 metres meant the defenders had great difficulty in making out their targets. Floundering through the mud, the attacking troops could barely keep up with the barrage but the German front line was reached by both the attacking companies of the 9th Royal Sussex. A Company on the left was able to continue over the front line to the German support line, their objective. B Company, to their right had more difficulty and by the time they moved forward to the support line at 5.10am had lost all their officers. A tenuous line had, however, been created and was reinforced by a machine gun and Stokes mortar that had been brought forward.[4] To the right the 2nd Leinsters suffered considerable casualties in moving forward, mostly from the Bois de Givinchy across the Souchez Valley, from which, when visibility allowed, came heavy machine gun and rifle fire. Although they did get small parties into the German support line by this point all their officers had become casualties and it was not long before it was decided to pull them back to about 40 yards in front of the old German front line, now designated the line of resistance in case of counter attack. During this attack, Corporal John Cunningham of the 2nd Leinsters showed immense courage in protecting the open flank and was awarded the Victoria Cross:

> For conspicuous bravery and devotion to duty when in command of a Lewis Gun Section on the most exposed flank of the attack. His section came under heavy enfilade fire and suffered severely. Although wounded he succeeded almost alone in reaching his objective (a position named Long Sap) with his gun, which he got into action in spite of much opposition. When counter-attacked by a party of twenty of the enemy, he exhausted his ammunition against them, then, standing in full view, he commenced throwing bombs. He was wounded again, and fell, but picked himself up and continued to fight single-handed with the enemy until his bombs were exhausted. He then made his way back to our lines with a fractured arm and other wounds. There is little doubt that the superb courage of this NCO cleared up a most critical situation on the left flank of the attack. Cpl Cunningham died in hospital from the effects of his wounds.[5]

At 11.30am all rifle and machine gun fire from the German side practically ceased although shelling continued.[6]

In the early hours on the other side of the Souchez Valley, C and D Companies of 46th Battalion, in reserve until now, moved to create the flank of the attack on the Pimple. In doing so they were detected by the Germans which, fortunately, only resulted in fire aimed too high to cause damage. Although coming under considerable machine gun fire D company was able to reach its objectives, creating posts in Carrion Trench, thus supporting the battalions on its right. C Company lost its way somewhat in the snowstorm but was able to establish itself in the quarries until later in the day

---

4   TNA: WO95/2217 War Diaries of H.Q. 73rd Brigade; TNA: WO95/2219 War Diaries of 9th Royal Sussex.
5   *Supplement to the London Gazette*, 8 June 1917, p. 5704.
6   TNA: WO95/2217 War Diaries of H.Q. 73rd Brigade; TNA: WO95/2218 War Diaries of 2nd Royal Leinsters.

when it was able to move to its objective line.[7] This, however, meant that the lines overlooking the Souchez Valley were not taken until that later hour, leaving its occupants free during the morning to fire across the valley at the advancing 73rd Brigade as has been seen. A combination of men losing their way, quite understandably with a snowstorm in the maze of destroyed trenches and the fact that there was a 300-yard gap between the attacks of the two brigades seems to have been a contributor to the losses inflicted on the British. Such losses were not experienced by the Canadian 50th Battalion attacking on the northern flanks of the Pimple. Having attacked at 5.00am, they reached all their objectives by 5.45am with a total of 54 casualties of which only one officer and three O.R. were killed. Their diary puts this down to the driving snow which made visibility so difficult for the defenders.[8] A good impression of how difficult the ground was to move over is found in the diary of the 44th Battalion where they state that movement in their advance was at a rate of 20 yards per minute which in no way was sufficient to keep up with the barrage. This, however, did not hinder the advance which, although meeting some opposition reached the objective in good time, taking a number of prisoners along the way. The severely cut up ground and poor visibility led to the right company actually going 300 yards beyond the objective before being brought back some way. Overall 77 prisoners of the *Fusilier/Garde-Grenadier-Regiment 5* were brought in with severe casualties being inflicted on a party of around 100 who attempted to escape to Givenchy. Casualties for 44th Battalion were 118 of which one officers and 27 O.R. were killed.

During the attack on Vimy Ridge, the remainder of *16th Bavarian Division* that had not been attacked directly had undergone a very similar bombardment to that suffered by those units further south. By the morning of the 12th they were in a sorry state and the decision had been made not to relieve the whole division by bringing forward *4th Garde Division* but to use two of this division's units to support the Bavarians. Thus it was that the Canadians actually attacked on the Pimple men of *I/RIR 93* and *Fusilier/Garde-Grenadier-Regiment 5*. There were many gaps in the line and this, plus the dreadful weather, made isolating and destroying pockets of German resistance, mostly *G.G.R 5*, reasonably straightforward.

During the pause that was required before moving down from the ridge there was some rearranging of units. The British 13th Brigade, attached to 2nd Canadian Division for the assault on the ridge, now withdrew back to its parent division, 5th British. To cover the gap created 1st Canadian Division took over 600 yards of the line previously held by the British, with 2nd Canadian Division covering the remainder. There was some evidence of German movement that pointed towards a counter attack on the Canadian's left and therefore the British 5th Division was moved in that direction to cover any eventualities.

All of the high ground of the ridge was now in Canadian or British hands and the next phase, delayed for a couple of days, of advancing onto the plain below, could begin. This was planned for the next day, 13 April, but it was already evident during the latter part of the 12th that the Germans had gone quiet. What had happened was that on the 11th, conscious that the attack would at some point be renewed and having already forbade any further counter attacks, Prince Rupprecht ordered that there should be a general withdrawal to the third line, usually called the Oppy – Mericourt line. This was to be carried out in such a way as to be completed by the morning of the 13th. The background to this move is the moving of Colonel Fritz von Loßberg to become Chief of Staff of *6th Army*. By this time Loßberg had become a kind of fireman, parachuted into every emergency and *Generalleutnant* von Kuhl (Rupprecht's chief of Staff at the Army Group)

---

7   War Diary of 46th Canadian Battalion.
8   War Diary of 50th Canadian Battalion.

said of him, "If anyone can straighten out this tangle, he can do it."[9] His advice was to pull the forces back from below the ridge to gain time.

Thus it is clear why diary reports from British and Canadian troops all along the talk of a quietening down of rifle and machine gun fire during the afternoon of the 12th. As troops began to move in the morning of the 13th reports came from up and down the Canadian lines south of the Souchez that the front trenches of the Germans were unoccupied. On the Canadian's left a similar situation was found by the advanced units of British 73rd Brigade and, following some active patrolling which found evidence of a hasty departure by the Germans, the 9th Royal Sussex and 2nd Leinsters, during the afternoon, pushed forward until they were able to create a series of outposts on the south western fringes of Angres along the road that runs down to Fosse 6. Some opposition was met in the mine areas of Fosse 6 but the men were able to advance in artillery formation with no casualties. During the night of the 14th, both battalions were relieved by 12th Royal Fusiliers. In the morning of the 14th this unit was first of all given the objective of a road about 1,000 yards to their front but as they approached this with no opposition, plans were widened to take in the area all the way to Bois de Riaumont, some 1500 yards further. This was also found to be unoccupied and thus the 12th Royal Fusiliers had advanced the line some 3,000 yards during the afternoon for a total of six casualties from shelling during the advance. They were able to make contact with the left of 95th Brigade, in the shape of 1st Duke of Cornwall's Light Infantry by evening on the 14th.[10]

On 4th Canadian Division's front, as patrols found the Germans had departed, the planned relief by 5th British Division was delayed until the front had been pushed forward. Although exhausted, the Canadians were able to push on and advanced the line, with little or no resistance. The 10th Brigade advanced, meeting no opposition until they came under machine gun fire after having reached the eastern edge of Bois d'Hirondelle. Here they handed over their positions during the late afternoon of the 13th to units of 95th Brigade (5th British Division) as planned for earlier in the day. To the right Canadian 11th Brigade was also able to move forward, cautiously at first, moving down off the ridge but then with an increased pace out into the plain beyond. By late afternoon they had been able to establish a line running from the south west of La Coulotte parallel to the German third line until it reached the Lens-Arras road where the long Cyril Trench met it. Then the line followed the road as far as La Chaudière. It was this line that the Canadians handed over to 15th Brigade (5th British Division) during the early part of the night 13 to 14 April. Thus the role within the First Battle of the Scarpe for 4th Canadian Division came to an end around 2500 yards beyond the ridge they had been tasked to conquer.[11]

The 5th Division employed two brigades for their dual action of taking over the Canadian 4th Division front before moving it forward in reaction to the German withdrawal. The 15th and 95th Brigades were on right and respectively. The 1st Duke of Cornwall's Light Infantry received orders to move forward to relief the Canadians which they did during the afternoon, halting for a while when it was decided that the Canadians should first advance behind the retreating Germans. The next morning, they pushed on a little but came under increasing machine gun fire as they cleared the woodland to the east of Bois d'Hirondelle where it became clear that the Germans were strongly holding the trenches of their third line, the Lens – Thelus on trench maps. This slightly advanced line was then consolidated and made ready for any possible German counter attacks.[12] On the right, 1st Devonshire Regiment, had a similar experience, being able to move their line

9   Rupprecht, *Kronprinz* von Bayern, *Mein Kriegstagebuch, Zweiter Band*, p. 140.
10   TNA: WO95/2217 War Diaries of H.Q. 73rd Brigade.
11   War Diary, Canadian 10th Brigade.
12   TNA: WO95/1577 War Diaries of 1st Duke of Cornwall's L.I.

slightly further forward but, upon finding the German trenches strongly held, stopped and dug in.[13] Both units were, in fact, generally on the line asked of them by the Operational Orders given by 95th Brigade for 14 April and therefore there was not a great deal of enthusiasm showed for any further action.[14]

The left hand battalion of 15th Brigade was 1st Cheshire Regiment with 16th Royal Warwickshire Regiment on the right. With similar rather vague and unambitious instructions to move forward, both battalions moved the line a few hundred yards but soon came under machine gun fire from the Lens – Thelus line and when brigade was asked for instructions the reply was not to push the attack. Both battalions thus commenced the process of creating a main defensive line back a little from the longest advance of the day before with outposts nearer the Germans.[15]

After a relatively quiet day 3rd Canadian Division learned (11 April) that the planned resumption of major offensive action was timed for the 12th, probably to coincide with the attack on the Pimple and was to take the Bloater Trench line that ran north east from Petit Vimy. During the day, however, this order was delayed 24 hours, without any reason being given. Therefore, the latter part of the 11th was used to rearrange units. This resulted in the front of the division being held by, from left to right, 49th Battalion, 58th Battalion and finally 60th Battalion. During the 12th these units managed to get patrols further down the hill into Bracken Trench but fire was too intense from Bloater Trench to consider moving further forward. During the night 43rd Battalion relieved 49th Battalion on the left. As similar patrols moved out during the morning of the 13th they found Petit Vimy empty of Germans but came under fire from Vimy. Slowly, as the day wore on, it became clear that the Germans had withdrawn; however, the German rear-guard comprising of a few machine guns in Vimy had caused the forward units to move forward cautiously. It was not until 2.55pm that orders were issued by the division to move past Vimy and occupy the railway line beyond. By evening troops had succeeded not only in doing this but also moved beyond, getting patrols as far as the Mont Forêt Quarries. Having had reports of the withdrawal of German troops the orders from Corps H.Q. were to renew the movement forward on the 14th to get in front of Fresnoy and Acheville. Although there was active patrolling by men of 43rd Battalion during the day there was no concerted attempt by the division to push the line much further forward. That only one battalion was committed made it was clear that there was no intention of the division to put more men into action. This was as far as the division intended to go.

It was a similar story with 2nd Canadian Division, the formation spending much of the 11th and 12 April consolidating and redistributing units, adjusting their line after the withdrawal of the British 13th Brigade. On the 13th, with 4th Canadian Brigade in the line patrols found Vimy unoccupied and thus they moved through and onto the rail line beyond. Overnight on the 13th and 14th, the 4th Canadian Brigade was relieved by 5th Canadian Brigade which moved the line forward to that around the quarries as shown on the map. No opposition was met and the men began to dig in and consolidate this position. This was only just in front of Mont Forêt Quarries, no attempt to assault the line ahead of them was made, their position being the first objective and no further orders pushing them further. In fact, in many ways the divisional commander had pre-empted Corps command as Byng gave instructions at the end of the 14th that no further

---

13   TNA: WO95/1579 War Diaries of 1st Devonshire Regiment.
14   TNA: WO95/1575 War Diaries of H.Q. 95th Brigade.
15   TNA: WO95/1514 War Diaries of H.Q. 5th Division; TNA: WO95/1568 War Diaries of H.Q. 15th Brigade; TNA: WO95/1571 War Diaries of 1st Cheshire Regiment; TNA: WO95/1557 War Diaries of 16th Royal Warwickshire Regiment.

attacks were to be made until sufficient artillery was brought up thus bringing the First Battle of the Scarpe to an end on this front.

Currie's 1st Canadian Division gave orders to its 1st Brigade to take over the front on the 10th and by morning of the 11th this was complete. They were to prepare and reconnoitre for an attack on the 12th, but, as has been seen, this was postponed 24 hours. Given this delay the front line troops changed yet again with 2nd Brigade taking over the line during the night of the 11th/12th. No reason is given for this rapid change over of front line troops, which must have been wearying for all concerned; getting into place by 10.00am only to find that you were to go back again that night. The 2nd Brigade's orders for the 12th were to carry out reconnaissance in preparation for advancing on the 13th. When the 13th came however, there does not seem to have been a great deal of activity until it was found that Willerval was empty of German troops and could be occupied by 8th Battalion. It was already late afternoon by this point. It was clear that the German withdrawal had left the Canadians feeling their way into an empty landscape. Patrols reached as far as the German wire in front of Arleux-en-Gohelle, reporting it uncut but not very strong. No further approach to the German line was made. Orders were to attack at 5.00am on the 14th but 2nd Brigade complained they hadn't the time to prepare and, due to the wire, they required artillery support. The advance began at 7.00am and although the left made good progress the right met opposition and also found that the British 2nd Division on its right had not advanced. Eventually a line was decided upon, some way from the German third line and the men dug in. Here they were to stay for the next few days; the First Battle of the Scarpe was over.

During 11 April, 51st Division was able to move into the Brown Line at last, a planned attack being made unnecessary by the withdrawal of the Germans. Patrols had come back reporting lights still burning in the dugouts and considerable material left behind. 154th Brigade were able to move into the line, 9th Royals Scots and 7th Gordon Highlanders moving out to create strongpoints a little beyond. This constituted the last of the action of the division in this area as during the evening and night through to 12 April it was relieved by 2nd Division of XIII Corps and thus the line along this section passed over to 1st Army. The three days from 9 to 11 April cannot be said to be 51st Division's finest hour. The poor levels of command and control that were exercised during the 9th and the delay in getting hold of the situation could, had German reserves been deployed closer, have led to a far different result on the northern sector of the offensive. The 1st Canadian Division were already concerned about their southern flank and German troops driving into that hole could have caused the Canadians to consider falling back, causing a chain reaction leading to the ridge not being taken fully at all on the 9th. The 51st Division history makes little comment on this stating, "The Division had finally reached all of its objectives after some Homeric fighting."[16] The volume continues with the outlandish assertion that 51st Division had been so successful that 2nd Division, entering the line at that time, was able to make considerable advances the next day. Not, unfortunately, a claim that can be supported by the evidence. The division was not, however, to get much of a rest, returning to the line further south over the night of the 15th/16th as the third division to be poured into the Roeux cauldron.

The first task of 2nd Division on 12 April was to consolidate its position and prepare for a planned attack on the railway line in front of it, with a bombardment timed for 2.00pm the following afternoon. Then at 12.20pm a message was received from the 1st King's Royal Rifle Corps stating that a patrol had reached the station on the railway close to Bailleul and a strongpoint created. Reacting quickly the planned bombardment was called off and patrols ordered across the front of the whole division. By late afternoon it was clear that not only was the railway

16   Bewsher, Major F W. *The History of the 51st (Highland) Division 1914-1918*. (Uckfield: Naval & Military Press, 1920), p. 159.

Remains of Vimy Church. (Author)

line now in British hands but that Bailleul itself was clear of German troops. This led to the advance of 5th Brigade on the left and 99th Brigade on the right to secure Bailleul and advance beyond to investigate whether the Oppy Line was held or not. Over the remainder of the 13th and into the 14th units of these two brigades did indeed capture Bailleul then, finding the German line strongly held and protected by thick wire, constructed a new line about 300 yards from the Germans. They had been able to do this at very little cost, mainly because of awful weather which kept the defenders quiet. The decision not to attack the Oppy Line was not a difficult one to take with the division had far outstripping its artillery support.[17]

The decision to withdraw made by Rupprecht a few days before certainly was shown to be a very wise one in the face of what happened in 1st Army's area. A delay had already been imposed on the Anglo/Canadian timetable by the difficulties in seizing Hill 145. Had the Germans, as planned, thrown reserves counter attacking the entrenched Canadians on the ridge, with all their artillery support in place, the result could have been catastrophic. The renewed attacks on the 13th and 14th could well have not only driven back the Germans back in confusion, but also made their way through the Lens – Thelus Line. As it was, the Germans had fresh troops to place in the reasonably prepared line which was well wired. Being overlooked from the ridge made the terrain given up pretty worthless and had put such a distance between themselves and the British and Canadian guns that it would be some days before any kind of concerted attack could be organised. The diary of the C.R.A. 5th Division makes it clear that during the period of 9 to 13 April there was little thought to moving forward as they remained within range. The sudden disappearance of the Germans and a rapid advance put them immediately out of range and so only on the 14th could

---

17   TNA: WO95/1296 War Diaries of H.Q. 2nd Division; TNA: WO95/1369 War Diaries of H.Q. 99th Brigade; TNA: WO95/1345 War Diaries of H.W. 5th Brigade.

the artillery begin to move.[18] The almost complete destruction of everything on the ridge now became a headache for the artillery and supply units. Roads were severely damaged all over the area and movement off those few threads of communication was close to impossible by all except those on foot, and even they with some considerable difficulty. It required no order from on high to halt the offensive in 1st Army, indeed the first order for any action that any division received was one of consolidation and wait for support to get up.[19] Reading the accounts of all the units over the four days after 10 April may give the impression of hesitation and lack of push. Although there does seem to have been some reluctance to move units forward quickly the context has to be borne in mind. Only Canadian 4th Division had been relieved by a relatively fresh division (it must be remembered that part of 5th Division had been involved already). The other three divisions were continuing a fight that they felt they had won, the taking of Vimy Ridge. Officers and men would have been exhausted and it is not surprising, given the loss of life on the 9th, that further losses were being avoided in already weak formations. Horne and 1st Army Headquarters must have been pleased with a job well done, not only was the ridge clear but the Germans had been forced to retire some distance. They could now await events to the south whilst licking their wounds and getting on with the enormous task of getting communications over the ridge back into some kind of effective link for moving troops, guns and supplies forward.

The magnificent Canadian Memorial on the present day site of Hill 145. (Author)

---

18   TNA: WO95/1522 War Diaries of C.R.A. 5th Division.
19   TNA: WO95/1522 War Diaries of C.R.A. 5th Division.

3rd Army – XVII Corps

Having achieved next to nothing on 10 April how was 3rd Army to pick itself up and gain the momentum again. An order went out from 3rd Army at 7.10pm on 10 April which read as follows:

> Corps are to reach the Green Line at all points tomorrow with their main bodies. Outposts to be on the line Fontaine-lez-Croisilles, Chérisy, Vis-en-Artois, Pelves, Plouvain, Greenland Hill. Cavalry Corps will move at 5am tomorrow and reconnoitre the Quéant-Drocourt Line and will assist in the attack of the Fifth Army as the situation permits. VII and VI Corps will advance at 5am and reach the Drocourt-Quéant Line. Dividing line the Arras-Cambrai road, Guémappe, Vis en Artois to VI Corps. XVII Corps will move forward and consolidate Greenland Hill, Plouvain.[20]

This order has been included here in the main text as it provides clear evidence of a number of issues with regard to command and control at this stage. The initial part of the order makes sense, in terms of 'let's finish the initial job you were given'. The next part makes partial sense in that the 5th Army's attack was due to commence at Bullecourt and 4th Cavalry Division had been attached to that Army for the possible exploitation of success there. However, orders to 'reconnoitre the Quéant-Drocourt Line' must have had commanders at Cavalry Corps questioning whether Army H.Q. understood the situation. Having failed to even get up to the German lines the day before they were now being asked to look at a line 8,000 yards, some 4½ miles, beyond the line held by the infantry at that moment. That order was, quite rightly, discounted. Again, given the information of how limited attacks had failed the previous day, an order to the two southern Corps to make another advance of over four miles is nothing more than absurd. Having, up to now, provided no real thrusting leadership, 3rd Army was now issuing the kind of orders that, as they filtered down through corps and division, would most likely be treated with silent contempt. Without any clear instruction then it would be down to Corps Headquarters to formulate what was to happen on the 11th. Only for XVII Corps were the 3rd Army orders clear and limited so as to provide positive instructions as to what they had to do. Finally, the timing of the order left very little time for corps to create clear orders for divisions and likewise for them to plan at a brigade level. VI Corps diary reports the 3rd Army order arriving at 8.05pm but interestingly only refers to it ordering the capture of the Green Line.[21]

Then a little later 3rd Army issued another telegram which, whilst well-meaning in content, came 24 hours too late:

> The A.C. [Army Commander] wishes all troops to understand that Third Army is now pursuing a defeated enemy and that risks must be freely taken. Isolated enemy detachments in farms and villages must not be allowed to delay the general progress. Such points must be masked and passed by. They can be dealt with by troops in rear.[22]

VI Corps H.Q. passed this last missive down to divisions at 9.05pm, which, given their experiences of the previous day, must have been greeted with amusement at best.[23] How these generally unrealistic and vague instructions from 3rd Army are now interpreted and carried out by the constituent corps will now be investigated, again starting in the north adjacent to the Canadian Corps.

---

20   Falls, *Military Operations, France and Belgium 1917 Vol. 1*, Appendix 45.
21   TNA: WO95/770 War Diaries of General Staff, VI Corps.
22   Falls, *Military Operations, France and Belgium 1917 Vol. 1*, p. 259.
23   TNA: WO95/770 War Diaries of General Staff, VI Corps.

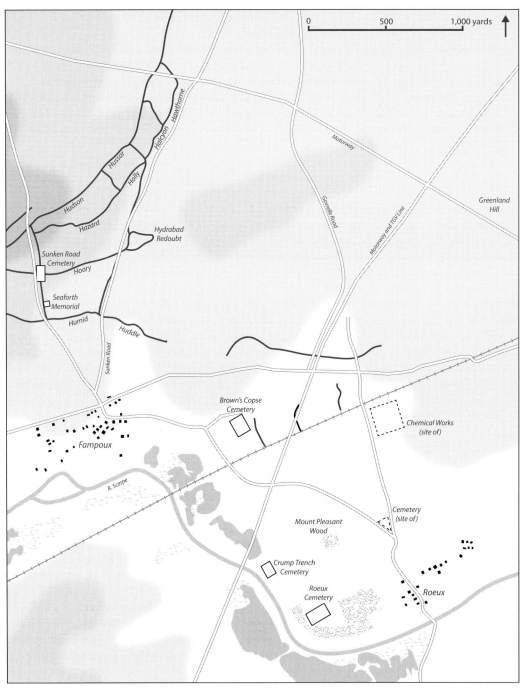

Roeux.

Having received the orders from 3rd Army with limited but clear objectives the first line of XVII diary for 11 April is a little surprising. "No important infantry action took place during the morning"[24] In fact, apart from some attempts by 51st Highland Division to finally clear the Brown Line nothing happened in the morning at all. In spite of being timed at 7.10pm on the 10th the XVII diary only makes mention of the order to take Greenland Hill just before describing that 4th Division finally went into the attack on this objective at 12.00 noon. They had issued that order, however, to 4th Division the previous evening. There is another interesting comment in the corps diary with a report from 3rd Army that Monchy-le-Preux had been taken but that "machine gun fire from the direction of the river was still very heavy."[25] Not surprising when the German troops in the vicinity of the river to the north had nothing happening on their front and could therefore happily look across the river and fire on any attacking troops there. Maybe hidden within the message from Army was a subtle admonishment that nothing was happening on XVII Corps front. In actual fact it was 4th Division themselves who, quite rightly, having experienced the fresh German troops in front of them the day before, wished for a proper artillery barrage on strongpoints that covered any attack. This meant a start time before noon was impossible, the lethargic movement of artillery, for whatever reason, still a factor even with a day in-between. Two battalions of 10th Brigade, not yet used in the offensive, were allocated for the attack in the north, namely 2nd Seaforth Highlanders and 1st Royal Irish Fusiliers. The only place they could possibly form up that was not under the possible fire of the Germans was the sunken road running down from the Hyderabad Redoubt to Fampoux.[26] During the morning the Seaforths, followed by the Irishmen filed into the sunken road to prepare to attack. Unfortunately, the movement had been registered by the Germans, aircraft having flown low over the road as the troops were assembling. Consequently, at 11.00am German artillery opened up on the road. The plan was for the two leading battalions, Seaforths on the left, to take the Gavrelle – Roeux road from the crossroads, just south of the inn, down to the chateaux. Following up The Household Battalion were to take Greenland Hill down to Plouvain railway station and 1st Royal Warwickshire Regiment to seize Plouvain. The Germans were clearly not subdued by the artillery preparation at all as when the men of the two leading units left the sunken road they were met by a hail of machine gun fire from the inn, station, chemical works, chateaux and the railway embankment. A party of the Royal Irish Fusiliers got within 200 yards of the station, covered a little by the embankment but were stopped there and forced to retire when in danger of being surrounded. Similarly, one small group of Seaforths got to a trench about 200 yards from the objective but were forced out, few returning. A chilling observation in the brigade diary is the fact that from the Hyderabad Redoubt a 500-yard line of dead Seaforths could be seen "where they were swept down by machine gun fire."[27] This line must have been so prominent that it was actually marked on trench maps produced for future attacks, not exactly an encouraging sight for those involved in those occurring later. 40 minutes after the first attack, advancing dutifully, the two support battalions attacked in support but to no avail, none of the men of either unit getting more than half way across the open ground in front of them before being driven back to the sunken road. The brigade operation orders had said that "boldness and energy are required"[28] for the assault. The men certainly gave this in full measure,

---

24   TNA: WO95/936 War Diaries of General Staff, XVII Corps.
25   TNA: WO95/936 War Diaries of General Staff, XVII Corps.
26   A memorial to the Seaforths can be found in the lane running north out of Fampoux to Sunken Road Cemetery. However, it must be remembered that they didn't attack from this lane but from the one which is now the D42E running from Fampoux to Gavrelle. The name of the cemetery (it was another sunken road) and the position of the memorial contributes to the mistake made by many visitors today.
27   TNA: WO95/1479 War Diaries of H.Q. 10th Brigade.
28   TNA: WO95/1479 War Diaries of H.Q. 10th Brigade.

but at a ghastly cost for no gain. Of the three companies of Seaforths and two companies of R.I.F. that attacked not a single officer returned unwounded and total casualties were 12 officers and 378 O.R. for the Scots and 11 officers and 287 O.R. for the Irish. At the end of the day the Seaforths could only muster 57 unwounded men from those that had attacked that afternoon, a casualty rate, including officers, of 87 percent. One company of the Seaforths, led by Lieutenant Donanld Mackintosh reached the road to Gavrelle but was forced back by German counter attacks. In attempting to urge his men to attack and subsequently retire, he was wounded three times, on the last occasion mortally.

> For most conspicuous bravery and resolution in the face of intense machine-gun fire. During the initial advance he was shot through the right leg, but, though crippled, he continued to lead his men and capture the trench. In the captured trench Lt. Mackintosh collected men of another company who had lost their leader and drove back a counter-attack. He was again wounded, and although unable to stand, he continued, nevertheless, to control the situation. With only fifteen men left he ordered his party to be ready to advance to the final objective, and with great difficulty got out of the trench and encouraged his men to advance. He was again wounded and fell. The gallantry and devotion to duty of this officer were beyond all praise.[29]

The support battalions were also badly hit with casualties for all ranks being 156 for the Household Battalion and 215 for the Warwicks. By the time the attack went in the Germans had managed to put some order into the units that had come up over the previous day and the attack of 11th Brigade went in against *I.R. 31* of *18th Division*, one of the relieving units and thus relatively fresh troops. The German account of the attack simply states that, "to the east of the *Polenwerk* [Hyderabad Redoubt] the attack withered away in the fire of the 1st Battalion"[30]

12th Brigade were also ordered to attack to the south towards Roeux village and allocated to the attack was the 2nd West Riding Regiment on the left with 1st King's Own (Royal Lancaster) Regiment to the right, reinforced with two companies of the 2nd Lancashire Fusilier Regiment. Some German trenches were cleared and the railway embankment taken around where the present road goes beneath it. A post was also established in a small wood but the line had to be created and consolidated well short of the village.[31] Another party made its way down the sunken road to the west of Mount Pleasant Wood but couldn't get into the woods at the southern end of it.[32] Feeling insecure and deeming the road not easily defended the party then withdrew. The attack of 12th Brigade succeeded in getting between the 1st and 3rd Battalions *I.R. 31* and caused some alarm for a while. Reserves from the 12th Company, a company of the newly arriving *I.R. 85* plus a machine gun section from the neighbouring *G.R. 119* were thrown into the gap and brought the situation under control by 3.30pm.[33] The divisional reserve, *III/Füsilier-Regiment 86* was brought forward to relieve the men of 2nd and 3rd Battalions of *I.R.31*.

---

29   *The London Gazette*, 8 June 1917, no.30122. His grave can be found in Brown's Copse Cemetery nearby along with a very large number of his Regiment close by.

30   Studt Hauptman d.R. a.D.Dr.Berhard, *Infanterie-Regiment Graf Bose (1. Thüringisches) Nr. 31 imWeltkriege 1914-1918*, (Oldenburg: Stalling, 1926), p. 186.

31   This small wood (properly Bois Rossignol) gave its name to Brown's Copse Cemetery which is almost but not quite on the same site.

32   This is the lane going past Crump Trench Cemetery and leading down to Roeux British Cemetery which lies in the woods the men couldn't enter on that afternoon.

33   Studt Hauptman d.R. a.D.Dr.Berhard, *Infanterie-Regiment Graf Bose (1. Thüringisches) Nr. 31 imWeltkriege 1914-1918*, p. 186.

A much smaller attack by 11th Brigade was planned to the north of 10th Brigade's attack which was, in the main, to create a secure flank for the latter. Only one company of 1st Somerset Light Infantry was involved and it could not meet its objective of getting to the inn on the Rocux – Gavrelle road, meeting the same kind of withering fire that its neighbours to the south had experienced. Managing about 200 yards of ground, the men then dug in and maintained this slightly forward position in front of the Hyderabad Redoubt. In these two flanking operations to the main attack 12th Brigade had 300 casualties of all ranks whilst 11th Brigade suffered 23.

What is clear from this afternoon slaughter of 10th Brigade is that no longer were any Germans on the run. Time had allowed the bringing up of substantial elements of German *18th Division* which had *I.R. 31* in the line, fresh troops given the time to dig themselves in and thus present a formidable force to remove. The artillery support that 4th Division received was totally insufficient for this task. Although they had managed to get four brigades of field artillery into action, two more than the previous day, ammunition was in short supply and the resulting creeping barrage spread across such a wide front became ineffective. Also on the evening of the 10th four army field artillery brigades and two heavy artillery groups had been transferred to 1st Army, cutting possible available support even more. The heavy artillery was now firing at considerable range with little or no time to target sufficiently the strongpoints of the freshly arrived Germans. A combination of unmolested strongpoints and ineffective barrage gave the men attacking across the open ground no chance at all. For once, whether or not the wire was cut, became immaterial as few of the assaulting troops got very far. The courage of the Seaforths and Irish Fusiliers that afternoon was magnificent but awful in its outcome.

At 2.50pm, when the division realised that the initial attack had failed Maj.-Gen Lambton telephoned that 10th Brigade were to renew the attack, "with a view to capturing the first objective at all costs."[34] According to the 4th Division diary this only arrived with the units involved at around 4.00pm by which time the remains of the brigade were digging in and Brig.-Gen. Gosling didn't consider it possible to carry out the order. Thankfully he was supported in this decision with an interesting aside in the divisional diary of "in the light of subsequent events there is no doubt that his decision was a wise one."[35] Allenby, during a meeting with Haig later that day, was very critical of Lambton at 4th Division not attacking early in the morning as he had ordered. Haig then goes out to visit divisions but interestingly only goes south of the Scarpe when a visit to ascertain what had happened to 4th Division would have been appropriate.[36]

Overnight, 9th Division was given instructions to attack through 4th Division, with one of the latter division's brigades being placed at the disposal of 9th Division. The vast amount of the next day, the 12th, was spent getting this attack ready as it was timed for 5.00pm. There is an interesting aside in the diary of the 9th Division H.Q. staff relating to the South African Brigade. That unit had sent a message to the Divisional Headquarters stating that the men had had no sleep for four days and no hot food since the 8th and "it was doubtful if men were in a fit condition for severe operations."[37] This was duly passed onto Corps which replied that "if attack was delayed we would not have such a heavy concentration of artillery to support our attack tomorrow."[38] A strange remark as surely more time would allow more artillery and ammunition to get forward and XVII Corps had no other area of concern than the one about to be attacked. The 27th and South African brigades were duly given the task of attacking the Roeux–Gavrelle Road and the

---

34   TNA: WO95/1446 War Diaries of H.Q. 4th Division. 10th brigade diary, TNA WO95/1479 War Diaries of 10th Brigade, has this call timed at 2.00pm.
35   TNA: WO95/1446 War Diaries of H.Q. 4th Division.
36   TNA: WO 256/15, Haig diaries, entry for 11 April 1917.
37   TNA: WO95/1738 War Diaries of H.Q. 9th Division.
38   TNA: WO95/1738 War Diaries of H.Q. 9th Division.

Chemical Works with 26th Brigade to take Roeux. The northern element was to attack at 5.00pm but the southern one by 26th Brigade later at 5.40pm and dependent upon the success of the other. Before the attack during the day was supposed to a period of softening up with heavy artillery; however, it is noted by both 27th Brigade and South African Brigade diaries that little or no such bombardment took place. With a few desultory shells falling sporadically here and there with no concentrated effort, the 27th brigade diary noted one shell falling on the Chemical Works between 10.00am and 1.00pm. The German histories tell a different story with reports of heavy destructive fire the whole day. One difference now being that the German artillery was not affected by this preparatory fire.[39] All the men had to make it towards the front line under observation and as a result, even before the attack began German artillery fire strengthened and casualties were incurred by both northern brigades even before zero hour. There was no artillery fire, even from field guns, before at 5.00pm the barrage opened up.[40] This opened up about half way between the two lines, to advance 100 yards every two minutes. What this meant, however, was that the trench lines of the Germans near the Roeux–Gavrelle road were under no bombardment whatsoever for the next 15 minutes. Thus, when the men of both brigades attempted to make their way forward at 5.00pm they were met by the withering fire of machine guns and rifles that had in no way been subdued, plus artillery. They even had no way of getting to and over the front British line, held still by 4th Division men, without being open to enemy fire. By the time the British barrage reached the German lines the assault was already over, the left having gained maybe 300 yards, the right even less. On the far left, 1st Rifle Brigade of 4th Division, tasked with creating a flank for 9th Division, suffered over 50 casualties trying to do so without success. On the left of 27th Brigade was 9th Scottish Rifles, in the centre 12th Royal Scots with their sister battalion the 11th on the right. The story of all three battalions is appallingly similar, numerous casualties whilst forming up and getting forward to the British front line, never even reaching the British barrage and coming to a halt a couple of hundred yards into No Man's Land; eventual casualties being between 180 and 220 men each.[41] The Royal Scots history sums up their efforts admirably with; "Under these circumstances the advance was a sacrifice rather than an attack."[42] Moving to the south the story does not become any more palatable as the results of the South African Brigade's attack are analysed. On the left, 2nd South African Regiment had a few survivors reaching points about 150 yards in front of the 4th Division line. In all they suffered casualties of 16 officers and 290 O.R. out of the 20 and 380 respectively that had attacked; 76 percent casualties. To the right 1st South African Regiment had a similar experience, suffering badly from machine guns that were missed by the bombardment falling south of the railway embankment.[43] Fortunately for the division as a whole the failure of the attack was successfully communicated and any advance by 26th Brigade was deemed unnecessary and they stood down. In the time between 4.30pm, when men began to form up for the attack, already under fire, and dusk when men and wounded could get back, any remaining fight in 9th Scottish Division had been extinguished. Men already freezing, exhausted and hungry had been asked to attack in what can only be described as the most appalling circumstances. By not relieving 4th Division, but attacking through them, none of the assaulting battalions could form up in any kind of protected circumstances thus suffering heavy

---

39   Berhmann & Brandt, *Die Osterschlacht bei Arras 1917 I*, pp. 174-175.

40   The German Official account mentions no such pause; Behrmann & Brandt, *Die Osterschlacht bei Arras 1917 I*, pp. 174-175.

41   TNA: WO95/1738 War Diaries of H.Q. 9th Division; TNA: WO95/1772 War Diaries of 9th Cameronians (Scottish Rifles); TNA: WO95/1773 War Diaries of 11th and 12th Royal Scots.

42   Major John Ewing, MC, *The Royal Scots 1914-1919, Volume 1* (Edinburgh: Oliver & Boyd, 1925), p. 409.

43   TNA: WO95/1777 War Diaries of H.Q. South African Brigade; TNA: WO95/1780 War Diaries of 1st South African Regiment; TNA: WO95/1781 War Diaries of 2nd South African Regiment.

casualties even before zero hour. Artillery support before zero hour was close to non-existent with the result that the German defenders were neither destroyed nor cowed. The barrage from the field guns was described by one unit as "thin", was already too far in front of the troops as they attacked and in no way did it subdue the defenders. The bravery of the men going forward was exemplary under such circumstances but all their courage and sacrifice was to absolutely no avail. It is even more disturbing when the German reaction to the attack is read where the defenders of *I/I.R. 31* under *Hauptman* Friederichs and *III/F.R. 86* under *Hauptman* von Knobelsdorff awaited the two brigades. After repelling the attack by *F.R. 86* were heard to say, "range practise with living targets – today we will meet our objectives."[44] They had not come away that day unscathed, however, with losses to *III/F.R. 86* of 150 men. The final nail in the coffin for any possibility of success for the South Africans though was the strengthening of the German positions in and around Roeux itself by elements of G.R. 119 who by now not only had the 1st Battalion in the line but the 2nd battalion in close support in Plouvain. The 3rd Battalion was in brigade reserve in Biache St. Vaast. The Germans were now in considerable strength just north of the Scarpe.

The only course of action remaining to VII Corps was to use the relatively unscathed 26th Brigade to hold the line, withdrawing the other shattered brigades of 9th Division and cut the line held by 4th Division too. During the night 12/13 April this movement was carried out so that by the morning 26th Brigade of 9th Division held the line from the River Scarpe to the Hyderabad Redoubt (exclusive) and 11th Brigade of 4th Division the actual redoubt and the line up to the Gavrelle Road where the Fampoux–Bailleul road crossed it. The following two days saw little activity on this front except for 34th Division pushing out a little on their left to align with the forward movement of 2nd Division. This was not a great distance as the Oppy Line was to the west of Gavrelle at this point and contact would soon be made with this formidable defensive position.

The First Battle of the Scarpe thus came to an end north of the River Scarpe. It had seen the greatest successes on 9 April, the taking of Vimy Ridge and an advance of over four miles eastwards from Arras. All the high ground that had formally dominated that city was now in British or Canadian hands. For a number of reasons that will be analysed later, the assault then faltered and where the initial advance had been the greatest, came to a standstill. Only in the north where the Germans recognised the dangerous position they were in, could the advance continue. This, however, was merely a withdrawal to a further position of strength which brought their line alongside the new positions of units nearer the river. The question is whether this level of advance was the greatest possible for the British and Commonwealth Army at this stage in the war and in these conditions or had the opportunity been missed for greater success?

3rd Army – VI Corps

The description of the events of 10 April left 37th Division tantalisingly close to achieving the objectives of the first day, namely the taking of the Green Line, which meant the taking of the village of Monchy-le-Preux; orders for the 11th were therefore clear, namely finish the job. Corps instructions to the artillery were to get up during the night and for heavy artillery to get as far forward as it could. This may have been a mistake in that reports all down the line from all units concerned in the attack on Monchy report no artillery or a very weak barrage. Reasons for this are difficult to ascertain as the diaries of both 70th and 71st Brigades R.A., of 15th Division, report moving up on the 10th and being ready by the evening, 71st Brigade mentioning firing by 6.00pm. Why then were they not firing on the 11th is a question not possible to answer but there is no evidence in divisional diaries of any properly formed orders for battery fire beginning at

---

44   Behrmann & Brandt, *Die Osterschlacht bei Arras 1917 I*, p. 175.

5.00am. It can only be assumed then that staff work in preparing for the attack did not extend to informing the artillery.[45] One rather curious clue as to some mix-up, poor staff work or otherwise is in the 111th brigade diary:

> At about 4.30am I was informed that the guns that had been supporting my Brigade up to this time had been taken away for some other task. At 5.00am when the attack started my Brigade had no artillery support, and I did not know what batteries had been allotted to me, or who was commanding them.[46]

Another clue to the reasons behind the confusion is the story found in a number of accounts that the attack was to be delayed because the artillery was not ready. This is not backed up by divisional diaries and stems mainly from the Heavy brigade diary where they talk repeatedly of a delayed start time. The cavalry diaries also carry something of that message but not consistently and as both cavalry and tanks congregated at Feuchy Chapel it is conceivable that it was there that this mix-up occurred. Whatever truth with regard to that morning, the fact is that the level of staff work in preparing for this attack had reached a new low.

The German defenders of Monchy were, by now, not the ragged remains of the units thrown out of their trenches on the first day of the offensive. On the right, up to the Scarpe, the remains of *I/I.R. 51* and *I/R.I.R. 99* that had been thrown into the fight at the end of the first day, were relieved by *III/I.R. 125* which put its 3 forward companies to work overnight creating a defensible line, due to arrive over the next day were the other 2 battalions of *I.R. 125*. South of them, down to the Arras-Cambrai road, remained various elements of *I.R. 162* and *I.R. 163* but these were being gradually being replaced by *I/ Bayerisches I.R. 17* of *3. Bayerische Divisionen* with the other Bavarian units creating a reserve, one west of the Bois du Sart and one in the wood itself.

On the left, astride the River Scarpe, 15th Division were to attack on a two brigade front, 45th Brigade on the left and 46th Brigade on the right, with orders to secure the high ground to the north east of Monchy-le-Preux between Pelves and Keeling Copse. 13th Royal Scots, 6th/7th Royal Scots fusiliers and 6th Cameron Highlanders were all sent into the attack for 45th Brigade and what followed can only be described as something of a shambles. No real line was held, units became intermingled and all the units veered right pushing across the line 46th Brigade was meant to follow. With little, or according to some diaries no artillery support, they all came under severe fire from rifle, machine gun and artillery from the Germans both near Monchy and north of the Scarpe. It must be remembered that on the other side the assault on Roeux was not due to begin until noon so all through the morning Germans around that village could concentrate on anything they saw to the south. The diaries of the Royal Scots and Fusiliers mention turning right to attack German machine guns that were firing at them and that eventually men entered the village. Interestingly, the Camerons also mention veering to the right but make no mention of entering the village, and they were on the right of the brigade. Only one battalion of the 46th Brigade was in the lead for the attack, the 10th/11th Highland Light Infantry. They complain bitterly about the lack of artillery and the movement across them of men of the neighbouring brigade. This, they say, caused them to move to their right as well and enter the village. Confusion certainly reigned

---

45   Colin Fox refers to an ordered delay that did not reach infantry or tanks, but there is no evidence of this having been sent in divisional nor corps diaries. The Heavy Branch diary for the attack says zero hour was delayed until 6.00am as the infantry was "not in position", then until 7.00am, but as the infantry and tanks attacked on time this statement is a little obscure. Fox, Colin, *Monchy-Le-Preux* (Barnsley: Pen & Sword, 2000), p. 29; KCLMA Fuller/1/4/1, Summary of tank operations 1 Bde Heavy Branch, 9 Apr–3 May 17.
46   TNA: WO95/2531 War Diaries of H.Q. 111th Brigade.

but clearly all of this left an enormous gap on the left of the division.[47] Fortunately, it does not seem that the men of *I.R. 125* north of Monchy were aware of the situation; folds in the ground do tend to obscure the view north west of the village. Thus, eventually, men of both brigades could eventually sort themselves out and create a line north west of the village, even though they found it impossible to get forward due to the heavy opposition of the fresh defenders of *I.R. 125*.

In the centre, 111th Brigade attacked Monchy on a two battalion front with the remaining units in support. 13th Rifle Brigade on the left and 13th King's Royal Rifle Corps, right, led the way with 10th and 13th Royal Fusiliers in support.

> Owing to natural obstacles and the enemy's fire the advance was at first rather slow, but the timely arrival of four tanks greatly assisted the advance and in a very short time the rifle battalions of the Brigade were in and through the Village, and were in time to catch the enemy with Lewis Gun fire as he retired over the open ground east of the Village.[48]

The individual units of 111th Brigade make very little comment about entering the village, with no mention of units of 15th Division at all. According to their diaries both rifle battalions were thorough the village without any street fighting, the Germans having evacuated the place. This is not easy to reconcile with the German reports of *I/Bayerische I.R. 17* which talk of bitter fighting and an eventual loss of almost all their company commanders and 223 other men before they had to abandon the village. The advance of units from the north, even though by accident, plus the appearance of one tank (see below) seems to have made the difference to the Bavarian defenders.[49] Six tanks were allotted to support the attack, three from the area of La Bergère, the crossroads to the south of Monchy on the way to Wancourt, three from an enclosure a little to the north west of the village. Of the ones heading to the enclosure 588 lost a track on its way up from Feuchy Chapel and 790 bellied somewhere similar. All three of the ones heading down the Cambrai Road made it to the crossroads. Here 600 with 2nd Lt. Ambrose was immediately bombed by Germans who also riddled the tank with armour piercing bullets. The crew, many wounded, tried to keep their Lewis gun in action and turned towards Monchy. Soon afterwards the tank was hit by artillery fire and eventually the tank had to be abandoned; four of the seven crew having been killed. Tank 597, with 2nd Lt. Toshack turned north at the crossroads and main some headway but was engaged again by artillery and hit whilst halted to change gear. Only three of the crew escaped, Toshack not being amongst them.[50] Tank 578, with Lt. Salter, first of all cleared a trench to the south of the Cambrai road and then turned north towards Monchy. He, like the others, was soon hit by shellfire which killed or wounded many of the crew. Salter and the remainder of the crew, having being cut off by artillery fire for some time, eventually made it back. Salter was responsible, with his single tank, for causing the German unit, part of *I/R.I.R. 84*, south of the crossroads to descend into panic. The German regimental history provides a vivid impression of what it was like for infantry, who had never fought against a tank before, to come against one of the steel monsters. As Salter reached the trench of 1st Company:

47 TNA: WO95/1914 War Diaries of H.Q. 15th Division; TNA: WO95/1943 War Diaries of H.Q. 45th Brigade; TNA: WO95/1950 War Diaries of H.Q. 46th Brigade; TNA: WO95/1945 War Diaries of 6th Cameron Highlanders; TNA: WO95/1946 War Diaries of 13th Royal Scots; TNA: WO95/1947 War Diaries of 6th/7th Royal Scots Fusiliers.
48 TNA: WO95/2531 War Diaries of H.Q. 111th Brigade.
49 Behrmann & Brandt, *Die Osterschlacht bei Arras 1917 II*, p. 78.
50 Toshack is commemorated on the Arras Memorial.

There could be no defence, fighting tanks with rifle and machine gun was useless, our own artillery was not shooting. Down the trench came the machine gun fire, hammering into the bodies of men, the killed falling silently, the wounded shouting and crying out. In this chaos *Leutnant* Hardow (commanding 1st Company) ordered "Evacuate the trench to the left!" All the men raced down the trench in mad haste, followed by the tank, towards 3rd Company.

As the troops reached the 3rd Company, that company commander, *Leutnant* Schnell, refused to move and there was thus a logjam of men which the tank then reached, killing more, including *Leutnant* Schnell, before:

> There was total panic. All of 1st and 3rd Companies sprang out of the trenches and ran, as fast as they had ever in their lives before, to the rear, followed by the machine gun fire of the tank which claimed more victims as if on a rabbit hunt.[51]

The one tank, 787 with 2nd Lt. Johnson, that had made it as far as the enclosure near the village, did some sterling work around the fringes. However, the account in the Heavy brigade diary is difficult to accept with its claim that the infantry only came up after the Germans had abandoned the village and that he had been to the east of the village before coming under artillery fire. Johnson's engine then seized and the crew had to abandon the vehicle. The artillery fire – corresponding to that which fell on the other tanks – is claimed by the crews to be their own artillery, coming down late because of the supposed delay in the attack. All of this can be discounted when all the other evidence is placed alongside. It is clear though, given the brigade commander's comments sited earlier, that the effect of the tanks was sufficient to aid 111th Brigade in taking the village. Johnson's tank, in the north, even if his account was probably a little exaggerated, is the one that probably made the greatest difference.[52]

The 112th Brigade was given the task on the 11th of reaching the Green Line where it runs south east of Monchy-le-Preux. Timed for 5.00am the brigade commander found he was not going to be supported at that time by 3rd Division on his right. They could not be ready by then but he decided to stay with the plan as given. On the left, 10th Loyal North Lancashire Regiment attacked at 5.00am with the aim of getting to the small woodland just to the north of the road from Monchy to St. Rohart Factory. This rather ambitious objective was never really an option as at first no artillery support was on hand and later only desultory fire was supplied. The Loyal North Lancs did manage to clear and occupy the sunken land that is now the main road up into Monchy from the Cambrai road and the same route for some distance down towards Wancourt. In this they were, as has been seen, aided by the tanks of C Company and then later by the cavalry. Apart from a few posts in shell holes, however, no further progress was possible. On their right the 11th Royal Warwicks attempted to make progress south of the Cambrai road but did not get very far.[53] Although 6th Bedfords had also come up in support there were few men in this advanced position on the right beyond the Cambrai road and a gap had formed between them and 3rd Division troops to the south.

By 9.00am the Monchy was declared clear of enemy troops and it was around now that the cavalry appeared. The 3rd Cavalry Division had orders to be ready to support the attack on the

---

51   Speck, Justizinspector William, *Das KöniglichPreußische Reserve-Infantrie-Regiment 84*, p. 188. It is not common for such behaviour to be included in regimental histories of any nation, demonstrating the significant effect the experience had on this regiment.

52   KCLMA Fuller/1/4/1, Summary of tank operations 1 Bde Heavy Branch, 9 Apr–3 May 17.

53   TNA: WO95/2536 War Diaries of H.Q. 112th Brigade; TNA WO95/2538 War Diaries of 10th Royal North Lancs and 11th Royal Warwicks.

Green Line around Monchy-le-Preux and should British forces take the village and beyond then they should provide units to move past and exploit the situation. Elements of the division were therefore in preparation for such a move when the news came in between 6.00am and 7.30am that elements of 111th and 112th Brigades had made some inroads into the village but that they were hung up in places. Another from 112th Brigade then saying that Monchy had fallen. In view of this 10th Hussars and Essex Yeomanry from 8th Cavalry Brigade were sent off at 8.30am to try and get up to and beyond the village. Similarly, 3rd Dragoon Guards of 6th Brigade were given similar orders. All these units had bivouacked east of Arras overnight and all had experiences great difficulty in watering and caring for their horses, which as a consequence, were suffering badly from exposure. The two units of 8th Brigade were tasked with taking all the area north of Monchy, up to and including Pelves, Bois du Sart and the two woodlands beyond, Hatchet and Jigsaw Woods; 10th Hussars on the left and Essex Yeomanry to the right. This plan soon came to naught as both units experienced heavy artillery and machine gunfire as soon as they came over Orange Hill. This caused both units to veer off to the right and enter the village at about the same time. Here the Essex Yeomanry moved to the east of the village and here set up strong-points using their Hotchkiss machine guns whist the 10th Hussars tried to leave the village in the northern area but coming under fire from both flanks at the edge of Monchy Wood, stopped there and also created strongpoints.[54] The German response to losing Monchy-le-Preux, however, was to bring down a heavy bombardment on the village and surrounding countryside.[55] With the better part of two cavalry regiments now in the village the result was a high casualty rate, especially amongst the horses. The high explosive shells exploding on the hard ground within the village are said to have been very destructive. The cavalry unit diaries are pretty scathing of the infantry at this point, claiming that they found no proper defence and only isolated groups of men sheltering in cellars:

> It was quite apparent that the infantry were [sic] not holding the village, though remnants of both the 111th and 112th Infantry Brigades were found in isolated cellars in and west of the chateau.[56]

The relevant infantry war diaries give no impression of being out of control in terms of defending the village. The O.C. 111th Brigade gives particular thanks to the cavalry for their support[57] but the fact that 111th Brigade Machine Gun Company had 12 of its guns positioned in Monchy during 11 April makes the extreme claim of the cavalry hard to take at face value.[58] The infantry brigade also had the 10th and 13th Royal Fusiliers in support at the western end of the village. The Fusiliers make some mention of small detachments being forward in the

---

54   TNA: WO95/1156 War Diaries of 10th Hussars & Essex Yeomanry. The German Official History unfortunately at this point enters the realms of fantasy describing a cavalry charge on their lines north of the village being destroyed, more likely it was simply the heavy fire which caused the cavalry to enter Monchy; Behrmann & Brandt, *Die Osterschlacht bei Arras 1917 II*, pp. 82-83.

55   In some modern accounts this is termed a 'box-barrage', i.e. surrounding the village; but from contemporary accounts it is clear that the whole village was placed under heavy fire and so the term is not appropriate on this occasion.

56   TNA: WO95/1156 War Diaries of 10th Hussars. Also TNA WO95/1156 War Diaries of 8th Cavalry Brigade, whose account probably feeds off that of the Hussars.

57   TNA: WO95/2531 War Diaries of H.Q. 111th Brigade.

58   Falls seems to accept the cavalry's accounts totally, claiming the defence "fell almost entirely upon the cavalry." There is no evidence in the communications with Falls during the completion of the History that he received any from members of 111th Brigade. Falls, *Military Operations, France and Belgium 1917 Vol. 1*, p. 265.

eastern end of the village at times but the bulk of their men remained in support. It is a severe criticism of the leadership of 111th Brigade to say that it was dependent upon the cavalry to lead the defence of the village during the whole day. On that day the cavalry of 8th Brigade were to suffer (especially for them) very severe casualties from the continuous and heavy artillery barrage; estimates of losses to horses in the brigade are somewhere around 85 percent, thus reducing it to an infantry unit. The Royal Horse Guards had tried to push up as support regiment but did not even reach the village, suffering so badly in the barrage that they turned back. In addition, the brigade had a serious loss in leadership in that the O.C. 8th Cavalry Brigade, Brig.-Gen CB Bulkeley-Johnson, whilst near the front wishing to see for himself the lines being held, was shot and killed. Given these losses it is perhaps understandable that a slightly exaggerated description of their role during the day should result; such losses will have smarted.[59] A further piece of evidence though to the poor showing of 111th Brigade is the comment by Lt.-Col. Dawson of the 6th Royal West Kents upon relieving the men in Monchy overnight between 11 and 12 April. He states that he only found cavalry to relieve with hardly a man of 111st Brigade to be found. One member of the Cavalry performed an act of immense bravery when manning a machine gun as a member of 8th Machine Gun Squadron; L/Cpl Harold Mugford was awarded the Victoria Cross:

> For most conspicuous bravery and devotion to duty when under intense shell and machine gun fire, L/Cpl Mugford succeeded in getting his machine gun into a forward and very exposed position. From this point he was able to deal more effectively with the enemy, who were massing for a counter attack. His No. 2 was killed almost immediately, and at the same moment he himself was severely wounded. He was then ordered to a new position, and told to go to a dressing station as soon as the position was occupied. He refused to go to the dressing station but continued on duty with his gun, begging his comrades to leave him and to take cover. Shortly afterwards this non-commissioned officer was removed to the dressing station, where he was again wounded in the arm. The valour and initiative displayed by L/Cpl Mugford was instrumental in breaking up the impending counter attack of the enemy.[60]

The 63rd Brigade had waited out the first part of the morning a little to the rear until they were told at 10.30am by 37th Division H.Q. that 15th Division were on the Hatchet Wood – Pelves line which prompted them to move forward.[61] This was, of course totally false and as soon as 10th Yorks and Lancs moved forward at 11.00am over the slight ridge in front of them they came under intense fire, mostly from across the river in Roeux. This halted the men in their tracks but they did manage to get into some practice trenches that the found in front of them. The order then changed to one of reinforcing Monchy-le-Preux. The 4th Middlesex and 8th Lincolns were ordered to the village, 4th Middlesex leading, the move being made south of the Yorks and Lancs to try and avoid the fire from across the river. The Middlesex men reached the village and having got in touch with 111th Brigade were asked by the cavalry brigade to cover the north east of the village, a platoon and two Lewis guns being sent there to create a strongpoint on the road to Roeux and Pelves. The remainder of the men were put in cellars, out of the artillery barrage, to support only when called

---

59   TNA: WO95/1156 War Diaries of 8th Cavalry Brigade.

60   *Supplement to the London Gazette*, 26 November 1917, p. 12329; Mugford survived the war but his wounds confined him to a wheelchair for the remainder of his life. He died in 1958. His medal is now in possession of the Imperial War Museum.

61   H.Q. of 37th Division had received a number of messages, beginning at 6.35am from 15th Division that its men were east of Monchy, all of which were not true; TNA: WO95/2513 War Diaries of H.Q. General Staff 37th Division.

upon. The Lincolns never even reached the village, getting hung up in trenches under heavy fire and went to ground to the right of the Yorks and Lancs.

The 6th Cavalry Brigade had similarly ambitious orders of first moving to the spur south of Monchy to then push further east and take Vis-en-Artois. The 3rd Dragoon Guards, however, found that just getting to La Bergère a difficult undertaking and they found themselves in an important, dismounted role of supporting 112th Brigade in taking and holding the line south of Monchy. Even the units acting as support in 6th Cavalry Brigade further back found themselves suffering badly from the German artillery bombardment. Once it was clear that their role of passing through to take Vis-en-Artois was not going to transpire, these supporting units moved further back beyond Feuchy Chapel into safer ground.[62] During the afternoon it appears as if there might be a serious threat of counter attack in this section and therefore Brig.-Gen Harman sent a dismounted squadron of the North Somerset Yeomanry forward as he had heard of the fragile nature of the front. In the sunken lane south of the Cambrai road Maj. West with B Squadron of the Yeomanry found about 30 men from four different battalions all mixed up and under the command of Private Batchelor[63] of the 6th Bedfords. Small arms ammunition for their own weapons running low, he had issued German rifles to the men of which there were ample. German troop concentrations clearly preparing for a counter attack were dispersed, as was a further one later in the evening.

The tactical prize of seizing Monchy was therefore achieved on 11 April, but not in what could be termed an example of a coordinated and smooth operation. It required the combined efforts of elements of three divisions plus tanks to complete the task. Communication during the day was extremely poor with over-optimistic messages being seemingly the norm, probably leading to much useless loss of life. The 111th Brigade does not seem to have had a firm grip on the situation at all and although the cavalry's claims are probably somewhat exaggerated, there seems to be more than an element of truth in them. The two brigades of 15th Division were particularly poor in almost all being drawn into the village when they should have been creating the left flank of the attack. Some excuse can be found for these failings, however, in the lateness of the attack on the other side of the river bringing extensive fire down from that direction. The fundamental problem faced on the day though is clearly a complete breaking down in the liaison between infantry and artillery. That a major attack, two days after the initial one, should receive such a paltry level of support is inexcusable, especially when it is clear that many guns were up and ready. The post war apologies of the difficulty of moving guns forwards are only one factor in the poor performance of the artillery, as contemporary diaries seem to show, there being little comment of facing such problems. The position on both flanks was nothing less than precarious and should a concentrated counter attack have developed during the day, as opposed to a number of rather half-hearted affairs, the situation could have become very serious.

The fact that a German attack did not materialise during the day is something of a wonder as it had been ordered as early as 7.00am that morning, almost as soon as the village was felt to be lost and in true German style of counter attacking when ground was lost. That an attack never came is down to the fact that the units in the area were in a very confused state with regards their organisation. It seems different units from four divisions were mixed together and thus nobody took the lead in organising a proper response. There is also comment that the artillery was again

---

62   TNA: WO95/1152 War Diaries of H.Q. 6th Cavalry Brigade; TNA: WO95/1153 War Diaries 3rd Dragoon Guards.

63   Major West does not identify the man in his report, but he is named (wrongly as Batchellor) in the Official History. It was George W. Bachelor who was, very deservedly, awarded the DCM, unfortunately dying of wounds during 3rd Ypres on 10 September 1917; he was all of 19 years old. Falls, *Military Operations, France and Belgium 1917 Vol. 1*, p. 267; TNA: WO95/1153 War Diaries of 1/1st North Somerset Yeomanry.

complaining of lack of ammunition for an attack. All in all, it seems that the lack of organised and dynamic leadership for once robbed the Germans of a possible coup in attacking what was at this point a poorly defended village.[64]

Many of the problems encountered by 37th Division's right flank were due to the Germans continuing to hold the village of Guémappe. On 10 April it has already been seen that this was not attacked by 3rd Division where that was still possible, another 12 hours or more for the German defenders to bring up reserves and strengthen their line. An attack was planned for the morning of 11 April to coincide with the assault on Monchy-le-Preux at 5.00am. For this attack 3rd Division replaced 112th Brigade of 37th Division in front of Guémappe. The attack was then delayed until 7.00am to give time for units of 76th Brigade to relieve those of 112th Brigade, which it will be remembered were already attacking by then. This does lead to the question of whether anyone from these two divisions was speaking to each other. So whilst the men of 112th Brigade were attempting to gain ground just south of La Bergère their right was totally uncovered until finally at 7.00am men of 8th King's Own Royal Lancasters on the left and 2nd Suffolks on the right finally attacked. This attack failed almost immediately, troops not even reaching the sunken road leading up to the crossroads held by 112th Brigade. Another attack in the afternoon, with the Lancasters again on the left but this time the 1st Gordon Highlanders on the right, failed again to gain any more ground and eventually the brigade, and thus the division, consolidated on a line about 500 yards west of and parallel to the sunken road.[65] Although the divisional and brigade diaries talk of fire from the flanks causing the lack of success, interestingly the battalions themselves speak of nothing but fire, mainly machine gun, from directly in front of them or from Wancourt that had not been subdued in any manner by artillery support. The Suffolk's diary sums up the failure in a way that would have been appreciated by most battalion commanders on this day:

The difficulties met with in the operations of 11 April were:

1. The troops were tired.
2. No time for personal reconnaissance and formation of plan of attack.
3. No artillery support.
4. WANCOURT was not in our hands.[66]

3rd Division had stalled yet again with no ground gained, leaving the taking of Monchy-le-Preux standing in somewhat of a salient, with ground north and now south of it being in German hands. The threat of some kind of major counter attack against the village could in no way be discounted in such a position given its prominent position in the landscape.

The night of the 11/12 April was a time of major alterations on the VI Corps' front with both 15th and 37th Divisions being relieved. During 11 April, 17th Division, hereto being part of the Cavalry Corps and as such under Army command, was transferred to VI Corps and ordered to relieve 15th Division. This it did, deploying 50th Brigade into the area north of Monchy. The 17th Division war diaries relate the relief of the line of 44th Brigade, when in fact units of all the brigades of 15th Division were scattered across the area. Although conditions did not aid in the relief, men of 15th Division often not arriving back until almost dawn on the next morning, by

64   Behrmann & Brandt, *Die Osterschlacht bei Arras 1917 II*, pp. 83-85.
65   TNA: WO95/1378 War Diaries of H.Q. General Staff, 3rd Division; TNA: WO95/1433 War Diaries of H.Q. 76th Brigade; TNA: WO95/1436 War Diaries of 8th King's Own Royal Lancaster; TNA: WO95/1437 War Diaries of 2nd Suffolk Regiment; TNA: WO95/1435 War Diaries of 1st Gordon Highlanders.
66   TNA: WO95/1437 War Diaries of 2nd Suffolk Regiment.

first light 50th Brigade were in position. In fact, the positions north of Monchy were so obscure that 8th Lincolns and 10th Yorks & Lancs of 63rd Brigade could not extricate themselves safely until the night of the 12th/13th.

The 37th Division were ordered to be relieved by 12th Division that night and therefore as the night fell on 11 April units began to fall back as the men of 36th and 37th Brigades relieved them. 37th Brigade relieved 111th Brigade in and east of Monchy itself and 36th Brigade took over the line held south of the village by 112th Brigade. In 37th Brigade, 6th Queens and 6th Royal West Kents were sent forward to relieve 111th Brigade. In reality, they actually relieved the remaining cavalry of 3rd Cavalry Division. They created a line on the eastern boundary of the village and then to the south as they could not gain contact with 36th Brigade on their right. The conditions at this time were appalling with a strong snow storm blowing, making visibility and movement extremely difficult. The 3rd Division had no such luck in being relieved and thus it fell to two battalions of 9th Brigade to relieve the exhausted men of 76th Brigade overnight, 11 and 12 April, these being the 12th West Yorks on the left and 1st Northumberland Fusiliers on the right.

VI Corps orders for 12 April were completely dependent upon what was happening on either side of them. There was no direct order to attack, simply to move, "as soon as situation on flanks makes advance possible."[67] This order led to the units of 17th Division spending the day north of Monchy waiting for developments and making ready for an attack should there be developments on the other side of the River Scarpe. Messages were received giving a mixed impression of what was going on there but eventually it was realised that the second phase of the attack on Roeux was not to take place. Unfortunately, an attack by 17th Division had already taken place. 6th Dorset Regiment had been tasked with attacking and taking the spur that runs from Monchy-le-Preux down to the lakes near Roeux. By the time the message arrived that no attack had taken place across the river the Dorsets had already advanced, taking heavy losses but actually gaining the ridge. From left to right D, C and A Companies attacked at 6.30pm, those on the left suffering particularly badly from machine gun fire, not surprising given that the Germans on the other side of the river were not under attack, the two left companies having only one officer remaining unwounded. Yet again the complaint is about almost zero support from artillery; what did arrive, "was observed to be extremely erratic."[68] The remnants of the companies and those sent up to support (all bar one platoon of the battalion was eventually sent forward) were ordered back to their start lines at 11.00pm; casualties being almost 100 all ranks.

This was the only action of 17th Division on this day, the only other movement being the relief of the Dorsets by 7th East Yorkshire Regiment, which was complete by daybreak the next day.[69] The 12th Division, having completed the relief of 37th Division were then told they were going to be relieved that night and as there was no movement on their left or right did little during the day.[70] Finally, on the right 3rd Division awaited developments on their right from VII Corps but a lack of any forward movement there condemned 9th Brigade, having moved up into the front line, to inactivity the entire day.[71]

The order to VI Corps for 12 April had led directly to a complete standstill, an attack that went in by mistake the only activity along the whole of the Corp front. That this attack was

67   TNA: WO95/770 War Diaries of H.Q. General Staff VI Corps.
68   TNA: WO95/1998 War Diaries of H.Q. 50th Brigade, report from C.O. 6th Dorsets.
69   TNA: WO95/1998 War Diaries of H.Q. 50th Brigade.
70   TNA: WO95/1824 War Diaries of H.Q. General Staff 12th Division.
71   TNA: WO95/1378 War Diaries of H.Q. General Staff 3rd Division.

partially successful, in spite of everything being against it, was perhaps evidence that, at least on the 17th Division front, action by this fresh division could have put the Germans under pressure. The spur that had been taken and then given up would have given some advantage to the troops who, over the coming days, would attack Roeux again and again. Their right would, at least, have been covered from some high ground across the river. What 14th Division, trying to take Wancourt to the south, thought of 3rd Division inactivity will be investigated when actions in VII Corps are examined. The German Official History is clear how 12 April was used. It describes the reorganisation of the mixed up units, feverish work on preparing the new lines that they occupied and similarly urgent movement of munitions for the artillery forward into position – in other words, every preparation necessary to ward off new attacks launched the following day.[72]

The original plan called for 29th Division to relieve 12th Division, after which there would be a general attack by the whole corps on 13 April. 29th Division reported that it had been held up and although able to take over the line overnight would not be in a position to attack on the 13th. Lt-Gen J.A.L. Haldane, O.C. VI Corps accepted this, thus the attack was cancelled. There was, however, during the day, an attack ordered by 3rd Division to take Guémappe, to take place late in the day. This had come about after the O.C. of 50th Division, finding themselves on the high ground south of Guémappe, realised that his division could not move forward without the village being in British hands. The two commanders thus arrived upon a scheme for attacking the village simultaneously from the south by 50th Division and the west by 9th Brigade of 3rd Division at 6.44pm with a complex arrangement of artillery. This was agreed by VI Corps H.Q. and thus orders went out to the two forward battalions of 9th Brigade. The men of 12th West Yorks on the left and 1st Northumberland Fusiliers on the right advanced with the barrage at the appointed time and reached the sunken road but as they got 200 yards beyond came under such rifle and machine gun fire that they were forced back to the road. No evidence of any support from the high ground above in the shape of 50th Division men was forthcoming, the Germans even seen standing on their parapets near Wancourt Tower firing down on the attacking British troops.[73] The only attack to be carried out on the 13th was therefore another costly failure, the brigade losing 313 men.[74] The C.O. of the Northumberland Fusiliers is particularly scathing at the fact that 29th Division had no knowledge of the attack and therefore could lend no support and that no attack came from the south, thus leaving his men in an isolated attack with the whole of the German defensive fire falling upon a narrow section of the front; he had a very valid point.[75]

The delay, caused by the tardy progress of 29th Division, led to the major effort of both VI and VII Corps being timed for early morning on 14 April. In order to allow 3rd Division to finally retire, one of the other brigades of 29th Division, 87th Brigade, was ordered to carry out the relief before dawn on the 14th. The corps was in this way reduced to two divisions, both of which were, however, fresh from reserve as compared to the units they replaced which had been out in the battle for five days in some quite horrendous weather. This led to yet another change of plans because it was this relief that led 29th Division to state that it could not attack at the appointed hour against Guémappe as it had insufficient time to prepare. The overall plan for the day was for the two Corps south of the river to attack at 5.30am behind a creeping barrage. For VI Corps the first objective was a line from the enclosures on the road east of Guémappe, through Hill 100

72   Behrmann & Brandt, *Die Osterschlacht bei Arras 1917 II*, pp. 100-101.
73   TNA: WO95/1427 War Diaries of H.Q. 9th Brigade.
74   Falls, *Military Operations, France and Belgium 1917 Vol. 1*, p. 287.
75   TNA: WO95/1378 War Diaries of 1st Northumberland Fusiliers.

east of Monchy-le-Preux and then down the spur to the right of XVII Corps. Further objectives included the St. Rohart Factory and the Bois du Sart. Haldane's plan to conform to Army instructions is difficult to understand. Knowing that there was to be no attack to the north of the river he must have been concerned about that flank. His reaction though was to give no orders to 17th Division for 14 April whatsoever. How 29th Division, had they been successful in moving thorough Hill 100 and beyond, were going to cope with the open flank to their left is not discussed or even raised anywhere. To the south, 87th Brigade had asked for, and been granted a delay in their attack. What did this leave in VI Corps? It left 88th Brigade the only unit in the corps carrying out an attack at 5.30am.

No attacking unit on the left and merely an artillery barrage of Guémappe on its right, the consequences of this decision were going to become very clear over the next few hours. For the attack 88th Brigade decided on a two battalion front consisting of 1st Essex Regiment on the left and The Newfoundland Regiment on the right. The first objective for both was a line over Hill 100 and at 5.30am they attacked from the trench dug east of the village by 2nd Hampshire Regiment over the previous two nights. At first all seemed to go well although the barrage was reported by the Newfoundlanders to be "deplorably thin."[76] On the left the 1st Essex reported at 6.30am that they had reached their first objective with three of their companies. A worrying addition to this message though was that German troops were seen massing to the north and north east around the Bois des Aubépines and Bois de Sart respectively. Also the flank company (X) had met difficulties almost immediately in trying to form defensive strongpoints to the north. Few of X Company, overwhelmed by superior forces whilst establishing, probably between 6.30am and 7.30am., a makeshift defence, were ever seen again. The loss of any flank cover to the north meant the end for those of the other three companies on the northern flanks of Hill 100. Most of these were also never seen again or if so, after the war was over. At the beginning of the day the battalion had 31 officers and 892 men, by the end it reported 17 officers and 644 other ranks killed, wounded or missing. It was confirmed later that 203 of those missing were prisoners of war.[77] To the right of the Essex the same fate awaited the Newfoundlanders as the lack of any kind of effort to their right meant no protection from the south either. They also got up onto the ridge with A Company endeavouring to cover the right by establishing a post in Machine Gun Wood, the small wood near the Monchy-le-Preux to St. Rohart Factory road. The first wave had stopped before the ridge and established strongpoints. The second wave plus some Lewis gunners who went over the ridge were never seen again. Germans advanced up the road from St. Rohart Factory but were beaten off by a strongpoint established just south east of Monchy. Clearly those troops who got beyond the ridge and moved towards Bois du Vert were all either killed or captured by the German defenders. Approximately 591 men went into action that morning of which 487 became casualties or were missing. Eventually 150 were reported as prisoners of war.[78] Shortly afterwards at around 9.00am the last remnants of both battalions made their way, as best as they could, back to their own lines under considerable pressure from the pursuing German infantry. Now the poor staff work of the division (and it must be said corps) almost led to the loss of Monchy-le-Preux itself. Before the exchange of divisions, the line from the River Scarpe to the Cambrai Road was held by two divisions with another the other side of the road (from the north 15th,

---

76   TNA: WO95/2308 War Diaries of The Newfoundland Regiment.
77   TNA: WO95/2309 War Diaries of 1st Essex Regiment; There are 181 names of Essex men, who died on 14th April and have no known grave, on the Arras Memorial. Only six 1st Essex men from that day have a known grave, scattered in cemeteries around the area and probably found much later.
78   TNA: WO95/2308 War Diaries of The Newfoundland Regiment. There are 130 names of those with no known grave from this day on the Newfoundland Memorial at Beaumont-Hamel on the Somme.

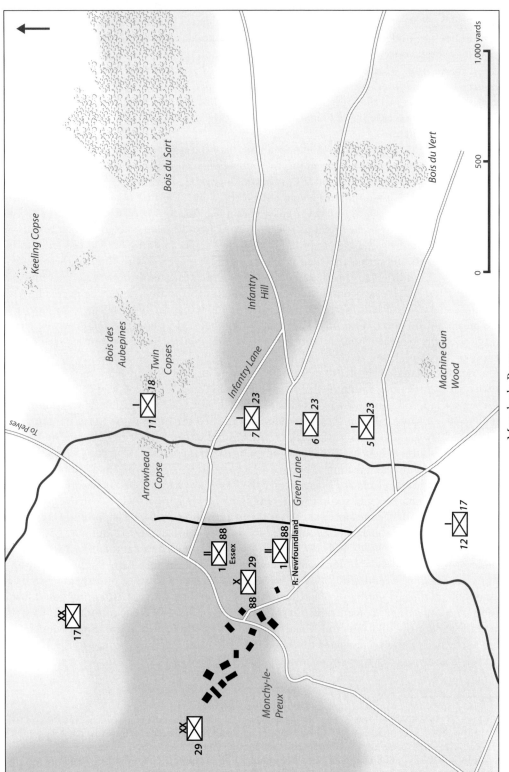

Monchy-le-Preux.

37th and then 3rd Divisions). It was now held by only two, 17th Division north (one brigade forward) and 29th Division south (one brigade Monchy, the other relieving 3rd Division the other side of the road). When the two battalions of 88th Brigade attacked, 4th Worcesters were in support but were located in the southern part of the front towards La Bergère, not in Monchy itself. 2nd Hampshires, having dug the assault trench had retired to Orange Hill as brigade reserve. The C.O. of the Newfoundland Regiment, Lt.-Col. J Forbes-Robertson had his H.Q. in the centre of the village and at 10.00am a wounded man of 1st Essex came in saying that all the battalion were killed or captured. Forbes-Robertson therefore sent his signalling officer, Lt. Keegan forward to try and find out what the situation was. Keegan returned 25 min later with the horrendous news that he found, "not a single unwounded man on the East edge of MONCHY and that 200 or 300 Germans were advancing only about 300 yards away".[79] All the telephone lines were down so the C.O. sent off the adjutant to make a report. Hastily scraping together what men from the Battalion H.Q. that were there, Forbes-Robertson hastened to the village edge. He vainly tried to turn a few slightly wounded or other stragglers on his way, eventually getting to a house on the edge where he could look out of a shell hole by means of a ladder. From there he saw the Germans already beginning to jump into the assault trench and half way between he spotted a hedge. He ordered a dash for the hedge which turned out to be the, "parapet of quite a good little section of trench."[80] Keegan, himself and seven other ranks took up positions. After some rapid fire to pin the Germans, Forbes-Robertson then ordered only fire at short range to conserve ammunition. About an hour and a half later the small group was joined by one man[81] who had been knocked out by a shell for a while but then crawled to them. There was some assistance from the left rear, probably one of the 88th Machine Gun Company guns that had not gone forward to support the attack (the latter were never seen again). This fire silenced a troublesome German machine gun to the left front, making life a great deal easier for the small band of men. No attack was made on the group and they accounted for about 40 of the enemy who tried to reinforce the men who had reached the assault trench. The group did observe a large body of men move south west across their front and attack south of the village. This attack, at around 12.30pm ran straight into the men of the 4th Worcester Regiment who were well placed with a result that, "the attack was completely shattered."[82] Approaching 2.00pm the sniping had died down and so Forbes-Robertson decided to send his messenger back with a call for reinforcements and that Machine Gun Wood should be shelled as it appeared to be a collecting point for a large body of German troops. Lt.-Col. Beckwith had already despatched one company to the North West of Monchy to guard against Germans moving around the village, after hearing of movement from Pelves.[83] He then ordered the whole of the battalion into the village which it reached after having avoided the heavy German bombardment. Therefore, as evening approached defences in the north-eastern and eastern approaches to Monchy-le-Preux were again in place. As it was the small band of brave men, who had been at the post in the south-eastern fringes of the village since just before 11.00am were only relieved by a platoon of the Hampshires at 8.00pm.

---

79   TNA: WO95/2308 War Diaries of The Newfoundland Regiment, from which the description of the action involving Lt.-Col. Forbes-Robertson that follows is taken.

80   As well as the two officers there was the provost sergeant and his corporal, a signal Corporal with two signallers, the Regimental messenger and a lone private of 1st Essex Regiment.

81   An orderly room corporal.

82   TNA: WO95/2309 War Diaries of 4th Worcester Regiment.

83   Falls, *Military Operations, France and Belgium 1917 Vol. 1*, p. 293 contains the report of the adjutant as the reason for the order forward but that would have meant a very long delay, more likely the messenger's desperate report was the prompt.

They were then able to make their way back to Arras where Forbes-Robertson's next task was to form a composite battalion out of the remains of the two that had begun the day in such a brave but futile attack. In actual fact it is clear that there was also a company of Hampshires in Monchy during this episode, but in the north eastern segment of the village along with two machine guns of No. 1 Section 88th Brigade Machine Gun Corps. The Hampshire diary makes two comments, both of which on separate occasions place X Company in Monchy. This is not to denigrate the achievements of the small band of men but perhaps its legendary status was encouraged due to the wish to deflect from the main events of the day.

What of the remaining brigade of 29th Division, 87th Brigade? Having asked for and gained a respite for having relieved 3rd Division what were its actions on 14 April. The derisory diary entry for the day is all that is required as a commentary:

> The 88th Brigade on our left attacked enemy position in front of Monchy-le-Preux. 2nd South West Borderers pushed forward patrols but unable to make much ground. In the afternoon the enemy counter-attacked the 88th Brigade re-taking the ground. We took over small portion of line from 88th Brigade.[84]

In summary then the sum total of VI Corps attempts to follow the 3rd Army instructions for the day was an unsupported, two battalion attack which, unsurprisingly, failed in the most catastrophic manner for the men of those units.

British prisoners, April 1917. (Private Collection)

---

84   TNA: WO95/2303 War Diaries of H.Q. 87th Brigade.

Captured British booty seized during the attack from Monchy on 14 April. (Private Collection)

This abject failure to carry out any kind of coherent, extensive and supported attack on this day seems to have received little or no commentary from above. The result of the Forbes-Robertson 'affair' seems to have been the legend of the men who saved Monchy from a major German counter attack, which led to a very false view of the failure of the two battalions of 88th Brigade in the first place. Almost immediately the decisive nature of the German response to the attack was put down to the Germans having planned an attack for the day and that the two British battalions unluckily happened to attack at the same time. Simultaneously to being destroyed they were then seen to have foiled a major German effort to retake the village. According to the 88th Brigade War Diary:

> It appears the brigade attacked at a time when the Germans were contemplating an attack on Monchy with two divisions. The attack of the 88th Brigade undoubtedly broke up and disorganised the German attack.[85]

This then found its way into the divisional history in 1925 relating that, "a strange thing had happened; attacks had been planned by both sides for the same morning; and we had only fore-stalled the Germans by an hour."[86] The strength of the German force was now at a division, the *3rd Bavarian*. The Official History then relates that prisoners taken from that division told of a major attack planned for the afternoon and that the temerity of the Bavarians in not taking the village being an opportunity thrown away. If the whole of the *3rd Bavarian* Division had been in the area and planning an attack then it would seem they did not perform very well, however, the records of that division do not support this. The line was being held on this day by *18th Bayersische I.R.*

---

85   TNA: WO95/2306 War Diaries of H.Q. 88th Brigade.
86   Gillon, Captain S., *The Story of the 29th Division* (Nelson & Sons: London, 1925), p. 283.

on the north and *23rd Bayerische I.R.* in the centre and *17th Bayerische I.R.* in the south. Having arrived over the previous couple of days the Bavarians had been able to dig themselves in and were organised in the usual way of one battalion forward, one in support and one further back, within each regiment. The main effort of 88th Brigade came against the *23rd Bayerische I.R.* so the two flanking battalions were not put under pressure in the attack. *17th Bayerische I.R.* report destroying the British that came against them, this probably being the right company of the Newfoundlanders. Similarly, to the north it will have been the forward battalion of the *18th Bayerische I.R.* that made short work of the company of Essex men trying to set up a flank, 50 prisoners are reported taken here. Only in the centre was the line broken through. Here *II/23 Regiment*, the forward battalion, was forced back by the assault. This also forced 11th Company of the *18th Bayerische I.R.* to pull back to form a flank. It was now 7.00am and the Germans recognised this as a turning point in the battle. Into the fray now came 11th and 12th companies of the *III/I.R. 23* who had, after working on the line in Pelves, come forward in support, along with the 9th and 10th Companies. On the southern flank 5th and 8th companies of the *23rd Bayerische I.R.* plus elements of *17th Bayerische I.R.* completed the almost comprehensive cutting off of the British troops. At this point the Germans reported large numbers of British troops surrendering, approximately 150. What the breaking through of the *23rd Bayerische I.R.* by British troops had led to, however, was the moving forward of the reserve battalions of the brigade. Unfortunately for the Germans, all their telephone lines had been broken and the order did not arrive at the lower units. It was not, therefore, possible to plan a counter attack before 4.30pm in the afternoon. However, when *Generalleutnant* Ritter von Wenninger, the divisional commander, asked for the necessary artillery support he was told it was not available and therefore the attack was called off.[87] The attacks that British troops had to repulse in the late morning and afternoon were simply the Germans of the battalions that had been involved earlier in the defence, counter attacking forwards. This clearly grants myth status to the idea that the 88th Brigade attack was merely 'unfortunate' in coming up against a planned German assault. Quite simply it was a foolish attack that was dealt with by the troops on hand who, equally foolishly perhaps, then tried to advance further. The British created myth, so formed, led to no comments or enquiry as to the performance of VI Corps on this day; reputations had been maintained.

3rd Army – VII Corps

Having held up attacks on 10 April until the afternoon and then made very little progress the VII Corps orders for the 11th were merely a repetition of those of previous days and in some ways no different to the original ones for the initial assault. An order going out at 10.55pm on the 10th made 6.00am the start time for 14th, 56th, 30th and 21st Divisions to continue their attacks. The 14th Division was tasked with assaulting Wancourt in conjunction with the neighbouring 3rd Division's attack on Guémappe. The 56th Division's orders were to get onto the high ground above Wancourt during the night and then "support advance of divisions on right and left at 6.00am."[88] The 30th and 21st Divisions had the rather optimistic orders, given the experiences of the previous two days, of being "prepared to work forward into the enemy's position during the

87   Reigel, *Hauptmann*, a.D., *Königlich-bayerischen 17 Infantrie-Regiment Orff* (52 Band Erinnerungsblätter deutscher Regimenter, bayerischen Kriegsarchiv, 1927); Ritter, Albrecht, *Königlich-bayerischen 18 Infantrie-Regiment Prinz Ludwig Ferdinand*, (47 Band Erinnerungsblätter deutscher Regimenter, bayerischen Kriegsarchiv, 1926); Behrmann & Brandt, *Die Osterschlacht bei Arras 1917 II*, pp. 109-112.
88   TNA: WO95/805 War Diaries of H.Q. General Staff VII Corps.

night if opportunity arises."[89] Should this turn out not to be possible then to attack at 6.00am and get to the original Green Line, the high ground above Héninel.

The 14th Division passed on the order to 41st Brigade in the line that they were to attack at 6.00am, even though they had been told only a few hours earlier that they would only attack when 56th Division had taken Hill 90. After discussion this was delayed until 6.30am with an attack by 56th Division timed for an hour earlier on Hill 90. When the time came there was little evidence of Hill 90 having being attacked and to make things worse:

> The barrage by 2 groups of field artillery, from which much had been expected, resolved itself into a little dispersed intermittent fire which beyond causing the infantry of the Brigade a considerable number of casualties had no influence on the attack.[90]

The plan was that the infantry retires 200 yards, the barrage would begin at 6.30am and then the attack would go in under the barrage. The result of so little artillery support and machine gun fire from Hill 90 was that the 7th King's Royal Rifle Corps and 7th Rifle Brigade could actually only get to their original trench line, suffering badly in the process. Many men had to lie out in shell holes for the rest of the day until they could get in after dark.

Meanwhile on 14th Division's right, 56th Division had informed VII Corps that they would not be able to clear Hill 90 the night 10/11 April. 167th Brigade was therefore given the task of taking the Cojeul Switch (Nepal Trench on trench maps) down to connect with 14th Division and carry Hill 90 as soon as possible.[91] This order is repeated in the brigade diary of the 167th at around midnight but it there is no indication of any concerted and supported attack on Nepal Trench which was the key to then taking Hill 90. On the left, 3rd London, who it will be recalled failed to take Nepal Trench the previous day, spent the day exchanging rifle and machine gun fire with the Germans to their front, until relieved later in the afternoon by 1/1st London. At no point was there any organised artillery attempt to cut the wire that had foiled them the day before nor a further attempt to take the German trench. 1/1st London's orders were to get into Nepal Trench on the left where 14th Division held it and bomb down all the way to the Hindenburg support line. Major Glover of the 1/1st London in reconnoitring the situation learned (how is not mentioned) that Nepal Trench for some distance to the north, since the previous morning, had not been in British hands. This was not true but as a result 1/1st London also made no attempt at that point to make any progress towards the objective of taking Nepal Trench. The 1/9th London, the Queen Victoria Rifles attached to 167th Brigade from 169th Brigade, started clearing the Hindenburg Trench system during the night around the Wancourt Line and around noon received orders from Brigade to continue down to the Cojeul River. This they succeeded in doing and as such, being in the rear of the Germans in Nepal Trench there was seen to be the beginnings of a retirement of the Germans back towards Héninel. This withdrawal then allowed, during the evening, men of 167th Brigade to finally get into Nepal Trench.[92]

To the O.C. of 90th Brigade of 30th Division, it remained clear that any frontal assault on the Hindenburg Line in front of him would only lead to high casualties with no gain. He therefore ordered 18th Manchester to enter the line in the 56th Division area at Panther Lane and to bomb down the front line. They were at Panther Lane by 4.30pm, by which time the Londoners had cleared the German Lines almost down to the river. Thus they followed the trench system down

---

89   TNA: WO95/805 War Diaries of H.Q. General Staff VII Corps.
90   TNA: WO95/1894 War Diaries of H.Q. 41st Brigade.
91   TNA: WO95/2933 War Diaries of H.Q. General Staff 56th Division.
92   TNA: WO95/2949 War Diaries of H.Q. 167th Brigade.

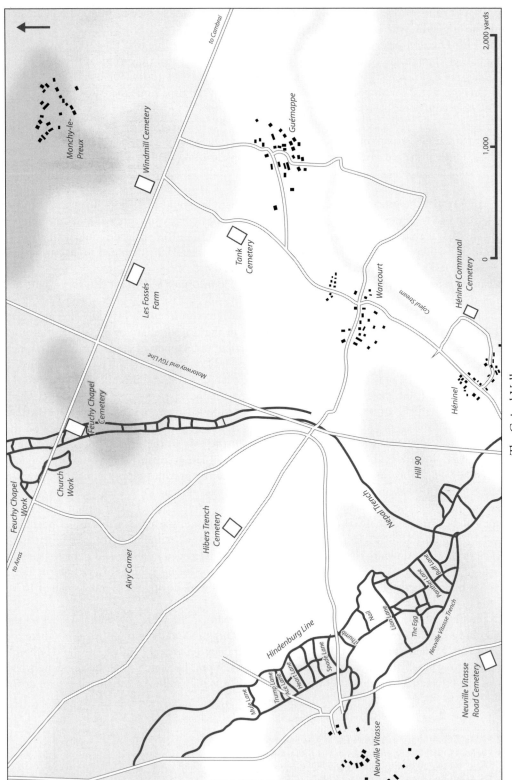

The Cojeul Valley area.

towards the river, one party attempting to bomb out along a trench leading towards Héninel but having to turn back. They were by now attached to 89th Brigade and were able to relieve the 1/9th Londoners in the complex of trenches near the river. Maj.-Gen Shea of 30th Division had ordered the 89th Brigade, in the shape of 2nd Bedford and 20th King's Liverpool, to attempt to use the small gaps in the wire, mostly on the right, to get into the front of the Hindenburg Line before them, starting at 6.00am. They came under heavy fire from a clearly undisturbed line in front of them as it was not going to be for some time before the troops of 56th Division and 90th Brigade on the left were going to get all the way down to the Cojeul; thus this attack achieved nothing.

The 21st Division had, following the loss of the small parts of the Hindenburg first line that they had held for a while, relieved 63rd Brigade and the line was now held by 62nd Brigade. They also had an attack set for 6.00am with the 10th Yorkshire Regiment left and 1st Lincolns to the right. The two units followed the barrage which had begun 22 minutes earlier but when they got to the wire the Yorkshires could only find one fully cut and one partially cut lane, the Lincolns finding three cut but all these were covered by German machine guns. The result was the usual brave but futile attempt to get through the wire with severe losses to both units and an eventual withdrawal back to the start line. Two companies of the Lincolns had lost all their officers during the action. Overall they had lost 156 casualties and the Yorkshires 125 all ranks.[93]

The 11 April for VII Corps can only be described as a mishmash of confused action, brave but unsupported and uncoordinated assaults with little hope of success and basically a poor show from 56th Division. The key to the objective of getting into Héninel and Wancourt, followed by the heights to the east, was Hill 90. This had been a key objective for 56th Division for two days, having not got to it on the 9th. During that time there was neither a coordinated artillery barrage nor attack on the high ground, merely a great deal of working and bombing through trenches, in the main down to the Cojeul. That task could have been undertaken by 30th Division, as in fact this division thought it had to do and allocated troops for it. The total casualties recorded for the period 10 to 13 April for the whole of 56th Division was 23 officers and 298 O.R.[94] It is not possible to distinguish casualties in 167th Brigade, the unit tasked with taking Hill 90, for the time they were attempting to do so. The brigade diary does not record casualties but using the individual battalion ones it can be calculated that between the 9th and 11th the brigade had casualties of a total of 585 all ranks; many of these will have been in the initial assault on the first day.[95] Although casualties can never be direct evidence of a lack of a will to carry out orders that the whole division lost less in four days in the line than a number of battalions did in one attack cannot pass without mention. The lack of any effort by 167th Brigade could have been excused and the saving of lives praised, had it not been for the fact that it led to heavy losses, over those four days, to the divisions on its flanks. Corps seemed to have little or no knowledge of what was happening or that its orders were not being carried out. There follows an extract from the diary of the 7th King's Royal Rifle Corps, ordered to attack on the 11th; the bitterness of the C.O. and author of the passage below is not difficult to decipher:

> At 1.00am [11 April] the Brigadier came up and talked over the situation. He agreed that it was quite impossible to push on until Hill 90 had been taken by the 56th Division and that all we could do was to remain on the defensive. Any advance up the valley was sheer madness

93   TNA: WO95/2152 War Diaries of H.Q. 62nd Brigade; TNA: WO95/2154 War Diaries of 1st Lincoln Regiment; TNA: WO95/2156 War Diaries of 10th Yorkshire Regiment (The Green Howards).
94   TNA: WO95/2933 War Diaries of H.Q. General Staff, 56th Division. Compare these casualties to the *battalion* casualties suffered in other divisions.
95   TNA: WO95/2949 War Diaries of 1/1st and 1/3rd London Regiment; TNA: WO95/2950 War Diaries of 1/7th and 1/8th Middlesex Regiment.

until the machine guns on Hill 90 which enfiladed the whole valley had been put out of action. The attached orders arrived and in spite of all protests we were ordered to carry them out. There was no time to copy them out and the originals had to be sent up to the forwards coys. B & C Companies, supported by the 8th Rifle Brigade were to advance up the valley and try and push on to WANCOURT. The 56th Division never left their trenches or made any attempt to take Hill 90. B Coy under WHITLEY made a most gallant attempt to push forward but from the start it was an impossible task & the Staff who had ordered the attack, if they had even come near enough to have looked at the ground they would have realised it too and would never have ordered the attack.[96]

The pressure exerted down the Hindenburg Line to the Cojeul stream did have the desired effect though of placing the German defenders on Hill 90 in a difficult position. With a danger of Héninel being taken the next day behind their backs the unit on Hill 90 used darkness to retire back, not merely into the valley but up onto the heights above. This had a chain reaction of forcing the Germans in Wancourt to also feel vulnerable given Hill 90 would be in British hands and therefore this village was also to be evacuated. The orders went out at 11.25pm and although to come into effect at 3.00am on the 12th the last men were busy blowing up stores and dugouts in Wancourt as the first British soldiers appeared above.[97]

Patrols sent out by 14th Division in the early morning of the 12th were the first to find Wancourt empty of the enemy apart from a few stragglers and snipers who were later made prisoner. 8th Rifle Brigade were therefore ordered to move passed Wancourt to the north with 8th King's Royal Rifle Corps to the south of the village. The information that 14th Division had received was that Guémappe was in the hands of the 3rd Division but that situation was soon dispelled when a patrol found trench west of the village held by Germans and another, attempting to join up with 3rd Division on the road between Wancourt and Guémappe was destroyed by the German defenders. That meant a change of orders for 8th Rifle Brigade, to now cover the north flank with one company whilst the remainder moved through the centre of Wancourt or to the south. Eventually getting to a line just the other side of the Cojeul stream, below the escarpment, there was a plan for a further push up the hill at 5.00pm but although a barrage timed for that time began it was decided, after some companies had not managed to get through the mud in the valley, that the men were too exhausted to attack. They had been fighting and out in the open for four days now and were at the end of their tether. The division was relieved that evening and overnight by 50th Division.[98]

The 56th Division history would like its readers to believe that Hill 90 was taken by a pincer movement by 1/2nd London bombing down from the north and 1/5th London from the south with a password of 'Rum Jar' for when they met.[99] There was probably no need for the password as the majority of Germans had retired and just a few stragglers were killed or taken prisoner. This began at 5.00am and by 5.35am, seeing the Germans leaving Héninel, A Company of 1/2nd Londons passed through the village and climbed the slopes on the other side. Although some outposts were created up towards the heights the main line was established by 169th Brigade in the valley alongside 14th Division.[100]

96   TNA: WO95/1896 War Diaries of 7th King's Royal Rifle Corps.
97   Behrmann & Brandt, *Die Osterschlacht bei Arras 1917 II*, p. 103.
98   TNA: WO95/1869 War Diaries of H.Q. General Staff 14th Division; TNA WO95/1894 War Diaries of H.Q. 41st Brigade; TNA: WO95/1895 War Diaries of 8th Rifle Brigade & 8th K.R.R.C.
99   Ward, Maj. D.H. Dudley, *The Fifty Sixth Division* p. 126.
100 TNA: WO95/2957 War Diaries of H.Q. 169th Brigade; TNA: WO95/2960 War Diaries of 1/2nd (City of London) Battalion (Royal Fusiliers); TNA: WO95/2960 War Diaries of 1/5th (City of London) Battalion

The 30th Division plan for 12 April was for the 18th Manchesters to clear the Hindenburg Line to the south of the Cojeul Stream, in front of 21st Division by bombing down the trenches. They had been involved in the trenches north of the river the previous day and during the night prepared themselves to cross the Cojeul and for C Company to take the fire trench whilst A Company dealt with the support trench. As with many plans over these days this went slightly awry when the bomb section of A Company under 2nd/Lt. S.M. Shirley, followed by the Lewis gun section under 2nd/Lt. C. Lawrence entered the fire trench, instead of the other, after a short barrage of rifle grenades and Lewis gun fire. Overcoming a sentry party, they advanced down the trench, with increasing resistance until bombs were running short about 400 yards in. 2nd/Lt. Westphal, commanding C Company, due to start later and realising the fire trench was already engaged, rushed into the support trench instead. With D company bringing up more bombs when daylight came more progress could be made and as the ridge was neared (where the line makes a slight right angled bend. See map) resistance became less and Germans could be seen moving back. Eventually posts were established by around 10.30am in both lines of the Hindenburg position just before the beginning of the bend and touch was made with 21st Division. The whole enterprise had cost six killed and 27 wounded, claiming to have killed over 100 Germans.[101] The *84th R.I.R.* deployed in that part of the line, had already been ordered to retire the previous evening and were in preparations to do so. The assault from their right therefore attacked straight into these arrangements but also explains why, although there was some resistance, it was not so severe that the line could not be cleared by mid-day. As the defending German regimental records (postwar) 25 killed or missing for that day the claims of the Manchesters seem to be somewhat exaggerated.[102] Whatever the case this was the last action for 30th Division for the First Battle of the Scarpe as they moved to XVIII Corps in 3rd Army reserve. In essence, their position had been pinched out by 21st and 56th Divisions and as such they did not need to be relieved by another unit.

The 21st Division expected to launch another that morning. Preparations were made before the attack got underway, 62nd Brigade receiving the welcome news that the objective was taken from the left. Thus their only task that day was to take over the line from 18th Manchesters. At 10.45am patrols from the 12th and 13th Northumberland Fusiliers entered the front line trench, finding it unoccupied and by 11.00am were in the support trenches. Here they found wounded men of 64th Brigade who reported that the Germans had left at 9.30am. They then made contact with men of 56th Division further down the line, further evidence that the success of the 18th Manchesters was a little less spectacular than claimed in their report.[103] 2nd Lincolns then pushed out beyond the Hindenburg support line on the spur and formed a flank there facing east. Later that afternoon, the 12th Northumberland fusiliers bombed further down the Hindenburg Line to the east, to a point, by the end of the day, where it curves back into a south easterly direction. From this point they reported the line remained strongly held.

By the close of 12 April, three days later than planned, VII Corps were near to the Green Line, even if not quite on it. They had taken the Cojeul Valley in the Héninel/Wancourt sector and could now set their goals on the dominating high ground to the east. The Germans had, in slowly

(London Rifle Brigade). The diaries of the 1/2nd Londons talk of two officers strolling down to Wancourt and finding it empty. The walk is a kilometre in full view of the Germans on the ridge so this is probably a mistake.

101   TNA: WO95/2339/3, War Diaries of 18th Manchester Regiment.

102   Speck, Justiczinspector William, *Das KöniglichPreußische Reserve-Infantrie-Regiment 84*, p. 195 and Casualty Table, p. 202.

103   Contemporary authors have also been misled by the Manchester's report. For example, see Stedman, Michael, *The Manchester Pals* (Barnsley: Pen & Sword, 2004), p. 173. This is not to demean the contents therein; it is merely that the planned retirement was misinterpreted as forced retreat.

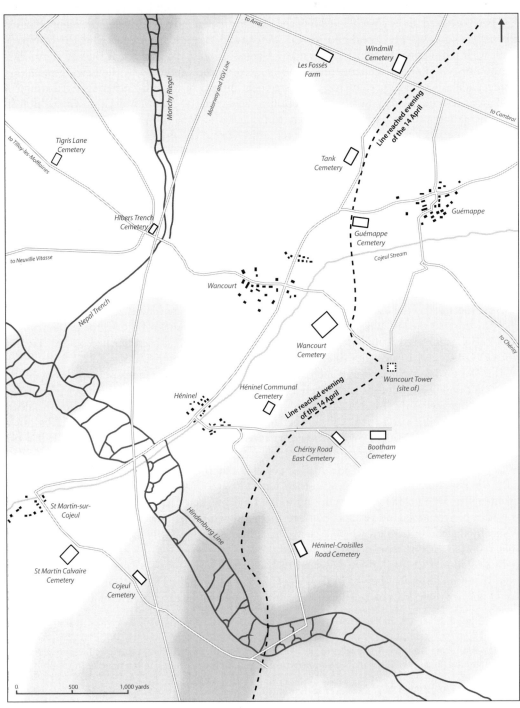

to Arras

Windmill
Cemetery

Les Fossés
Farm

Line reached evening
of the 14 April

to Cambrai

Monchy Riegel

Motorway and TGV Line

Tank
Cemetery

Guémappe

to Tilloy-les-Mofflaines

Tigris Lane
Cemetery

Guémappe
Cemetery

Hibers Trench
Cemetery

Cojeul Stream

to Neuville Vitasse

Wancourt

to Chérisy

Nepal Trench

Wancourt
Cemetery

Wancourt Tower
(site of)

Héninel Communal
Cemetery

Héninel

Line reached evening
of the 14 April

Chérisy Road
East Cemetery

Bootham
Cemetery

St Martin-sur-
Cojeul

Hindenburg Line

Héninel-Croisilles
Road Cemetery

St Martin Calvaire
Cemetery

Cojeul
Cemetery

0   500   1,000 yards

Cojeul Valley.

losing ground in the Hindenburg trenches themselves, been forced off the vital positions on Hill 90. How much this was a key to the area can be seen by the full withdrawal of *86th R.I.R.* and *84th R.I.R.* back to a line on the heights between the Hindenburg Line west of Fontaine-les-Croisilles and Guémappe. It is clear from the histories of both of these regiments though that they were far from beaten and that any further attempts to make progress across that high ground for the British would not be straight forward.

On the night of 12/13 April the remains of some of those battalions of *18th Reserve Division*, engaged in fierce fighting for four days, were relieved by units of *35th Division* that had been arriving. Around Guémappe the *II/I.R. 176* took over the defences whilst *III/I.R. 141* took over the high ground above Wancourt down to the road from the latter village to Chérisy.[104]

The 50th Division had, at the beginning of the campaign, been in 3rd Army reserve, although it is worth repeating here that General Allenby had to gain GHQ permission before putting this division in the line. That permission was given on the evening of 11 April, the same time as that for 33rd Division, also to VII Corps. Therefore, by the morning of 13 April, 151st Brigade of 50th Division had taken over the front line area from 14th Division and Maj-Gen. P.S. Wilkinson, G.O.C. 50th Division, had taken over command in the sector. He had the 1/9th Durham Light Infantry take over the valley position and instructed to try and get up onto the heights, especially around Wancourt Tower.[105] The brigade diary reports men of the D.L.I. getting up to the vicinity of the Tower but one report that they were 50 yards east of it was later corrected to the same distance west. What they failed to do was subdue fire falling onto 3rd Division as has already been seen. Unfortunately, the diary of the 1/9th gives us no further clues as to what happened. With a slender toehold on the high ground, the instructions for the next day were to continue the advance to the east.[106]

Unfortunately, the 56th Division's operations on 13 April demonstrates the same level of confusion that had been seen over preceding days. As far as the divisional diary is concerned it had received orders to advance on Chérisy and that at 12.50am on the 13th it had ordered 169th Brigade to do just that.[107] The first line of the 169th brigade diary for the day is; "Attack as ordered for 13th was postponed."[108] There is no evidence of any reason in the diaries or the divisional history. No pressure was therefore placed on the German defenders in front of them, giving them yet more time to strengthen their positions. What is notable at the end of the entries for the day in the divisional diary is that prisoners of *Infantrie-Regiments 84, 86* and *99* had been taken that day. These units had been in the line since the first day, no new units had been forced to take over from reserve and none of their casualties had been high.

On the right, 21st Division attempted to continue progress in the direction of Fontaine-les-Croisilles both down and behind the Hindenburg Line. The 12th Northumberland Fusiliers, with the task on the left could make little progress, noting that the division on their left (56th) had not moved. Some gains was made in the Hindenburg but two companies of 19th Brigade, in support,

---

104 Behrmann & Brandt, *Die Osterschlacht bei Arras 1917 II*, p. 107.

105 1/9th D.L.I. was under the command of the remarkable Lt Col Roland Boys Bradford VC MC. Awarded the MC as a Lieutenant in February 1915, he became temporary Lt Col and C.O. of the battalion in August 1916 at the age of 24. Awarded the VC on 1 October 1916 he was to receive it from the King after this battle in June 1917. He was promoted to Brig-Gen (now 25, the youngest ever without privilege) in November the same year but was killed 20 days later. His brother George, a Lt. Commander in the navy was killed at Zeebrugge in April 1918, was awarded a posthumous VC; the only brothers awarded the decoration during the war.

106 TNA: WO95/2838 War Diaries of H.Q. 151st Brigade; TNA WO95/2840 War Diaries of 1/9th Durham Light Infantry.

107 TNA: WO95/2933 War Diaries of H.Q. General Staff 56th Division.

108 TNA: WO95/2957 War Diaries of H.Q. 169th Brigade.

had to be sent forward to fill the gap that had formed between the division's left and the right of 56th Division.

The 13 April therefore saw little progress along VII Corps front. One whole fresh division from reserve, another bringing in a barely committed brigade and a division that had suffered relatively few casualties in the preceding three days made no progress against the very same three regiments that had been holding this part of the line since the morning of 9 April. Orders for the 14th were comprehensive and demanding; the valley of the Sensée stream was to be reached including the village of Cherisy and beyond almost to Vis-en-Artois.

Across No Man's Land, the Germans used the fresh units of the newly-arrived *35th Division* to replace the original units of *18th Division* during the night to the 14th. Thus the newly ordered renewal of the attack would meet fresh troops of *I.R. 176, I.R. 141* and, to the south, *I.R. 61.*[109] What difference a day can make.

Already, during the night, concern was raised within 151st Brigade that the position on their left, almost left rear, in Guémappe was going to make moving forward extremely difficult. Then at 3.10am the brigade learned that 29th Division was not going to be attacking the next morning. Plans to follow up to 56th Division's attack were substituted for orders to form a defensive flank on the left. The position at 5.30am was that one and a half companies of 9th D.L.I. were up on the ridge near Wancourt Tower, the remainder in the valley with 6th D.L.I. also in the valley to their right. In support in the valley behind was 8th D.L.I. It is difficult to ascertain from the relevant diaries what the 9th D.L.I. did during the day, but the situation map culled from the brigade diary gives the impression that very little was achieved, the unit in question remaining stationary. They were clearly given the task of covering the left although no orders can be found in the diaries.[110] 6th D.L.I. started up the slope, W and X Companies in front, both of which, after they reached the ridge were not seen for the remainder of the day.[111] Y and Z Companies also reached the ridge but under the intense fire from the front and also the left from Guémappe they could go no further. The 8th D.L.I. came up in support but could get no further. Casualties in the two companies of the 6th D.L.I. that were still in communication had been severe and adding to the confusion were men of 56th Division who had veered off into their area. The 8th D.L.I. had suffered 58 casualties of all ranks during the day, up to their relief. Casualties were far worse for the 6th D.L.I. The remains of W and X Companies were eventually found holding out in the training trenches on the hill but when all men had got back in the battalion it had suffered somewhere around 200 casualties in total, including five officers killed and eight wounded. For their actions on the hill the two company commanders of W and X Companies, Capt. R.S. Johnson and Capt. H. Walton were awarded the M.C.[112]

The 56th Division's 169th Brigade also attacked at 5.30am. The divisional diary first claims a gap of 500 yards between its left flank and the right of 50th Division and then that units of the 50th came across its left rear. None of the attacking units made any progress and eventually in one area were two battalions of 56th and two battalions of 50th Division. The attacking battalions, 1/9th London (Queen Victoria Rifles) and the 1/16th London (Queens Westminster Rifles) both

---

109 Behrmann & Brandt, *Die Osterschlacht bei Arras 1917 II*, p. 113.

110 TNA: WO95/2840 War Diaries of 1/9th Durham Light Infantry. The diary entries for the 12th to 14th are sparse in the extreme and give the impression the unit was not in action and provided no assistance to establishing the events of the day; TNA WO95/2838 War Diaries of H.Q. 151st Brigade.

111 Ainsworth MC, Captain R.B., *The Story of the 6th Battalion Durham Light Infantry, France April 1915 to November 1918*, (London: St. Catherine Press, 1919), p. 37. TNA: WO95/2840 War Diaries of 1/6th Durham Light Infantry.

112 The regimental history also notes that Corporal Betts was awarded the DCM and *Croix de Guerre*. In fact, his award was the MM not the DCM.

Remnants of the formidable Hindenburg Line on the Héninel heights. (Author)

suffered very badly from machine gun fire and made little progress, in spite of very heavy casualties, the men pushing on very bravely. The brigade diary complains about the 50th Division being in the wrong place as it feels its left flank should have been on the tower when in fact 1/6th and then 1/8th D.L.I. were using the tower as their left flank.

A glance at situation maps of both divisions immediately answers the question of confusion. That of 50th Division shows the position of its attacking units in the valley; the road rising up onto the ridge from the valley half way between Héninel and Wancourt being its right. A glance at the situation map for 56th Division, for the evening of 13 April, clearly shows that the division felt that the whole area, almost to Wancourt was within its operational remit. Given that, how it could be determined that there was a gap on the left is difficult to understand and the confusion of troops is not difficult to comprehend. There seems to have been little or no coordination between the two divisions as to boundaries or objectives. Small wonder both major units complain about the intrusion of men into what they felt was their space during the attack.[113]

The analysis provided by 21st Division is very succinct: The "5.30am attack commenced. Little progress made."[114] The fresh 19th Brigade (33rd Division) which had arrived in support from army reserve, had been fed into the battle under the command of 21st Division in an attempt to provide further operational impetuous to no avail. 5/6th Cameronians were to attack behind the Hindenburg Line towards Fontaine-les-Croisilles whilst the 1st Cameronians were to take over the task of bombing down the Hindenburg Line. The summary by 21st Division H.Q. is a little

---

113 TNA: WO95/2933 War Diaries of H.Q. General Staff 56th Division; TNA WO95/2838 War Diaries of H.Q. 151st Brigade.
114 TNA: WO95/2327 War Diaries of H.Q. General Staff 21st Division.

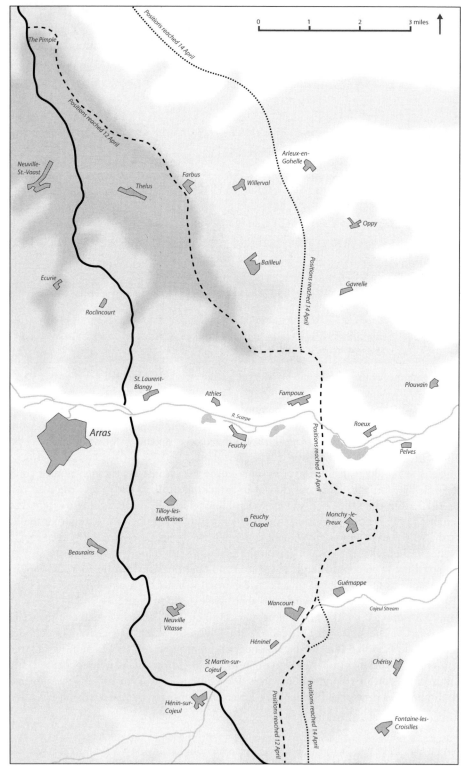

The Pimple

Positions reached 14 April

0   1   2   3 miles

Positions reached 12 April

Neuville-
St.-Vaast

Farbus

Thelus

Arleux-en-
Gohelle

Willerval

Oppy

Bailleul

Positions reached 14 April

Ecurie

Gavrelle

Roclincourt

St. Laurent-
Blangy

Athies

Fampoux

Plouvain

R. Scarpe

Arras

Feuchy

Roeux

Pelves

Positions reached 12 April

Tilloy-les-
Mofflaines

Feuchy
Chapel

Monchy-le-
Preux

Beaurains

Guémappe

Wancourt

Cojeul Stream

Neuville
Vitasse

Héninel

Chérisy

St Martin-sur-
Cojeul

Positions reached 14 April

Hénin-sur-
Cojeul

Fontaine-les-
Croisilles

Positions reached 12 April

Arras front, 14 April 1917.

harsh as the 5/6th Cameronians made around 800 yards of ground before they were stopped by machine gun fire and had to dig in. The 1st Cameronians had also made a little progress down the Hindenburg Line although bombs seemed to be short in supply for some reason. The 5/6th War Diary is bitter with regard to the lack of cooperation from 56th Division on the left. There was no liaison, 5/6th alone suffering 216 casualties of all kinds in the attack.

VII Corps finished the First Battle of the Scarpe approximately on the Green Line, their final objective for the first day. Whilst this can be viewed as a critical statement, it must be remembered that Hindenburg Line was opposite two thirds of the corps frontage. The last day of this initial stage in the Battle of Arras provided, however, a perfect example of what had gone wrong since 9 April. Communication between corps appears to have gone from bad to worse. The 56th Division was clearly in the wrong place, but in all subsequent analyses by this unit they claim it was not them, but those around that failed. Mitigation is that there is no evidence that divisional boundaries were established by Corps Headquarters. Thus the divisions were left to fend for themselves. This would have not been a problem had it been common practice for divisional commanders to share their interpretation of where said boundaries should be. The consequence of none of this being in place was a confused attack which troubled the German defenders little and an exposed flank that troubled 5/6th Cameronians greatly. The German official account dismisses the attacks of 50th and 56th Divisions in several paragraphs. Indeed, the machine guns of *2nd Comp. / Maschinengewehr-Scharfschützen-Abteilung 3*[115] and *3rd Comp. Maschinengewehr/I.R. 61* cut the attackers down in the valley within 300-400 metres from their lines. Following this, counter attacking troops gathered in hapless prisoners from the assaulting divisions.[116]

The First Battle of the Scarpe was at an end but fighting in the Arras sector went on into late May 1917. Only after the war was this rather artificial nomenclature decided upon. On the ground there will not have been any significant change to men's experience bar those in High Command. The decision to prepare for a major push along the front after artillery support could be properly planned and prepared did not mean a cessation to the fighting. It is now necessary to place the fighting from 9 to 14 April in the context of the remainder of the war in terms of how far had the British Army evolved before fleeting success could be transformed final victory.

---

115 'Machine gun marksman detachments'; The presence of one of these units, consisting of three companies of at least six machine guns, meant that between them 12 or more machine guns would be engaging the attackers.

116 Behrmann & Brandt, *Die Osterschlacht bei Arras 1917 II*, pp. 113-114.

10

Epilogue and Conclusions

His Last message home
"I Did My Best"
       CWGC epitaph of a soldier killed on 9 April 1917.

Epilogue

To place the events of the 9 to 14 April in context, it is necessary to continue a brief narrative to bring some kind of conclusion to the overall Battle of Arras. After the date upon which the Battle Nomenclature Committee deemed that the overall Battle of Arras was over have been covered, the events of the first six days will be discussed in terms of where success had been achieved and where remained vestiges of an army not yet fully prepared to obtain victory.

It has been generally propagated that the decision to send General Allenby to the Middle East later in the year was one based upon his performance as commander of 3rd Army. There is little in the way of solid evidence backing the assertion although there was also no love lost between the 3rd Army commander and his Commander-in-Chief. Much has been made of a conference between the officers commanding 17th, 50th and 29th Divisions on 15 April. It has been said that the conclusions of this conference led to the Generals communicating directly with Haig, remarking about the piecemeal way their units had been committed and that this had to stop. The basis for this rather mutinous and highly unusual description of events is based upon a letter sent to Edmonds after the war. It has subsequently gained acceptance and is referred to in a large number of texts summarising the Arras offensive.[1] The relevant divisional war diaries make reference to the conference, held at 12.30pm on the 15 April and it does indicate a decision to ensure that further attacks are made with due attention to cooperation and sufficient preparation. There are two problems with regarding this conference as some kind of mutiny in the ranks (albeit high ranks). Firstly, the timing of the conference and Haig's instructions to Allenby do not form evidence that one forced the other, entirely the opposite in fact as the order to delay further attacks preceded the conference.[2] Secondly, the actions of the previous few days were not a result of specific instructions from 3rd Army but were more or less a consequence of decisions emanating from divisions themselves. The conference was held by three Maj-Generals who had only recently entered the fray and were meeting quite naturally, not to mull over previous attacks, but to form policy for the days ahead. Here is the text of the resolution:

---

1   For example, see Sheffield, G. & Bourne, J., *War Diaries and Letters 1914-1918*, (London: Orion, 2005), p. 495; Beckett, Ian F. & Corvi, Stephen J. (eds), *Haig's Generals*, (Barnsley: Pen & Sword, 2009), p. 27; making it now almost accepted fact.

2   The delay in the offensive to 23 April is often cited as a result of the 'mutiny', clearly nonsense when the chronology is followed. Horne in fact asked for the delay as 1st Army would not be ready any earlier.

In view of the fact that the Germans are in considerable strength east of MONCHY, with flanks thrown out to the North and South of it, it is thought desirable:

1. To concentrate on improving the defences and communications of the MONCHY position;
2. After these defences have been made good, to advance simultaneously with the troops North of the SCARPE rather than to face concentration of the enemy's guns on a small front, which tends to futile losses without adequate gains.[3]

Handwritten the same day beneath the typed resolution is the reply from the VI Corps staff officer who had attended the conference that the "Army Commander concurs with the above resolution, and wished every effort made to render MONCHY secure against hostile attack". This was not a revolt by divisional commanders, nor was Haig involved as the timing of the conference and the reply allows insufficient time for the C-in-C to have been sent and reply to the resolution. Finally, Haig makes no comment in his diary for the period which is further evidence he was not aware of the conference or the resolution. It was Robertson, back in London that proposed Allenby to Lloyd George for the role on the Middle East. He knew that there was no love lost between Haig and Allenby and when Smuts turned the job down it seems to have been good management on the C.I.G.S. to move the 3rd Army commander out of France.

What is clear is that the decision was made to refrain from major attacks until there had been sufficient pause to ensure a coordinated effort. It seems that at this stage in the war, only attacks made with the kind of staff work that went into the initial offensive had any chance of success. The diaries of all the units now at the front in 3rd Army now fill with the pages of Operational Orders laying down all the typical instructions and guidelines for an attack to take place. During a conference on the 16th, this attack was originally planned for the 20th. Up to that date there were a number of small scale efforts to be made, usually to attempt to gain a better position for the subsequent general attack. The major of these was to be the taking of Guémappe but the corps commanders, Snow and Haldane were not enamoured of this plan and wanted it to be part of the major attack. Also, the next day Horne asked for a postponement as he felt the weather was hindering his preparations. Finally, Gough of 5th Army, who were also to renew their efforts on the 20th asked for this not to take place until 3rd Army had gained the Sensée Valley. Haig acquiesced to all of these requests, postponing the attack to the 23 April. Some fighting did occur, however, during the period of 15 to 23 April. Much of this was in the area of Wancourt Tower which was lost and regained several times by 50th Division until finally on the 17th it was taken and consolidated by men of the 1/7th and 1/6th Northumberland Fusiliers. Fighting also continued around Roeux where German counter attacks actually made the position less favourable by the 23 April, especially for those attacking on the south of the river.

On 23 April, 1st Army was to attack and take the Oppy Line, whilst 3rd Army were yet again ordered to advance over Greenland Hill north of the Scarpe, take Vis-en-Artois on the Cambrai road and advance over the Héninel heights and into the Sensée Valley south of the Scarpe. There were partial successes on the day, including the taking of Gavrelle by the 63rd (Royal Naval) Division and the advancing of the line across the plateau above Héninel to the high ground overlooking the Sensée Valley. Overall though the day can only be described as fulfilling the function of pinning German forces from any movement of resources down to meet the French offensive on the Aisne. By this point in time it was clear that the latter offensive, although gaining some substantial ground, was not the breakthrough promised by Nivelle.

---

3   TNA: WO95/2281, Diary of H.Q. General Staff, 29th Division.

In the face of what was clearly not the resounding success that the French had hoped for there were, between 18 and 26 April, a number of discussions and meetings between both politicians and military commanders at which the question of how to continue was raised. The French leaders were clearly unhappy with Nivelle and might well have replaced him there and then had it not been for the support of Field Marshal Haig. In fact, the Field Marshal's decision making now becomes odd when reviewed in light of his attitude during the early part of the year when presented with Nivelle's plan. At that time, he was adamant that should the breakthrough not occur he should be able to turn to his original wish to attack in the Ypres sector and the corollary insistence that French forces take over some of the line held by British troops in order to free up reserves for the projected northern offensive. He now reversed that demand and in fact asked Robertson to inform the French War Minister, Painlevé "that if the French offensive were stopped it would be considered a breach of faith"[4]

It is difficult to understand this change of approach by Haig. He had, after the 23rd attacks, positions around Arras that were advantageous to his troops; Vimy Ridge, Pont du Jour, Monchy-le-Preux and the Héninel heights all in his hands. The Official History disagrees with this view stating that; "The "good defensive line" postulated by the Commander-in-Chief had nowhere been completely attained."[5] Walking the ground of the lines held after 23 April refutes this observation, the positions are all positive ones either for future offensive or, should it be necessary (as it was in 1918), defensive action. It would have been perfectly possible for him to site the agreements made in January and February, close down the Arras campaign and, having asked for some of the line around St Quentin to be taken over by the French, turned his attentions to Ypres. Instead he authorised 1st Army to carry out the attacks on the Oppy Line that were impossible on 23 April, now timed for the 28th and what became known as the Battle of Arleux. At the same time attacks were to be renewed by 3rd Army on Roeux and Greenland Hill. The attacks of 1st Army had only one positive outcome which was the capture of the village of Arleux by the Canadians. There were some small local successes around Oppy and Gavrelle, fighting continuing into the next day, but the bulk of the German lines remained in their hands and the success at Arleux was only partial as the trench taken in front of the village was a loop, another line lay behind in front of Fresnoy.

The 3 May had been set as the date for the next major offensive on 1st, 3rd and 5th Army fronts, even before the actions of the 28th. News filtering down to Haig as the date approached did not give him confidence that the French were likely to continue their offensive; in fact it looked as if Nivelle's days were numbered. The Field Marshal did not, however, reduce the plans for 3 May which also included a further attack by 5th Army at Bullecourt. His decision to coordinate the whole attack at a time of darkness at 3.45am[6] led to confusion and near disaster for the men of 1st and 3rd Armies. Casualties were enormous and the day could be said to be one of the blackest of days for British and Australian armies with the only success being that of the Canadians in taking Fresnoy.

Although actions after the 3 May were never of the same scale, fighting continued with some successes, but also a major setback when Fresnoy was lost to a German counter attack. A success to the south was the eventual taking of the infamous Roeux Chemical Factory by elements of 17th and 4th Divisions. In many respects the fighting that continued on this front for the remainder of the summer was no longer made up of large scale attacks but were intended to pin down opposing

---

4   Falls, *Military Operations, France and Belgium 1917 Vol. 1*, p. 411.
5   Falls, p. 431.
6   3.30am was requested by I Anzac Corps, the staff of which knew the lay of the land and wanted to achieve surprise. The subsequent compromise when Allenby observed that 3rd Army required daylight was a mere quarter of an hour later. It is interesting to note that S.S. 135 makes it clear that attacks in darkness should not be undertaken if at all possible and only over known ground.

troops to support the new initiatives in the north on Messines Ridge and subsequently the Third Battle of Ypres.

Conclusions

Planning for the Arras offensive reached levels of sophistication not as yet seen in the history of the British Army. As soon as the decision to attack in the area was made by Field Marshal Haig, following his willingness to comply with the overall policy for the year, little was left to chance. Plans were not confined to the allocation of troops to the operation but extended to all possible facets. Lessons in logistics and all the other myriad lines of communication necessities to modern twentieth century warfare were all taken into account to ensure that when the offensive was launched it was not to lack for anything. There is little evidence that, in spite of Haig's preference for offensive action in Flanders, he approached the impending Nivelle plan with anything but a high level of commitment. There are some interpretations of the relationship between the two generals that emphasise the tensions and disagreements[7] but the correspondence between them is cordial, even if embedded in the usual formalities of the day and military strictures. It does seem to modern observers that Haig was dragging his feet in some ways, certainly the railway problem, although not an invention, was used by the Field Marshal to buy time. On the other hand, he was correct in foreseeing that, once the Joffre pattern of continuing small scale assaults had been replaced by a major offensive, such an undertaking could not be rushed if materials were not in place. The fact that staple requirements such as road metal were not in sufficient numbers by the launch of the offensive gives some insight into the fact that a delay until April was, in many ways, a necessity. It must also be remembered that Haig had been told that the RFC would not be ready until mid-April and that more tanks were going to be available during February and March. He could not foresee that in fact the RFC would still be stretched in April due to poor aircraft and that the promised tanks would never arrive. The overall timing of the offensive then was as early as could be expected. Spears often comments that the delay, in comparison to Joffre's plan, played into the German Army's hands in allowing them time to catch breath and reinforce.[8] What Spears fails to recognise, however, is that the German withdrawal was designed precisely to combat what Joffre had in mind. The advance of the British and French armies during February and March was what would have occurred under Joffre. Spears was correct, however, in condemning the lack of urgency of the French troops of G.A.N. in chasing the German withdrawal. General d'Espèrey should have been given a free hand in launching a major attack. That he wasn't is a clear indicator of the state of Nivelle's mind at that moment; full of indecision, fear of what was happening in Paris and stubbornness. All the way through the various stages of political turmoil during the first four months of 1917 Haig's instructions to his Army chiefs never wavered. Both Horne of 1st Army and Allenby of 3rd Army had clear instructions as to the offensive and made their plans. The only time Haig became involved in those plans was over Allenby's artillery plan and in this he was correct to intervene. The advances in artillery techniques, although substantial by early 1917, were not as yet sufficient to guarantee the advancing troops the kind of support they would require. What should have worried Haig, however, was Allenby's insistence on Snow's VII Corps attacking the Hindenburg Line frontally. Here is an example of what was not the first, nor was it to be the last, occasion where a Corps commander disagreed with his Army commander, with good reason, but was overruled. Haig's command style had always been, from the beginning of his command of all British forces in France, one of delegation and then not unduly interfering.

---

7   Philpott W., *Attrition* (London: Abacus, 2014), p. 257.
8   Spears, *Prelude to Victory*.

This has been commented upon by a number of writers over the years[9] and indeed Haig himself put forward his ideas to General Rawlinson when the latter was in command of 4th Army on the Somme in August 1916

> Actual execution of plans, when control by higher commanders is impossible, subordinates on the spot must act on their own initiative, and they must be trained to do so.[10]

He then argues, however, that;

> Close supervision by higher commanders is not only possible but is their duty, to such extent that they find necessary to ensure that everything is done that can be done to ensure success.[11]

Travers speculates that this would lead to confusion and lack of focussed direction at times, citing examples in late 1917 and in 1918. In the case of the April offensive objectives were clear, allocation of forces was clear and neither Allenby nor Horne felt under pressure to do anything contrary to their own ideas during the planning process. It was their job to turn the overall objectives into ones to be carried out by formations under their command and Haig left them to it. There is no evidence that Haig was aware at the time of Snow's concerns over the plans for VII Corps. He will also not, as overall Commander-in-Chief, have had the time nor inclination to look in detail at, say, allocation of artillery assets to various corps. Haig's involvement in the appointment of Geddes to sort out transport in France does show, however, that he was fully aware of his responsibilities to allow his army commanders to carry out their plans without the infrastructure required for modern warfare breaking down.

One element of the offensive that Haig did hold close under his control was the use of reserves. Even Falls, in the Official History, is not in agreement with this state of affairs, comparing it with a brigade commander not being able to use a reserve company under his command without reference to the Divisional H.Q.[12] He hints that it may well have been Haig's concerns over the lack of reserves overall that led to this decision. Another view might be that he did not want them committed to an unsuccessful assault and thus reduce the capabilities of his armies in any switch of emphasis to Flanders. One flaw ascertained in hindsight to the planning of reserves was their positioning. Although they had been brought up to as near to the front as was deemed possible the use of two divisions as follow up formations on the first day (4th and 37th Divisions) meant that a lot of area behind Arras was taken up by these two units. What was not in place and could have facilitated a closer proximity of at least two divisions was a plan for the advance of elements of 17th Division and/or XVIII Corps when the former two units had moved forward.

Horne and Allenby, therefore, were free to plan as they saw fit and each in their turn delegated more precise objectives and resources to their respective corps commanders. Therefore, in Horne's 1st Army it was to General Byng that the planning for the taking of Vimy Ridge was left. Horne's decision to have an even longer preliminary artillery bombardment must be placed in the context that the task ahead was deemed to be a very difficult one and, as an artillery man, he wished to do all in his power to support the Canadians. The staff work in preparing the Canadian Corps and attached British units cannot be faulted in terms of producing a comprehensive and thorough plan.

---

9   Travers, Tim, *How the War Was Won*, (Barnsley: Pen & Sword, 1992), pp. 14-15; Brian Bond & Nigel Cave (eds), *Haig: A Reappraisal 80 Years On* (Barnsley: Pen & Sword, 1992).

10   Bond & Cave, *Haig*, p. 94.

11   Bond & Cave, *Haig*, p. 94.

12   Falls, *Military Operations, France and Belgium 1917 Vol. 1*, p. 280.

Contrary to many accounts, nothing in that plan was unique to the Canadians and Operational Orders all along the front for the attack on 9 April have a similarity due to following S.S. 135. The choice of a different system of objective lines is one that is difficult to comprehend. The insertion of an intermediate Red Line, not evident on any other part of the assault, was not, in itself, the problem. That was an internal matter within the corps and would not have had any negative effect on the neighbouring XVII Corps. What must have been irritating to local commanders was the fact that where the armies met both the Black and Blue Lines were not the same and therefore there was room for confusion over where units of 1st Canadian and 51st Highland Divisions were supposed to be at a particular time. In both armies the important lines, Black, Blue and Brown were decided upon at their respective Army Headquarters. That there should be a discrepancy at where these lines met is not mentioned at any level in any correspondence, it seems that 51st Highland Division was simply told to cope and carry on. It did this by simply telling the appropriate unit to push forward posts to connect with the Canadians. Not a recipe for good cohesion. Also with dubious origins within this latter divisional front was the 'New Black Line'. This line has no geographical prominence to account for its addition[13] and in reading attack accounts, simply served as an additional element of confusion. Amidst all this increased complexity of planning came what could have been the most significant decision and this was made at divisional level by Maj-Gen. Harper, O.C. 51st Division. XVII Corps Commander, Lt-Gen. Sir Charles Fergusson had laid down that all his three divisions should attack with all three brigades up. Harper decided against this and was allowed to attack with only two brigades, each having a supporting battalion from the remaining brigade. It is difficult to understand why this was allowed as the reasoning for the decision from corps was sound and should have been adhered to. If there is one place where a corps commander can influence a battle most it is at the planning stage but here Fergusson was willing to waive his authority for no other reason than the tradition of not depriving divisional commanders of their liberty of action. The result of this abrogation of responsibility has been clearly seen. The additional battalion in each brigade was never used as it was unclear who commanded it and the attack was starved of men with a result of not achieving the objective; this knock on effect being the failure of the neighbouring division to do the same on that flank. The lack of any real post-offensive critical analysis allowed Harper to emerge unscathed from his divergence from orders given, thus perpetuating this tendency of his at Cambrai later in the year when he refused to accept the best method of working with tanks. Unsurprisingly this led again to problems in the offensive. Therefore, even in the planning stage, where the British Army had honed its skills in preparing set piece assaults on prepared positions, elements of traditional top-down leadership created unnecessary problems for lower echelon commanders and were to do so for some time to come.

A further problem that was never recognised at the planning stage, yet was to be an element in eventual failure on the first day, was the position of VII Corps. The German withdrawal to the Hindenburg Line had meant that everywhere on the front south Tilloy-les-Mofflaines had to be advanced to come within striking distance of the German front line. 14th and 56th Division seemed to have been able to carry out this manoeuvre without undue difficulty. It meant creating an advanced new front line and also consequently assault trenches even nearer to the enemy, all of which was successfully carried out. On 30th Division front, however, this was not fully achieved. The taking of Hénin-sur-Cojeul, quite strongly held by the Germans, on 2 April, pushed forward the men of the division along the Cojeul Valley and in fact allowed them to occupy St.-Martin-sur-Cojeul in the night before the main assault and attack from a reasonable distance. This was

---

13   There is brief mention in the 152nd Brigade War Diary of a German battalion headquarters, but this seems a questionable reason for adding a new objective line.

not mirrored in the north, however, whereby 21st Brigade had a substantial distance to cover before they would be actually assaulting the Hindenburg Line. The failed attempt to take a post in a windmill on the Hénin-sur-Cojeul to Neuville Vitasse road resulted in the whole brigade not being able to use this road as their initial jumping off point. There was no excuse in the run up to the main offensive not to clear this road by a properly supported attack and allow 21st Brigade to be further forward and in line with its neighbour. Both brigades could have then attacked together instead of in the staggered nature forced upon them.

Within XVII Corps and VI Corps, however, there was a planning element that was both new and bold and showed a clear indication that the British Army was developing its skills on the battlefield. Already on the Somme battlefields the notion that a unit should attack and simply keep going with further units coming up in support had been clearly seen to be faulty. What in many of the Operational Orders as the 'leap frog' approach was an operational development of the method of moving past the first objective. One unit to obtain the first objective, quite near, whilst a second then passes through (i.e. 'leap frogging') to move on the next. This had become normal procedure in the latter stages of the Somme and was embodied in the new training pamphlets that arose out of experience in that battle. Much more revolutionary though, was the idea that a brigade might pass through a newly won position. This had been tried on the Somme and because of the integrity of a divisional formation was not seen to be too difficult and was well practised. Planning for the Arras battles though took this a logical, but difficult step forward. For the first time a whole division was to continue the offensive, not by relieving the initial attacking division but by physically moving through its positions and attacking onwards. Two headquarter staffs with all the administrative paraphernalia somehow cooperating on a single front, one of which was to be actually carrying out an attack, was indeed an audacious step forward in tactical thinking. Clearly, however, if a substantial advance against a series of fixed positions was to be successful, this was a means of continuing the fight with fresh and strong units, as opposed to experiences in the past where tired and worn out battalions were tasked to keep moving. The success of this manoeuvre north of the Scarpe demonstrated the power of this initiative, less so in the south. The southern attempt involved more than one division in front of the one coming through and this meant that when things did not go quite to plan in the initial attack the whole thing fell apart somewhat. There were still good lessons though to be learned from the experience in terms of command and control.

At unit level, planning clearly reflected the innovations that had arisen out of reflections at all levels on the experiences of the Somme. The fact that S.S. 135 and the subsequent S.S. 143, covered earlier, can be seen embedded in much of the Operational Orders of divisions down to battalions is quite remarkable given their recent publication. That can only mean that such practice had already become common practise in many units and that the opportunity to carry out training before the attack allowed any misconceptions to be ironed out. New advances in weaponry had been assimilated properly into fighting units and were beginning to be accepted into the instructions to units. The sophistication of how an assault was planned can be grasped by perusal of Appendix III where instructions for 11th Royal Scots for the morning of 9 April are reproduced in full. Examination thereof, especially the section pertaining to companies, demonstrates that such movements were rehearsed during spells out of the line with white tapes representing the German trench lines. The new techniques of platoon manoeuvre and combined firepower, as seen throughout the narrative, were utilised to successfully overcome stubborn defences.

The overall operational planning, once the allocation of forces to particular operations was clear, then turned to how artillery was going to be used. It has already been noted in an earlier chapter that how the artillery assets were allocated does not seem to have been even handed across 3rd Army and when 1st Army is brought into the comparison; the whole scheme becomes even more uneven. The category of artillery piece of particular interest is that which is capable of firing with the new 106 fuse, i.e. the 6", 8" and 9.2" howitzers. These three types of piece had, because of the new fuse, a dual role. They could fire high explosive at wire, with the 106 fuse, and obtain excellent wire cutting ability or be used as part of the mainstay heavy artillery to attack strongpoints, headquarters and all the other tasks usually allocated to the Royal Garrison Artillery. If these three types are totalled for four corps the following is the result:

Canadian Corps	240 pieces	XVII Corps	158 pieces
VI Corps	108 pieces	VII Corps	136 pieces

That amounts to almost 400 pieces north of the Scarpe but less than 250 south of the river without any significant difference to frontage attacked nor depth of objective lines. In fact, the limited nature of the objectives on Vimy Ridge only serves to increase the fall of shell possible on that area of the front. It has proved impossible to pin down the allocation of the limited number of new type fuses to different corps but there is mention of Horne, commanding 1st Army and a gunner by training and inclination, of making certain that he obtained a fair share, if not more of the precious article. Then, when the allocation of artillery is examined, it becomes clear that in VII Corps, either there cannot have been sufficient 106 fuses to allow the heavies to participate in wire cutting or there was not the acceptance in the various C.R.A. in the corps that it is what they should be doing. VII orders continually comment on the use of 18pdr guns to do the wire cutting and how difficult it was because of the distance to the wire they had to shoot from. It was well known by this stage in the war that when the trajectory of the shell was too steep, i.e. from long range, the capability of the 18pdr firing shrapnel was close to useless. Yet this is what they did in VII Corps with the result that the wire, the thickest to been countered on the attack frontage, was either virtually untouched or had, as in the case of 21st Division, inadequate lanes for the attack. Nobody, at any stage, examined the preliminary bombardment with any overall view as to how it might perform when underway. At this stage of the war uncut wire in front of the enemy front line meant almost certain failure of an attack, however gallant the men and however well they functioned under the new platoon tactics. No tactics on earth are going to get the men through the wire once the barrage has left the enemy trench. Where they could get in, trench mortars sometimes could save the day but they had to be able to get within range. On 30th Division front, there was nowhere for them to do this task, for some reason on 56th Division front nobody seems to have had the idea and where assistance was given in front of 21st Division the mortar crew paid for it with their lives. The one remaining tool for clearing the wire was of course the tank. The very limited number and quality of the vehicles available meant that their effect in this role would be limited. Where they did not break down and actually reached the line it has been seen how often they were able to assist in the advance by driving over the wire. They could not be everywhere though and were missing, for one reason or another, in many of the places most needed with tragic results. Many reports after the war talk of the lack of observation of the wire and thus that it was not known that the wire was uncut. Walking the ground puts such comments in great doubt as observation on 90 percent of the area is good enough for observers to have been perfectly aware of the state of the wire.

Inconsistencies aside, what is clear is that the introduction of the 106 fuse and the use of tanks at Arras was the future of a wire cutting methodology that might not require days of preliminary bombardment implemented at this period of the war. Barbed wire obstacles could be dealt with in the hurricane style bombardment which was in Allenby's mind at this time but for which resources and experience were not yet sufficient. Another element in the preliminary bombardment which might also become possible within a shorter time scale when skills improved was that of nullifying in some way the enemy artillery batteries. The emergence of new skills in both flash spotting and sound ranging was just beginning to give the artillery a capability of hitting what it wanted to, even if not within sight. Pulled, with some institutional resistance, into the twentieth century by scientific improvements, the artillery arm had at last accepted that the days of galloping up to within sight of the enemy and firing off some rounds were finally gone forever. There remained kinks in the system to iron out, but the foundations for the kind of artillery support enjoyed by the troops in the latter phases of the war were finally here. What was still clearly lacking was the command and communication structure to enable such support to be continued once the initial breaking of the front lines had been accomplished. Some plans were in place to move batteries forward as the troops advanced but on the whole the eventual movement and control of batteries was incoherent and inefficient. Much more thought was required in planning for future phases, beyond the first day.

Throughout much of the war, when a major offensive was envisioned, the cavalry was central to exploitation. Arras was no different with Cavalry Corps, minus 1st and 4th Cavalry Divisions, being allocated to Allenby for use in the classic role. Unlike other arms of the service, however, the cavalry had never really been able to carry out this intended role and therefore little had been learned of how tactics might have developed to meet the modern age of warfare. There remained a notion that the infantry would create some kind of gap and the cavalry would gallop through and cause mayhem in the rear, thus forcing a general retreat of the enemy. At Arras the plan was not much more detailed than that and in many ways it could not be, as no one foresaw where the breakthrough would occur. The role was essentially opportunistic by its very nature. For this reason, the employment of cavalry was within normal usage but where it was allocated for use is questionable. Both divisions being earmarked for use, en masse, south of the Scarpe was a strange decision as the sector attacked by VI Corps had probably the most difficult terrain with two ridges (Observation Ridge and Orange Hill), the valley of the Cojeul to cross, Monchy-le-Preux and the heights above Wancourt. It is difficult to envisage how both divisions could have been utilised in this area, even had the attacks here been more successful. On the other hand, the area north of the River Scarpe is very open in nature once the heights of the Pont-de-Jour are taken, yet here no cavalry was due to operate. The idea of the massive breakout was still high in the minds of commanders and thus dominated planning.

At this stage of the war the role of the tank remained uncertain with no clear policy for its use had emerged. Although Travers remarks on the schools of thought on tank employment that fell into two camps; those who saw tanks as the mainstay of an attacking force and those who deemed them as assistants to the infantry.[14] Until the quality and numbers of tanks reached a sufficient level, and at Arras neither of these circumstances had reached sufficient numbers, the tank could never be the mainstay of an attack. Planning at Arras was thus based around how a tank might add the attackers as opposed to the prime mover role. Who was in command of this planning was also obscure and open to dispute. The Heavy Branch Machine Gun Corps would have liked to have been an independent force, making its own decisions as to the allocation and implementation. This they were not, in essence they were subordinate to Army Headquarters and it distributed to the various Corps. And it was within Corps that their deployment occurred. By distributing them to Corps, 3rd Army began the process of creating penny packets of tanks much to the dismay of tank proponents. Moreover, the allocation of 12 tanks to 5th Army thinned the numbers even more, as well as tempting Bullecourt planners to attack in a way that was not operationally and technologically viable at the time. Thus these vehicles would have been far better employed in the main attack. In addition, the allocation of eight tanks to 1st Army was optimistic in the extreme when a casual glance at the ground, once the massive artillery bombardment was even half way through its job, would have deemed the terrain impassable to any kind of vehicle. Thus one third of the

---

14   Travers, *How the War Was Won*, pp. 41-46.

force was already unavailable to the three central corps involved and of the remains only eight were given to XVII Corps. Tank planning was thorough with arrangements for all the necessary requirements for refuelling etc. in place. Each tank had its route planned, in all cases to follow up the infantry once the Black Line was taken. There can be no criticism raised over the level of detail that was in place; however, the thinness of the vehicles on the ground was not to the H.M.G.C.'s liking.

> Nothing like sufficient Tanks could be put into the field to enable a sound tactical distribution in depth being adopted and no reserve could be held in hand. The whole operation from a Tank point of view was make-shift.[15]

In summary, it can be seen that planning for the first day was sophisticated, thorough and in high detail. Staff work was almost invariably of a very high standard with all, down to the individual soldier, being clear as to their role in the upcoming offensive. The detail had been dealt with, the flaws, however, being more in the wider tactical employment of resources. Also missing was a clear indication of what would come next should objectives be reached so that smaller unit commanders from division downwards would be able to plan the next steps without having to wait for the next orders to arrive.

The uneven allocation of artillery assets has already been examined above. Leaving that aside for the moment, the question is how advanced was the British artillery in April 1917? The answer can be seen in a vast number of unit diary entries, already quoted in relevant sections earlier. Where sufficient resources had been allocated the wire formed little or no problem, nor did the defenders who were often still cowering in their dugouts. Horne, as he admits himself, over egged his preliminary bombardment, leaving a devastated enemy but also an impassable terrain. In the short term though, his limited objectives led to this not being a serious problem. In XVII Corps the effect of the preliminary bombardment plus subsequent creeping barrage allowed a high level of success, only really marred by the mistakes of 51st Division. The failure of units to the south was, for the most part, due to diminishing resources, not artillery performance. Decision making with regard to allocation of types of artillery pieces led to wire being uncut with the usual results. When the men could follow the barrage, success almost invariably was the outcome. Units had developed the art of being up with the barrage to a high degree, at times being on the parapet of the German trench at the precise moment the barrage lifted off it. A far cry from the 300 or more yards of No Man's Land still to cross after the German defenders emerged as seen in the early days of the Somme battles. The speed of the barrage was a problem at times, possibly being in places a little too slow, as were the difficulties caused when men lost the barrage. There was clearly a fine line between these two related problems but the consequences of losing the barrage meant that erring on the slow side in moving the barrage forward was probably a good decision; where success was quick and decisive, such as in XVII Corps, the next complaint was the standing barrage during the pause between operational phases. Units were almost literally champing at the bit with nothing opposite, an enemy in flight, but their own barrage falling in front of them hindering any pursuit. This also was contrary to recent instructions embodied in S.E. 135 where pursuit was strongly encouraged to take advantage of what might be a fleeting opportunity. In the British Army's development as an attacking force there clearly remained some dichotomies in decision making where boldness on the one hand was hindered by the desire for security against counter attack on the other. There also remained some discussion over the type of creeping barrage, an argument over

---

15 KCLMA Fuller/1/4/1, Summary of tank operations, p. 7.

the mix of shrapnel and H.E. and how smoke should be used (even if at all). The learning process was still occurring, sometimes against conservative opposition, but it was clearly there.

Engaging the enemy's artillery was honed to a fine degree for the first day of the Arras battle. The desultory nature of the German barrage, as related in countless descriptions of the attack, is testament to the recently developed skills of the gunners and the bravery of the R.F.C. in its brave and costly role of spotter. German accounts talk of firing S.O.S. signals and nothing happening, not only making their defensive role that much more difficult but having a serious effect on morale. The realisation that it was not necessary to completely destroy the enemy artillery but to neutralise it using gas as a main weapon was a significant step forward. As the battle moves into subsequent days, German artillery became far more destructive, an indication of the increasing inability of the British to counteract it. In terms of development then the British had almost perfected the destruction, or at least neutralisation of enemy artillery but only for a limited time in an offensive. What was required was for the development to continue with an increasing ability to find and stop new German batteries where and when they appeared.

One of the primary reasons given in many accounts of the first days of the Battle of Arras is that the success of 9 April could not be replicated on subsequent days due to the poor weather and state of the ground hindering the movement of support troops, especially artillery. Whilst some of this is true, what has been demonstrated above is that diminishing artillery support does not lie wholly in this aspect of the battle. Crucial to following up the attacks of the first day was deployment of sufficient assets forward to allow attacks to be supported to a reasonable extent. The advance of the first day often meant that the next attacks would be against positions improvised over the previous day and night. Certainly attacks north of Roeux on Greenland Hill were against trenches newly dug and hastily wired. To support such attacks does not require heavy artillery in the same way that smashing your way through well prepared and wired defences does. What was required was the coordinated field artillery of at least the division carrying out the attack, supported by whatever else could be got forward. The fact that some of these units did not move over the night of 9/10 April was not just due to mud or snow but simply because they were not ordered to. The coordination of artillery and infantry over the five remaining days of the First Battle of the Scarpe was poor to say the least and is probably best described as appalling. Falls is less critical in his final analysis of the battle, stating; "Liaison between field artillery and infantry in the Battles of Arras was generally fairly satisfactory."[16] He is generous in the extreme with this view, as he would have reviewed the diaries and the constant reports of poor artillery support. Again and again an attack was ordered, was promised a barrage but finds that it goes in with, at best, a desultory one and at times none at all. The subsequent rise in the average casualty rate is therefore not difficult comprehend. There was clearly a great deal of work to do within divisions and corps to ensure artillery efficacy in the follow up to an advance. The need for that analysis and subsequent changes in methodology was never recognised, the whole fiasco obscured by the ready excuse of poor ground conditions.

In his summing up of the days following 9 April, Falls lays much of the blame for the missed opportunities at the feet of the troops and junior leaders. After praising them in the conditions prevalent on the first day he then goes on to say;

> When the conditions provided for ceased to exist, to be replaced by conditions calling for speedy decisions and unrehearsed action, troops and junior leaders were found wanting.[17]

---

16   Falls, *Military Operations, France and Belgium 1917 Vol. 1*, p. 545.
17   Falls, p. 145.

It is the lack of training for open warfare that he states as the cause of this failure. It has been shown, however, again and again in the narrative above that the lack of any kind of real success was not the inability of troops to carry out their tasks. The fault lay not at brigade, battalion and below, but at division and higher. Divisions acted alone, with little cooperation amongst those on flanks or acted in the wrong fashion or prevaricated allowing the enemy to recover. Griffith identifies the difference between the state of mind of generals before and after the initial onslaught.

> Impatient generals cast aside their admirable earlier acceptance of such things as logistical build up, rest and breakfast for the assault troops, reconnaissance, rehearsal, detailed coordination and briefing of all participants …. and kept on simply demanding instant results.[18]

Examples of the above will have been recognised when following the narrative but an example for each will be used here for the sake of clarity and emphasis. The most notorious of the first fault, that of units acting alone, was the attack of 88th Brigade east of Monchy-le-Preux on the 14th with absolutely no support on left or right. Leading, with awful inevitability, to the destruction of the two attacking units, the decisions that led to this attack must be laid at the feet of the divisional commanders on the spot. 17th Division came into the line on the southern banks of the Scarpe on 12 April and should have been the unit providing flank cover for 88th Brigade. They did virtually nothing, in fact Maj-Gen. P.R. Robertson, commanding, ordered very little during the days being covered in this book. The divisional history passes over the days, dismissing the 14th with a few paragraphs and certainly no mention of the disaster that befell the brigade they should have been supporting. Instead he chronicles the halting of a German counter attack, the myth that has been here thoroughly dismissed. Given the total loss of two battalions, the telling line "The fighting died down with no important result for either party" is disingenuous.[19] The second fault, that of acting in an unacceptable fashion, can be laid at the door of 56th Division. S.S. 135 is very clear in its instructions as to the carrying out of attacks, making the bombing down of trenches an unacceptable method of carrying out an attack; "It may be taken for granted that once an attack has come down to the bombing stage the operation has come to a standstill."[20] Yet this is exactly what Maj-Gen. Hull ordered to be done from the evening of the 9th onwards, orders that rarely varied over the next few days. This led to 14th Division being unsupported on their right and an extremely slow advance over the days under consideration here. Had it been in a very small section of the Hindenburg Line this could be forgiven but they had got well behind that line during 9 April. The eventual withdrawal of the Germans once Wancourt and Héninel had fallen is a clear indicator of what could be achieved by advancing behind instead of down the trenches. Griffith notes, "The BEF's commanders did nevertheless face a serious problem of dissemination when they tried to cut back the bomb culture, since it was already very deeply rooted."[21] Unfortunately, the decision making of the same Officer Commanding can yet again be questioned within the third fault, that of prevarication. The reasons for his demand for a delay until midday on the 10th cannot be justified but the results can be clearly seen in the narrative. Hull is not alone in the blame for the outcome, however, as the decision was accepted and then allowed to become the order for all other units south of the Scarpe. A dubious request by one divisional commander was allowed to dictate the pace for the entire second day of two corps. Therefore, at the precise moment when the

---

18   Griffiths, *Battle Tactics,* p. 75.
19   Atteridge, A.H., *The History of the 17th (Northern) Division* (Glasgow: Maclehose & Co., 1929), p. 209.
20   S.S. 135, p. 70.
21   Griffith, *Battle Tactics,* p. 68.

successes of the first day could have offset the failures, to a greater or lesser extent, Allenby allowed prevarication to reign. These are only three examples of where, at a divisional level, decisions were made that had a significant effect on the success or not of actions between 10 and 14 April. The performance of divisions, as units, was not in any way even. The Canadian divisions had, on the whole, performed well except for some criticisms that could be laid at 4th Division. These have some foundation in the raiding policy of the division in the lead up to the offensive, condemning some weak battalions to attack, thus making their task difficult to complete. This, combined with the tenacity of the German defenders, caused the hiccup on 9 April. The 4th Canadian Division is, though, also a good example of a division operating efficiently, in the way decision making during the day allowed the objective to be later taken, reserves being used intelligently. The valour of the men then allowed this decision to convert earlier partial failure into success. On the contrary, decision making in 51st Division was anything but laudable. The initial decision to not follow Corps instructions and attack three brigades up was a major contributor to the problems that ensued. Lacking the necessary punch, it required the intervention of supporting troops to take initial objectives, leading to a general weakening of the attacking force. This is the one occasion where Fall's assertion that junior officers failed can be supported with the assault veering off in the wrong direction. The subsequent loss of subalterns and N.C.O.s in the initial phase though could have contributed to this error and therefore again it comes back to the initial decision by Maj-Gen Harper. Added to this was the fact that Divisional H.Q. had no idea about the error until well into the second day; all in all, a poor show by a division of repute. The 34th Division may not have reached the Brown Line all along its front but it is difficult, even in hindsight, to ascertain how much this was due to the failures of 51st Division on their left. The 9th and 4th Divisions, with the highly successful operation of one division passing through another and completing the taking of the ambitious Green Line in places, was a clear example of how good staff work at divisional level had become for a set piece attack. The days that followed and the failure to take advantage of the successes of the first day has been seen to be the result of decision making at the next level, that is Corps, plus the original plan. It was Lt-Gen. Fergusson, commanding XVII Corps who, on the 10th, decided that cavalry could seize Greenland Hill when, due to lack of artillery, the infantry could not. The eventual lack of any kind of action that day was deplorable, especially when seen in the context of what later transpired in front of Roeux. Even the usually supportive Falls is critical of Fergusson and also the failure to put any kind of pressure on moving artillery pieces forward. The fact that the original plan had the Cavalry Corps positioned to attack south of the Scarpe and the first call on them was north of the river did not aid the situation. 34th Division had also had its artillery taken away from it on the afternoon of 9 April in order to support the Cavalry Corps, yet again a strange decision at a high level. Moving forward when the Germans retired on the Oppy Line, 34th Division had done little wrong when coming out of the line exhausted and suffering from the extreme cold. Both 4th and 9th Divisions could also be proud of their achievements in the First Battle of the Scarpe. The one criticism that could be laid at divisional level was the same all along the line – that coordinating artillery support failed, much to the chagrin of brigade and battalion commanders. There is no evidence north of the Scarpe that lack of training contributed to any of the failures. On the contrary, officers and men displayed courage and bravery time after time in the face of a resolute defence.

Smaller episodes can eventually, if allowed to, dominate the larger picture and this is generally what happened over the six days of the battle in VI Corps. There was not one overarching poor decision at any level that led to the stalling of the offensive but a number of small poor judgement calls which can be seen as indicators that the British Army was not yet ready to succeed beyond the initial phase. Things began to go wrong on the 9th, due to resolute defensive actions of the Germans. Again it is not the actions or abilities of the men or junior leaders which are the cause but in this case the rigidness of the plan of attack. It seems that within different divisions the ability to control the artillery barrage differed. On the one hand when held up at the Railway Triangle, 15th Division were able to recall the barrage in order to get through the problems it faced and eventually reached Orange Hill and managed to push through the defences there. On their right 12th Division, having struggled against some of the redoubts on or behind Observation Ridge, lost the barrage and finished the day well short of the Brown Line. Two elements of higher command were at fault on 12th Division front. First, the inability to react to events and adapt the creeping bombardment during the afternoon advance to the Brown Line. With the relatively long pause between the timings for the advance to the Blue and then the Brown Line this was a feasible option, as demonstrated elsewhere across the front. Secondly, the inordinately long time it took for the command in 12th Division to use the hole in the German lines created by 15th Division. The redoubt at Feuchy Chapel having been determined to be a tough position to seize, it was not until midday on the 10th that units were pushed through the gap to outflank the German defenders. This resulted in the Brown Line's capture with little opposition. This delay was not the fault of Maj-Gen Scott, commanding 12th Division as he was ready at 5.00am to carry out this manoeuvre but was halted by the general order for a midday attack. The 3rd Division started well, Tilloy-les-Mofflaines posing problems but not insurmountable ones. Somehow, however, the leading units lost the barrage although diaries are unclear on this. The Brown Line was not taken although some blame can be laid at the neighbouring 12th Division's failure to cover their left flank. Subsequent days do not read so kindly for Maj-Gen. Deverell. His men easily took the Brown Line on the 10th but he decided this was all that was required of him even though for a brief moment Guémappe and the Green Line could have been in his grasp. Subsequent days were spent in piecemeal attacks against the village, none of which appear to have the kind of artillery support required nor were they adequately coordinated with neighbouring divisions. The necessary drive on that moment of the 10th was lacking and Deverell's increasingly exhausted men paid dearly for that error in the days until the 13th when they could withdraw.

The problems of 15th and 12th Divisions meant that 37th Division, moving up to take over the mantle of attack on the 9th and drive for Monchy-le-Preux never had a reasonable chance of succeeding in taking their objectives. Division command and control is immediately in question, control of 111th Brigade appearing to have been completely lost. If it had carried out its orders correctly it could have passed through 15th Division onto Orange Hill and subsequently by the end of the 9th the German lines to the south would have been badly outflanked, probably forcing a retirement during the night. All the subsequent movements against Monchy-le-Preux, give the impression of units acting in an uncoordinated manner. Divisional and even brigade diaries are unclear as to the subordinate unit movements and the impression of a whole division blundering about in front of and then within Monchy-le-Preux without a great deal of centralised control is obtained. Had it not been for the cavalry entering the village on the 11th the impression is gained that the Germans could have and probably would have regained it. In any analysis of the battle Maj-Gen. Bruce Williams, commanding 37th Division, does not show the leadership required for a fluid battle, nor does he seemed to have instilled such in his brigade commanders. Even the withdrawal on the 11th/12th was fraught with uncertainty with some units being left stranded for a while at the front because nobody was sure where they were. Posterity has awarded 37th Division with the accolade of capturing of Monchy-le-Preux. Let the village monument remember the men who fought there, not their brigade and divisional commanders for whom 9 to 11 April could not be deemed their finest hour.

The performance of VII Corps is perhaps the most difficult to analyse due to two factors. The strength of the line it had to break and the uncertainty over the means they were given to carry out that task. Lt-Gen. D'O. Snow was not seen by some of his contemporaries as a particularly able corps commander:

Snow was of course quite useless; he was an old man and ought to have been sent home long before.[22]

He did, however, discern the magnitude of the task given to his corps and was correct in attempting to downgrade the effort into one where no direct attack on the Hindenburg Line would take place. Once this was refused the die was cast on what was to become a costly failure as Snow's command over the divisions within his corps seems to have been limited in the extreme. In 14th, 56th, 30th and 21st Divisions he had a very capable force of experienced units therefore the question of where lay the overall failure of the corps has to be raised. Again, there is no evidence that any of the failures were due to a poor performance of men or junior leaders. Whether attacking in favourable conditions, such as 14th Division's taking of the Harp, or in gallantly attempting, as did 64th Brigade, to get through the wire and into the Hindenburg Line, the bravery and tactics of the small unit was of a high standard. On the contrary, it was decisions at division and above level that led to failure. The initial errors were in planning and available resources. The allocation of fuses and heavy artillery was simply not up to the task of assaulting the Hindenburg Line head on. Compounding this error was the decision not to ensure that the assault line was as close to the German major defences as it could be. This pushed the artillery back and made its difficult task even harder. Wire cutting became a lottery; heavy artillery not used for the task (probably due to the lack of 106 fuses) and field artillery too far distant to be effective; only in 14th Division was this not a problem. It also led to the complicated timing of the attack with three different start times within the corps. Corps Operational Orders had dealt with this in one way by making each attack dependent upon the success of the earlier one to its left. The success of 14th Division on Telegraph Hill and the fall of Neuville Vitasse thus allowed the lunchtime attack of 30th Division to go ahead. That it failed was not a surprise when the fact was that the Hindenburg Line and its defenders were virtually untouched. It was within the power of Maj-Gen. Shea at that point to call a halt to the attack of his right brigade. He knew the wire was uncut in front of his right brigade and it was therefore not difficult to predict the outcome of an attack. Similarly, the domino effect was supposed to come into play on 21st Division front with 64th Brigade only attacking to follow up success on the heights above it behind Neuville Vitasse. It is to the discredit of both divisional commanders that they did not fall back on their orders and call off the attacks of two brigades which cost so many lives. Snow then basically hands over the resulting days in the First Battle of the Scarpe to his divisional commanders and the one destined to dictate proceedings was Maj-Gen. Hull of 56th Division. The weakness of Snow, in consenting to Hull's request for a late start on the 10th, was in error. This led to the loss of crucial hours during the most offensive's opening day. Hull was so fixated by the Hindenburg Line that almost all his division was devoted to bombing efforts down it with subsequent slow progress as predicted in S.S. 135. This leaves 14th Division attempting to progress with an open right flank when it is *behind the Hindenburg Line* and any progress here makes that line untenable. Hull was told on two occasions to take Hill 90, subsequent to his failure to take it on the first day, the key to taking Héninel and Wancourt and on each occasion makes very little effort to do so. His is perhaps the poorest performance of any of the divisional commanders over the six days of battle. Indeed, from the first day onwards, he had little grasp of what is required if a major enemy line is to be broken through and a substantial advance is to be made. The cooperation and communication between 56th and 14th Divisions seems to have been almost non-existent with diary entries of both blaming the other for not being able to advance. Hull then repeated that failure when 50th Division came up on his right, the situation as

---

22   TNA: 45/116 Official History correspondence, Brigadier B.L. Montgomery to Falls, 8 October 1938. This is, of course, Montgomery of Alamein fame.

to where troops were supposed to be inserted almost descending into farce. It is perhaps indicative of Hull's approach that the casualties of 56th Division are the lowest of any similar sized unit over the six days. Hull's experience of Gommecourt and subsequent battles on the Somme may have been a reason for this apparently over-cautious approach once his command reached objectives, but this is mere speculation as he was never questioned over the performance of his division over these days.

To suitably examine these apparent command and control failures, two managerial factors require investigation; namely that of the General Staff and also that of corps and divisional leadership. Prior to the war the British Army could count only a handful of divisions, but by the time of the Arras offensive the BEF had risen to over 60 divisions in five armies on the Western Front alone and was continually on the search for competent staff officers. The administrative role at battalion level was carried out by the adjutant, but it was not here that serious administrative problems began. The first proper staff officer was found at Brigade, where there would normally be a staff captain and a Brigade Major. It is the latter of most concern, as the role was looking after G matters; that is operations, intelligence and organisation amongst other tasks.[23] When orders came down from division, his role was to turn these into orders for battalions. With a scarcity of trained staff officers, those who held the coveted psc (passed staff college) were usually to be found at divisional level and above. There were other training opportunities for junior staff officers[24] but lack of training and experience of these vital officers would dog the army until the end of the war. The attack of 88th Brigade is an example of where poor staff work can lead to a crisis. Leaving aside the decision to attack (a leadership issue, not a General Staff one), the fact that no troops were ordered to occupy the trenches when the attacking battalions had left them was down to orders not being drawn up by the Brigade Major, usually a routine matter. "As a result, when the Germans counter attacked, there was practically nobody in our front line at Monchy and disaster nearly ensued"[25] At divisional level, there would be a larger staff, the G area of concern usually manned by a GSO1, GSO2 and GSO3 of diminishing rank. This command ladder often meant that promotion was possible for those gaining experience in action; however, even so almost a quarter of those holding GSO1 were those without psc after their name. The fact that only a limited number of officers passed out of Staff College meant that the more competent of these would be coveted by GHQ and at army level with the consequence that many at divisional level were perhaps not the best or at least not as well trained. One of the criticisms laid against staff officers at divisional level was their isolation from the front that they "tended to lead a secluded and relatively luxurious life far behind the firing line where, immersed in office work, they had no time for personal contact with the front-line troops."[26] The friction between front-line officers and the 'red tabs' is thus understandable but did not lead to the kind of teamwork required, especially when the attack was underway and rapid decisions were required to be acted upon in an efficient manner. The number of occasions sited above, where orders reached the fighting troops either too late to carry out the required preparations or even after the time they were supposed to be implemented, is a sign that staff work was not at its best. At corps level the problem was exacerbated in the British Army by the continuing redeployment of divisions within corps. "I hate changing corps because they generally run things a little differently and one has to get into new ways."[27] Even worse this policy could lead to an even more enlarged distance between the fighting units and Corps H.Q.:

---

23   The staff captain looked after A and Q matters, A personnel and Q supplies, quartering etc.
24   Robbins, *British Generalship,* p. 42.
25   TNA: CAB 45/116, Letter Maj-Gen C.G. Fuller to Falls, 8th July 1938.
26   Col. T.T. Grove, quoted in Robbins, *British Generalship,* p. 46.
27   Archibald Home, GSO1 of 46th Division quoted in Messenger, *Call to Arms,* p. 348.

A corps staff which had been well dug-in for a year on a quiet front resembled nothing so much as the menial hierarchy of a ducal palace – with the duke away. Never having had a division on their hands for more than a month or so they had come to regard them as persons to be employed but not encouraged.[28]

The decision to transfer divisions between VI Corps and XVIII Corps has to be seen in this light and it is therefore not surprising that the three divisional commanders should decide to meet for their own conference on 15 April as related above. They will have had little affinity for a corps staff, preferring to have their own staff officers organise their activities rather than an unknown corps equivalent.

At this point during the war the development of staff work had clearly made significant progress. It was capable to organising and administering a major offensive with all that entails, with newly developed techniques such as complex bombardment and creeping barrage plans and the passing of divisional size units through another; all with substantial levels of success. This very positive aspect was, nonetheless, overshadowed by an inability to cope with movement at a large scale. One clear indication of this was the extremely poor cooperation between infantry and artillery once the British lines had been vacated and the troops were a number of miles ahead. Another was the poor communication of orders down from corps to division and then further to the fighting units. Finally, there was the poor communication in the opposite direction with divisional staff sometimes blissfully unaware of where their troops were, leading to corps staff reaching very false conclusions about operations, thus leading to poor decision making at all levels.

However, staff officers are merely an administrative arm to ensure the orders are disseminated in a clear and unambiguous manner. The quality of those orders would depend upon the decision making capabilities of commanders at every level from army to battalion. Decisions were made upon information at hand and it has already been intimated that the quality of that information will have moved from excellence before 9 April to poor, if not miserable by some way through that day. The quality of leadership in the British Army throughout the war has been a subject for debate for decades. When the arguments are put forward, however, it must be remembered, exactly as in the case of staff officers, that the army expanded massively within a very short space of time, creating a requirement for officers that could not be met. The consequence of this dearth of officers, especially at a senior level, was that it took a very long time for incompetent men to be removed. Even as late as 1918 Field Marshal Haig remained unhappy about the standard of leadership remarking, "the truth is that we have more vacant appointments than qualified officers to fill them."[29] Advancement to the higher positions was, in the early years of the war, almost automatic with only five out of 30 divisional officers of the 1914-16 period failing to obtain corps (all adjudged too elderly) and five army command.[30] The old Regular Army dominated this leadership pool and many of its members had never experienced warfare on a large scale. It is, therefore, entirely understandable that many were found to be wanting when coming face to face with it. But replacing incompetence was impossible with no one else to promote. Even those at brigade and battalion level of command had to be appointed quickly as the BEF expanded, resulting in the quality at this level being anything but consistently good or better. Many battalion commanders were sent home very quickly and those found to be of a good quality were soon commanding brigades. This process, however, was a slow one for the reasons previously stated. One case to illustrate the process

28 Chapman, Guy, *A Passionate Prodigality: Fragments of an Autobiography*, (London: MacGibbon &K ee, 1965), p. 141.
29 TNA: WO 256/27 Diaries of Field Marshal Sir Douglas Haig, entry for February 11th 1918.
30 Robbins, *British Generalship*, p. 53.

was that of Maj-Gen. Charles Ross who, having retired in 1912, was reinstated to command a brigade before becoming commander of 6th Division in November 1915, despite having little experience of active command. According to one source he failed "to exercise any command over his division, leaving his brigadiers a free hand to go their own way."[31] He did not move to a home establishment division until August 1917. The long drawn out battle on the Somme sealed the fate of many older divisional commanders, a notable example being Maj-Gen. Ivor Philipps who was removed from command of 38th (Welsh) Division, a political appointment (he was a friend of Lloyd George) subsequently reversed during the crucible of the Somme offensive. The process was still underway by the time of the April 1917 offensive with Maj-Gen. Shea being relieved of his command of 30th Division before it was moved up to Flanders at the end of April.[32] In summary then it is unsurprising that the performance of leaders at a number of levels should be inconsistent and that many should be unable to cope with the move from a well prepared siege attack to the demands of a quick decision, rapid moving situation. It required a further year of experience and culling before sufficient quality leaders were on hand to turn initial success into victory:

> The failure to conduct significant manoeuvre at the tactical level was the root cause of the inability of armies to achieve strategic success during the First World War. Successful operational manoeuvre depended directly on success at the tactical level.[33]

Robbins' rather simplistic statement has truth at its core whilst ignoring the fact that unless other circumstances allowed, such manoeuvres would founder under a rain of enemy machine gun and artillery fire. The truth at its core was the fact that an advancement in technology and techniques away from the infantry would only lead to eventual victory if, at the same time, there was a development in small unit tactics. The year 1917 was the tactical turning point. The Somme taught leaders, through hard and bitter experience, that waves of men advancing in the general direction of the enemy was not a remedy for success. Poor use of developing armaments such as the rifle grenade and Lewis gun added to their frustrations, giving rise to the innovative ideas that some leaders put forward during the latter months of the Somme campaign. This led, as has been discussed in an earlier chapter, to the publication and distribution of S.S. 143 and a change in training techniques, these new ideas being first tested on a larger scale at Arras. It was not the end of innovation in tactical methods, as the basic platoon principals were altered to some extent as the war progressed until by August 1918 they were able, in a unified combined arms assault, to be the (relative) masters of the battlefield. What remained evident, however, was that such tactics came to naught if troops were set impossible tasks. Again, it must be said that Falls' assertion that the loss of momentum once the initial attack had more of less succeeded was the fault is, on careful examination, false and hides the actual reasons for failure. It was not the failings of the junior officers in the Seaforths and Irish Fusiliers on 11 April at Roeux which led to such horrendous losses or the lack of training in the Newfoundland and Essex regiments on the 14th that led to their destruction. All of these units were committed in a way that had not changed over the previous two years and, unfortunately, was to continue in months to come. Tactical innovation in the infantry had to be mirrored by a similar advance in how all the services were used together, not only in the initial assault, but in those days following. The Battles of the Scarpe were stark reminders that although artillery employment had reached an adequate level in quality and quantity for the initial assault it failed to provide the necessary suppression of the enemy in subsequent days. A combination of difficulty in

---

31   Grove memoir quoted in Robbins, Simon, *British Generalship,* p. 55.
32   The sacked Shea subsequently took charge of 60th (London) Division in Palestine.
33   Robbins, *British Generalship,* p. 98.

getting guns forward but also a loss of good command and control led to very poor artillery support for almost all the enterprises from 10 to 14 April. Over the months to come the major advances in artillery were to be based around the increasing ability to register targets allowing a change in preliminary bombardments before the initial assault. Beginning at Cambrai in November 1917, the lengthy preliminary bombardment was to be replaced by either none at all or a short hurricane one. This reflected the increase in the artillery's ability to neutralise both the defenders in trenches and opposing artillery, the increasing availably of reliable tanks that were able to support the infantry and wider availability of the No. 106 fuse for all calibre of gun and howitzer.[34] By April 1917 this was still in the future and therefore only the ability to neutralise the enemy artillery and how to create a really effective creeping barrage were the significant steps forward and these limited to the initial assault. A missing element of the eventual successes as achieved at Amiens in 1918 was tank availability. Given the paucity of vehicles and that more advanced versions were not at hand, it is hardly surprising that the tank does not figure highly in the April battles. That a mere handful, having traversed difficult terrain and overcome innate mechanical frailties, should have had such an impact is a remarkable demonstration of operational and tactical potential. On two occasions the action of one single tank allowed the attack on the first morning to be as successful as it could be in the circumstances. On a later occasion only the fact that four tanks had a significant effect on the defenders made the capture of Monchy-le-Preux possible. Only when the two arms of artillery and tanks were in conjunction in more reliable machines advancing over terrain that had not been pulverised by a multi-day bombardment would the real possibilities of the tank be realised. The battles on the Scarpe would not furnish sufficient experiences to further the case for the tank, its leaders still fighting its perceived role as an assist to the infantry. It would require Cambrai much later in the year before the real potential could be seen and lessons learned.

The importance of the air arm at Arras demonstrated the flowering of a fledgling body of men and machines. So new in the scheme of things and in the ebb and flow of type and quality of aircraft, the RFC found itself at a low point and suffered accordingly but still managed, by means of a huge sacrifice in men, to perform vital duties. The losses in March have already been given above as 101 hours per casualty but this was to be even worse in April with the figure dropping to 92, the worst for any month of the whole war. The 316 flying crew killed or missing was also the highest number in any month of the war. The ability to bring artillery to bear on their German counterparts, to allow the production of maps to facilitate accurate planning of attacks down to platoon level and to then report on progress when the attack went in were all incredibly important facets to the success of the first day. That things then did not progress cannot be laid at the door of the RFC. They continued to provide support, despite of horrendous losses and the difficulties of a more fluid situation. From this experience it is clear how the RFC's role continued to develop until it gained complete air superiority in late 1918. Perhaps its development was due to the fact that, as a completely new arm, it could develop at a fairly even pace, its role growing as its aircraft improved in quality, without significant interference from any of the 'old school' who might find it difficult to adapt to change, as was the case in the tank fraternity.

In addition to the more dramatic new advances in warfare developed since 1914, there were many other smaller, but nonetheless vital technologies, embraced by the British Army before the Battle of Arras. The strengthening of the fire power of the humble infantry battalion with heavy machine guns, effective trench mortars, portable automatic weapons and an effective, mass produced bomb combined with a unit organisation for employment thereof. The opening day

---

34　By 1918 the 106 fuse was available not only in large numbers, but also for the 18 pdr. gun which could therefore resume its previous wire cutting role thus allowing heavier guns to concentrate on strongpoints or rear area targets.

of Arras demonstrated that when the wire was cut and creeping barrage closely followed, final resistance was overcome. Reports of combined use of Lewis guns and rifle grenades allowed the infantry to overcome all opposition. However, what is also clear from subsequent days is that where preparation was inadequate and artillery support lacking, such advanced tactical drills came to naught. As mentioned above, this was not as a result of faulty small unit leadership or the men themselves. Unsubdued enemy artillery, machine guns and riflemen made any kind of manoeuvre in the open, even by the most highly trained of units, a deadly affair. Thus a platoon could bring one enemy machine gun under fire whilst other men manoeuvred around it, but it could not do the same against four or five when under severe bombardment. The terrible truth of the disaster that befell 10th Brigade at Roeux on 11 April was that its component units never even got near enough to the objective to carry out any kind of manoeuvre. Trench mortars, especially now that the excellent Stokes Mortar had been delivered in numbers, was used to great effect when could brought within range. Expertise in their use was still fairly nascent, especially when ensuring that mortars advanced with the attackers. Another problem was ammunition not being brought up in sufficient quantities. As well as being used in the offensive barrage, the machine gun was also accompanying troops forward and the insertion of this powerful weapon into the new front line meant that counter attacks could be engaged with direct fire when artillery was unavailable. All in all, given optimum conditions, the infantry accompanied by supporting arms, was up to the task of storming strongly held positions. More importantly, when the enemy's position was a hastily constructed one, or the garrison shaken, assault troops could advance through uncut wire or against minor opposition by application of the new fire and movement tactics.

> Simple communication is exactly that, simple. However, often in large organisations planning events maintaining a holistic view of the operation can be difficult. Plans can get developed in isolation and there is always that natural adversity to sharing ideas or working in partnership.[35]

This statement originates from a modern commercial company that specialises in C3 solutions, that is helping organisations that require efficient command, control and communications – the three 'C's. This volume has attempted to show that the first of the two 'C's, namely command and control, were at times sadly lacking in the latter stages of the offensive. But how much was this influenced by the final 'C', communication? In 1917 communication, both within formations and units, from corps to division to brigade and the other way, and across units, say from division to division, was not at all easy. It relied for the most part on the telephone, with overland or buried cables being laid either in preparation for an attack or rapidly once underway. Cables were prone to cutting by enemy shellfire and thus communication devolved on to signal flags, runner or pigeon. Wireless was in its infancy and held suspect by many whilst power buzzers were used infrequently or to transmit pre-arranged messages such as "1st objective achieved", etc. The delay in the transmission of an order to a recipient could be measured in hours. Although an order from army to corps and in most cases from corps to division and division to brigade, could also be communicated by telephone. However, this was often impossible once Battalion H.Q. moved forward. It was then down to runners to carry the orders to Battalion H.Q., then, after further processing, to company commanders who passed on the directives. All of this was lengthy and time consuming process. No problem at all in the luxury of the days leading up to 9 April where multi-page Operational Orders could be processed down to precise company level plans. A different reality would be in place from 10 April onwards. It will have been clear from the narrative that very often orders the previous evening at corps level at times only reached battalions in the early hours, a time elapse of 8 to 10 hours. The question that has to

---

35   See <http://foamhand.com/our-services/command-control-communication/>.

be posed is how much the communications difficulties were the result of battlefield conditions that contributed to some of the more questionable command and control decisions. Beginning at the highest level it is clear that the kind of information being received at the various Army Headquarters was often at best over-optimistic and at worst wrong and only clarified after a delay sometimes measuring days rather than hours. In such circumstances observations such as from Allenby's famous "The enemy is defeated …" on 12 April can be readily understood and are more difficult to criticise. Even at corps level the message throughout the first 3 days is an overtly optimistic one; however, the position of most units was known by the end of the first day. The initial critical error then, of allowing a late start all across the front on 10 April, cannot therefore be laid at the door of poor communications. The delay in transmission of orders exacerbated the situation at divisional level where at times orders are received either very late or too late at brigade and then battalion level. Yet again, these delays cannot be sited as the reason for the poor decisions contained in these orders. What the delay does succeed in doing though is making the task of the attacking battalions even more difficult. Lack of preparations, reconnaissance and rushed orders to companies adds to the agony of those units asked to attack in often unsupported attacks on unnecessarily narrow frontages. In summary then, although advances in communication devices had substantially improved, the transmission of orders remained problematic. What remains unrecognised is that it was not technology that was required, but the understanding that there would always be delays and hastily formed decisions were often fatal. This narrative also finds no mitigating circumstances with regard to divisional commanders and their decision-making process. Almost were made with full knowledge of the situation as it stood and have to be judged in that light.

Where then does the First Battle of the Scarpe fit into First World War operational and tactical development and does it deserve a great deal more attention in the literature? In the final analysis, the case has been made that the battle was, at the time, consigned to the status of a side show and therefore not of particular importance, a view that has continued to the present day. Nevertheless, it is also clear that the opportunity to increase the rate of development of the British and Dominion was thereby missed. At a number of levels, it has also been demonstrated that lessons had been learned and that, at battalion level, an effective combined arms approach was already in place. Unfortunately, at corps, division and brigade, command and control remained flawed. This would improve over the next 18 months but never to a completely satisfactory level, as can be expected in an army expanding in leaps and bounds during active operations. It could be argued that a full analysis of the Battle of Arras might have accelerated the process of removal of incompetents from various levels of command, but, trained commander and staff officers being at a premium, where were the replacements to come from? The fact that there was a Second and a Third Battle of the Scarpe is an indication that higher command had yet to fully appreciate the diminishing returns from continuing an offensive beyond what could be achieved. Only at Amiens in August 1918, not to mention the subsequent "100 Days" series of offensives, would this finally be appreciated. The mould for success had been created for the Arras offensive; what remained was the improvement of certain elements from which a successful army could be forged. Improvements in artillery methodology, in the numbers and quality of tanks, types and numbers of aircraft, and the meritocratic rise of capable commanders would ensure that the final product was as efficient as possible. That it still had its faults is unsurprising when the rapid developments from a colonial military force to continental size army, backed by an Empire placed on a total war footing, is taken into consideration. Thus, although the effective operational and tactical seeds were sown on the Somme, the roots of that imperfect, but successful fighting force of summer and autumn 1918 were grown at Arras in April 1917.

Appendix I

Agreement signed at Anglo-French Conference, 26-27 February 1917

1. The French War Committee and the British War Cabinet approve of the plan of operations on the Western Front as explained to them by General Nivelle and Field Marshal Sir Douglas Haig on 26 February 1917.

2. With the object of ensuring complete unity of command during the forthcoming military operations referred to above, the French War Committee and the British War Cabinet have agreed to the following arrangements:

    (1) Whereas the primary object of the forthcoming military operations referred to in paragraph 1 is to drive the enemy form French soil, and whereas the French Army disposes of larger effectives than the British, the British War Cabinet recognises that the general direction of the campaign should be in the hands of the French Commander-in-Chief.

    (2) With this object in view, the British War Cabinet engages itself to direct the Field Marshal Commanding the British Expeditionary Force to conform his plans of operation to the general strategical plans of the Commander-in-Chief of the French Army.

    (3) The British War Cabinet further engages itself to direct that during the period intervening between the date of the signature of this agreement, and the date of the commencement of the operations referred to in Paragraph 1, the Field Marshal Commanding the British Expeditionary Force shall conform his preparations to the views of the Commander-in-Chief of the French Army, except in so far as he considers that this would endanger the safety of his Army, or prejudice its success, and, in any case where Field Marshal Sir Douglas Haig may feel bound on these grounds to depart from General Nivelle's instructions, he shall report the action taken, together with the reasons for such action, to the Chief of the Imperial General Staff, for the information of the British War Cabinet.

    (4) The British War Cabinet further engages itself to instruct the Field Marshal Commanding the British Expeditionary Force that, after the date of the commencement of the forthcoming operations referred to in Paragraph 1, and up to the termination of these operations, he shall conform to the instructions of the Commander-in-Chief of the French Army in all matters relating to the conduct of the operations, it being understood that the British Commander will be left free to choose the means he will employ, and the methods of utilising his troops in that sector of operations allotted to him by the French Commander-in-Chief in the original plan.

    (5) The British War Cabinet and Government and the French Government, each so far as concerns its own Army, will be the judge of the date at which the operations referred to in

Paragraph 1 are to be considered as at an end. When so ended, the arrangement in force before the commencement of the operations will be re-established.

(Signed)   M. Briand   (Signed) Lloyd George
(Signed)   Lyautey   (Signed) W.R. Robertson, C.I.G.S.
(Signed)   R. Nivelle   (Signed) D. Haig, F.-M.

Calais, 27 February 1917

Appendix II

14th Division Orders and Instructions & Communication Arrangements for 9 April 1917[1]

1   TNA: WO95/1869 War Diaries of H.Q. General Staff 14th Division.

S E C R E T   Copy No. 20

14th DIVISION OPERATION ORDER No. 112.

Reference 1/10,000 and 1/20,000 Maps of   4th April, 1917.
   the BEAURAINS Area and map issued with
   14th Division S.G.2518 dated 30/3/17.

1.   The Third Army is to break through the enemy's defences
   and advance on CAMBRAI.
      Simultaneously, the First Army is making an attack on the
   VIMY RIDGE.

2. (i). The task allotted to the 14th Division and to the 56th
   Division on our right and 3rd Division on our left is to capture
   and consolidate the hostile position as far as the Brown Line.

   (ii). The boundaries of the 14th Division, the successive
   objectives (Red, Blue and Brown Lines) and the boundary between
   the two assaulting Infantry Brigades are shown on the map issued
   with 14th Division S.G. 2518 dated 30/3/17.

   (iii). After the Brown Line has been secured the two southern
   Divisions of the VII Corps and certain Divisions of the VI Corps
   have the further task of securing the line HENINEL - GUEMAPPE -
   MONCHY-le-PREUX.

3.   Present information indicates that the hostile forces opposite
   and near the front allotted to the Division are the 23rd Reserve
   Division (Saxons) from the COJEUL River to TILLOY, with the 11th
   Division (mixed, Prussians and Silesians) to the North of TILLOY.

4. (i). The assault will be delivered on "Z" day.   The preparatory
   bombardment will be carried out on "V", "W", "X", and "Y" days.

   (ii). The hour of zero on "Z" day will be communicated later.

5.   The Division will attack with two Brigades in line, 43rd
   Infantry Brigade on the right and the 42nd Infantry Brigade on
   the left.   The 41st Infantry Brigade will remain in Reserve.

6.(i).The boundaries allotted to assaulting Infantry Brigades are
   shown on the map mentioned in para. 2 (ii)

   (ii). The 43rd Infantry Brigade is allotted the task of
   capturing those portions of the Red, Blue, and Brown Lines
   falling within its boundaries.

   (iii). The 42nd Infantry Brigade is allotted the task of
   capturing the portions of the Red and Blue Lines within its
   boundaries.   The 42nd Infantry Brigade will also be responsible
   for maintaining touch with the 3rd Division during the advance
   from the Blue to the Brown Line up to a point approximately
   at M 9 c 4.7.

   (iv). The Blue and the Brown Lines will be consolidated as
   soon as each is captured and made secure against counter-attack.

7.   By zero hour on "Z" day Infantry Brigades must be in their
   positions of assembly.   The necessary moves to take place in
   accordance with orders already issued.

                                                             - 8.

2.

8.   (i). A map illustrating the time table for the lifts of
the Creeping Artillery Barrage up to and including the capture
of the Blue line is issued herewith - Map A.   A similar map
illustrating the Creeping Barrage from the Blue to the Brown
Line will be issued later.

(ii).   The dotted lines indicate the approximate lines on
which the Barrage will be placed and the figures on or at the
end of th se lines indicate the time counting from Zero hour
at which the Creeping Barrage will lift off the line concerned,
i.e., the Creeping Barrage lifts off the line marked 2.20 at
2 hours and 20 minutes after Zero.

(iii). The Creeping Barrage comes down on the line marked
2.12 at 2 hours 4 minutes after Zero.   It therefore will remain
on this line for 8 minutes.   The hour plus 2 hours 4 minutes
will be marked by all guns forming this barrage opening with a
salvo of shrapnel.

9.   At Zero the 3rd Division is advancing to the attack of
the German first system of trenches on their front and on our
flank

10. (i) At 2 hours 4 minutes after Zero the leading Infantry
of the 43rd and 42nd Infantry Brigades will advance from their
assembly trenches and creep up as close to the Artillery Barrage
as possible ready to go forward close to the Barrage when it
begins to creep back.

(ii). At 3 hours 12 minutes after Zero the Creeping Barrage
lifts off the last portion of the Blue Line and goes back to
form a Protective Barrage about 300 yards east of the Blue
Line.   The rate of fire on the Protective Barrage gradually
decreases until the time fixed for the commencement of the
advance from the Blue to the Brown Line, when the rate of fire
again rises to the rate fixed for the Creeping Barrage.

(iii). At a time to be notified later the Infantry of the 43rd
Infantry Brigade detailed for the assault of the Brown Line
and the Infantry of the 42nd Infantry Brigade detailed to keep
in touch with the right of the 3rd Division will creep forward
as close as possible to the Artillery Barrage and will follow
that Barrage up to the limits assigned to them.   After the
capture of the Brown Line a gradually decreasing Protective
Barrage will be formed as before.

11.   It is most important for all ranks to realise that, to
ensure success, it is necessary to keep as close to the creeping
barrage as possible ready to deal with the defenders of any
trench as soon as the Barrage lifts off that trench.

12.   At 2 hours 4 minutes after Zero, the 41st Infantry Brigade
will commence leaving the Caves and will occupy the old
British Front Line System between HALSTEAD and HOOGE Streets
and the Northern boundary between the VII and VI Corps.
As the troops of the 42nd Infantry Brigade move forward to the
assault the 41st Infantry Brigade will occupy the old German
front line system between PREUSSEN WEG and the left boundary
of the Division as these trenches are vacated by the 42nd
Infantry Brigade.

13.   H.Q. of the 41st Infantry Brigade will, until a definite
task has been allotted to the Brigade, remain in direct telephonic
communication with Divisional H.Q.

- 3 -

14. (i). 16 Tanks will assist the attack of the 3rd and 14th Divisions on The HARP and 4 of these will subsequently assist in the attack on the COJEUL SWITCH.

(ii). The Tanks will endeavour to be up in time so as to start with the leading infantry.

(iii). All ranks are to be warned that they are no account to wait for the Tanks should the latter get delayed.   The pace of the Infantry is to be regulated according to the Creeping Barrage as explained in para. 10.

15. (i). Directly the Blue Line is captured the 14th Divisional Group of Field Artillery comes under the orders of the G.O.C. 14th Division.

(ii). As soon as the Blue Line is captured the C.R.A. will move up one Field Artillery Group to positions about M 12 c. for the purpose of assisting in the advance from the Blue to the Brown Line.

(iii). It may be necessary to move a second Field Artillery Group forward soon after the one mentioned in sub-para. (ii) above.   The C.R.A. will arrange accordingly.

16.   As soon as the Brown Line is consolidated the 14th Division becomes part of the VII Corps Reserve.   Assaulting Infantry Brigades will reform on the ground gained, the probable distribution being -

    (i). 43rd Inf. Bde. on the Brown, Blue and Red Lines.
    (ii). 42nd Inf. Bde. on the Blue and Red Lines.
    (iii). 41st Inf. Bde. in the old German Front Line System.

17. (i). The Field Coys. R.E. and Pioneer Coys. at present working under Infantry Brigades will be at the disposal of the C.R.E. from 6 a.m. on "Y" day.

(ii). The C.R.E. will detail -

    (a) One Field Coy. R.E. for making a tram line on the old German formation level running through M 12, M 18, N 13 and 14.
    (b) 3 Sections of a Field Coy. R.E. to assist the Artillery in the construction of the gun positions about M 12 c.
    (c) Two companies Pioneers for clearing the road from BEAURAINS to TELEGRAPH HILL via the cross roads in M 6 c, and for making two mule tracks, one from HAZEBROUCK STREET to the North of TELEGRAPH HILL and the other from about M 4 d 7.5 past the South of TELEGRAPH HILL to the COJEUL SWITCH.

(iii). The above work to commence as soon after Zero plus 2 hours as the situation permits.

(iv). The remaining Field Coys. R.E. and Pioneer Coys. to remain in Reserve.

18. (i). Contact aeroplanes will be in the air from Zero to dusk.

(ii). The distinguishing mark of VII Corps contact planes is a black stripe and streamer under the starboard lower plane.

/(iii).

- 4 -

16

18 (cont'd)

(iii). Contact aeroplanes will call by Klaxon Horn for flares
to be lit by the leading troops as nearly as possible at the
following hours -

Zero plus 3 hours 30 minutes.
"   "   7   "   30   "
"   "   8   "   30   "
"   "   11   "

(iv). Only red flares will be used.   Each of the three Infantr
Brigades will arrange that each platoon carries at least 30 flares.

19.   Watches will be synchronized daily from "V" day onwards
through Signals at 9 a.m. and 6 p.m.

20.   Divisional H.Q. will remain at WARLUS.

Map A is issued with
  starred copies only.

Issued at 11.30 p.m.

Lieut Colonel
General Staff.

Copies to -

* No. 1.   14th Div. Artillery.
  2.   C.R.E.
* 3.   41st Infantry Bde.
* 4.   42nd Infantry Bde.
* 5.   43rd Infantry Bde.
  6.)
  7.) A.A. & Q.M.G.
  8.   14th Signal Coy.
  9.   11th King's Liverpool Regt.
  10. 14th Div. Train.
  11. S.S.O.
  12. 14th Div. Supply Col.
  13. A.D.M.S.
  14. A.D.V.S.
  15. D.A.D.O.S.
  16. A.P.M.
  17. 14th Div. Depot Battn.
  18. 14th Div. Gas Officer.
  19. Camp Commandant.
* 20. VII Corps. — *map No. 23*
* 21. VII Corps H.A.
* 22. 56th Division.
* 23. 3rd Division.
* 24. 1st Bde. Heavy Branch M.G.Corps.
* 25. 8th Squadron R.F.C.
* 26. War Diary.
* 27. File.

SECRET
=============

H.Q. 7TH CORPS.
G.C.R 604/269
Received 3.4.1.7
Despatched...........

14th Division
S.G. 2584.

14th DIVISION SIGNAL COMMUNICATIONS FOR THE OFFENSIVE.

1. Diagrams and Map.

(i).   The accompanying diagrams Nos. 1 and 2 show the various means of communication which will be established at Zero and after the capture of the Blue Line.

(ii).   The Map No. 3 shows the existing system in advance of the Advanced Divisional Exchange in CHRISTCHURCH Cave and the proposed extensions to TELEGRAPH HILL.

2. Buried Cable Routes.

All cable routes East of DAINVILLE and as far as Advanced Brigade Command Posts are buried at least 6 ft. deep or are laid in tunnels or sewers.

3. Communication by telephone and telegraph.

A.   Artillery.

The Group Exchange will be in CHRISTCHURCH Cave, providing telephonic and telegraphic communication from C.R.A. to Groups.
There is no O.P. Exchange, each battery having a direct line to its O.P.   For observation after the capture of the objectives each Group will have an O.P. line put through as far as LOWEN SCHANZE, or further according to progress made, before Z day, and these lines will be extended by ground lines as soon as possible.

B.   Infantry.

Each of the Infantry Brigades is in direct communication with the Division and each has an alternative route through the Advanced Exchange in CHRISTCHURCH Cave.
Before Zero the battalions of the assaulting Infantry Brigades will be connected through to their respective Advanced Brigade Command Posts.
During the advance to the Blue Line Advanced Signal Stations will be established at approximately M 6 d 4.3 for the left brigade, and M 12 d 8.5 for the right brigade. Wires will be run out to these stations from each Advanced Brigade Command Post.   An exchange will be established at each of these advanced stations and battalions should run out lines to them as soon as the situation permits.

4. Liaison between Infantry and Artillery.

The Artillery Liaison Officer with each Infantry Brigade will be connected to the Group Exchange.   The two F.O.Os. will be in direct telephonic communication with their respective Liaison Officers.

5. Runners.

As soon as the situation permits, runner posts will be established as follows :-

Left Bde.   No.1.   Advanced Brigade Command Post.
            No.2.   Junction of TELEGRAPH LANE and
                        CORDITE TRENCH (M 6 a 3.5).
            No.3.   Advanced Signal Station (M 6 d 4.3).

Right Bde.   No.1.   Advanced Brigade Command Post.
             No.2.   M 11 b 9.3.
             No.3.   M 12 d 1.4.
             No.4.   Advanced Signal Station (M 12 d 8.5).

All Runner Posts will be marked by notice boards, and routes marked by sign posts.

/6.

- 2 -

6. Visual
   Signalling.

The central receiving station is at G 35 a 1.3 (call VS) and two transmitting stations are at M 5 a 70.05 (call K R) and M 5 b 6.9 (call Z D B).   Two receiving stations for forward work are being established at M 5 d 7.3 (call Z D C) and M 5 b 6.9 (call Z D B).   The receiving station Z D C and transmitting station K R will be connected by telephone. When the first objective has been carried, each Brigade will establish an advanced signal station, the left brigade at M 6 d 4.3 (call B P) and the right brigade at M 12 d 8.5 (call Z Z).

For the advance from the Blue to the Brown Line a receiving station (call T S) will be established on TELEGRAPH HILL about N 7 c 1.9.   Communication from T S to Z Z will be by runner till other arrangements can be made.

Battalions will send their messages to these stations by runner, for transmission.

7. Pigeons.

The Pigeon Loft to be used by this Division is close to SIMENCOURT and is connected by telephone to the Divisional Exchange.

A forward dump of pigeons, probably not more than 4 pairs, will be established at G 35 a 0.7.   It is hoped to be able to supply the Right Brigade with 6 pairs of birds and the Left Brigade with 4 pairs.

Messages arriving at the Loft will be telephoned to the Divisional Signal Office and sent by telegraph to addressee.

8. Power Buzzer.

(i).   An Amplifier is to be installed at LOWEN SCHANZE. Each Brigade will be allotted a Power Buzzer which should be sent forward with a selected Battalion Commander.   The calls for these Power Buzzers will be - Right Brigade C Q, and Left Brigade C S.   Four signallers who have undergone a Wireless course should be appointed to operate and carry the Buzzer.

(ii).   For the advance from the Blue to the Brown Line, a second Amplifier will be sent forward as far as possible. The advancing battalion will take one Power Buzzer (call C R) forward to work back to the Amplifier.   Base lines must in all cases be parallel to a North and South line

9. Wireless.

A Trench Wireless Set, sending and receiving, will be placed at the disposal of each Brigade Commander.   These sets will work back to the Corps directing station near ACHICOURT.   An officer and four men who have undergone a Wireless Course, must be detailed to carry each set and encode and decode messages.

The calls for these sets are - Right Brigade Y M, Left Brigade Y M M and for Corps directing station YU.

10. Aeroplane
    Contact.

Signalling from the front line will be by Flares in accordance with orders to be issued later.

Battalions and Brigades will carry with them the following equipment :-

French Lamp or Signalling Panel.
Ground Signalling Sheet.
Signalling Strips.
Flares as ordered.

Three signallers must be detailed to carry and operate this equipment, and must keep in close touch with the Battalion Commander so that he may avail himself of the

/opportunity

- 3 -

opportunity when a contact aeroplane is overhead.
The distinguishing mark of the contact aeroplane is - Black band beneath the lower starboard plane, with a streamer behind.
The sending of messages to aeroplanes is only to be used in case of emergency, when other means are not available.
Messages are to be confined to the code laid down on page 71 of S.S.135.

11. Supply of   (i). An advanced Signal dump under an officer detailed
    Equipment.   by 14th Div. Signal Coy. will be made at G 35 a 0.7.
                  Pigeons, cable, and other stores will be available here.

                                   Artillery Brigades, Infantry
    Brigades and Battalions can draw on this dump on a written
    indent signed by the Signalling Officer concerned.
    (ii). Smaller dumps of cable will be made at the
    Advanced Brigade Command Posts.

                                        Lieut Colonel
                                        General Staff
    April 2nd, 1917.   14th (Light) Division

    Copies to -

        14th Div. Artillery.
        41st Infantry Brigade
        42nd Infantry Brigade
        43rd Infantry Brigade
        C.R.E.
        14th Div. Signal Coy.
        11th King's Liverpool Regt.
        Q Branch.
        A.D.M.S.
        D.A.D.O.S.
        A.P.M.
        Div. Gas Officer.
        VII Corps. —— *no map.*
        VII Corps H.A.
        56th Division
        3rd Division.

11th Royal Scots Operation Orders for 9 April 1917[1]

---

1   TNA: WO95/1774 War Diary of 11th Royal Scots Regiment.

O P E R A T I O N   O R D E R   No 15   Copy No
By Lt. Col. W.D.Croft. D. S. O.   2/4/17

Ref. Map
Arras 51b. N.W.
Edition 7a
Scale 1/10,000

1. **Information**   The 27th Brigade will attack and consolidate the
Black, Blue and Brown Lines, its left moving from
ST. PANCRAS inclusive through road junction at
CHANTECLER and thence along HELFER GRABEN to 2nd
Objective at Railway Cutting, then to POINT DU JOUR.
Its right moving practically due East from 150 yards
S. of CUTHBERT CRATER.
Its direction will be by the right.
The 34th Division will attack on the left of the
27th. Brigade and the S.A.Brigade will be on the
right of the 27th. Brigade.

2. **Intention**   The Battalion will assault the Blue Line (Railway
Cutting) and thereafter the Brown Line.

3. **Distribution** C. and D. Coys. will form up in the vicinity of the
Craters in position already rehearsed with K.O.S.Bs.
after the latter are in position.
1. The first Wave will mop the 1st. line trench and
its central trench.
The 2nd. Wave will mop 2nd Trench (CHANTECLER).
The 3rd. and 4th. Wave will mop 3rd. line from
junction of ZIEGELI and AL-Z along SEBALD and SALZACH
to HELFER inclusive.
2. When the 1st. Wave has mopped up the 1st. trench
it will rejoin the 2nd. Wave in CHANTECLER where
they will reorganise.
3. At Zero plus 30 mins. A and B Coys. will move in
artillery formation N. of and parallel to AUGUST
AVENUE and parallel to OCTOBER AVENUE. Battalion
Scouts will guide the columns to the various bridges
over Works Line etc.
4. At Zero plus 1 hr. 45 mins. the first two waves
of C and D will move from CHANTECLER passing through
and picking up 3rd. and 4th. Wave and moppers of
K.O.S.Bs. and will cross OBERMEYER GRABEN at
5. Zero plus 2 hrs. and will get as close as possible
to the barrage which is 300 yds. E. of OBERMEYER.
At the same time (Zero plus 2 hrs.) the head of A Coy.
(followed by B. Coy.) in HELFER TRENCH will pass
OBERMEYER TRENCH.
6. The Battalion Scouts will ensure that the progress
of A. and B Coys. is not impeded during its passage
along HELFER to the RAILWAY CUTTING.
7. Zero plus 2 hrs. 6 mins. Barrage leaves stationary
line in front of OBERMEYER for Y1 and Y2 trenches.
Four minutes before moving forward, guns as a
warning will fire intense shrapnel for 2 mins. which
gives white smoke instead of black of H.E.; then change
to 2 minutes H.E. to allow waves to get close before
lifting forward at Zero plus 2 hrs. 6 minutes.
N.B. Troops can get closer up to H.E. than Shrapnel.
8. Zero plus 2 hrs. 12 mins. Barrage lifts off "Y" and
sits on Blue Line (2nd. Objective, Railway Cutting).
A and B Coys. (latter less 1 platoon) will immediately
flood Y trench from where the barrage will be watched.
9. At Zero plus 2 hrs. 40 mins. barrage will lift off
Railway Cutting (Blue Line 2nd Objective) giving a
2 minute Shrapnel and 2 mins. H.E. before doing so.
A and B will form up in 2 Waves and will move forward

2.

so as to get close up to the barrage before it lifts off the Railway Cutting.
D. Coy. will support this advance, C Coy. being in Battalion Reserve and moving to Y as soon as the trench is clear of A.B. and D Coys.
The Platoon of B. Coy. left in HELFER will watch the left flank and will block any trenches running North of HELFER.
10. As soon as A.B and D Coys. have cleared to dug-outs in the Railway Cutting they will advance at least 150 yds. from the Railway Cutting and dig in. B Coys. left flank resting on ZWEIER GRABEN.
O. C. B Coy. will send a patrol along ZWEIER GRABEN to make a stop, the position depending on the barrage which is stationary 300 yds. from the Railway Cutting. This Patrol will be reinforced by a Lewis Gun.
O.C. C Coy. will occupy ZWEIER GRABEN from the Railway Cutting inclusive to B. Coy. inclusive.
O.C.E. Coy. will place 2 Lewis Guns to rake the RAILWAY CUTTING to the North.
Battalion Scouts will link up with 15th Royal Scots and will watch left flank.
Negative reports every 15 minutes to C. Coy.
O.C. A Coy to maintain touch with 9th Scottish Rifles.
11. At Zero plus 6 hrs. 46 mins. the stationary barrage starts advancing to 3rd Objective giving a warning 3 mins. shrapnel and 2 mins. H.E. before doing so.
A.D and B. Coys. (right to left) will be formed up in four waves and will move forward with the barrage.
C Coy. in artillery formation 300 yds. in rear and echeloned on the left flank.
Battalion Scouts on the left flank of B Coy.
12. Zero plus 8 hrs 4 mins. barrage lifts off Brown Line. The Battalion will digg in at least 100 yds clear of any existing German Trenches.
Each Company will send out patrols and Lewis Guns to cover consolidation.

(Sgd) W. Loftus, Capt.

3/4/17   Adj. 11th (s) Bn. The Royal Scots.

APPENDIX A

Forming up of C and D Companies

C and D Coys. will move at such an hour as to insure that,

   a. They do not reach the positions of assembly before the K.O.S.Bs. are in position.

   b. They are in position in time for Company and Platoon Commanders to ascertain that every wave is in its proper place before Zero.

As C and D will move from ARRAS on Y/Z night and as the position of their billets is at present uncertain it is impossible to give a starting time.

C Coy. will move by AUGUST AVENUE.

D Coy. will move by OCTOBER AVENUE

Both these routes will be carefully reconnoitred and timed from their Mouths North of ST. NICHOLAS to the places of assembly, the exact situation of which they will get from their opposite numbers in the K.O.S.Bs.
These routes must be reconnoitred and timed at least twice by representatives of each Company.
A report to be rendered to Orderly Room.
C and D are not bound to use these routes and if preferred they may march overland.
The important point being that they reach their destination at the proper time.
It will be easy to add the required time necessary for the move from ARRAS Billets to the mouths of OCTOBER and AUGUST AVENUES.

APPENDIX B.

Arrangements for A and B Coys. on the Y/Z night.

1. A Company will be in dugouts in and around the two
present Battalion Headquarters near AUGUST AVENUE.
B Company will be in NICHOLS REDOUBT.
They must be ready to move at Zero plus 30 minutes.

2. O.C. A and B Coys. will draw from Battalion H.Q. on
Y day and allot the following additional loads which
have to be carried up to and dumped at HELFER TRENCH.
75 tins (petrol) of water per Company.
38 slings containing 2 Stokes bombs per Company.

3. A Hot Meal and a Rum Issue must be served as late as
possible before moving.
To be arranged by Q.M.Ss. under instructions from
Company Commanders.
Men who are not going into Action will be detailed as
Mess Orderlies and for any other job in order to save
those who are going into action as much as possible.

4. Greatcoats will be collected and dumped at convenient
places by men not going into action after the troops
have moved.

5. O.C. Coys are responsible that the sector is carefully
reconnoitred at least twice before W/Z night and that
situation of Bridges are known.
The closest liaison will be maintained between them
and Lt. Tredgold who is responsible that sufficient
bridges are placed in position on Y/Z night.
Company Commanders will satisfy themselves that every
man has his proper equipment before moving.

It cannot be too strongly impressed on all ranks that
the throwing away of equipment etc. apart from it being
unsoldierly may be the cause of disaster.
A large surplus of Rifle Grenade Cartridges will be
carried by Officers and N.C.Os. as well as Rifle
Grenadiers. All stores such as Rifle Grenades, Green
Very Lights, ground flares, rifle grenade cartridges,
smoke bombs, S.A.A., shovels etc. will be drawn from
Bde. Dump on Y Day.
All Chewing Gum, Rations, Sandwiches, cold tea will be
issued by Quarter Master on Y Day.
It is hoped to obtain and issue Cigarettes on Y Day.

APPENDIX C.

A hot meal will be served to C and D Coys. at the latest possible time before moving.

All fatigue work will be performed by men not going into Action.

Greatcoats will be collected as soon as the Companies have moved off.

A small Bottle of Rum containing sufficient for a half ration of rum for each section will be issued to Section Leaders to issue to their men at the latest possible minute before Zero.

It is calculated that 20 bottles per Company (including 4 Lewis Gun Sections) will be sufficient.

Coy. Commanders will satisfy themselves that every man is in possession of his proper equipment before moving off.

It cannot be too strongly impressed on all ranks that the throwing away of equipment etc. apart from it being unsoldierly may be the cause of disaster.

A large surplus of Rifle Grenade cartridges will be carried by Officers and N.C.Os. as well as Rifle Grenadiers. All stores such as Rifle Grenades, Green Very Lights, Ground Flares, Rifle Grenade Cartridges, Smoke Bombs, S.A.A., Shovels etc. will be drawn from the Brigade Dump on Y Day.
All Chewing Gum, Rations, Sandwiches, Cold Tea, will be issued by Quarter Master on Y Day.
It is hoped to obtain and issue cigarettes on Y Day.

APPENDIX D.

List of things to be carried on the man

Normal Fighting Equipment.
Box Respirator (P.H.Helmet to be left with Pack)
Shovel on back (under haversack)
2 Sandbags tied on to the braces.
100 rds. S.A.A. plus 10 in Magazine.
Cold Tea in Water Bottles (no milk or sugar).

In the Haversack

One complete Iron Ration with 5 fresh Complete Biscuits.
1 Large Meat Sandwich,
1 Packet Chewing Gum.
Unexpended portion of days ration.

Exceptions to above.

a. One Section in each Coy. will carry 100 rds. S.A.A. 2
   smoke rifle grenades and 4 Mills Rifle Grenades (with
   rods and cartridges) in double haversacks like rifle
   grenadiers.

b. Rifle Grenadiers, no shovels, 20 rds, S.A.A.
   2 haversacks each containing 5 grenades.

c. Lewis Gunners. No shovels.

d. Rifle Sections. C and D Coys. will carry 150 rds. S.A.A.
   per man.

e. 16 Grenade Cups in each Coy. by Rifle Grenadiers.

f. All N.C.Os. will carry wirecutters in addition to those
   fixed on the rifle and carried by the men.

   Aeroplane Flares. Every Officer and N.C.O. will carry one
   signal flare.

APPENDIX E.

COMMUNICATIONS

1st Objective

In the attack the following means of communication will be carried out. Battalion H.Q. will be at junction of CANNON STREET and AUGUST AVENUE.

By wire

1½ hours before Zero a wire will be run out from Battle H.Q. to forward lip of CLARENCE CRATER and a full reel of cable jointed on. The K.O.S.Bs. will carry this wire forward to OBERMEYER via SALZACH and HELFER dropping stations on the way.

Messages to H.Q. from forward Coys. when beyond 3rd German trench may be handed in to K.O.S.B. H.Q. or any forward station for transmission by wire. If wire is not "through" runners must be employed.

Visual

K.O.S.B. Head Quarters in ZIEGLEI will be in communication with Brigade by visual. Brigade receiving station will be at G.5.d.5.2. at top of DECEMBER AVENUE.

"B" Battalion when "A" Battalion Head Quarters move forward, will send two runners with them so that they may guide "B" H.Q. to "A" H.Q. at the appropriate time.

2nd Objective

When the objective has been gained "B" Battalion H.Q. will move forward to the advanced H.Q. of the K.O.S.Bs. in ZIEGLEI. The senior Officer of the reserve Coys. will remain behind at the ("C" Work) Headquarters in order to be in telephonic communication with Brigade. "B" Battalion will carry forward the wire laid by "A" Battalion. No wire will be laid forward of Battalion H.Q. until it has finally settled down when a wire will be pushed through at once via HELFER to furthest trench reached. One lineman station will be dropped between OBERMEYER and the advanced Battalion H.Q. and another between Battalion H.Q. and the Railway. The wire will then be maintained by "B" Battalion from their first lineman station to the second objective.

Visual

"A" Battalion will establish a visual receiving station in OBERMEYER to read signals sent by "Bs" visual party from the second objective (or while on its way to the second objective). This party will move with Battalion H.Q. and on capture of second objective will establish a visual station in the second objective or in the furthest trench reached. They will inform the Coys. when they have done this.

Power Buzzer

One Power Buzzer will be taken by "B" Battalion and established at H.Q. when the second objective has been taken. It will be used for bridging a gap over which it may be possible to keep the wire in repair. A message must be sent by it even if the cable is holding out. The receiving set will be in the mine gallery about CUTHBERT CRATER. Messages will be sent from here to Brigade report centre.

Runners

When "B" Battalion moves forward for the second objective, "A" Battalion will establish a relay post in OBERMEYER to which "B" Battalion runners will deliver messages. "As" relay post will carry these messages to Brigade relay post at "A" Battalion H.Q. These relay posts will be near the telephone line.

3rd Objective

Brigade H.Q. will probably have moved to OBERMEYER and Brigade Report Centre to second objective or to Battalion H.Q. of one of the Battalions holding this objective.

Wire

Wire will be laid across the open. Again no wire will be laid forward of Battalion H.Q. until it has actually settled down. Lineman stations will be dropped as before.

Visual

Before the attack commences a Brigade receiving station will be set up on the high ground just W. of OBERMEYER. The visual party of the leading Battalion will move forward with Battalion H.Q. and get into communication as soon as circumstances require with a Brigade transmitting station which will be established on the spur just E. of the Railway in case communication with OBERMEYER is not possible.

Power Buzzer

This will not be moved forward but will remain in the same position with its personnel.

Runners.

Two Brigade Runners will go forward with the attacking Battalion and will take back the first report to Brigade. A relay post of runners will be established by Brigade at transmitting visual station above alluded to. Telephone Stations throughout the operations will be denoted by a small triangular blue and white flag, and Battalion H.Q. by a small square one.

Messages

Messages handed in to Signals must have a time in the "Address Form". Without the time a message is often valueless.

Contact Aeroplanes

Aeroplanes call for flares by a succession of A's (. -) sent on the Klaxon horn. If the Horn fails to act or if no reply is received the Aeroplane will fire a white light. Care must be taken that there is no obstruction between the flare and the Aeroplane. If it is not possible to reply at once, a repetition of the signal should be awaited before lighting flares otherwise they may be lit when the observer is not in a position to see them.

When these flares are called for it is essential that they should be lit by the more advanced troops.

Signallers at Battalion H.Q. will be ready to communicate with Aeroplanes if required to do so.

APPENDIX F.

BATTALION MEDICAL ARRANGEMENTS

Aid Posts. By Z. hour Medical Officer with Orderlies and 8
attached R.A.M.C. bearers will be at Aid Post at
top of OCTOBER AVENUE.
They will move forward when 1st objective has been
taken to K.O.S.B's. Aid Post. When 2nd objective
has been taken an Aid Post further advanced will be
selected this Aid Post to be relatively well advanced
in order that should there be no suitable site between
2nd and 3rd objectives it could be used for 3rd objective until a more suitable place be found or made.

Evacuations. To Aid Post. By Regimental Stretcer Bearers; these
will move off with Companies. They will not evacuate
cases lying nearer than 1st objective at once but leave
them to R.A.M.C.,
From Aid Post. By R.A.M.C. attached to Aid Post .
They evacuate to the Field Ambulance's most Advanced
Dressing Station.

Captain MacDowell Report, 9 April 1917[1]

1 War Diaries of 12th Canadian Infantry Brigade, RG9, Militia and Defence, Series III-D-3, Volume 4907, Reel T-10699 File: 326.

107

C O P Y of Dugout approximately Junction
CYRUS and CLUTCH 8 a.m.
Original Report. 9-4-17.

O. C., 38th Battalion, C. E. F.

Objective reached but am afraid is not fully consolidated. The mud is very bad and our machine guns are filled with mud. I have about 15 men near here and can see others around and am getting them in here slowly. Could "D" Company come up in support if they have stopped in the front line.

The runner with your message for "A" Company has just come in and says he cannot find any of the Company Officers. I don't know where my Officers or men are but am getting them together. There is not an N.C.O. here. I have one machine gunner here but he has lost his cocking piece off the gun and the gun is covered with mud. The men's rifles are a mass of mud, but they are cleaning them. My two runners and I came to what I had selected previously as my Company H.Q. We chucked a few bombs down and then came down. The dugout is 75 feet down and is very large. We explored it and sent out 75 Prisoners and two Officers. This is not exaggerated as I counted them myself. We had to send them out in batches of 12 so they would not see how few we were. I am afraid few of them got back as I caught one man shooting one of our men after he had given himself up. He did not last long and so am afraid we could not take any back except a few who were good dodgers, as the men chased them back with rifle shots. The dugout is a very large one and will hold a couple of hundred. The men were 11th Regiment R. I. R.

I cannot give an estimate of our casualties but believe they are severe. Will send back word as soon as possible. There is a field of fire of 400 yards or more and if there were a couple of Brigade Machine Guns could keep them back easily as the ground is almost impassible. Horrible mess. There are lots of dead Bosche and he evidently held well.

I can see 72nd men on our left. The 78th have gone through after we reached here. The barrage was good but the men did not keep close to it enough and held back. There are no shovels here found yet so will just get our rifles ready. No wire is here and cannot spare men to send out.

The line is obliterated, nothing but shell holes so wire would not be of much use. Men are pretty well under at present. There are no artillery Officers here. His fire is very weak and suppose he is going back. This is all I can think of at present.

Please excuse writing.

(SGD) T. W. MACDOWELL,

Captain,
O.C. "B" Company 38th Canadian Inf. Battn.

108

C O P Y of Original Report.

10·30 a·m· 9/4/17·

O·C· 38th Battalion C· E· F·

Have been along the line. The dugout we occupy is at the
corner of CYRUS and BABY. It has three entrances well distant from
each other, and will hold easily 250 men at the very least. A tunnel
leads down towards our lines, which I did not explore. It has a
winch and cable for hoisting. There are only 15 men with us of whom
two are stretcher bearers. The rifles are one mass of mud. I have
two Lewis Guns and only four pans. Thexxxx Both guns are out of
action on account of the mud. We have a very few bombs as we had to
bomb several dugouts.

The 78th I have no trace of but there are two German
Machine Guns just in front of us. They are firing constantly. Snipers
are also busy. We cannot locate them as yet. The ground is
practically impassible. His aeroplanes came over and saw a few of my
men a t dugout entrance and now we are getting his heavies from our
right and his left. I have no N.C.O's. whatever and unless I get a
few more men with serviceable rifles, I hate to admit it, but we may
be driven out. Three of the men are wounded as it is so I might as
well tell you the facts of the case.

The runner has just come in with your message. We are in
BABY TRENCH slightly to the right of CYRUS. I was wrong in my other
message as to my location as I had just arrived and I will try to
get in touch with MAJOR HOWLAND, but don't like to leave here as
mentioned above have not an Officer or N.C.O. There are a lot of
wounded out in front of here as I can see by the rifles sticking up.

His heavy battery from the right is working very well at
present.

(SGD) T. W. MacDOWELL, Captain,
O.C. "B" Company, 38th Battalion.

C O P Y *of Original* XXXXXXX.   109
2.45 p.m. 9/4/17.

O. C., 38th Battalion C. E. F.

While exploring this dugout KELTY and I discovered a large
store of what we believe to be explosives in a room. There is also
an old sap leading away down underground in the direction of No. 5
Crater. This was explored down to a car, got no further as it may
be wired.

Would you get in touch with Brigade as quickly as possible and
ask that either a party of 176th or 182nd Tunnelling Company come up
and explore these. We have cut all wires for fear of possible
listening posts. The dugout has three entrances so will accommodate
easily 250 or 300 men with the sap to spare. It is 75 feet under
ground and very comfortable. The cigars xxxi are very choice and my
supply of Perrier water is very large. If I might I would suggest
that you take it up with the Brigade that this place be occupied in
strength as there is a great field of fire to the North and West as
well as to the East. This you see makes it a very strong supporting
post to our left flank, and I would strongly recommend that it be
occupied by Brigade Machine Guns. I cannot locate them as I have no
N.C.O's. to leave in charge here to look for them myself. It is quite
alright for anyone to come up here. They are firing at us all the
time with their heavy guns from the South-East but I have no casualties
to report since coming in except being half scared to death myself
by a big brute. I cannot impress you too much the strength of this
position and value of it as a strong supporting point to the left
flank by which they will undoubtedly make their counter attack.

Observation is good here on the whole far side of LENS and
other VILLAGES. Battery positions can be seen. We have taken two
machine guns that I know of and a third and possibly a forth will be
taken tonight. This post was a machine gun post and held by a
Machine Gun Company. I believe they were Prussian Guards. All big
strong men who came in last night. They had plenty of rations but we
had a great time taking them prisoners. It is a great story. My
two runners KOBUS and HAY did invaluable work in getting them out of
the dugout as we had to conceal the fact that we were only three in
number. I don't think they all get back though.

Please have these Engineers sent up at once to examine wire
further as this is a great dugout and should not be destroyed. I belie
the sap runs into No. 7 Crater and might help in being an underground
C.T. There are a large number of wounded in front of here I can see
by the rifles stuck in the ground. I can't think of anything
further. Tell Ken to come up to tea to-morrow if it is quiet. Sorry
to hear of C.O. and HILL and the others.

(SGD) T. W. MacDOWELL, Captain,
O.C. "B" Company 38th Battalion.

Note on Sources

Prelude to Victory

Brig.-Gen. Spears[1] was a liaison officer in 1914 and held a number of posts throughout the war, usually of a similar nature. In 1937 he published *Liaison 1914*, a vivid account of his work during the difficult days of the great retreat of the British and French armies. His style and the descriptive nature of his narrative, placing the reader in the scene with him, was a success. He followed up this work with *Prelude to Victory* in 1939. The problem with this second volume is that he was not, unlike in *Liaison*, present at the majority of the scenes he describes although this would be assumed by the reader. Indeed, the narrative is so convincing that contemporary readers have accepted his descriptions as though Spears had personally witnessed them. He had, however, to rely on others and limited sources. The result is at times misleading as much of it should be regarded as hearsay as opposed to secure evidence. Thus there is a personal reason for the strong animosity towards Lloyd George, its foundations rooted in the manpower scandal in the first half of 1918. At this time there was an accusation that Lloyd George had misled Parliament before *Kaiserschlacht* with regard to BEF strength statistics. Having its origins with the bitter Major-General Sir Frederick Maurice – the recently dismissed Director of Military Operations – the affair influenced Spears as he was writing *Prelude to Victory*. Moreover, his secretary and mistress whom he would eventually marry was Maurice's daughter. Thus most modern accounts of the notorious Calais Conference are based on Spears, the primary source being his biased father in law. Therefore, *Prelude to Victory* must be read with caution. For example, Spears ignores the fact that St.-Martin-sur-Cojeul was taken before the assault and, curiously, he describes the assault on the Pimple as having taken place on 9 April. Although eminently readable, *Prelude to Victory* is, in parts, loosely based on sources of a questionable nature.

German Sources

I have tried to utilise as many German sources as possible. The German official account is very variable in its content, much depending upon the source of its information. For example, the events at Monchy on 14 April, compliment available British sources available sources thus placing operations thereabouts in a different light. Conversely, the poor descriptions of events at St. Laurent-Blangy, with vivid descriptions of non-existent flame throwers, are easily debunked. German regimental histories vary in quality. Some are short descriptions of little value to the historian. When chronicling Prussian units, these publications are often the only remaining source, as most of the primary sources were destroyed in an air raid during the Second World War. Unfortunately, some are so unreliable as to be almost useless, but do shed some light on personalities involved. One or two, such as that of the *R.I.R. 84* are extremely good, displaying an unvarnished narrative. What German sources do demonstrate though is that reserves were certainly not on hand over the first two days and that the military situation could have developed more favourably had certain British divisions performed better.

---

1   His surname was actually Spiers at the time. It was changed in 1918, but as he wrote under the altered Spears, it will be used throughout.

Bibliography of Published Sources

Ainsworth, Captain R.B., MC. *The Story of the 6th Battalion The Durham Light Infantry, April 1915 – November 1918*. London: St. Catherine Press, 1919.

Atkinson, C.T. *The History of the South Wales Borderers*. London: The Medici Society, 1931.

——. *The Royal Hampshire Regiment, Volume 2, 1914-1918*. Glasgow: University Press Glasgow, 1952.

Atteridge, A.H. *A History of the 17th Northern Division*. Glasgow: MacleHose & Co., 1929.

Bailey, Sgt. O.F. and Hollier, Sgt. H.M. *The Kensingtons', 13th London Battalion*. Uckfield: Naval Military Reprint, 2002.

Beckett, Ian F. & Corvi, Stephen J. (eds), *Haig's Generals*. Barnsley: Pen & Sword, 2009.

Behrmann, Franz & Brandt, Archivrat Walther. *Die Osterschlacht bei Arras 1917 I. Teil*. Oldenburg: Stalling, 1929.

Bennett, Captain S.G., M.C. *The 4th Canadian Mounted Rifles*. Toronto: Murray, 1926.

Berhard, Studt Hauptman d.R. a.D. Dr. *Infanterie-Regiment Graf Bose (1. Thüringisches) Nr. 31 im Weltkriege 1914-1918*. Oldenburg: Stalling, 1926.

Bernard, Philippe. *The Decline of the Third Republic 1914-1938* (translation). Cambridge: University Press, 1985.

Berton, P. *Vimy*. Toronto: McClelland & Stewart, 1986.

Bewsher, Major F.W. *The History of the 51st (Highland) Division 1914-1918*. Uckfield: Naval & Military Press reprint of 1920 edition.

Bond, Brian & Cave (eds), Nigel, *Haig: A Reappraisal 80 Years On* (Barnsley: Pen & Sword, 1999).

Bond, R.C. *The History of the 9th King's Own Yorkshire L.I. Regiment*. Uckfield: Naval Military Press reprint, 2004.

Boyle, A. *Trenchard: Man of Vision*. London: Collins, 1962.

Braun, Maj. a.D., Heinrich. *Das K.B. 25 Infanterie-Regiment*. München: Verlag Bayerisches Kriegsarchiv, 1926.

Brigade, Members of the London Rifle. *The History of the London Rifle Brigade*. London: Constable & Co. Ltd., 1921.

Bromet, Group Captain G.R., D.S.O. O.B.E et al. *Naval Eight*. London: Signal Press, 1931.

Brown, Ian Malcolm. *British Logistics on the Western Front: 1914-1919*. Westport, USA: Praeger, 1998.

Brumwell, P. Middleton. *The History of the 12th (Eastern) Division in the Great War*. London: Nesbit & Sons, 1923.

Buchan, John. *The History of the Royal Scots Fusiliers (1678-1918)*. London: T. Nelson and Sons, Ltd., 1925.

——. *The History of the South African Forces in France*. London: Nelson & Sons, 1920.

Campbell, Christy. *Band of Brigands*. London: Harper Perennial, 2007.

Cassar, George H. *Lloyd George at War, 1916 – 18*. London: Anthem Press, 2009.

Cave, Nigel and Robinson, Phillip. *The Underground War: Vimy Ridge to Arras*. Barnsley: Pen & Sword, 2014.

Chandler, David. *A Guide to the Battlefields of Europe*. Ware: Wordsworth, 1998.

Chapman, Guy. *A Passionate Prodigality: Fragments of an Autobiography.* London: MacGibbon & Kee, 1965.

Civrieux, Commandant de. *L'Offensive de 1917.* Paris et Bruxelles: Van Oest, 1919.

Clarke, Alan. *Donkeys.* London: Hutchinson, 1961.

Clements, Captain Robert. *Merry Hell, The Story of the 25th Battalion 1914-19.* Toronto: University of Toronto Press, 2012.

Cowper, Col. J.M. *The King's Own, The Story of a Royal Regiment, Vol. 3, 1914-1950.* Aldershot: Gale and Polden, 1957.

Dudley Ward, Major C.H. *The Fifty Sixth Division 1914-1918.* Uckfield: Naval & Military Press reprint of 1921 edition.

Dutton, David. *The Politics of Diplomacy.* London: Taurus, 1998.

Dziobek, Otto, *Geschichte des Infanterie-Regiments Lübeck (3. Hanseatisches) Nr. 162.* Oldenburg: Gerhard Stalling, 1922.

Edmonds, Brig.-Gen. Sir James E. and Wynne, Capt. G.C. *Military Operations, France and Belgium 1915 Vol. 1.* London: Macmillan and Co., 1927.

Edmonds, Brig.-Gen. Sir James E. *Military Operations, France and Belgium 1914.* London: Macmillan and Co., 1922.

——. *Military Operations, France and Belgium 1916, Vol. 1.* London: Macmillan and Co., 1931.

Egremont, Max. *Under Two Flags, The Life of Major General Sir Edward Spears.* London: Phoenix, 1998.

Elstob, Lt-Col. Wilfrith, VC, DSO, MC. *Sixteenth, Seventeenth, Eighteenth, Nineteenth Battlions, The Manchester Regiment, A Record 1914-1918.* Manchester: Sherratt & Hughes, 1923.

Ewing, John, MC. *The History of the Ninth (Scottish) Division.* London: Murray, 1921.

——. *The Royal Scots, 1914-1919, Volume 2.* London: Oliver and Boyd, 1925.

Falls, Captain Cyril. *Military Operations, France and Belgium, 1917, Volume 1.* London: MacMillan, 1940.

Farndale, General Sir Martin. *History of the Royal Regiment of Artillery: Western Front 1914-18.* London: Royal Artillery Institution, 1998.

Farr, M. *Winter and Discontent: The December Crisis of the Asquith Coalition, 1915-1916. Britain and the World.* Edinburgh: University Press, 2011.

Fetherstonhaugh, R.C. *The Royal Canadian Regiment 1883-1933.* Uckfield: Naval & Military Press reprint of 1936 edition.

——. *The 13th Battalion Royal Highlanders of Canada 1914-1919.* Uckfield: Naval & Military Press reprint of 1925 edition.

——. *The 24th Battalion, C.E.F., Victoria Rifles of Canada 1914-1919.* Uckfield: Naval & Military Press reprint of 1930 edition.

Förster, Sigismund von. *Das Reserve-Infantrie-Regiment Nr. 31.* Oldenburg: Stalling, 1921.

Fox, Colin. *Monchy-Le-Preux.* Barnsley: Pen & Sword, 2000.

Franks, N. "A Father's Love." *Over the Front, Vol. 10* (1995).

Fraser, David. *Alanbrooke.* London: HarperCollins, 1982.

Gemmingen-Guttenberg-Fürfeld Oberst, Freiherr von. *Das Grenadier-Regiment Königin Olga (1 Württembergisches) Nr. 119 im Weltkrieg 1914-1918.* Stuttgart: Belser, 1927.

Girardet, Jacques and Duclos. *Somewhere on the Western Front.* Arras: Degeorge, 2007.

Gliddon, Gerald. *VCs of the First Wrold War, Arras & Messines 1917.* Burton-on-Trent: Wrens Park, 2000.

Götz, August. *Das K.B. 8 Infanterie-Regiment, Großhertzog Friedrich II von Baden.* München: Verlag Bayerisches Kriegsarchiv, 1926.

Greenhalgh, Elizabeth. *Foch in Command: The Forging of a First World War General.* Cambridge: University Press, 2011.

——. *The French Army and the First World War*. Cambridge: University Press., 2014.

Grey, Maj. W.E. *2nd City of London Regiment (Royal Fusiliers) in the Great War 1914-1919*. London: The Headquarters of the Regiment, 1929.

Griffith, Paddy. *Battle Tactics of the Western Front: The British Army's Art of Attack 1916-18*. New Haven & London: Yale University Press, 1994.

Grimwade, Captain F. Clive. *The War History of the 4th Battalion The London Regiment (Royal Fusiliers) 1914-1919*. London: The Regiment, 1922.

Hankey, Lord. *The Supreme Command 1914-1918*. London: Allan & Unwin, 1961.

Harris, John. *Covenant with Death*. London: Hutchinson, 1961.

Hart, Peter. *Bloody April*. London: Cassell, 2006.

Hayes, Geoffrey, et al. *Vimy Ridge: A Canadian Reassessment*. Ontario: Wilfred Laurier University Press, 2009.

Heinicke, Lt. d.Res. a.D., Karl & Bethge, Lt. d.Res. a.D., Bruno. *Das Reserve-Infanterie-Regiment Nr. 263 in Ost und West*. Oldenburg: Stalling, 1926.

Hindenburg, Field Marshal Paul von. *Out of My Life*. London: Cassell, 1920.

Hooton, E.R. *War Over the Trenches*. Hersham: Ian Allen, 2010.

Jones, H.A. *The War in the Air Volume 3*. Oxford: Clarendon Press, 1931.

Lindsay, Lt.-Col. J.H. *The London Scottish in the Great War*. Aldershot: Regimental Headquarters, 1925.

Lloyd George, David. *War Memoirs of David Lloyd George*. London: Nicholson & Watson, 1933-1936.

Ludendorff, General Erich von. *Meine Kriegserinnerungen*. Berlin: Mittler & Sons, 1919.

Lupfer, Captain Timothy. *The Dynamics of Doctrine: The Changes in German Tactical Doctrine During the First World War*. Sevenoaks: Pickle Partners Publishing, 1981 (2014 edition).

Majendie D.S.O., Major V.H.B. *A History of the 1st Battalion Somerset Light Infantry – July 1st 1916 to the end of the War*. Taunton: Goodman & Son, Phoenix Press, 1921.

Messenger, Charles. *Call-To-Arms, The British Army 1914-18*. London: Cassell, 2005.

Murphy, David. *Breaking Point of the French Army, The Nivelle Offensive of 1917*. Barnsley: Pen & Sword, 2015.

Neill, H.C. *The Royal Fusiliers in the Great War*. London: Heinemann, 1922.

Nicholls, Jonathan. *Cheerful Sacrifice*. London: Leo Cooper, 1990.

Nollau, Oberstlt. a.D. Herbert. *Geschichte des Königlich Preußischen 4. Niederschlesischen Infanterie-Regiments Nr. 51*. Berlin: Kolk, 1931.

O'Neill, H.C., O.B.E. *The Royal Fusiliers in the Great War*. London: Heinemann, 1922.

Paland, Wolfgang. *Die Abenteuer des Musketiers Albert Krentel*. Norderstedt: Books on Demand, 2015.

Petre, F. Loraine, O.B.E. *The History of the Norfolk Regiment 1685-1918, Vol. II, 4th August 1914 to 31st December 1918*. Norwich: Jarrold & Sons, 1924.

Prior, Robin & Wilson, Trevor. *Command on the Western Front*. Oxford: Blackwell, 1992.

Radley, Kenneth. *Get Tough Stay Tough, Shaping the Canadian Corps 1914-1918*. Solihull: Helion, 2014.

Reid, Walter. *To Arras, 1917, A Volunteer's Odyssey*. East Linton: Tuckwell, 2003.

Ritter, *Oberstleutnant* Holger a.D. *Geschichte des Schleswig-Holsteinischen Infanterie-Regiments Nr. 163*. Hamburg: Leuchtfeuer Verlag, 1926.

Robbins, Simon. *British Generalship on the Western Front*. London: Frank Cass, 2005.

Robertson, Field Marshal Sir William. *From Private to Field Marshal*. London: Constable, 1921.

Rupprecht, Kronprinz von Bayern. *In Treue Fest: Mein Kriegstagebuch, Erster band*. Berlin: Mittler & Sohn, 1929.

——. *Mein Kriegstagebuch, Zweiter Band*. Berlin: Mittler & Sohn, 1929.

Sandilands, Col. J.W. & MacLeod, Lt.-Col. Norman. *The History of the 7th Battalion Queen's Own Cameron Highlanders*. Stirling: Eneas MacKay, 1922.

Sassoon, Siegfried. *Counter attack and Other Poems*. New York: E.P. Dutton, 1918.

Schacky, Siegmund Frh. Von. *Das K.B. Reserve-Infanterie-Regiment Nr. 1*. München: Bayerische Kriegsarchiv, 1924.

Schütz *Generalmajor* a.D., Wilhelm v. & Hochbaum *Leutnant. Das Grenadier-Regiment König Friedrich Wilhelm II (1. Schlesisches) Nr. 10*. Oldenburg: Stalling, 1924.

Scott, Maj.-Gen. Sir Arthur B. *The History of the 12th (Eastern) Division in the Great War 1914-1918*. London: Nisbet & Co, 1923.

Shakespear, Lt.-Col. J. *The Thirty Fourth Division*. Uckfield: Naval Military Press Reprint, 2010.

Sheen, John & Stewart, Graham. *Tyneside Scottish*. Barnsley: Pen & Sword, 1999.

——. *Tyneside Irish*. Barnsley: Pen & Sword, 1998.

Sheffield, G. & Bourne, J. *War Diaries and Letters 1914-1918*. London: Orion, 2005.

Sheldon, Jack & Cave, Nigel. *The Battle for Vimy Ridge – 1917*. Barnsley: Pen & Sword, 2007.

Sheldon, Jack. *The German Army in the Spring Offensives 1917*. Barnsley: Pen & Sword, 2015.

——. *The German Army on Vimy Ridge 1914 – 1917*. Barnsley: Pen & Sword, 2008.

Spears, Brig.-Gen E.L. *Prelude to Victory*. London: Jonathan Cape, 1939.

Spears, Edward. *Liaison 1914*. London: Cassell, 1930.

Speck, Justizinspektor William. *Das Königlich Preußische Reserve-Infanterie-Regiment 84*. Zeulenroda: Sporn Verlag, 1937.

——. *Das Königlich Preußische Reserve-Infanterie-Regiment 84*. Zeulenroda: Sporn Verlag, 1937.

Stedman, Michael. *Manchester Pals*. Barnsley: Pen & Sword, 2004.

Stewart, Lt.-Col. J., D.S.O. & Buchan, John. *The Fifteenth (Scottish) Division 1914-1919*. Edinburgh & London: William Blackwood & Sons, 1926.

Studt, *Hauptmann* d.R. a.D. Dr. Bernhard. *Infantrie-Regiment Graf Bose (1. Thüringisches) Nr. 31 im Weltkrieg 1914-1918*. Oldenburg: Stalling, 1926.

Sutherland, Captain D., MC, TD. *War Diary of the Fifth Seaforth Highlanders*. London: Bodley Head, 1920.

Taylor, Colin. *I Wish They'd Killed You in a Decent Show*. Brighton: Reveille Press, 2014.

Terraine, John. *Douglas Haig, The Educated Soldier*. London: Cassell & Co., 1963.

War Office, *S.S. 135, Instructions for the Training of Divisions for Offensive Action*. London: H.M.S.O., 1916.

War Office, *S.S. 143, Instructions for the Training of Platoons for Offensive Action*. London: H.M.S.O., 1917.

War Office, *Statistics of the Military Effort of the British Empire During the Great War 1914-1920*. London: H.M.S.O., 1922.

Wavell, Archibald. *Allenby, A Study in Greatness: The Biography of Field-Marshal Viscount Allenby of Megiddo and Felixstowe*. New York: Oxford University Press, 1941.

Williams, Jeffrey. *Byng of Vimy*. London: Martin Secker & Warburg Ltd., 1983.

Wyrall, Everard. *The East Yorkshire Regiment in the Great War 1914-1918*. London: Harrison & Sons, 1928.

Zabecki, David T. *Chief of Staff, Vol. 1: Napoleonic Wars to World War 1*. Annapolis: Naval Institute Press, 2008.

Index

INDEX OF PEOPLE

INDEX OF PLACES

INDEX OF ALLIED FORMATIONS & UNITS

INDEX OF GERMAN MILITARY FORMATIONS & UNITS